the Comprehensive Guide to Lingo

For Windows & Macintosh

the Comprehensive Guide to Lingo

Creating Interactive Applications With Macromedia Director

For Windows & Macintosh

Gary Rosenzweig

VENTANA

The Comprehensive Guide to Lingo: Creating Interactive Applications With Macromedia Director

First Edition 9 8 7 6 5 4 3 2 1
Printed in the United States of America

Ventana Communications Group, Inc.
P.O. Box 13964
Research Triangle Park, NC 27709-3964
919/544-9404
FAX 919/544-9472
http://www.vmedia.com

Limits of Liability and Disclaimer of Warranty

The author and publisher of this book have used their best efforts in preparing the book and the programs contained in it. These efforts include the development, research and testing of the theories and programs to determine their effectiveness. The author and publisher make no warranty of any kind, expressed or implied, with regard to these programs or the documentation contained in this book.

The author and publisher shall not be liable in the event of incidental or consequential damages in connection with, or arising out of, the furnishing, performance or use of the programs, associated instructions and/or claims of productivity gains.

Trademarks

Trademarked names appear throughout this book, and on the accompanying compact disk or floppy disk (if applicable). Rather than list the names and entities that own the trademarks or insert a trademark symbol with each mention of the trademarked name, the publisher states that it is using the names only for editorial purposes and to the benefit of the trademark owner with no intention of infringing upon that trademark.

Macromedia End User License Agreement

By opening the CD-ROM packaging, the end user agrees to the terms of the End User License Agreement included at the back of this book.

President/CEO
Josef Woodman

Vice President of Content Development
Karen A. Bluestein

Managing Editor
Lois J. Principe

Production Manager
John Cotterman

Technology Operations Manager
Kerry L. B. Foster

Technical Director
Dan Brown

Product Marketing Manager
Jamie Jaeger

Creative Services Manager
Diane Lennox

Art Director
Marcia Webb

Acquisitions Editor
Sherri Morningstar

Developmental Editor
Scott Janssen

Project Editor
Jessica A. Ryan

Copy Editor
Marion Laird

Assistant Editor
Patrick Bragg

Technical Reviewer
Alan Levine

Desktop Publisher
Patrick Berry

Proofreader
William R. Stott

Indexer
Richard T. Evans, Infodex

Cover Designers
Laura Stalzer
Alice Whicker

Interior Graphics
William Follett

About the Author

Gary Rosenzweig is a multimedia software developer, entrepreneur, and writer. His business, CleverMedia, does consulting and Internet publishing and creates games, applications, and utilities. He has worked as a senior engineer for Ingenius, a Reuters/TCI education multimedia company. Gary holds a master's degree in journalism from the University of North Carolina at Chapel Hill and a bachelor's degree in computer science from Drexel University. He now lives in Denver, Colorado. You can contact Gary at the following addresses:

World Wide Web:
http://www.csn.net/~rosenz
http://clevermedia.com

E-mail:
rosenz@aol.com

Acknowledgments

First, thanks to those who directly affected the writing of this book, the "pit" crew at Ingenius: William Follett, Ken Gadoua, Rob Martin, Andy Schmit, Jay Shaffer, John Sturman, Jenny Thomas, and Phil Waters. They are the multimedia authors I used as my sample target audience for this book. They are also great friends who continue to have very positive influences on my career and my life.

Thanks to David Ferguson, who first hired me at Ingenius, and Heath Stewart, with whom I learned Lingo and first discussed the idea of a book. Thanks also to Heath Burr and John Nyquist for helping me with ideas and encouragement.

Thanks to Sherri Morningstar for bringing the book and me to Ventana. Also thanks to the team that put the book together: Jessica Ryan, Scott Janssen, Alan Levine, Marion Laird, Patrick Berry, JJ Hohn, John Cotterman, and the CD-ROM team.

There were also those who had a more indirect influence, removed by years or distance: Jeffrey Popyack, David Magagnosc, Sheila Dresser, Kevin Schwartz, Jody Lichty, Stacey Crown, Michael Tirenin, Rick Kaspar, Jerry Kramer, and Courtney Love.

Also many thanks to my entire family, including Jaqueline, Jerry, and Larry Rosenzweig, Rebecca Jacob, and Barbara and Richard Shifrin.

Contents

Section V: Lingo Reference A–Z

Section VI: Appendices

Introduction

It was about two years ago that I first got the idea to write a Lingo book. That was only six months after I was in a bookstore looking for one. I needed the book because I had just gotten a Lingo programming job. Although I had extensive knowledge of Hypercard's scripting language and other programs and programming languages such as Asymetrix Toolbook, C, FORTRAN, and Pascal, I knew very little about Lingo.

All I needed was a quick way to get up to speed on this latest language. I remembered how useful Danny Goodman's Hypercard 2.0 Handbook was as a reference for me, and I figured that a similar book must exist for Director, which was gaining popularity fast after the release of the first Windows version.

But the only books I found on the shelves were about animation and using the score and cast. The best guide I had for picking up Lingo was the Lingo Dictionary that came with the software. So I learned as I went along. Fortunately, I was immersed in Lingo for eight to twelve hectic hours a day to make a deadline on a huge project. That helped me learn fast. Soon I was creating things in Director that people thought you needed C++ programmers to do.

The idea for a book came naturally. Being a journalist as well as a computer programmer, I felt I had a knack for communicating technical ideas. Encouraged by the lack of published material available and my growing expertise on the subject, I began making plans in the fall of 1994.

The problem was that I didn't know my way around the publishing industry. I did things backward—writing the book first. I called it "Lingo Scripting for Authors & Artists." The 32-chapter workbook was specially designed for multimedia authors with backgrounds in graphic arts or printing. I could relate to them, having worked my way through college with desktop publishing and journalism jobs.

The book didn't have a publisher, and Lingo was not as hot a topic then as it is now, so I became my own publisher. First, I uploaded the text file to America Online. Then I put an HTML version on my Web page.

The e-mail started flooding in. People were thanking me for my book. The download count on AOL topped one thousand, and the hits on my Web page jumped into the hundreds per week. I especially enjoyed getting e-mail from other countries.

In November of 1995, Shockwave came along. I placed my first game, a crossword puzzle, on my Web page on the day of the public beta release. In the following months, my Space Pirate and Pretty Good Golf games caused my Web hits to increase exponentially—and my e-mail as well. Plans for Director 5 started to come to light about this time too. I began to think about the next version of my book.

Then along came Ventana Communications and the chance to get my book into stores. The editors at Ventana wanted a "comprehensive" approach, and I saw that as a great way to set my text apart from the few other books that had been published up to that time.

The result is in your hands now. "The Comprehensive Guide to Lingo" is a "brain dump" of what I know about the subject. I start off with a "Beginner's Workbook," which is based on the same teaching methods that made my online book so successful. Switching from the tutorial style, I then go into detail about advanced techniques. In addition, there is a section on Shockwave, which makes Lingo a more powerful language than Java, or anything else, when it comes to browser applets. The book ends with a full reference section, including an alphabetical rundown of all commands, and a collection of useful tables and charts.

In addition to the text, there is a CD-ROM disc and an Online Companion. The CD-ROM contains Director movies created with the scripts used in the book chapters. This allows you to immediately test out the programs you are reading about. There is also a helpful collection of third-party products and demos.

The Online Companion provides up-to-date information and allows for reader input. There are also links to other Internet resources.

It is my hope that you find this book enjoyable as well as informative, and inspiring as well as useful.

Happy scripting,
Gary Rosenzweig

How to Make the Most of This Book

This book is organized into sections so that Lingo users at various levels of experience and expertise can focus on information geared to their particular needs. The material is divided into five main sections, each of which is described below, so you don't have to read the *Comprehensive Guide to Lingo* from cover to cover in order to find what you need to begin working with the program.

Read the following descriptions of the book sections and decide where you want to start. Many readers will start with the "Beginner's Workbook," but if you think you're ready to jump into more difficult concepts, then go ahead and see if you're comfortable. If you get lost, you can always go back to preceding sections for guidance.

Section I

The first section, "Beginner's Workbook," is geared toward Macromedia Director users who are familiar with the general workings of Director but have never dabbled much in Lingo. The chapters are written with the assumption that the reader has no previous programming experience.

Not only should first-time Lingo programmers start with the "Beginner's Workbook" section, but so should others who feel that they do not have a firm grasp of how Lingo works. Many computer users, for instance, have learned to adapt some simple *on mouseUp* or *on exitFrame* scripts from other books or demonstration products. They have learned *how* to use a few select commands but aren't sure *why* they do what they do.

Each chapter in the "Beginner's Workbook" section builds upon what was learned in previous chapters. By going through the chapters one by one and trying all the examples, you will gain a good understanding of basic Lingo and be ready to use it in your projects.

Most chapters also include a "Try It Yourself" section to help you get your feet wet with some hands-on scripting. These exercises take the lesson in that chapter one step further to reinforce what was taught. Everything you need to figure out the problem presented in the Try It Yourself exercise will have already been explained in that or a previous chapter.

The "Beginner's Workbook" section covers the following:

- The basics of Lingo
- Using the message window to test commands
- Scripts that let the user navigate through a movie
- Making custom buttons and getting them to behave properly
- Changing and animating graphics using Lingo
- Letting the user control elements on the stage
- Controlling the sprites, sounds, transitions, tempo, and palette of a movie
- Global variables
- Simple Hypertext

Section II

Once you have mastered some elementary concepts, you're ready for the "Advanced Lingo" section. These chapters are designed for beginners who are ready to move beyond the basics and for developers who have a good foundation in Lingo but wish to get on with learning more difficult techniques.

"Advanced Lingo" starts off with a quick course in computer science. These concepts can be of a lot of help to Lingo programmers, many of whom come from nonscience or nonengineering backgrounds. Then the focus shifts to advanced Lingo commands. These chapters can be used as a continuation of the learning process that started in the first section, or they can be referred to as needed.

"Advanced Lingo" covers the following:

- Programming concepts
- Creating better hypertext
- Asking the user questions
- Menu bars
- Lingo-style lists
- File input and output
- Debugging

Section III

"Expert Lingo" addresses the needs of those who have a solid understanding of Lingo. Again, the chapters can be read through or used as reference. The material covers a variety of topics, but the focus is on the importance of creating a good piece of multimedia and on methods to help Lingo programmers achieve that goal.

"Expert Lingo" covers the following:

- Object-oriented programming
- Selection lists

- Creating your own scrolling graphics
- Pull-down menus
- Movies in a window
- Graphics tricks
- Digital video control
- MIDI control
- Creating and altering the score from Lingo
- Building your own tools
- Xobjects

Section IV

The fourth section, "Shockwave," shows you how to make Director movies for the Internet. Thanks to the Shockwave plug-in for Netscape and other browsers, you can embed small Director movies in World Wide Web pages. You can use this plug-in to create anything from simple animated banners to complex interactive games that you can add to your Web site. You'll learn how to optimize your movies for the Internet and how to use special commands to take advantage of this new medium for Director-based content.

Section V

Finally, the book ends with "Lingo Reference A-Z," a run-down of all Lingo commands and how to use them. In this section, designed for quick reference, you can refresh your memory as to how any command operates, and discover ways to easily fix problems you might encounter while programming.

Moving On

Now it is time to get started. The "Beginner's Workbook" is divided into "Lessons" with each chapter containing two to five of them. These lessons are designed to be learned initalliy in one sitting, but it will take longer than that to absorb the content and try the example.

Each lesson builds on the previous one, so make sure you understand all of the concepts presented in each before moving on.

SECTION

I

Beginner's Workbook

2 Combining Lingo & Director

Before you can write Lingo scripts, you need to understand the basics of using Director and how Lingo works with it. While you can use Director without Lingo, you cannot do much Lingo programming without using the standard Director functions. Let's review Director, see how Lingo fits in, and then try a few Lingo commands.

Lesson 1: Director Basics

This lesson reviews the basic elements of Macromedia Director. It will definitely help those unfamiliar with Director to understand these concepts before they attempt to program in Lingo.

If you are already familiar with Director elements like the cast and the score, you may want to read this lesson anyway, as it contains several hints on how to set up your Director movie for scripting. The rest of the lessons assume you have a pretty good grasp of this information.

The Movie

Director files are called *movies*. They look something like the illustration in Figure 2-1 when sitting on the Macintosh desktop. In Windows, they are files with a .dir extension.

Think of a movie as an entire multimedia production with a cast, crew, and script. It has a beginning, middle, and end, as well as plot twists and special effects. Or, you can think of a movie as just a scene—one of many movies that make up your entire production.

Figure 2-1: *A Director movie is the primary type of Director file.*

Each movie consists of a *score*, which is sort of like stage direction or choreography for the actors to follow—it is divided into *frames*. The actors in your Director movie are called *cast members*. The screen is called the *stage*. When cast members are placed in frames in the score, they appear on the stage during those frames of the movie.

The Cast

The cast is just a collection of multimedia elements such as graphics, sounds, text boxes, buttons, digital video, and basic shapes. They can all be seen or heard on the stage if they are placed in the score.

Lingo scripts are also cast members. Think of them as the movie's crew, not visibly appearing on the stage at any time, but necessary for going beyond anything but the simplest production.

Each cast member can be referred to by its number or name. The number is automatically assigned, according to the member's position in the cast member list. The name, however, must be assigned by you.

The entire cast is shown in the cast window in Director, pictured in Figure 2-2. Each cell in this window contains a representation of a cast member (its *icon*), its number, and its name. If you double-click on the icon, a new window opens with that single cast member in a graphic, text, or information box. You can also use the cast window to rearrange or delete cast members. One way to rearrange them is to use the standard cut or copy, and paste.

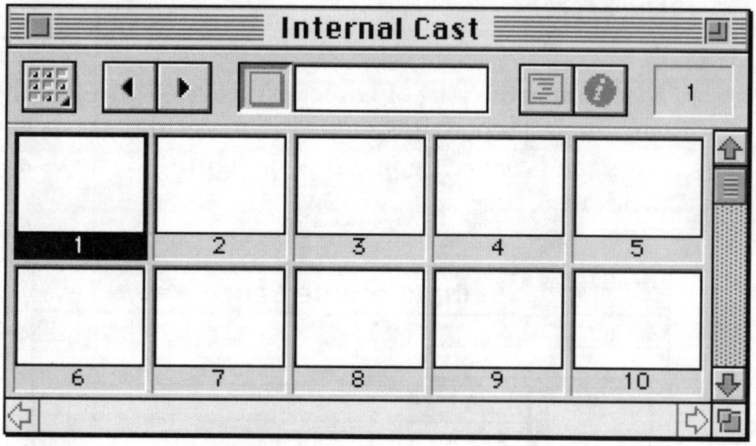

Figure 2-2: *The cast window.*

It is best to give every cast member a name and only use that name, not the number, when referring to it in Lingo. You can do this by selecting the name field of each cast in the cast window or in the individual cast member's information box or display window. This way, you can move your cast members around in the cast without confusing the scripts.

For instance, a script can refer to member 22. But, if you rearrange the cast members at some point, then the cast member that was previously member 22 in the list now has a different number and your script will refer to the wrong member. However, if you named the cast member "graphic1" and refer to it by name, it won't matter what number in the list the cast member is, the script will find it.

Cast members also contain other bits of information about themselves. A text box might have a margin or border width, for instance. These are called *properties*.

All cast members can have Lingo scripts attached to them. A button, for instance, can contain all the scripting necessary to govern the button's behavior and function.

Each movie contains its own internal cast. In addition, casts can be saved as individual files. This means you can have multiple casts being used by the same movie, and multiple movies using the same cast.

The Score

The score is the part of Director that controls what the cast members do and when. It is made up of a grid that has *frames* going across and *channels* going down. Figure 2-3 shows an empty score window.

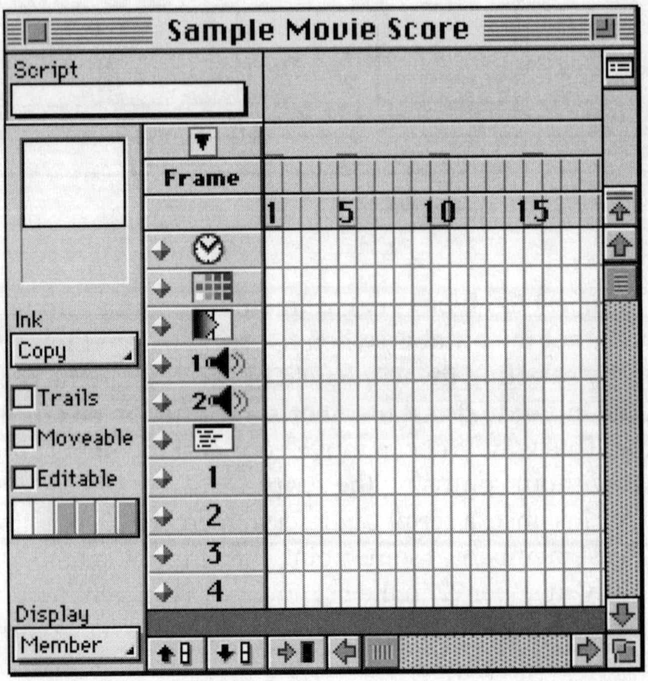

Figure 2-3: *The score window.*

There are 48 *channels* in the score—they are numbered. The little box that forms the intersection of a frame and a channel is called a *cell*, just like in a spreadsheet program. Each cell can contain a cast member.

For instance, if you want frame 1 of a Director movie to contain three elements, you might put the three cast members in frame 1, channels 1, 2, and 3.

A cast member in a channel is also called a *sprite*. Sometimes channels are referred to as sprites as well.

Each cell, in addition to containing a cast member, also holds information about the position of that cast member on the stage. You can have the same cast member appear twice in one frame by placing it in two sprites, say sprite 3 and sprite 4, but the location information for each sprite is different, so they appear on different parts of the screen.

Each cell can also have a script associated with it, in addition to the cast member. You can use the same script more than once by assigning it to different sprites in the same frame. This way, several buttons in your movie can behave the same without requiring duplicate scripts to be written for each one.

Scripts can also control an entire frame by placing them in the script channel of the frame. The script channel is right above the numbered channel rows in the score. You can assign these scripts, and the ones for the sprites, by selecting the cell and using the pop-up menu at the upper left-hand side of the score.

There are several other special channels at the top of the score. These include channels for sounds, transitions, color palette, and tempo.

To create animation using the score, you can simply have several nearly identical frames next to each other, but with one or more elements offset slightly. For instance, one sprite could contain a cast member that is a graphic, and it will appear on the left side of the screen. On the next frame, however, all of the other sprites stay the same, except that your animated sprite has moved a few pixels to the right. Continue this pattern over many frames and it will look as if the graphic is moving to the right when the Director movie plays. In fact, it is acting like a paper flip book or filmstrip, showing you different images through time and creating the illusion of movement.

Using Lingo you can do the same animation without using more than one frame in the score. You can even vary the behavior of the animation depending on the user's actions.

Think about it—if you want a line to float across the screen, you can easily do that with a dozen frames in the score. But if the line needs to be red at times and blue at other times, you will need two sets of frames, one for the red line and one for the blue. That's 24 frames.

What if the line can be three different widths? This means you need three sets of frames—one for each length—and each of those has to have a red and a blue version. That's 72 frames.

Now, consider if the line can be 10 different lengths. Now we are talking about 720 frames, all to make a line float around. Imagine what you will need for more complex animation!

With Lingo, the above example can be done in one frame, no matter how many variations are involved.

States of a Director Movie

If you are familiar with creating Director movies, you know that you open the movie file in Director, create or make changes to the score, then press Play to start the movie. Later, you press Stop to make more changes. These items are available in Director's control panel, shown in Figure 2-4, or they can be accomplished by several different keyboard combinations.

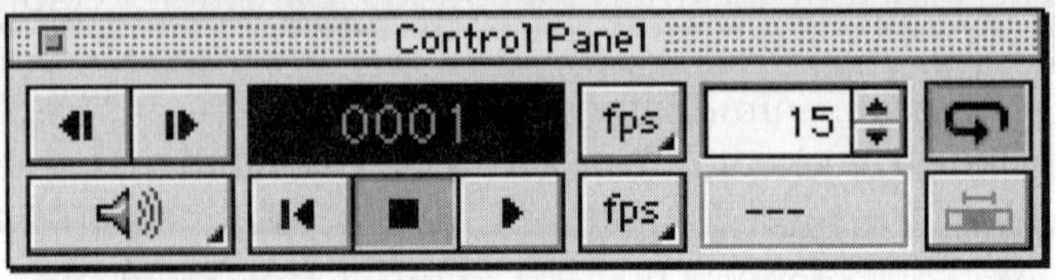

Figure 2-4: *The control panel.*

This process shows that there are two different states of Director movies: stopped and playing. You can also think of these as authoring and viewing, or program and run states.

The important thing to remember is that Director does virtually nothing on its own when in stopped mode. It just waits for your commands, accepts changes to the score, cast, and scripts, and allows you to save and load different movies. In play mode, however, Director takes your score, cast, and scripts and executes what the current movie has been programmed to do.

A projector, an application created by Director from a movie, only has a play mode. It begins running immediately, and although it can "stop," it will not let the user alter the cast, score, or scripts.

Most of your work done in Director will result in the creation of projectors. To allow users who do not have Director to play your movies, you would make a projector. This makes your movie a stand-alone application. With Lingo, that projector can load other movies, create floating dialog boxes, allow user input, and do almost anything you see in computer applications and CD-ROM products.

Lesson Review

Director Terms	Definition
Movie	The primary type of Director file. It has a score and a cast.
Score	The chart that shows you what cast members are in which frames.
Script	A list of English-like Lingo statements that control the flow of a Director movie (see next lesson for more details).
Frames	Each moment in a movie, in chronological order.
Cast member	A graphic, piece of text, button shape, or script used in a movie.
Cast	The collection of all cast members.
Channel	One of 48 rows in the score where cast members can be placed.

Cell	The intersection of a frame and a channel in the score.
Sprite	A cast member placed in a channel of the score.
Icon	A small representation of a cast member in the cast member window.
Properties	Pieces of information associated with a movie, frame, sprite, or cast member.
Play State	When the movie's play head is moving.
Stop State	When the movie's play head is not moving and you can make changes to the score and cast.
Projector	A stand-alone application created from a movie.

This lesson was meant to serve as a review of the elements of Director. Now that we have them fresh in our minds, we can move on to learn about how Lingo enters the picture.

Lesson 2: Lingo Basics

Understanding the basics of Lingo requires one to learn a lot of "lingo"—terms such as *script, handler, variable,* and *message* that are about to become part of your vocabulary. This lesson describes what these terms mean to you when you're working with Lingo and Director.

Scripts

Lingo scripts are collections of instructions for your Director movie to follow. They are stored in cast members, just like the rest of the Director elements.

At first glance, a Director script cast member may just look like an oddly formatted piece of text. The words are all in English, and they almost make sense.

Lingo scripts are actually nothing more than instructions strung together in such a way that Director can follow them. "Understanding" language requires very complex intelligence, more than you can expect from a multimedia application (or indeed any computer program available at present). However, if you restrict the vocabulary and phrase structure of a language enough, a program can recognize (understand) the elements and execute the instructions you provide.

For instance, you might say to a person: "Could you go over there and get me that coffee mug?" A computer program would have an easier time understanding your request presented this way: "Go there," "Get mug," "Bring back."

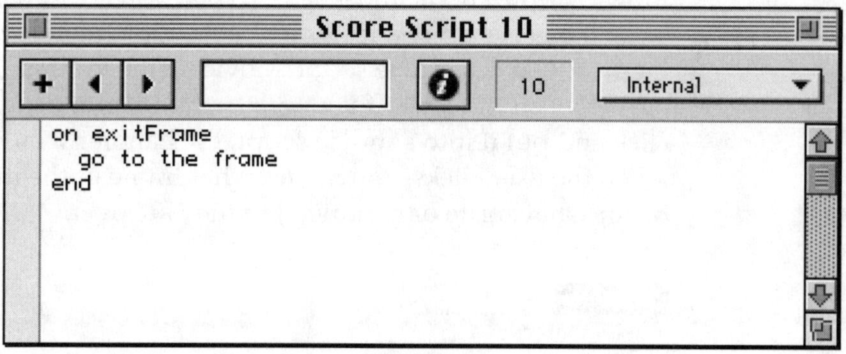

Figure 2-5: *What a Lingo script looks like.*

A Lingo script looks like a block of text. Figure 2-5 shows a very simple Lingo script. You edit the script the same way you would edit text. You can open the script edit window from the menu bar, or by using the Cmd+0 (zero) keys on the Macintosh or the Ctrl+0 keys on a PC in Windows. There are also other ways to open the script window, like double-clicking on an already existing script cast member.

You can have as many script cast members as you like. The reasons for having multiple script cast members are: you may want to divide your scripting for organizational purposes, or you may want different scripts to give instructions to different elements in a movie.

Inside each script cast member a script is broken into smaller pieces, called *handlers*—so called because each set of instructions should be designed to *handle* a certain situation. For instance, a handler may manage the situation where the user clicks the mouse. A script cast member may contain one or several handlers.

You can easily spot handlers in scripts, because they are always aligned with the left side of the scripting window and they always start with the word *on*.

Types of Scripts

There are four basic types of script cast members: movie scripts, frame score scripts, score sprite scripts and cast member scripts.

Movie scripts

Movie scripts are the most basic. When you create a script from scratch by selecting Script from the Window menu, as shown in Figure 2-6, it is a movie script. Movie scripts contain handlers that are active all the time. If you wrote a handler to handle a mouse click and put it into a movie script, the handler would do its thing when the user clicks—no matter what frame of the movie they are on, or what sprite or cast member they are over.

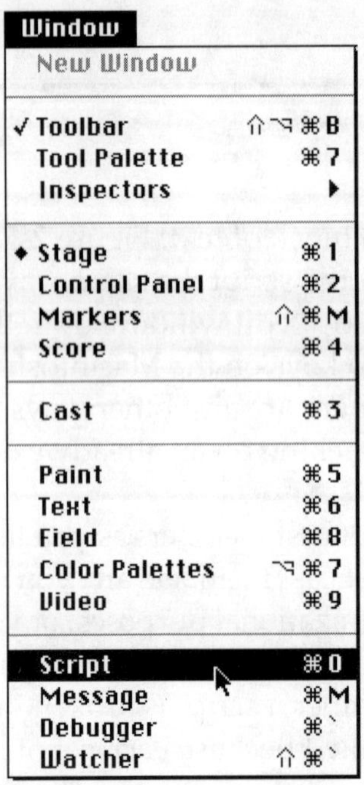

Figure 2-6: *Selecting the script window when starting from scratch will automatically bring up a blank movie script.*

Frame score scripts

These are not active in the entire movie. They look the same as movie scripts, but if you bring up the information box about the script, it will show that it is a score script instead of a movie script. These can be attached to an entire frame of the movie's score.

You can create a frame score script by selecting "new script" from the script pull-down menu in the score window. Figure 2-7 demonstrates this. Make sure you have selected the script channel of the score before creating the script.

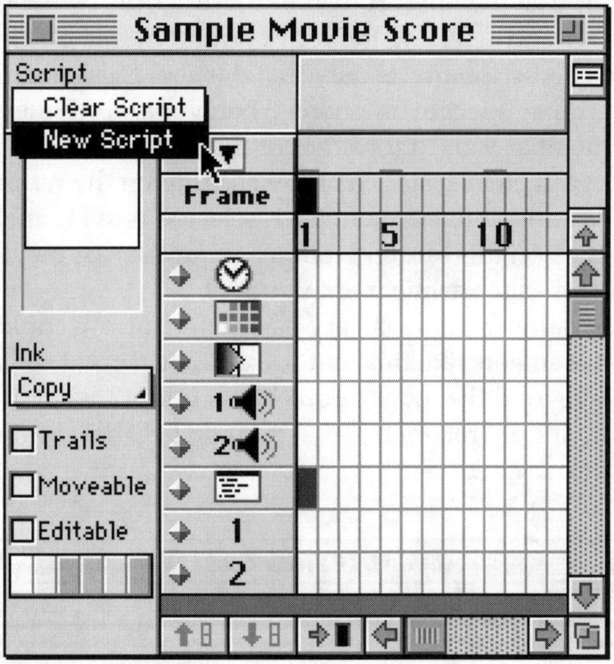

Figure 2-7: *Creating a new frame script.*

The handlers in this script are only active when the movie is in that frame. The same script can be applied to more than one frame in a movie.

Sprite score scripts

Basically the same as frame score scripts, but sprite score scripts are attached to a specific cell in the score. They only affect the sprite in that particular frame. You can attach the same script to more than one cell in a frame and to cells in other frames as well.

Sprite score scripts can be created the same way as frame scripts. Just select a sprite channel before creating the new script.

Director considers frame score scripts and sprite score scripts to be the same: just score scripts. Since their use is very different, we shall refer to them as different things.

Cast scripts

Cast members have scripts that perform specific functions for a specific cast member. You enter these scripts by opening the cast member and selecting the script button in that cast member's window. This script affects only that particular cast member but performs those specific functions wherever and whenever the same cast member is used throughout the movie.

You can create cast scripts by clicking on the script button in the cast window while a member is selected (see Figure 2-8). You can also click on this button while viewing the cast member in its own window—such as the paint window.

The paint window is very basic Director. We could explain Director elements like this, but it would be a good 50 pages of stuff that's beyond the focus of this book. I didn't want to leave out the paint window reference here, though, because most users will find that info useful.

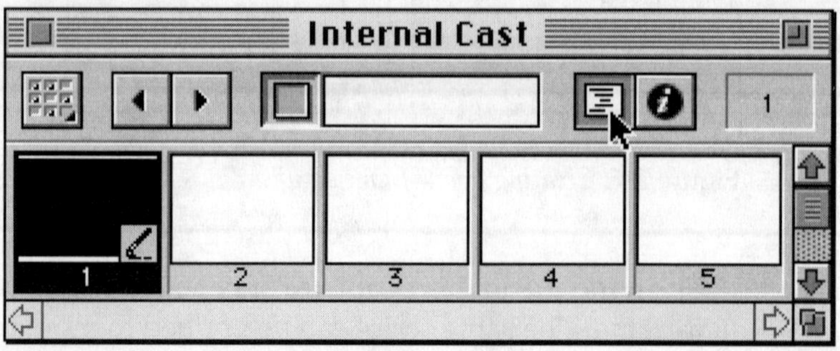

Figure 2-8: *Creating a cast member script.*

Switching Script Types

If you have accidentally created a score script when you really wanted a movie script, or vice-versa, you can change the type of script by selecting the "information" (using the little "i" icon) about the script. Figure 2-9 shows what this dialog box looks like and how you can switch script types.

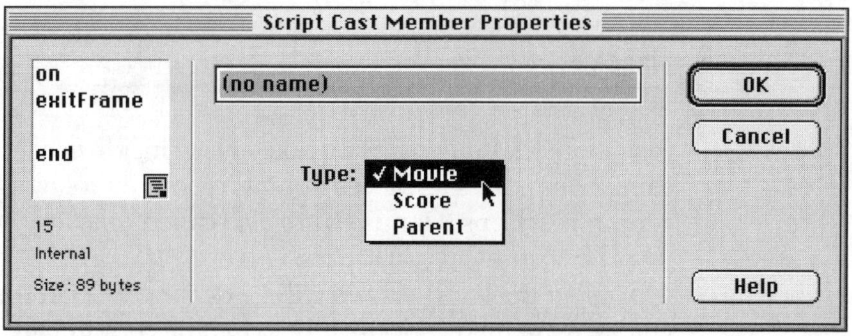

Figure 2-9: *Changing the script type in the script's information window.*

Events & Messages

You can simplify reality by saying that time is a series of events, each one following the previous one. Director movies can be described in exactly that way.

Each time something important happens, it is called an *event*. While things like clicking the mouse button may not seem very important to us, it is important to a computer—which is busy counting 1's and 0's all day.

Events are things like the mouse button being clicked, the movie reaching the end of a frame, or a key press.

Every time an event takes place while a movie is playing, Director sends out a message to announce the occasion. For example, if the user clicks on the mouse button, an immediate "mouseDown" message is sent. This is probably followed quickly by a "mouseUp" message as the user releases the mouse button. Then, the current frame in the movie ends and Director sends out an "exitFrame" message to signify that it is done with that frame. It follows with an "enterFrame" message to announce that it has started on the next frame.

But where do these messages get "sent"? Well, they have various destinations and uses. Director, for instance, gets these messages so that it can interpret ones like the user pressing the Escape key. However, we can intercept these messages using Lingo and use them as triggers for our programs, as you'll see in later chapters.

Handlers

Just about all Lingo activity takes place inside *handlers*. You can think of handlers as pieces of Lingo grouped together to perform certain functions. Handlers are also called *functions, subroutines, procedures,* or even just *scripts*.

Most of the handlers we will be dealing with in the next few chapters are made specifically to handle certain Director messages, such as "exitFrame" or "mouseDown." By naming these handlers appropriately, we can set them to automatically intercept the messages. For instance, in order to have a handler that reacts to the "mouseDown" message, we should name the handler "on mouseDown." We'll be seeing examples of these types of handlers in the coming chapters.

Another type of handler is one that doesn't react to any Director-generated message but instead waits for us to activate, or "call," it. These handlers can have any names we wish to give them.

Our own handlers can do two very important things in addition to containing many pieces of code. For one, they can accept *parameters*. This means we can pass numbers or text into a handler and it will react in a prescribed way. For example, we may have a handler that causes a graphic on the screen to flash several times. We can pass the number of times it is to flash into the routine as a *parameter*.

The second important thing a handler can do is return a value. For instance, it may be a handler's task to do a complex piece of math. When the task is completed, it returns the value so that the original handler that called our math handler can use it.

Script Elements

Lingo scripting is made up of commands, functions, variables, and special syntax.

Commands

Commands are actions that you want your Director movie to perform. For instance, the command *put* is the most basic. You can write a piece of lingo code that says: *put "Hello World" into field "aTextField"*.

What this will do is take the words *Hello World* and put them into a text cast member named "aTextField."

When scripting, you have to be very careful to make sure that the command you are asking Director to perform is possible. For instance, if there is no cast member named "aTextField," then Director will not know how to carry out the above command. It will complain with an ugly error message.

Functions

A command that asks a question, such as "What time is it?" is called a function because it returns a value rather than performing an action. However, some functions both perform an action and return a value.

There are many predefined functions in Director. These usually are referred to with the word *the* in front of them. For instance, *the mouseDown* refers to whether or not the mouse button is down at the present moment.

Variables

Variables are simply pieces of information stored for later use. Think of the variables themselves as boxes that contain information. Each box has a label. For instance, a box labeled "time" may contain the current time. They are called variables because the information they contain can vary while the program is running. For instance, you could put the number 3 into a variable called "myNumber." Later on, you could replace the 3 with the number 6.

Special Syntax

In addition to commands, functions, and variables, Lingo contains some elements that control which pieces of code get executed. These are English-like structures that allow you to control the rest of the script. For instance, an *if...then* statement allows you to specify a certain condition that must be met before a Lingo instruction is executed. A *repeat while* statement allows you to repeat a command or series of commands many times.

The Most Important Lingo Command

All of the commands in Lingo control aspects of a Director movie. A command can make a graphic on the screen change, the movie jump to a different frame, or a sound play. A combination of commands can perform very complex operations.

The most important command, however, is unique in that it does absolutely nothing. It looks like this: "--"

This command is used for commenting your code. Anything that appears after a "--" on the same line will be ignored by Director. You should use this to write comments next to lines of code so that months later you can remember what a line does, or a colleague can figure things out without bugging you. A "--" can appear on a line by itself as well, to provide comment for the next or previous line of code.

Those Odd Lingo Words

Although Lingo is not really case-specific, it has become conventional to capitalize certain letters when writing a Lingo command or creating a variable. Usually, these names are several words strung together, like *mouseDown*. The first word starts with a lowercase letter, and every word thereafter is capitalized. This makes these multiword names easier to read. Other examples are *exitFrame*, *puppetSprite*, and *myFirstVariable*.

Lesson Review

Lingo Terms	Definition
Script	One or more handlers stored in a cast member.
Function	A handler that returns a value.
Procedure	Another name for a handler.
Subroutine	Another name for a handler.
Event	Something that happens during a movie, such as a mouse click.
Message	A signal created in reaction to an event.
Command	A single piece of Lingo that performs an action.
Variable	A "container" that stores a number or text.
Handler	Many Lingo commands strung together to perform a certain function. Often a handler is built to react to a message, such as *on mouseDown*.

If you have ever programmed in a computer language before, especially one similar to Lingo, such as HyperCard's scripting language, you probably already know much of the information offered in this lesson. However, if Lingo is your first experience with programming language, then this stuff is all new. You may want to remember to come back to this lesson after you have a few scripts under your belt so that you can better understand some of these concepts.

Now that you have an overview of what is in store, let's move on to getting our feet wet with some Lingo commands.

Lesson 3: Getting Started

Lingo syntax:

```
put, set
```

If you look ahead to the reference section of this book, or if you have flipped through the manual that comes with Director, you will see that there are hundreds of Lingo commands (most of which you will use infrequently). The commands in this lesson and the next few lessons are the most common Lingo syntax—the ones you'll use most of the time.

In order to learn new commands, we will use Director's message window. This is a good way to learn, and this window can also be helpful as a constant companion when you're developing new programs.

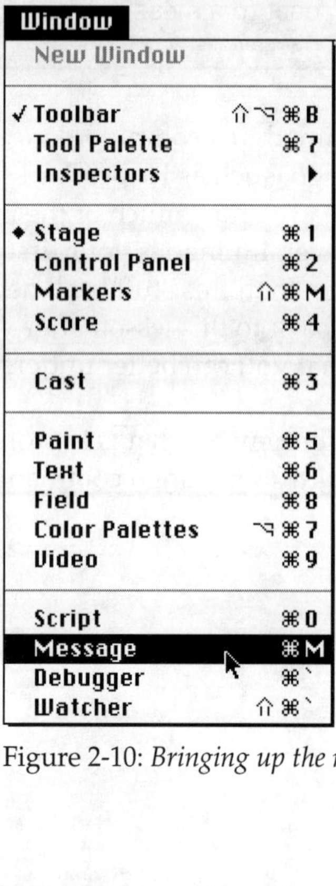

Figure 2-10: *Bringing up the message window from the menu.*

To get the message window up, just press Cmd+M on a Mac, or Ctrl+M on a PC, or use the menu bar, shown in Figure 2-10. It brings up a simple window where you can type text (Figure 2-11). Each line of text you type, however, is interpreted by Director as a line of Lingo code as soon as you press the Return key.

Figure 2-11: *The message window.*

For instance, try typing the following line in the message window:

```
put 3
```

After you press Return, the message window will "answer" your message with the following line:

```
-- 3
```

Using the *put* command without any further instructions as to where you want the result to be put will result in the object being put into the message window, as we see here. The message window prefaces all of its "answers" with a double-dash.

Here is another example. Just input the first line, and Director will answer with the second:

```
put "Hello World"
-- "Hello World"
```

Director can actually do things with the *put* command, not just regurgitate what you typed. Try this:

```
put 3+4
-- 7
```

The drawback of the message window is that it only allows you to test one command at a time. But since we will be learning Lingo one command at a time, it will be useful as we go along to demonstrate single lines of code outside of their more complex scripts.

Let's use it right now to learn about variables. Suppose we want to store the number 3 for future use. We can use the *put* command to do this. Type this into the message window and press return.

```
put 3 into myFirstVariable
```

Nothing happened, right? Ah, but something did. Several things, in fact. The first thing that Director did was to create a variable, or empty box. In this case it was labeled "myFirstVariable." There is nothing special about this name—we just made it up. You could just as easily call it "Fred."

The next thing Director did was to fill that empty box with the number 3. Now we can retrieve the contents of that box by typing the following:

```
put myFirstVariable
-- 3
```

There we go! Director remembered what we told it. The name of the variable is important; if we had named the variable "Fred" to begin with, we would need to ask for that name instead of "myFirstVariable."

You can also use the *set* command to create or change variables. For instance:

```
set myFirstVariable = 4
put myFirstVariable
-- 4
```

We can also put text into variables. Try this:

```
put "It's a piece of text!" into mySecondVariable
put mySecondVariable
-- "It's a piece of text!"
```

In Lingo, you need to put quotes around pieces of text in order to prevent Director from trying to interpret them as commands.

Things You Can Put in Variables

Integers 5, 75, 0, –23

Floating-point Numbers 0.42, 56.9, –5.3, 7.0

Strings "Hello", "The quick brown fox", "g"

Boolean Values TRUE, FALSE, 1, 0

Variables represent a valuable part of programming in any language. They allow you to store numbers and text for later use and pass them on to other handlers. Most important, you can change the value of a variable by performing operations on it.

For instance, you can add 1 to a number variable:

```
put 3 into a
put a
-- 3
put a+1 into a
put a
-- 4
```

In this case we used a variable called "a". We placed the number 3 into it and took a look at the contents. Then we placed a new number, equal to the original number, plus 1, into the same variable. When we take a second look at the variable's contents, we see a 4.

You can perform all sorts of operations on variables, including the standard mathematical functions: addition, subtraction, multiplication, and division.

Try It Yourself

Use the message window like a calculator. Try balancing your checkbook or performing simple math. Use variables as the equivalent of a calculator's memory function to store and retrieve numbers.

Moving On

In addition to being a good place to learn about new scripts, the message window is also invaluable for testing and debugging in more advanced work.

Now that you know how to use some basic Lingo commands, in the next chapter we'll create some scripts.

3 Frame Scripts

The most constantly used type of script is the frame script. Some Lingo programs consist entirely of frame scripts, while other Lingo programs combine frame scripts with other types of scripts. Let's familiarize ourselves with some basic frame scripts and see what they can do for us.

Lesson 4: Simple Frame Script

Lingo syntax:

```
go, the frame, on exitFrame, on mouseDown
```

Now that we know how to type Lingo into the message window, let's create a script cast member that actually does something useful.

One of the most common scripts is one placed in a frame in the score to cause the movie to wait for a mouse click to continue to the next frame.

Since you want to control an entire frame, you need to put the script into the script channel of the frame you want to control.

You will need two pieces of Lingo to perform this operation. The first is the *go* command. This command asks the Director movie to jump to a frame in the score. For example, *go to 3* will make the play head of the Director movie jump to frame 3.

The other piece of Lingo syntax you will need is *the frame*. This is a predefined Lingo function that will return the number of the current frame you are on. Try it in the message window:

```
put the frame
-- 1
```

In the above example, Director returned a 1, to show that the movie is currently in frame 1. If you use the score window to select a cell in another frame, it will return the number of that frame instead. When a movie is playing, *the frame* will return the number of the frame currently showing.

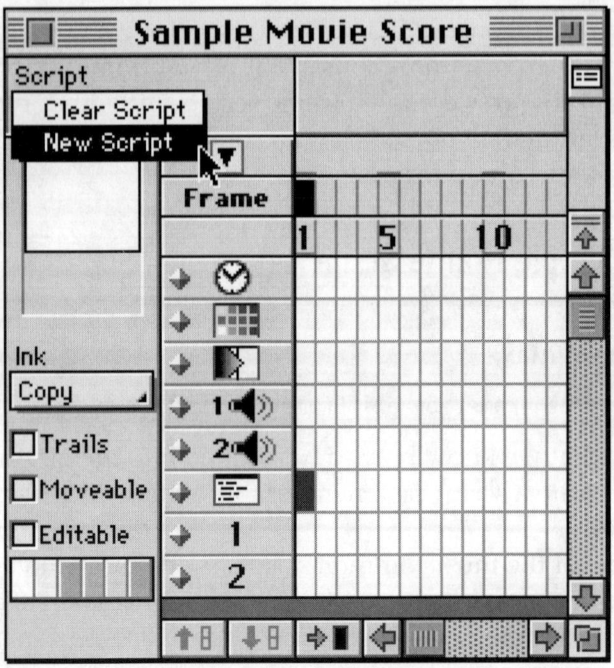

Figure 3-1: *Creating a new score script.*

Now, let's build a frame score script to do what we want. In the score, select the cell in the column of the frame you are interested in, and select the script row. Then go to the script pop-up menu in the upper left side of the screen and pull it down to select New Script. Figure 3-1 shows how this should look. A scripting window will appear. Type in the script in Figure 3-2.

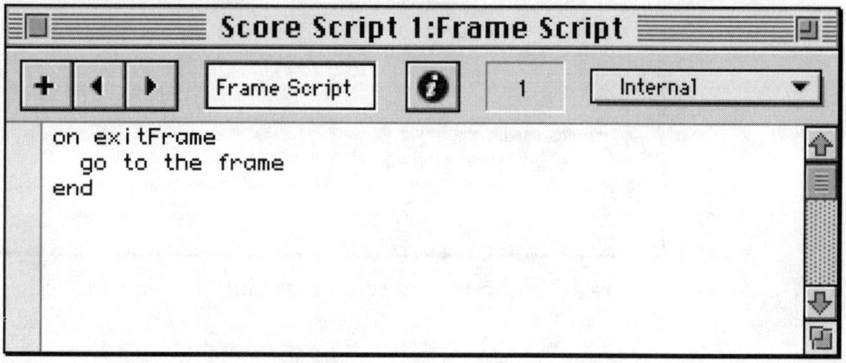

Figure 3-2: *The most basic frame script.*

There are plenty of things to explain here. Let's go through it word by word. The first line is referring to an event, *exitFrame.* Events are simply a set of things that can happen in the Director world. *exitFrame* is an event that takes place every time a frame in the score is done playing.

You can intercept these events and cause them to trigger scripts by using handlers. The *on exitFrame* handler shown above will execute every time the *exitFrame* event occurs.

Since this particular script is a score script that appears only in one frame of the score, it will only work when the *exitFrame* event occurs on that particular frame.

The only line of code in this handler is *go to the frame*. This simply tells the movie to jump to the current frame—in essence, causing the movie to loop on the current frame. Every time the frame is done, an *exitFrame* event happens. That event triggers our handler, which tells Director to start that frame all over again. So it stays there forever.

We need to add something to the script to allow the user to get out of the looping frame. Add another handler to your script so that it looks like the one in Figure 3-3.

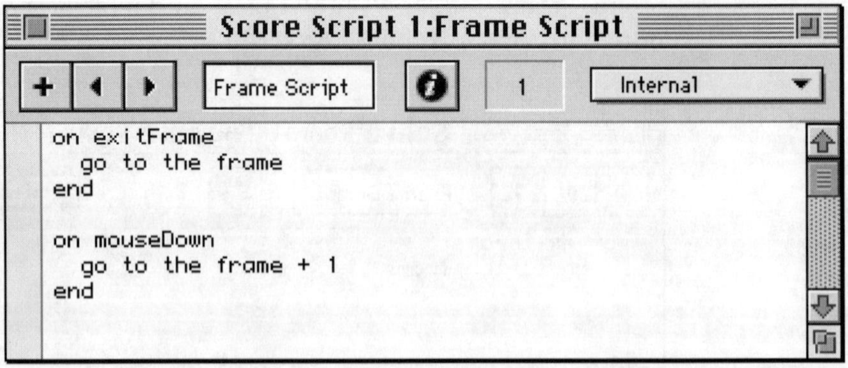

Figure 3-3: *A frame score script that waits for a mouse click.*

The new handler in the script only reacts to the event of the user pushing down on the mouse button. This creates a *mouseDown* event that your script handles.

Your *on mouseDown* script also has only one line. This line tells Director to move to the current frame, plus 1. The play head jumps out of its loop and continues with the very next frame.

You can place this same frame script in many places in any Director movie. It acts as a sort of "pause" for the movie.

If you are familiar with the score tempo elements, you know you can create an effect similar to this script by using the "wait for Mouse Click or Key Press" tempo setting. But we have already moved beyond that because our script is specific in looking for only a mouse click. In addition, with our method, the play head keeps moving; it is just stuck looping on the same frame over and over again. This will allow other Director effects, like looping sounds or more scripts, to continue while it waits.

Later, we design similar frame score scripts that do much more complex functions.

Try It Yourself

Test out this script yourself. Create a new movie and make several consecutive frames of whatever you want. Try just placing various elements such as text, shapes, and bitmaps on the first few frames.

Now create the above script and place it in the frame channel of those frames. Try playing the movie. What happens if the script is only in some of the frames? In all of them?

We have taken our first steps in Lingo. Make sure you understand these basic frame scripts; we will need to use ones like them in most of the rest of the chapters.

In the next lesson we will explore using the keyboard as a way to jump around in a movie's score.

Lesson 5: Simple Frame Navigation

Lingo syntax:

```
if…then, on keyDown, the key, go previous, go next, go loop,
marker
```

The last lesson used the mouse button as user input in a frame script. We can also use other methods of user input in Lingo, such as the keyboard. Let's look at a basic way to incorporate keyboard input into frame scripts.

What if we take the script in the last lesson a little further. Instead of having users click the mouse button to go to the next frame, we'll have them use the keyboard. This means that our *on mouseDown* script will have to be replaced by an *on keyDown* script.

The two handlers work in pretty much the same way for our purposes. Take a look at the script in Figure 3-4.

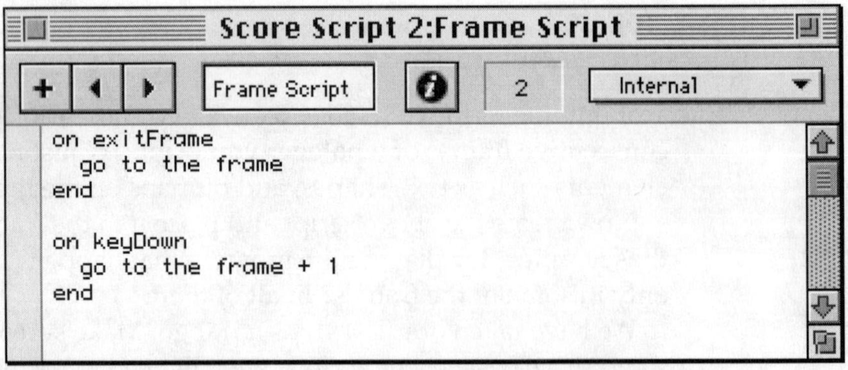

Figure 3-4: *A basic frame score script that waits for a key to be pressed.*

Remember that this script should be a score script, not a movie script, and should be assigned to the script channel of the frame you wish it to control.

We could also add the *on mouseDown* handler back to this script and make both options available to the user.

Now that we are using the keyboard, we can add some more detail to the script's functionality. Suppose we only want to have the movie move forward when the user hits the spacebar? Maybe we also want the movie to move back one frame when we hit another key.

We now are asking Director to do different things in different situations—in this case, depending upon which key the user pressed. To do things like this, we need the *if...then* Lingo structure.

The *if...then* structure works in much the same way it does in the English language and in other programming languages. Between the *if* and the *then* we need to put a true or false statement. After the *then*, we need to put a Lingo command that will only be obeyed if the true or false statement is true.

In English, we might say: "If it is raining, then take your umbrella." The lingo command follows the same structure:

```
if the key = " " then go to the frame + 1
```

Breaking the line apart, we see that we placed the true or false condition *the key = " "* between the *if* and the *then*. *the key* is another one of those predefined Lingo functions. It returns the character representing the last key typed on the keyboard. We are checking to see if it is a space. If it is, then *the key* = " " has the value of true, otherwise it is false.

Writing if...then Statements

Simple *if...then* statements are usually kept on one line:

```
if the key = " " then go to the frame + 1
```

However, they can also be separated into several lines that perform exactly the same function:

```
if the key = " " then
  go to the frame + 1
end if
```

The advantage of the second method is that you can include more than one line of code inside the statement.

After the *then* we see our familiar *go to the frame + 1* command. Now if we place the line into the *on keyDown* handler, we get our desired effect. Figure 3-5 shows the completed script.

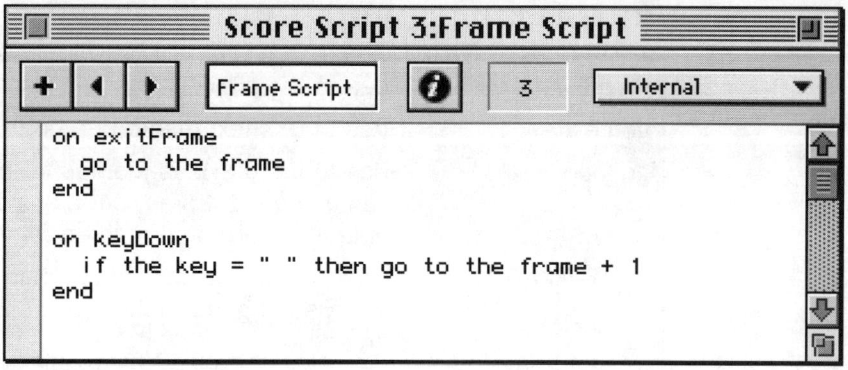

Figure 3-5: *A frame score script that waits for the spacebar to be pressed.*

You can alter the *on keyDown* script to do more specific things. For instance, you can allow the user to move back one frame in the score by pressing the "b" key. To do that, just add this line:

```
if the key = "b" then go to the frame -- 1
```

Now if you place that script in every frame of the movie, you get user-controlled backward and forward movement between the frames, similar to a slide show. However, if there is no script in the previous frame, then the *go to the frame - 1* command will only result in the movie moving back one frame and then quickly moving forward to the original frame.

Another useful line might be to offer the user a way to get back to the beginning or end of a movie. Say we label the first and last frames in the score "startFrame" and "endFrame." Then we can add the following lines to the *on keyDown* script:

```
if the key = "s" then go to frame "startFrame"
if the key = "e" then go to frame "endFrame"
```

If you are creating a corporate presentation that you or a colleague may be showing, and you want to be able to jump quickly from one important frame to another, you can add lines that make the movie jump to a certain frame when you press the respective number key on the keyboard.

Markers, or frame labels, are a great way to facilitate navigation like this. If you label the frames in your movie, then there are several Lingo commands you can use, instead of just *go to frame*. Here is a list:

go previous	Goes to the previous marked frame.
go next	Goes to the next marked frame.
go loop	Goes to the previous marked frame if you are in an unmarked frame, but loops to the same frame if you are on a marked frame.
go marker(0)	Loops on the current frame if it is marked; otherwise, it goes to the previously marked frame.
go marker(x)	Moves x markers ahead in the score.
go marker(-x)	Moves x markers back in the score.

Note that *go loop* and *go marker(0)* are exactly the same.

Try It Yourself

To try what we have learned, create a slide show presentation using the above script. Make several frames with different imported pictures on them. Assign the script to each of the frames, so that there is one key the user can use to move forward, and another key the user can use to move back.

These simple navigation techniques will enable you to make your movies much more sophisticated. In the next lesson, we will add *time* as another element that can cause the movie to break out of a looping frame.

Lesson 6: Timed Frame Script

Lingo syntax:

```
repeat…while, exit repeat, the ticks, the mouseDown
```

We have added the element of user interaction to our movies with the previous two lessons' frame scripts. In this lesson, we will build upon that by adding the element of time to the scripts.

A common need in kiosks and CD-ROM introduction screens is to pause over a certain frame for a given period of time. However, if the user clicks on the screen before the time has passed, you may want the movie to move ahead immediately.

The previous lessons had scripts that looped on a frame while waiting for the mouse button to be clicked or a key to be pressed. Those scripts will wait forever for this. But instead of waiting for user input, this next script will wait 10 seconds and then continue to the next frame on its own.

To do this, we will need to ask Director about the current time. First, we will need to see what time it is when the wait begins, then we will need to keep checking the time to see if too much time—10 seconds, in this case—has elapsed.

To tell the time, we will use *the ticks*. This Director function will return the number in 1/60 of a second since the computer was started. Try it in the message window:

```
put the ticks
-- 387132
```

You will get a different number, depending on how long your computer has been on. Type the same command again and compare the two numbers. Your message window might then look something like this:

```
put the ticks
-- 387893
```

The two numbers differ by exactly the amount of time, in 1/60 of a second, between hitting the Return key at the end of each command. In this case, the difference is 761 ticks, or a little under 13 seconds.

To create a script that will loop for a specified length of time, we need to introduce the concept of *loops*. This is similar to how our old frame script works, by going to *the frame* every time an "exitFrame" message happens, but this loop takes place entirely inside a handler.

The command for loops is *repeat*. There are two flavors of *repeat* loop. We'll deal with one right now: the *repeat while* loop.

After the command *repeat while*, you must give a condition, just as in *if...then* statements. As a matter of fact, *repeat* loops and *if...then* statements are very similar. The first checks to see if a condition is true, and then executes the code inside. The second checks to see if a condition is true, and then executes the code inside over and over again until the condition is no longer true.

To signify the end of the section of code that a *repeat* loop should repeat, we use an *end repeat* statement. Inside the *repeat* loop we can place any additional Lingo script we choose, including other *repeat* loops—or we can place nothing, as we do in this script.

Frame Loops Vs. Repeat Loops

We now have two types of loops at our disposal: looping on a frame in the score with the *go to the frame* command, and the Lingo *repeat* loop.

The fundamental difference is that frame looping keeps the play head moving so that things are allowed to happen inside other loops. The score still has control over the movie. Tempo settings determine the frequency of the loop. Other handlers are allowed to react to other messages, such as "mouseDown."

Repeat loops, however, freeze the entire movie while the commands inside the loop execute. Control of the movie is not returned to the score until the *repeat* loop is done. Even messages like "mouseDown" are ignored unless dealt with inside the *repeat* loop.

Another function we will need for this script is the ability to store and retrieve numbers. We can do this by using variables. We will put the initial time that the frame was supposed to end in a variable called "endTime." Then we'll add 10 seconds worth of ticks to it so that it represents the time when the loop should end and the movie should be moving on. We will use the *repeat* loop to constantly compare this variable to *the ticks* until *the ticks* has passed "endTime."

Figure 3-6 shows the score script that we need to place into the frame script channel in the score to make this all happen.

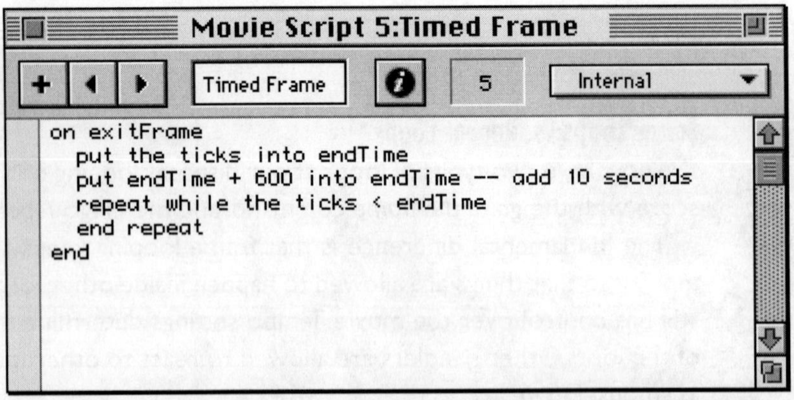

Figure 3-6: *A frame script that waits 10 seconds to go to the next frame.*

The other piece of functionality we need to add to the script is the ability to move forward immediately if the user clicks the mouse. To do this, we will keep checking the predefined Lingo function *the mouseDown* to see if the user has pushed the mouse button.

the mouseDown is similar to *on mouseDown*, except that the first one is a function, which returns a true or false value, and the second one is a handler that accepts "mouseDown" messages. *the mouseDown* is a piece of Lingo that we use inside a handler, while *on mouseDown* actually *is* a handler.

Make changes to the previous script so that it matches Figure 3-7, and test it out.

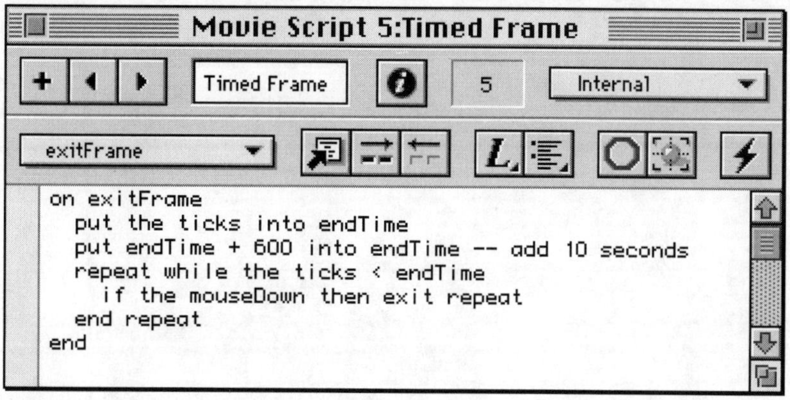

Fig 3-7: *A frame script that waits 10 seconds, or until the user pushes the mouse button, to go to the next frame.*

When *the mouseDown* is equal to true, we use the *exit repeat* command to tell Director to jump out of the *repeat while* loop. This way there are two ways that our *repeat* loop can end: the time allotted can expire and the *repeat* loop ends normally, or the user pushes the mouse button and Director jumps out of the *repeat* loop. Either way, when the *on exitFrame* script is over, the movie will move on to the next frame.

Try It Yourself

Create a slide show-type presentation that moves forward every five seconds if the user just waits, but will allow the user to click on the mouse to advance without delay.

Moving On

In this lesson we introduced repeat loops, a very important part of any programming language. In the future, we will be using repeat loops for many things, and even have repeat loops inside of other repeat loops.

In the first lesson of the next chapter we will introduce buttons, a screen element that can be used to let the user navigate through a movie.

4 Buttons

Buttons are the most-used interface elements in multimedia. Whether they look like rectangles, circles, real physical push-buttons, hovering surfaces, or are completely invisible, all buttons share similar behaviors. Let's learn about Director's buttons, how to make your own, and how to create the scripts that make them behave properly.

Lesson 7: Navigation With Buttons

Lingo syntax:

```
on mouseUp
```

The previous lessons described how to use Lingo to allow the user to move to different parts of the movie while it is playing. A better way to do this is to use buttons.

You may need to have a screen in your project that has several buttons, each one allowing the user to jump to a certain frame in the movie. That frame, in turn, may have more buttons on it, to let the user explore further, and maybe a button to take them back to the original screen.

Creating simple buttons that perform the function of jumping from one frame to another is easy. First, use the Director Tools palette to draw a button on the screen.

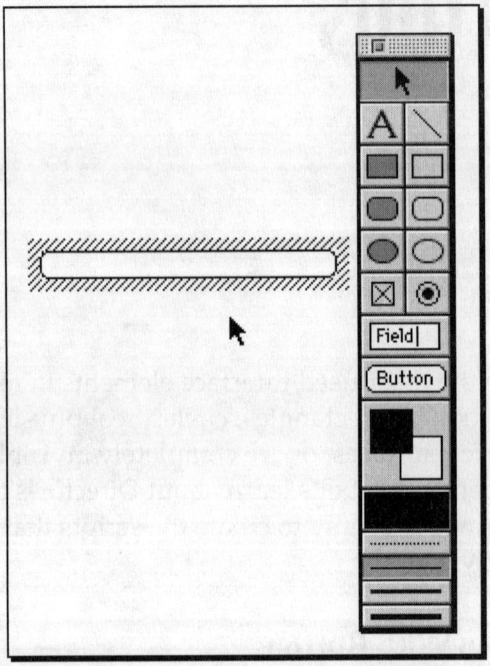

Figure 4-1: *The Button option on the Tools palette lets you draw buttons right onto the stage.*

Now, bring up the cast window and select the new cast member of that button. Hit the scripting button in the cast window to edit the script of that button.

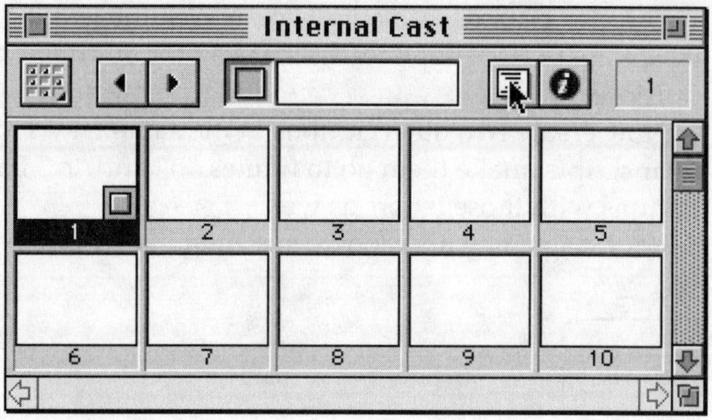

Figure 4-2: *The cast window shows your newly created button in cast member 1.*

The script window opens up. It immediately fills the script text with a blank *on mouseUp* handler. *On mouseUp* is similar to *on mouseDown*, but it takes effect when the user completes a mouse click by releasing the mouse button.

Let's complete the script ourselves. Look at Figure 4-3.

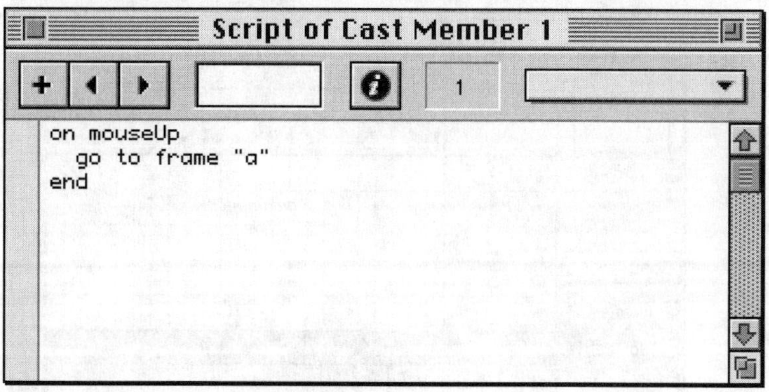

Figure 4-3: *A basic button script.*

Director buttons also allow you to edit the text that appears inside the button. Type **"a"** in that text for our demonstration purposes.

Now create two other buttons in the same way. However, in their scripts, make them go to frames "b" and "c." Label the buttons with those letters as well.

Your stage may now look something like Figure 4-4.

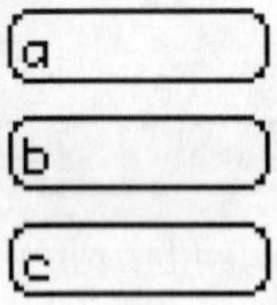

Figure 4-4: *Three buttons on the stage.*

Now go to the score and label any three frames "a," "b," and "c." Label the frame that has the three buttons "start."

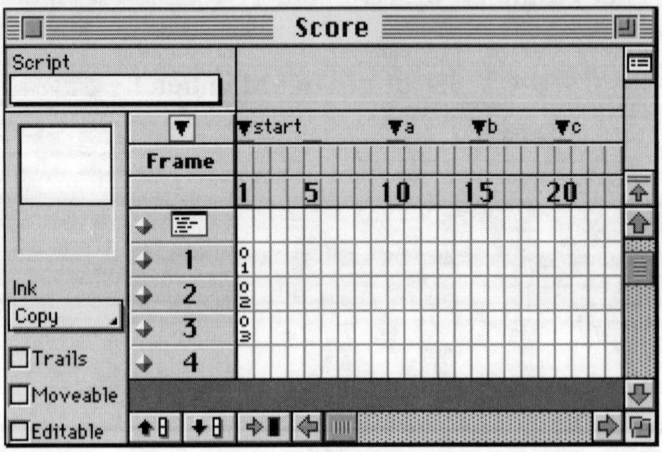

Figure 4-5: *The score showing four labeled frames.*

Click on a cell in your frame "a" to move the movie head there. Create a fourth button and place the script in Figure 4-6 in it.

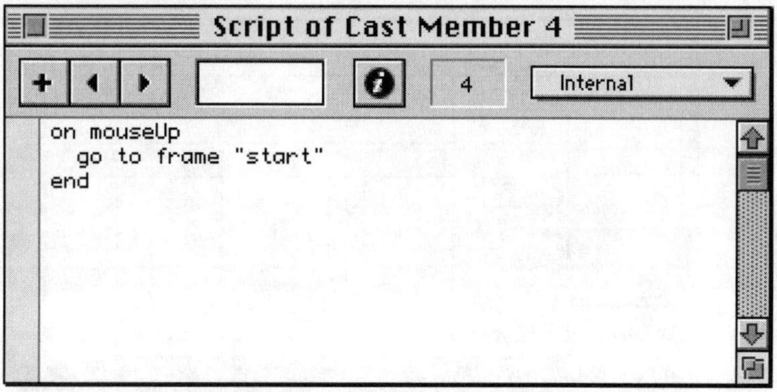

Figure 4-6: *A button script for a "return" button.*

Label this button "return." Now use copy and paste to place the "return" button in all three frames: "a," "b," and "c."

To finish up our demonstration movie, place the same looping frame script, shown in Figure 4-7, in each frame. You would do this by creating only one new script, and then placing that single script in several frames of the score.

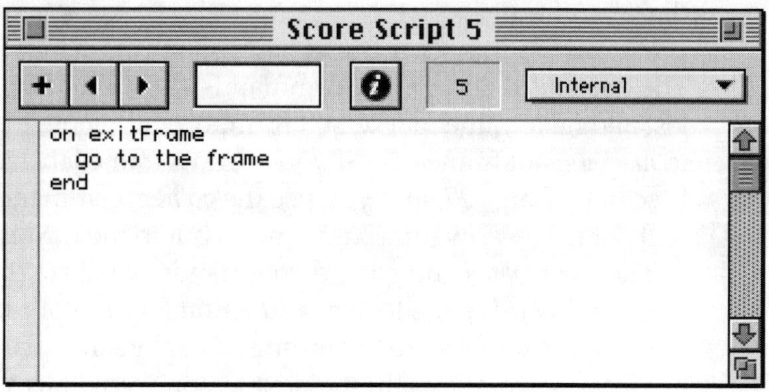

Figure 4-7: *Your basic looping frame script.*

Your final score should look like Figure 4-8.

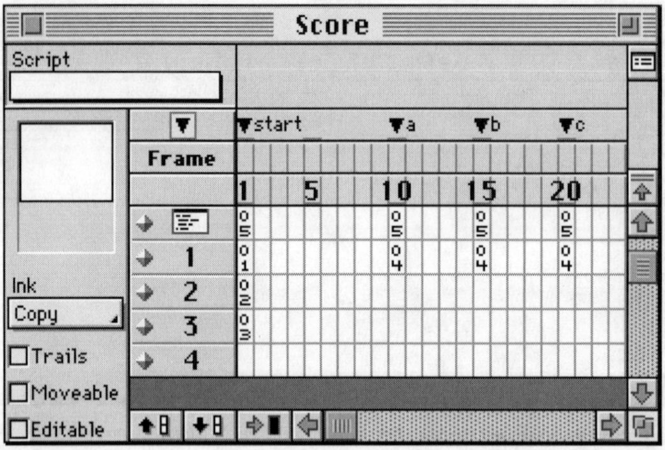

Figure 4-8: *The score showing the "start" frame and all three branches with the return buttons in place.*

If you play the movie now, you should get the initial screen with the three buttons. Click on any button to go to one of the three other frames. Keeping the score window open will allow you to see where Director's play head is positioned. Hitting the "return" button in any of these three frames will take you back to the "start" frame.

We can use our other frame navigation commands here as well. The *go previous* and *go next* commands will jump the movie to the last and next frame markers. It is important to note that this jumps to *markers*, not frames. So, if you are on a frame labeled "b," which is actually frame 27, and you use the *go next* command, the movie will not necessarily jump to frame 28 but to the next marked frame.

The *go previous* and *go next* commands are useful for creating a page backward, page forward functionality to your movies.

Now our movies are beginning to behave like real programs, not just presentations. In the next lesson we will leave the simple Director-style buttons behind and move on to using our own custom ones.

Try It Yourself

Take some of your own content and use this simple navigation system to create a nonlinear slide show. You can divide your content up into subjects so that users can quickly find what they need.

What about going beyond the one "main menu" of buttons and have a second menu on one of the other pages?

Lesson 8: Building a Better Button

Lingo syntax:

```
the memberNum of sprite, the number of member, updateStage
```

Normal buttons in Director are pretty boring. They are simply rounded rectangles with text inside. In order to create a professional presentation, you will probably want to ditch them altogether and create your own graphically appealing buttons.

A better button might be made by a small bitmap image that has the same style as the rest of your presentation. A button done this way can be beveled, have a shadow, look like it sticks out of the screen, look like it is engraved into the screen, or be a toggle switch, a glowing orb, an electric socket, or just about anything.

The simplest way to create a button like this is to use a bitmap cast member in place of a Director button. You can assign an *on mouseUp* script to that bitmap just as easily as you could to a button. In addition, you can select the Highlight When Clicked option in the bitmap's information box, as in Figure 4-9. This will give the bitmap a highlight effect when the user clicks it.

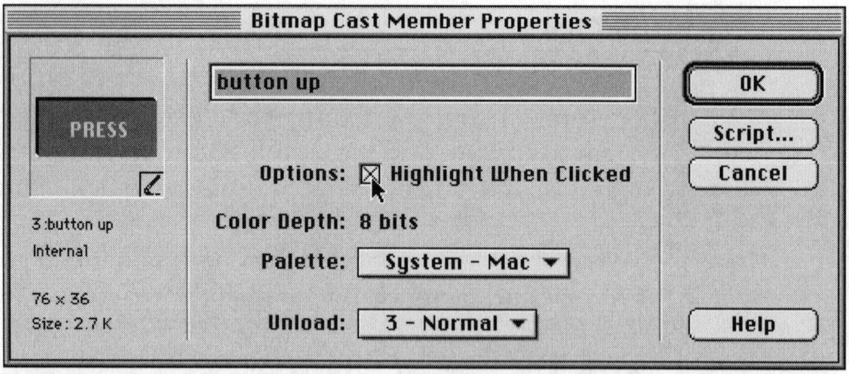

Figure 4-9: *The Highlight When Clicked option can be used to make a bitmap image more like a button.*

A better way to make your own buttons is not to use the Highlight When Clicked option but instead make your own up and down *states* of the button. You need to create these two states and place them in two cast members. Figure 4-10 shows some examples.

Figure 4-10: *Some examples of the up and down states of buttons.*

Let's use the first example: simple raised buttons. The first state shows the light hitting the bottom and right side of the button and a shadow being cast in the proper direction. We'll call this the up state of the button. The second state shows the button pushed closer to the stage. The shadow has been reduced and the button has moved slightly down and to the right.

Registration Points

To create bitmap buttons, you can use either Director's paint window or any other graphics program, and import them into Director. The important thing to remember is to match the graphics' registration points, so that when the two graphics are interchanged on the stage, they give the illusion of movement that you desire. This can usually be done quickly by trial and error, and eventually you will get a "knack" for it.

The script we need to develop will take two such graphics: an up state and a down state. Name these cast members "button up" and "button down." Place the graphic of the up state of your button in the channel you want—in this case, let's use channel 1. You can position it on the screen anywhere you want for now.

Before we write the script that handles this button action, let's try a new command in the message window:

```
put the memberNum of sprite 1
-- 1
```

the memberNum of sprite returns the number of the cast member that is currently in that sprite channel. In this case, it returned 1, which is where the cast member "button up" is located. In your case it may return a different number, depending on where you have that member in the cast .

We could also assign *the memberNum of sprite* by using the *set* command. This is what we will do in the script. You can try this in the message window. Place the "button up" bitmap on the stage and in sprite channel 1. Make sure that "button up" is the first cast member and "button down" is the second cast member.

```
set the memberNum of sprite 1 = 2
updateStage
```

You should see the bitmap change to the "button down" bitmap as soon as you hit Return after *updateStage*. This is a pretty straightforward command. When you make changes to the stage using the *set the memberNum of sprite* command, the changes will not take effect until you issue an *updateStage* command. This will allow you to make several changes, and then have them all occur at once, as far as what the user sees.

The updateStage Command

It is sometimes hard for beginners to understand when to use the *updateStage* command. You need to use it any time you change something on the stage using Lingo. Director is oblivious to these changes you are making until you tell it to *updateStage*. At that point the stage will visually change to match your alterations.

One of the most common problems users encounter with Lingo scripts is that after writing a handler that should be making changes to the stage, nothing happens. Usually, it is because the *updateStage* is missing.

Another piece of Lingo we will need is *the number of member*. Try this:

```
put the number of member "button up"
-- 1
put the number of member "button down"
-- 2
```

The result here is the number of the cast member with a specific name. In this example, 1 and 2 are the numbers of the cast members with those names. You may have different numbers.

Another predefined function in Director is *the clickOn*. This is a very useful one for developing button scripts. This function will return the number of the sprite channel that was last clicked. Let's test it with the simple score script, shown in Figure 4-11, and assign it to the button we have placed on the stage.

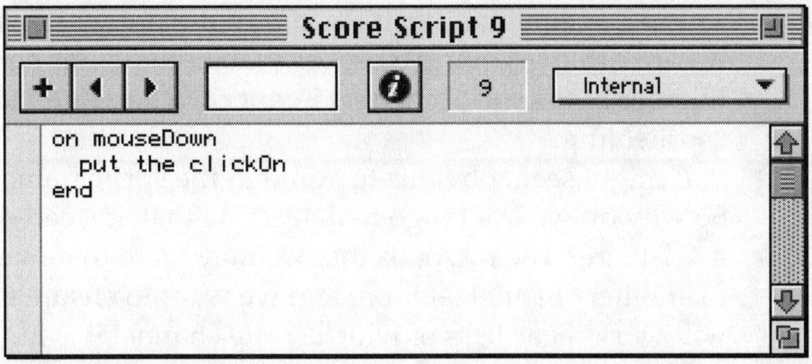

Figure 4-11: *A little script that will put the number of the sprite that was clicked into the message window.*

Before trying this out, place a simple frame script in the score to make it loop, as you did in previous lessons. Now, open the message window and position it so that it doesn't cover the button on the stage. Play the movie.

When you click on the button, a "-- 1" gets thrown to the message window. This is your piece of code telling you what value is returned by *the clickOn*.

Try putting the button in another sprite channel. The number thrown to the message window will change accordingly.

Let's try to use these pieces to make our script. Type in the script shown in Figure 4-12 as a score script. Then assign it to that cell in the score instead of the score script of the entire frame.

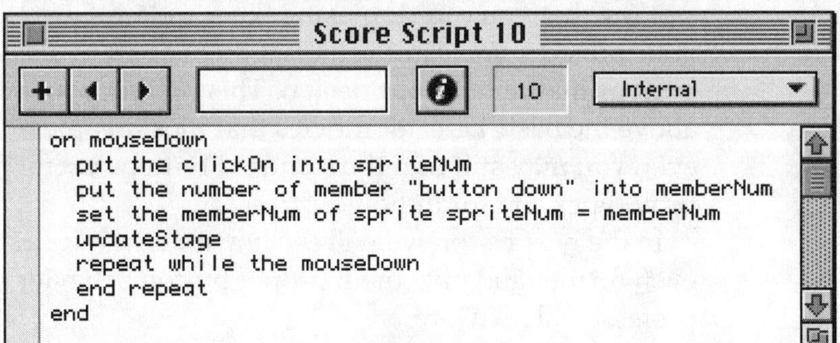

Figure 4-12: *A button script that waits for the mouse to be released before it acts.*

The first thing we need to do is figure out which sprite channel we are dealing with. We use *the clickOn* to do this and store the number of the sprite channel in our own variable, called "spriteNum."

It might seem obvious to you that the sprite number will be 1. So why do we use Lingo to determine that, instead of just placing a "1" there? The reason is that we may want to move this button to another channel later on, and we want to ensure that this script will work regardless of which sprite channel it is in.

The next thing we do is get the cast member number of the down state of the button. We place that into our variable "memNum."

Now we make our change. We set the member number of the target sprite to the number of the "button down" bitmap. The sprite channel that previously contained the up state of the button now contains the down state. We use *updateStage* to make the change visible to the user.

Next comes our *repeat* loop. We want the down state of the button to continue to show as long as the user is holding down the mouse button. We use *the mouseDown* as our condition.

Our little *repeat* loop does nothing except loop endlessly until the mouse button is lifted. Once that happens, the script ends and our temporary cast member switch reverts back to the original "mouse up" cast member.

If we wanted this button to actually do something, we could place a command, like *go to the frame+1*, at the end of the script.

Now that you can stop using the standard Director buttons in your projects, you can start to set them apart by using styled buttons that reflect your design. This will set your products a level above the basic Director movies that most people produce. However, you may still find the standard buttons useful for creating prototypes and for in-house projects.

In the next lesson we will see how to take our custom buttons even further and give them proper button behavior similar to professional software.

Try It Yourself

Take the exercise from the previous lesson and update it to include bitmap buttons instead of the Director-style buttons. Take this opportunity to practice developing a "style" for your buttons.

Lesson 9: An Even Better Button

Lingo syntax:

```
rollover, the name of member
```

The button handler we wrote in the previous lesson allowed us to use any bitmap we want as a button. The button had an up state and a down state and a script that waited for the user to release the mouse button in order for the button to perform its action.

However, our handler is far from perfect. A good button should react to a mouse click in the following way:

- It should change to a down state when pressed.
- While the mouse button is still down and the cursor is over the button, it should remain in its down state.
- While the mouse button is still down and the cursor has been moved from over the button, it should return to its up state.
- When the mouse button is released, it should return to its up state, and only perform its action if the cursor happens to be over the button at that time.
- The button should not react if the user clicks elsewhere and then moves the cursor over the button while holding down the mouse button.

It sounds complex, but if you try the buttons in just about any program on the Macintosh or Windows, you'll see that they follow these rules. We can create a button handler script that does this for us as well.

First, we need to learn some new commands. The *rollover* function tells you if the cursor is over a particular sprite. You can test this in the message window. Place a bitmap on the stage and into sprite channel 1. Bring up the message window. Type in the following Lingo, but position the cursor over sprite 1 on the stage before you press Return.

```
put rollover(1)
-- 1
```

The 1 in the above command means that we are interested in whether or not the cursor is rolling over sprite channel 1. Try the same thing with the cursor not over the sprite and you will get a 0.

The only other command we need is *the name of member*. This is the companion command to *the number of member*. As you may have guessed, this returns the name of the cast member when you supply its number.

To use the script, you need two cast members, the up state of a button, named "button," and the down state, named "button down." Place the up state on the stage and assign to it the score script shown in Figure 4-13.

Score Script 3:Button Handler

Button Handler | 3 | Internal

```
on mouseDown
  -- get the sprite number and the two cast numbers
  put the clickOn into spriteNum
  put the number of member "button" into upNum
  put the number of member "button down" into downNum

  -- set the cast member to the down state
  set the memberNum of sprite spriteNum = downNum
  updateStage

  -- repeat as long as the user holds down the button
  repeat while the mouseDown
    if rollover(spriteNum) then -- cursor over button
      set the memberNum of sprite spriteNum = downNum
    else -- cursor not over button
      set the memberNum of sprite spriteNum = upNum
    end if
    updateStage
  end repeat


  if the memberNum of sprite spriteNum = downNum then
    -- set the cursor back to the up state
    set the memberNum of sprite spriteNum = upNum
    updateStage

    -- add the button's function here

  end if
end
```

Figure 4-13: *A good button behavior script.*

Notice that the script is an *on mouseDown* script, not an *on mouseUp* script. This is important. We need to perform the button behavior in the time between the mouse button being pushed down and the button being lifted. Using an *on mouseUp* would mean that we would miss our opportunity to perform the button behavior.

Walking through the script, we start by getting the number of the sprite that contains the button. We place that in a variable, "spriteNum." Then we get the numbers of the two cast members—the up state and down state of the button.

Next, the script sets the button to the down state, so even if the user does the quickest of mouse clicks, the button appears to go down for a moment.

The *repeat* loop continues until the mouse button is lifted. Inside, there is an *if...then* statement that is a little more complex than in previous lessons. The first difference is that we divided a single *if...then* statement over several lines. This way, you can include several lines of code between the *if...then* line and the *end if*. This is also our first use of the command *else*. As you may have guessed, the code after the *else* statement only executes if the *if...then* condition is false.

We use the *if...then* statement to set the sprite to the down state if the cursor is over it, and up if the cursor is not.

When the mouse button is lifted, the *repeat* loop ends. The next thing the handler does is set the button back to its normal up state. Most of the time you will not need this part, as the button action will whisk away the movie to another frame anyway. After the button is returned to the normal state, you can add code that will describe what the button actually does, such as go to another frame in the movie.

We can do a little better with this button behavior script. In the previous script, we needed to include the names of the up and down state buttons in the script. This is called "hard-coding"; you use it when you place an important piece of information, one that may change, in the script. Since we know what sprite was clicked on by using *the clickOn* command, we can then go further and use *the name of member* command to get the name of the button. Then we can append the word *down* to the name and get the name of the down state. That way we can match button states by naming them appropriately: "button" connects to "button down," "switch" connects to "switch down," etc.

A better script would get the names of both the up and the down states automatically. Look at the script in Figure 4-14.

Score Script 5:Button Handler

Button Handler | 5 | Internal

```
on mouseDown
  -- get the sprite number and the two cast numbers
  put the clickOn into spriteNum
  put the memberNum of sprite spriteNum into upNum
  put the name of member upNum into upName
  put (upName&&"down") into downName
  put the number of member downName into downNum

  -- set the cast member to the down state
  set the memberNum of sprite spriteNum = downNum
  updateStage

  -- repeat as long as the user holds down the button
  repeat while the mouseDown
    if rollover(spriteNum) then -- cursor over button
      set the memberNum of sprite spriteNum = downNum
    else -- cursor not over button
      set the memberNum of sprite spriteNum = upNum
    end if
    updateStage
  end repeat


  if the memberNum of sprite spriteNum = downNum then
    -- set the cursor back to the up state
    set the memberNum of sprite spriteNum = upNum
    updateStage

    -- add the button's function here

  end if
end
```

Fig 4-14: *A better button behavior script, without hard-coded numbers.*

We use one new Lingo element in the script: *&*. This symbol concatenates two strings together. Try it in the message window:

```
put "learning"&"lingo"
-- "learninglingo"
```

If you use *&&*, you can get an automatic space inserted between the two strings.

```
put "learning"&&"lingo"
-- "learning lingo"
```

In the above script, this is how we get "button down" from "button."

The most important message in this lesson is to remember not to hard-code numbers or names into your scripts. The more independent of specific numbers and names a handler is, the more useful it will be.

In the next lesson, we will get to a better implementation of this same script, so that we can assign the button handler functionality to as many buttons as we want, without copying-and-pasting the script in every spot where we need it.

Try It Yourself

Try using the button behavior script. Try assigning it to two different buttons on the stage. Now, try adding an action for the button to perform. How about this line:

```
go to frame upName
```

This will cause the button named "button" to let the user go to a frame named "button." Another button with another name will go to its own frame.

Lesson 10: A Pretty Good Button Handler

Lingo syntax:

```
return
```

Now that we know all of the Lingo necessary to create proper button behavior, we need to make a button handler that works in many situations. If we have three buttons that do three different things, we want to be able to use the same button handler for all of them, even though they might perform very different actions.

This makes good programming sense. Whenever you have a piece of code that you need to use several times, it is best to create your own handler and call it when needed, rather than copying-and-pasting the same code in different spots. This will not only minimize the amount of scripting you have to do but also make it easier to make changes to your code later on because you'll only have to change it in one place.

To create our own handler, we just need to place it in a movie script and give it a name that will not conflict with anything that Director is already using. Let's call our handler "buttonClicked" and place it in a movie script.

```
Movie Script 6:button Handler
button Handler    6    Internal

on buttonClicked
  -- get the sprite number and the two cast numbers
  put the clickOn into spriteNum
  put the memberNum of sprite spriteNum into upNum
  put the name of member upNum into upName
  put (upName&&"down") into downName
  put the number of member downName into downNum

  -- set the cast member to the down state
  set the memberNum of sprite spriteNum = downNum
  updateStage

  -- repeat as long as the user holds down the button
  repeat while the mouseDown
    if rollover(spriteNum) then -- cursor over button
      set the memberNum of sprite spriteNum = downNum
    else -- cursor not over button
      set the memberNum of sprite spriteNum = upNum
    end if
    updateStage
  end repeat

  if the memberNum of sprite spriteNum = downNum then
    -- set the cursor back to the up state
    set the memberNum of sprite spriteNum = upNum
    updateStage
    return TRUE
  end if
  return FALSE
end
```

Figure 4-15: *A good button handler for all occasions.*

This script is basically the same as the one used in the previous lesson. However, it is not an *on mouseDown* handler in a score script but rather our own custom handler in a movie script. This is so we can call it from anywhere inside the movie.

The handler is called "buttonClicked." That is a name we just made up. There is no "buttonClicked" event in Director—we just created it. You could call it anything you want. The handler will never react to a message, since there is no "buttonClicked" message; it will be specifically called by us, from another script.

The handler also includes a new command: *return*. We follow this command with either *TRUE* or *FALSE* in this handler. This will be the value of the function "buttonClicked" when we call that handler. What *return* does is immediately exit the handler and assign whatever value we want—just as if it were a variable. Figure 4-16 shows a simpler example.

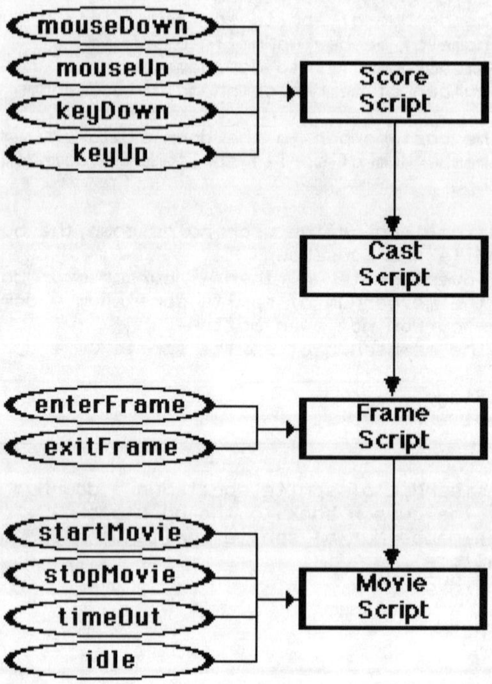

Figure 4-16: *A simple handler that returns a value.*

If we call this handler from the message window, this is what we get:

```
put fortytwo()
-- 42
```

Returning Values From Functions

A function that returns a value usually needs a place for that value to be stored. Just calling *fortytwo( )* will get you nothing if you don't try to store the result somewhere: *put fortytwo( ) into myNumber.*

Notice that we place a set of parentheses after the handler name when we call it. This is so that Director understands that it is a handler and not a variable. Later, we will be placing parameters inside these parentheses.

In the case of our button handler, when we ask for "buttonClicked" we will get the result *TRUE* if it is a valid click, or we'll get *FALSE* otherwise. Now we can use our handler in small score or cast scripts assigned to buttons on the stage. Let's take one of our buttons and place a script like the one in Figure 4-17 in the cast member that represents the up state of the button.

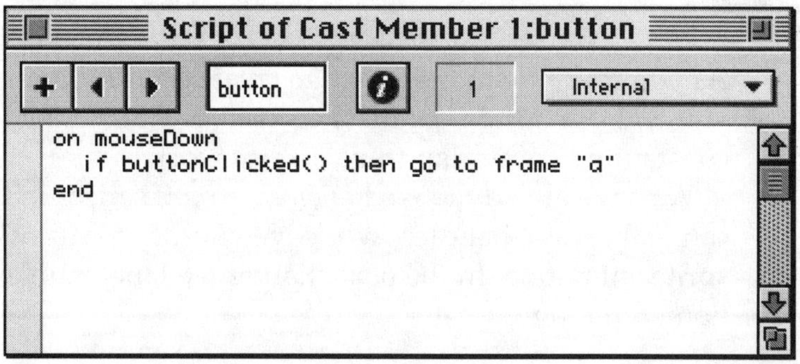

Figure 4-17: *The cast script of a button that uses our button handler.*

Our script simply calls the "buttonClicked" handler, which does all the fancy up state/down state work for us, and then returns *TRUE* only if it was a valid button press. We can now go on to create as many buttons as we want, knowing that the complex code for the button handler is only in one spot. Notice that we put a set of empty parentheses ( ) after the call to "buttonClicked." This is to make sure that Director does not try to interpret "buttonClicked" as a variable but instead looks for and finds our handler.

The ability to create our own handlers is essential to making anything beyond the most basic of Lingo programs. Handlers like *on mouseDown* or *on exitFrame* are already reserved in Director to react to certain events. Handlers that we create ourselves are called by these, or other, handlers.

Try It Yourself

Apply this lesson's button handler to the buttons you used in the previous lessons' exercises. Then add some more screens and buttons to it to see how easy it now is to create new buttons that call the button handler.

Moving On

As you continue to use Lingo to create your multimedia projects, you will use button handlers, as well as other standard handlers, constantly in your day-to-day script work.

We have already looked at *on exitFrame* scripts in Chapter 3. We can make these handlers work even harder for us by doing simple sprite animation. In the next chapter we'll begin to explore animation with Lingo.

5

Animation

Director started off as an animation tool, and is still used by many as just that. Lingo can extend the animation ability by adding user interaction, elements of randomness, and programming logic. We can even create simple games by animating with Lingo.

Lesson 11: Flashing Sprite

Lingo syntax:

```
not, the visible of sprite
```

A very simple special effect for a frame is to have a single sprite flash on and off. You could use this for a flashing arrow on a map, Christmas lights on a tree, or anything you want to draw attention to.

We will introduce two new pieces of Lingo for this script. The first is *the visible of sprite*. This will return a true or false depending on whether the sprite is visible.

In addition, we have the power to make any sprite visible or invisible by setting this variable. Figure 5-1 shows the little diamond-shaped switches, to the left of the sprite channels in the score window, which you can use to do this job manually while authoring.

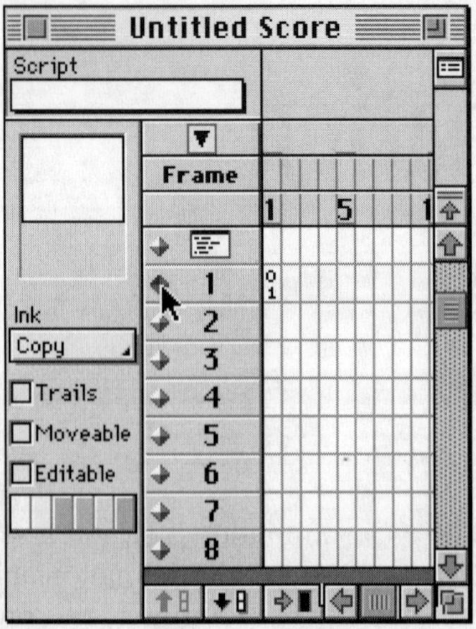

Figure 5-1: *The diamonds on the left side of the score allow you to manually set the visibility of a sprite channel while authoring.*

Make a simple graphic, such as a drawing of a light bulb, in a cast member, then stick it in sprite channel 1. You should see it appear on the stage. Now use the message window to play with the visibility of this graphic.

```
put the visible of sprite 1
-- 1
set the visible of sprite 1 = FALSE
put the visible of sprite 1
-- 0
set the visible of sprite 1 = TRUE
```

The first line you typed will return a 1, since the sprite is certainly visible. Then we changed the value by using the *set* command. Notice that you need to use the *set* command to change a Director variable like this. As a rule of thumb, every time you need to change a Director-defined variable, the ones that start with the word *the,* you must use the *set* command; *put* will not work.

Also, note that you do not have to use the Lingo command *updateStage* when setting the *visible* property of a sprite.

As soon as you press Return at the end of this line, you should see the graphic disappear from the stage. You should also see the change in the diamond-shaped switch next to sprite channel 1 in the score window.

When you test this value with the next line, you will see that it is now 0. Then, set it back to 1.

Note that we use the word *TRUE* to represent 1, and *FALSE* to represent 0. In cases like this, they are interchangeable in Lingo. We use words instead of numbers to make our code easier to understand. As a rule, you should try to use *TRUE* and *FALSE* rather than 1 and 0.

The other command you need for this script is *not*. This simply reverses the true-false value of anything. Try it in the message window:

```
put not TRUE
-- 0
put not FALSE
-- 1
put not 1
-- 0
put not 0
-- 1
```

Figure 5-2: *A drawing of a light bulb to use in our flashing sprite script.*

Now you have the pieces to create your flashing graphic script. Create a graphic in a cast member and stick it on the stage in sprite channel 1. You can use a simple drawing of a light bulb as in Figure 5-2. Or it can be anything you want: a shape, a bitmap, or text. Type in the script shown in Figure 5-3 and make it the score frame script for that frame.

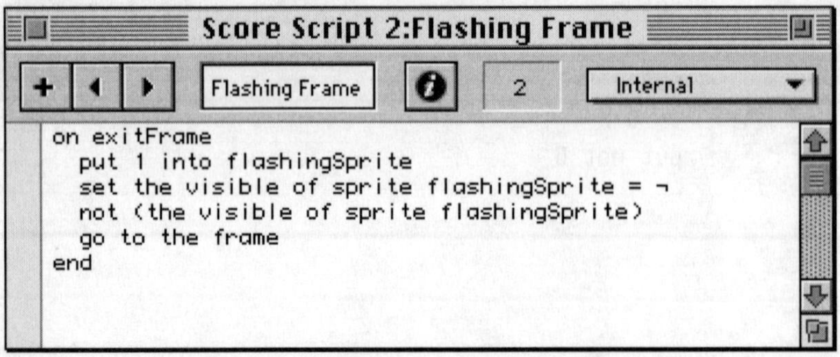

Figure 5-3: *A score script that causes sprite 1 to flash on and off.*

Notice the odd character at the end of one of the lines: "¬." This character is created when you hit Option+Return (Alt+Return in Windows) instead of Return. It signifies that the two lines are actually one. You have the option of using this in your code or letting Director's scripting window automatically wrap text for you. We have used an arrow (→) throughout this book to make sure it is clear when lines of code continue. You may want to use a continuation character to make your code easier to read.

In the handler, since we want to deal with sprite number 1, we store the number *1* in a variable called "flashingSprite." We could have just written *the visible of sprite 1*, on the next line, instead of using the variable; but remember that it is better to store numbers like this in variables before using them instead of "hard-coding" them.

Examining the script, all it does is constantly change the visibility of a sprite. When the *on exitFrame* script executes, it reverses the visibility of the sprite and loops back into the same frame. This script will loop on the same frame over and over.

The speed at which the flashing occurs depends on the frame rate. If you set the frame rate to one frame per second, the sprite will disappear one second and reappear the next.

Let's do something else with this script. Suppose we want two graphics to flash on and off. That by itself seems simple enough: we just need to double the code in the script to do it for two sprite channels. But what if we wanted it to alternate between the two—so that while one sprite is on, the other is off?

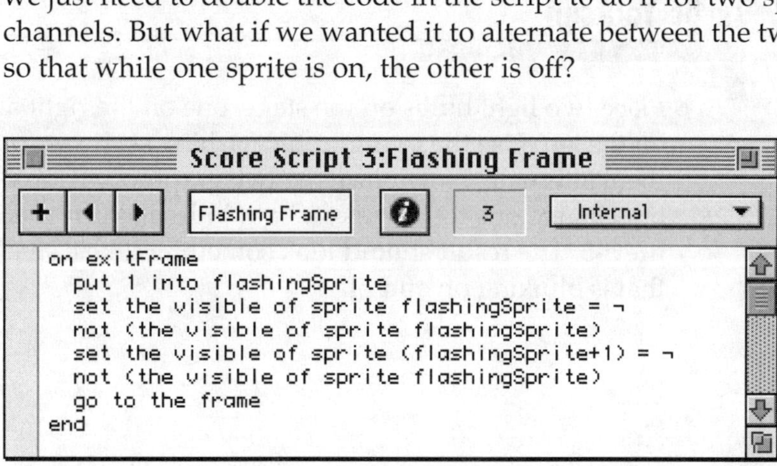

Figure 5-4: *A score script that causes sprites 1 and 2 to alternate on and off.*

The script in Figure 5-4 still relies on only one sprite number. We assume that the other sprite we'll be changing is in the very next channel, so we only need to add 1 to the first sprite number to get the other.

After setting the visibility of the first sprite, we simply set the visibility of the second sprite to the opposite of that. Notice that you need to put parentheses around the *flashingSprite+1*. This is to prevent any confusion about which sprite we want to set the visibility of. Otherwise, Director will assume that we want *(the visible of sprite flashingSprite)+1*. It is always best to include parentheses when in doubt.

One of the problems with this script is that when the movie leaves the current frame—say, by the user clicking a button—the visible settings of any sprites remain set, and any sprites that are not visible remain that way in every frame thereafter. You can fix this by making sure you set *the visible* of any sprite you have used to *TRUE* in the button scripts that make the movie jump to another frame.

In the next lesson we will go a step further than just turning sprites on and off. We will use *the puppetSprite* command to actually change the cast member in a sprite channel.

Try It Yourself

Place two light bulbs on the stage, one on the right and the other on the left. Use the two-graphic flashing sprite script to make them alternate. Now place the two graphics on top of each other, but change one to look like a light bulb that is turned off, as in Figure 5-5. The result should look something like a single light bulb that is blinking on and off.

Figure 5-5: *A drawing of a light bulb turned off.*

Lesson 12: Alternating Sprite

Lingo syntax:

`puppetSprite, case…of`

Lingo gives us much more than just the power to make sprites visible and invisible. We can actually change the cast member of a sprite. We did this in several previous lessons with our graphic buttons. The changes we made to the button sprites were temporary, however, and the sprite reverted to the cast member that was assigned to it in the score when our handlers were done.

We can make changes to a sprite and have those changes stick by using the *puppetSprite* command. The name of this command gives us some clue as to what it does—it is sort of like attaching strings to a sprite so that we can manipulate it in Lingo.

In previous script, we didn't need to use *puppetSprite* because none of the changes we made needed to stick around when the handler was done. In the button handler scripts, for instance, the button always returned to its original state at the end of the handler.

Once we *puppetSprite* a sprite, any changes we make to it will be permanent until we make other changes, or until we turn off the puppetSprite.

Talking Puppets

Although technically *puppetSprite* is not a verb, it is often used as one among Lingo programmers. You can also say: "I turned on [or off] the puppet of a sprite," or "I puppeted a sprite." You can interchange "That's a puppetSprite" with "That sprite is puppeted."

We can use the message window to test out our new command. First, create two bitmapped graphics and name them "graphic 1" and "graphic 2." You can make them anything you want, or even import some graphics you have lying around. Figure 5-6 shows two states of a waving hand that might be used for this example.

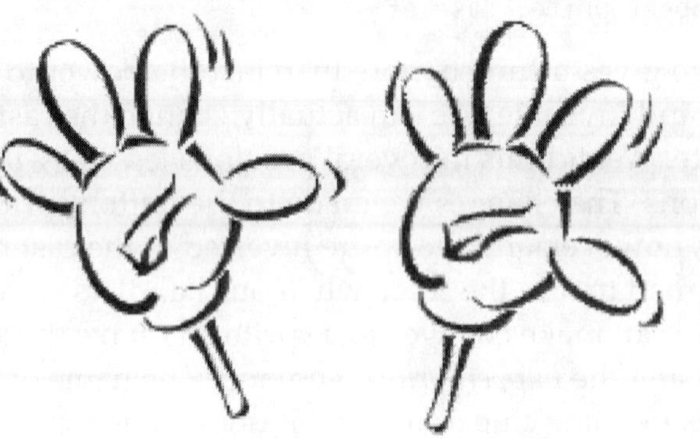

Figure 5-6: *Two bitmaps representing a two-step animation of a waving hand.*

Move the first graphic onto the stage and into sprite channel 1. Make the message window visible and try these commands.

```
puppetSprite 1, TRUE
set the castNum of sprite 1 = the number of cast "graphic 2"
updateStage
```

After the *updateStage* command, you should see the graphic on the stage change to your second graphic. Actually, to make this change happen, we didn't need to use the *puppetSprite* command at all. If you tried the same thing without the *puppetSprite 1, TRUE,* you would have gotten an identical result.

However, there is a difference when we use it. Try putting the same graphic in sprite channel 2 of your movie but positioning it on another part of the stage so that you can see both sprites. Now try the following in the message window.

```
puppetSprite 1, TRUE
set the castNum of sprite 1 = the number of cast "graphic 2"
set the castNum of sprite 2 = the number of cast "graphic 2"
updateStage
```

At this point, both sprites appear to have changed to the second graphic. Now type this line:

```
go to the frame
```

You should see sprite 2 change back to its original graphic (the one placed in the score) while sprite 1 stays with "graphic 2." This was because we puppetSprited sprite channel 1 but not channel 2.

We can use this *puppetSprite* concept in a frame script to make the sprite alternate between two graphics.

```
on exitFrame
  puppetSprite 1, TRUE
  put the memberNum of sprite 1 into cNum
  put the name of member cNum into cName
  if cName = "graphic 1" then
    put "graphic 2" into cName
  else
    put "graphic 1" into cName
  end if
  put the number of member cName into cNum
  set the memberNum of sprite 1 = cNum
  go to the frame
end
```

Figure 5-7: *A frame script that alternates sprite 1 between two bitmaps.*

The *on exitFrame* handler in Figure 5-7 starts off puppeting sprite 1. This is only necessary the very first time the script runs but will harmlessly execute on each loop through the same frame.

Next, we grab the number of the current cast member in sprite channel 1. Then we convert the number to a name. We test this name and set our "cName" variable to the opposite cast member. Then we convert the name back into a number and set the sprite to that cast member.

Notice that we don't need to do an *updateStage*. This is because a *go to the frame* will have the same effect.

We can also make this script alternate sprite 1 among more than two graphics. The following script will take the sprite from "graphic 1" to "graphic 2" to "graphic 3" and back around again. We can still use our waving hand drawings for this—by creating a middle state for the animation, as in Figure 5-8.

Figure 5-8: *A third, middle state for our waving hand graphic.*

The script in Figure 5-9 uses the *case* statement instead of an *if...then* statement. A *case* statement is exactly like a simple multiple-part *if...then* statement, dealing with only one variable. You simply state the variable name in the initial line, in this case "cName." Every "case" after that will be something to compare the variable to. If a match is found, the code in that section of the *case* statement will be executed.

Score Script 4:Alternating Graphic

Alternating Graphic | 4 | Internal

```
on exitFrame
  puppetSprite 1, TRUE
  put the memberNum of sprite 1 into cNum
  put the name of member cNum into cName
  case cName of
    "graphic 1":
      put "graphic 2" into cName
    "graphic 2":
      put "graphic 3" into cName
    "graphic 3":
      put "graphic 1" into cName
  end case
  put the number of member cName into cNum
  set the memberNum of sprite 1 = cNum
  go to the frame
end
```

Figure 5-9: *A frame script that alternates sprite 1 between three different cast members.*

Case Statements Vs. if...then Statements

Case statements are new for Director 5.0, but they have always been part of other languages. They are similar to using a long, multiple-part *if...then* statement but are actually much simpler.

In a *case* statement, you can only specify one variable to be tested. The statement then compares that to different values to figure out which one matches. *if...then* statements allow you to test multiple things and create very complex tests.

One problem with a script like this is that it moves too fast. We could slow down the frame rate of the movie, but that might affect other things we have going on. In the next lesson we will see how to slow down the script so that the animation happens at any rate we want.

Try It Yourself

Another way you can use this script would be to swap out several graphics that represent a spinning object—giving the illusion that that object is spinning on the screen. You could create any simple stand-in-place animation like that and use this script to animate it.

Lesson 13: Timed Alternating Sprite

Lingo syntax:

```
mod
```

The Director score gives you plenty of control over what happens on the stage without the need for a single line of Lingo. You can control the speed at which a frame plays by setting its rate in the tempo channel, choosing the palette that the frame uses in the palette channel, defining which transition Director should use when entering that frame in the transition channel, and placing a sound in either or both of two sound channels. Figure 5-10 shows these controls.

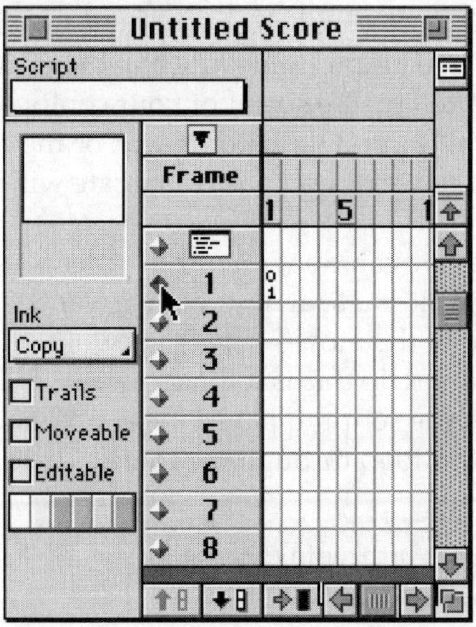

Figure 5-10: *The top portion of the score allows you to control the behavior of each frame.*

You can also do all of these things in Lingo—and you can do them better. Handlers you write will go beyond the basics of these frame controls.

Let's take a look at *timing*. The previous lesson contained a script that alternated between two graphics. The rate of change was equivalent to the frame rate. The frame rate of the overall movie can be set in the control bar shown in Figure 5-11. The frame rate of an individual frame can be set in the score.

Figure 5-11: *You can control the frame rate of the movie in Director's control panel.*

If you set your frame rate to 15 frames per second, then our alternating graphics handler will change sprite 1 a total of 15 times every second. The maximum frame rate at which Director can display a movie is limited by the speed of your computer. If the graphic is large enough, and your computer, or the computer of your target user, is slow enough, the frame rate will slow down to compensate.

One of the things we can do with our handler is to use *the ticks* to make the graphic alternate at any rate we want, without having to adjust the tempo of the movie.

The first way we can do this is to place a piece of Lingo in our handler that causes the script to pause for one second before proceeding with the next loop through the frame. The code will look like this:

```
put the ticks + 60 into delayTime
repeat while the ticks < delayTime
end repeat
```

This is similar to the code used in the timed frame script in an earlier lesson. We place the current time, in ticks, plus 60 ticks into a variable called "delayTime." Then we wait around inside a *repeat* loop until the always advancing *the ticks* catches up to our variable. The script is shown in Figure 5-12.

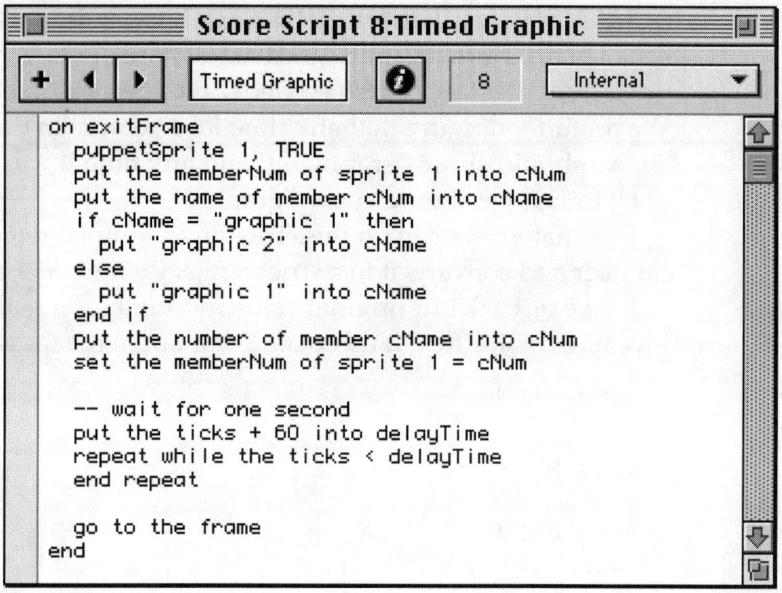

Figure 5-12: *An alternating graphic script that waits one second between changes.*

This will seem to do the trick if we place it in our alternating graphics script. You can put any number in place of the "60" to get different wait times. Remember that ticks are actually 1/60 of a second, so 60 ticks are equal to 1 second.

The script is not a good one to use, however, as it simply pauses the entire Director movie for one second and lets nothing else happen. If the time were longer, say, 10 seconds, your users would notice that mouse clicks and key presses would not respond while this script was in "wait" mode. Also, any other animation going on would freeze.

Another problem with the "wait" method of timing is that the other Lingo commands also take time to execute. The whole graphics-switching piece of our handler may take several ticks to run. This may not seem like much, but it might mean that our entire script will take 64 ticks, not 60 ticks, to run. If you were trying to synchronize animation, this small time difference could foul things up.

A better way to time your Lingo animation is to use *the ticks* to set a tempo for the changes, instead of pausing it. What if *the ticks* went from 0 to 119, or two seconds, and then started over again. We could then figure that any time *the ticks* was in the range of 0 to 59, we should show "graphic 1," and any time it was in the range of 60 to 119, we should show "graphic 2."

Fortunately, we can do this. The Lingo command *mod* takes any number and converts it to a strict range. Using *mod 4,* for example, will give us back our original value for numbers less than 4 but will give us 0 for 4, 1 for 5, and so on. Try it out in the message window:

```
put 1 mod 4
-- 1
put 2 mod 4
-- 2
put 3 mod 4
-- 3
put 4 mod 4
-- 0
put 5 mod 4
-- 1
put 6 mod 4
-- 2
put 453 mod 4
-- 1
```

The actual range of numbers when we use *mod 4* is 0 to 3. No matter how high we go, the *mod* command will always stick to that range. We can use this function in our timed alternating graphic script. Figure 5-13 shows just such a script.

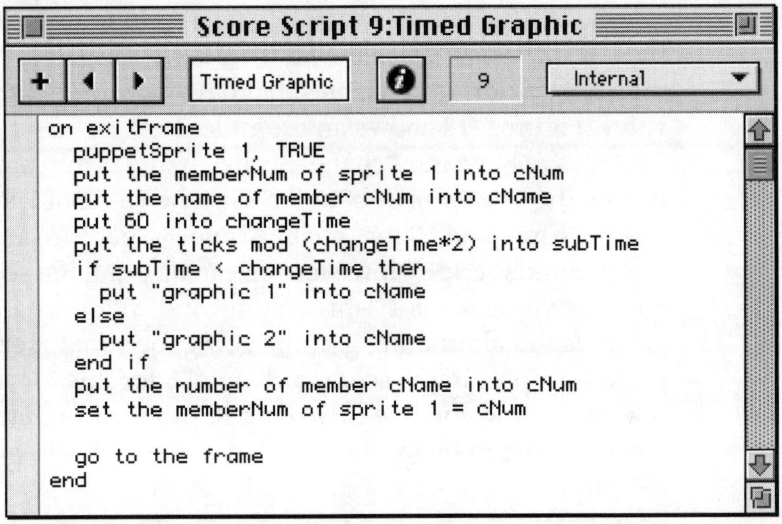

Figure 5-13: *A timed animation script that uses mod to keep the timing honest.*

Notice that we placed the number 60 in the variable "changeTime." Then we used that value, multiplied by 2, to determine the range of the variable "subTime." Then we used the "changeTime" again as the halfway mark in that range to determine which graphic should be showing.

Now let's make some changes to the script to make this whole concept come alive. Suppose we want to have more than one graphic alternating at the same time. Suppose, further, that these graphics are to alternate at different rates. We can do this using basically the same script.

First let's pull the code out of the *on exitFrame* script and create our own handler called "changeSprite." There are two important pieces of information that we need to tell this new handler: the sprite we want it to change and the rate at which it should change.

We can pass values like this into handlers by using parameters. We list the variables that will be passed into that handler in the *on handlerName* line. In this case we list "spriteNum" and "changeTime."

When we call this handler now, we need to include values for these parameters. Once the handler is running, it treats these parameters as normal variables that have been preset to a certain value. Figure 5-14 shows an example.

Once we have our "changeSprite" handler in place, we can call it from the *on exitFrame* handler with the value of 1 for "spriteNum" and 60 for "changeTime" to get the same result as our previous script. However, we can also call it a second time with the value of 2 for "spriteNum" and 25 for "changeTime" to get a second alternating graphic going. Be sure to remember to place a graphic in the score in channel 2 for this to work. Director does not allow you to easily puppetSprite sprite channels that have nothing in them.

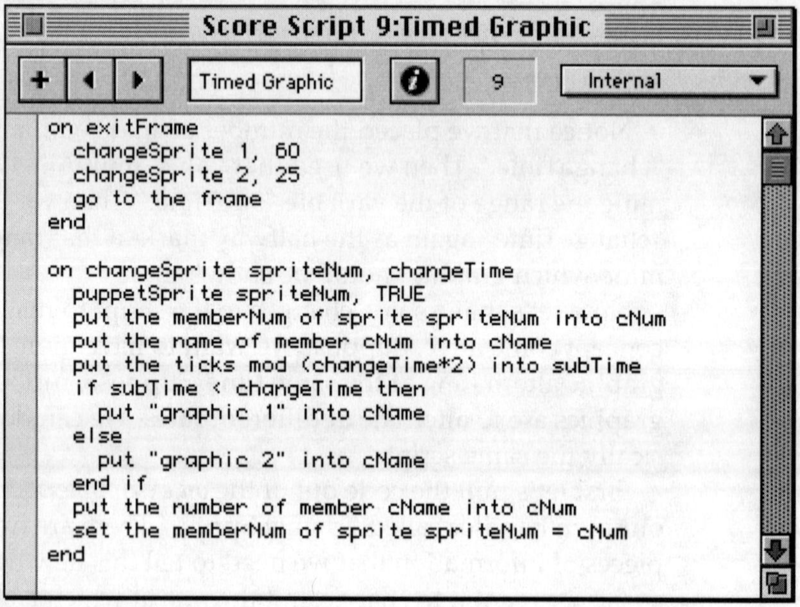

Figure 5-14: *A script that will animate two sprites at the same time, and with different change rates.*

This last script demonstrated a powerful programming concept: the ability to use a single handler to create multiple effects. With the use of parameters, our *on changeSprite* handler can be used many times, each time producing a different effect.

In the next lesson, we will go on to use puppetSprites to alter more than just the cast member—we will change the location of the sprite on the stage as well.

Try It Yourself

You don't have to stop here. You can have many more graphics alternating at the same time. You could add more parameters that define which graphics you are supposed to swap, so that different calls to *on changeSprite* use different bitmaps. You could even make the handler swap out three graphics instead of two as we did in the previous lesson.

Lesson 14: Racing Sprites

Lingo syntax:

```
the locH, the locV, random
```

Without Lingo, the common way to create an animation is to use several similar frames in the score and change one or more sprites in each frame to reflect movement. For instance, in the first frame of a sequence, you might have a graphic on the left side of the stage. On the next frame, the graphic would be a few pixels to the right of the previous position. The next frame would have the graphic even more to the right. By the end of the sequence, the graphic would be all the way on the right side of the stage. When this sequence is played in Director, the graphic appears to actually move to the right.

Using Lingo, you can accomplish the same thing in only one frame. We will use the *puppetSprite* command again. In addition to being able to switch cast members in Director, you can also change other things about the sprite—like its position on the screen.

To do this, we will use *the locH* and *the locV* properties of a sprite. The first is the horizontal position of a sprite on the screen, the second is its vertical position. The values of these properties are in pixels. Put a graphic into sprite 1 and try this in the message window:

```
put the locH of sprite 1
-- 320
set the locH of sprite 1 = 300
updateStage
```

After the *updateStage* you should see the graphic move a little to the left. The number 300 might be different, depending on where you originally placed the sprite and how big your stage is.

Remember that the original position of the sprite is still recorded in the score. If you continue in the message window with the following, the sprite will be restored to its original value:

```
go to the frame
```

If we have also puppetSprited the sprite, it would have stayed put.

Now let's build a script that will use this technique to create animation. First, draw or import a graphic—say, that of a cartoon character. Then place it on the stage in sprite channel 1. Put it all the way over on the left. In the same frame use the script in Figure 5-15.

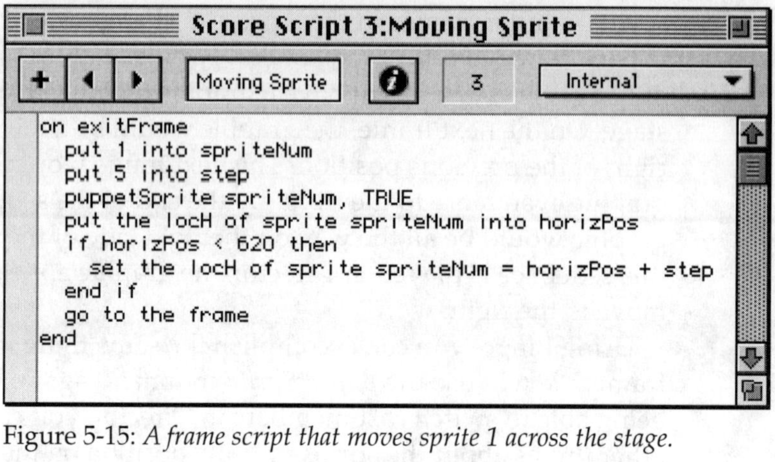

Figure 5-15: *A frame script that moves sprite 1 across the stage.*

The variable "spriteNum" contains the number of the sprite channel we are dealing with. The variable "step" determines how many pixels the animation moves with each iteration of the script.

We puppetSprite sprite 1 to start things off. The only time this really does anything is the first time the *on exitFrame* script is executed. After that the *puppetSprite* command is redundant and essentially ignored.

We use *the locH* function to determine the horizontal position of the sprite. We test this to see if it is greater than 620. Assuming the stage is 640 pixels wide, which is a typical width, then 620 is a good measure of when the sprite reaches the right side of the screen. Use a lower number to have the sprite stop sooner, or a higher number to place it closer to the right side of the screen.

If the sprite is not yet to the right side of the screen, we take the horizontal position of the sprite and add "step," in this case 5, pixels to it. This will move it over a bit to the right.

When the sprite reaches its destination, the *if...then* statement is no longer true and the sprite stops moving. The script then tells Director to loop back and start the frame again. The frame rate will determine how fast this animation will run.

In addition to *the locH* function, *the locV* function could be used to move the sprite vertically instead of horizontally. You could use both to move it diagonally.

Let's create a handler that will provide more advanced sprite movement. Let's make parameters out of the maximum horizontal distance that the sprite moves and the speed at which it moves. We will also make a parameter out of the sprite that the handler is dealing with. Figure 5-16 shows this more advanced handler.

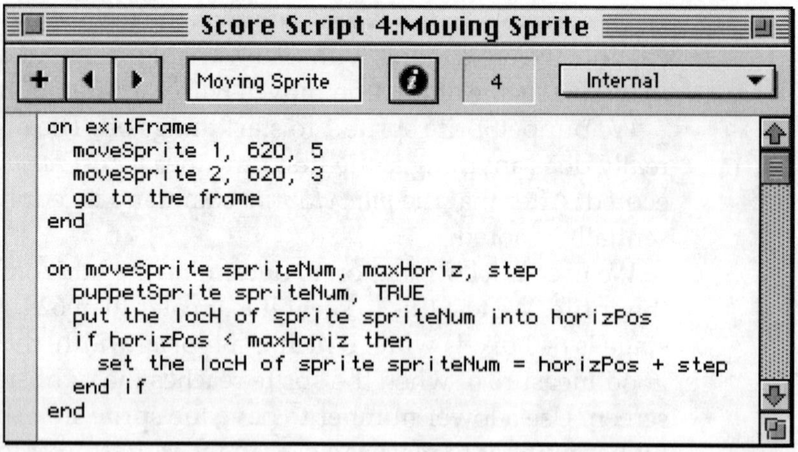

Figure 5-16: *A handler that makes two sprites move across the screen at different rates.*

This script is already set up to race sprite 1 and sprite 2 across the screen. If you start the two sprites in the score in the same horizontal position, sprite 1 will always win, since it is always given a faster speed.

We can make this script a little more fun by adding a random element to it. *the random* command in Lingo returns a random number between 1 and x. Try it in the message window:

```
put random(3)
-- 2
put random(3)
--3
```

You will most likely get different results, of course.

The alteration of our script shown in Figure 5-17 will race three sprites across the screen. Notice that the *on moveSprite* handler is identical to the previous one. We simply changed the parameters that are calling it. Also notice that we have sprite 2 moving at a constant rate of 5, while sprites 1 and 3 are moving at rates that change each time.

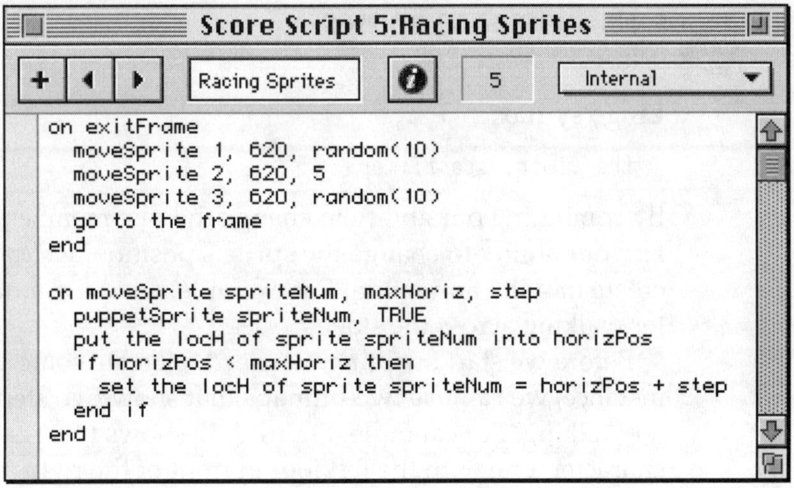


```
on exitFrame
  moveSprite 1, 620, random(10)
  moveSprite 2, 620, 5
  moveSprite 3, 620, random(10)
  go to the frame
end

on moveSprite spriteNum, maxHoriz, step
  puppetSprite spriteNum, TRUE
  put the locH of sprite spriteNum into horizPos
  if horizPos < maxHoriz then
    set the locH of sprite spriteNum = horizPos + step
  end if
end
```

Figure 5-17: *Using the* on moveSprite *handler and the* random *function to race sprites across the screen.*

Remember to place a cast member—a car, bicycle, or rocket ship, for instance—into all three sprite channels so the *puppetSprite* command has something to grab. Alternatively, you could place three different cast members in the sprites too.

The idea of racing sprites across the screen, with no predetermined outcome is an excellent example of something that is impossible to do in Director without using Lingo. We also demonstrated in this lesson the possibility of dramatically changing what a handler does by sending different parameters. Our *on moveSprite* handler takes on a whole new dimension by passing a random number into the "speed" parameter.

In the next lesson we will combine the concepts of moving a sprite and changing its cast member to create some complex animation.

Try It Yourself

Build a movie that races five sprites across the stage. Finish it off by adding background elements like a start line and a finish line.

Lesson 15: Animating Sprites

Lingo syntax:

```
the timer, startTimer
```

By combining our ability to change the cast member of a sprite and our ability to change the sprite's position, we can use Lingo to create moving animation. For example, we can animate a character walking across the stage.

Before we start scripting, we need to create some graphics. For instance, we can use two bitmaps that show two steps of a character walking. For example, Figure 5-18 shows two snapshots of a character: one with the left foot in front of the right, and one with the right foot in front of the left. The idea here is to animate the character as it floats across the screen to make it look like it is walking.

Figure 5-18: *Two graphics that represent a man walking.*

Make sure that the bitmap registration points for these cast members line up. A good way to do this is to put the graphics in adjacent cast members and flip back and forth between them. By moving their registration points, you should line up the images so that the animation is just right when you flip between the two cast members. Figures 5-19 and 5-20 show how our example looks in the paint window with the registration point visible.

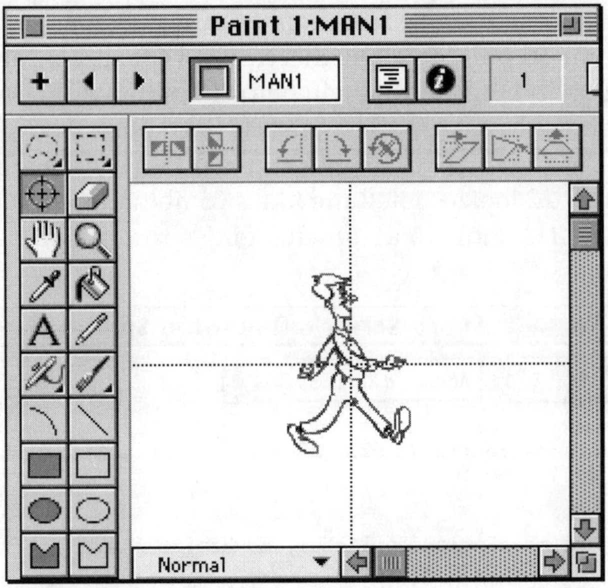

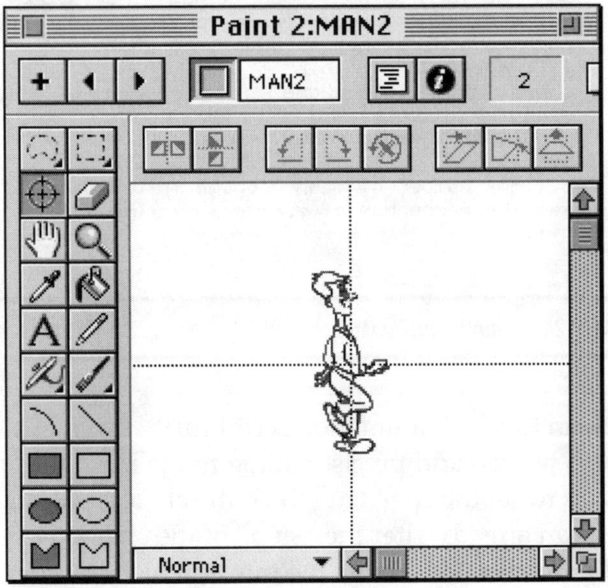

Figures 5-19 and 5-20: *The registration points on each bitmap should match up to make the animation smooth.*

Director 5.0 somewhat automatically centers each picture by its registration point to make this easier. There is also an "onionskin" function in Director that will help animators do this.

Name the first graphic "MAN1" and the second "MAN2" in the cast. Put "MAN1" into sprite channel 1. Our animation script in Figure 5-22 looks something like a combination of our previous *on moveSprite* handler and our changing sprite script.

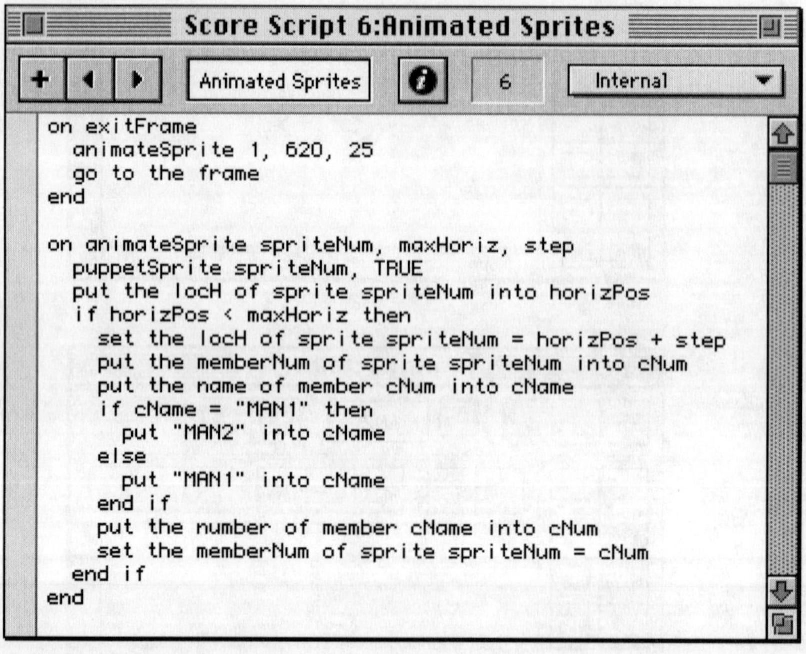

Figure 5-21: *A sprite animation script.*

We can take this animation script further in many directions. For one, we can add precise timing to the handler. This would allow us to set the speed at which the character walks.

You can already alter the "step" of the character in our handler, but that would not change the rate at which the character takes steps, or just how many pixels each step represents on the screen.

First, we can try incorporating a piece of our timed alternating graphic script. The result would be as shown in Figure 5-22.

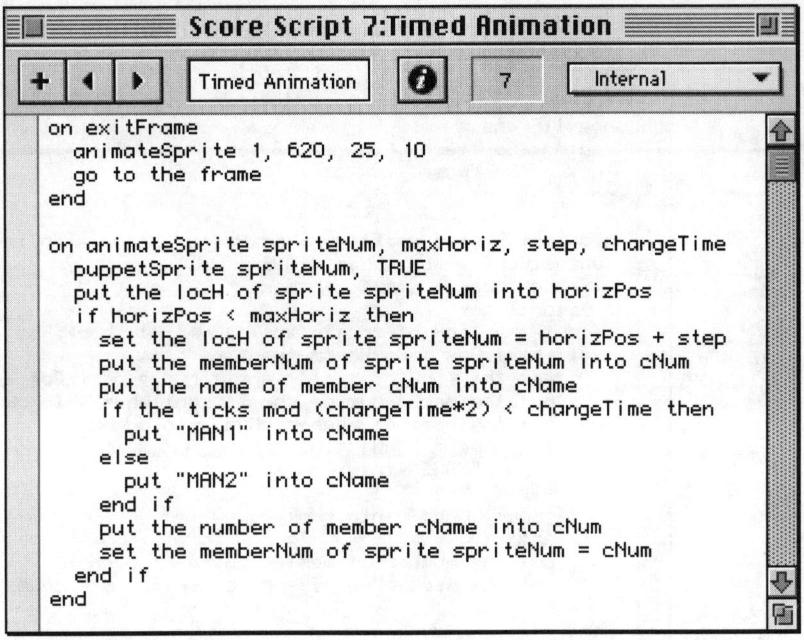

Score Script 7:Timed Animation

Timed Animation | 7 | Internal

```
on exitFrame
  animateSprite 1, 620, 25, 10
  go to the frame
end

on animateSprite spriteNum, maxHoriz, step, changeTime
  puppetSprite spriteNum, TRUE
  put the locH of sprite spriteNum into horizPos
  if horizPos < maxHoriz then
    set the locH of sprite spriteNum = horizPos + step
    put the memberNum of sprite spriteNum into cNum
    put the name of member cNum into cName
    if the ticks mod (changeTime*2) < changeTime then
      put "MAN1" into cName
    else
      put "MAN2" into cName
    end if
    put the number of member cName into cNum
    set the memberNum of sprite spriteNum = cNum
  end if
end
```

Figure 5-22: *A sprite animation script that alternates between graphics according to the clock.*

This type of animation is only a little better than the previous script. We still have no way to control the time it will take the graphic to reach the other side of the stage, or just how often the bitmaps switch. To do this we need to be able to record the starting time of the animation and proceed with the next step in the animation every time enough time has elapsed.

There is another Lingo function called *the timer*. This is basically the same as *the ticks*, but instead of constantly increasing as time moves on, we can reset *the timer* to 0 by using the *startTimer* command.

We can use these two commands to make sure that each step in our animation occurs only at certain time intervals. When *the timer* exceeds the time allotted for each step, we perform our animation and reset *the timer*. Figure 5-23 shows the new script.

Score Script 8:Timed Animation

Timed Animation | 8 | Internal

```
on exitFrame
  animateSprite 1, 620, 25, 30
  go to the frame
end

on animateSprite spriteNum, maxHoriz, step, stepTime
  puppetSprite spriteNum, TRUE
  if the timer > stepTime then
    startTimer
    put the locH of sprite spriteNum into horizPos
    if horizPos < maxHoriz then
      set the locH of sprite spriteNum = horizPos + step
      put the memberNum of sprite spriteNum into cNum
      put the name of member cNum into cName
      if cName = "MAN1" then
        put "MAN2" into cName
      else
        put "MAN1" into cName
      end if
      put the number of member cName into cNum
      set the memberNum of sprite spriteNum = cNum
    end if
  end if
end
```

Figure 5-23: *A sprite animation that has a set time for each step.*

Try It Yourself

We can now race the sprites again. Try placing graphics in sprite channels 1, 2, and 3. Add Lingo scripts to deal with these sprites in the *on exitFrame* script. You can use set values or the *random* function, as in the previous lesson, to create a real race.

Moving On

In this lesson we learned how we can combine elements from different scripts into a new one. To create moving animation, we took the scripting needed to make a sprite move across the screen and combined it with the scripting needed to make a sprite alternate between bitmaps. Then we added scripting that we had used before to time the animation.

6 Games

Interactive multimedia isn't very interactive if all the user is doing is clicking the mouse every once in a while. Using Lingo, you can allow the user to manipulate items on the stage.

Lesson 16: User-Controlled Moving Sprite

Lingo syntax:

```
the mouseH, the mouseV, cursor(x), the clickLoc
```

You might be familiar with the "moveable" setting for a sprite in the score. With a script, you can accomplish the same thing but do it exactly the way you want.

Let's first try to make a sprite follow the cursor around the stage. We need a few new Lingo functions to do this. *the mouseH* and *the mouseV* return the horizontal and vertical positions of the cursor at the current time. Let's use the message window to test them out:

```
put the mouseH
-- 357
put the mouseV
-- 202
```

Of course, you will get different numbers, depending upon where your cursor is relative to the upper left corner of the stage. These coordinates are measured with the horizontal 0 being on the left side of the screen and the vertical 0 on the top of the screen. From that corner, the coordinates move across to 640 for a typical screen, and down to 480.

Now that we know the position of the cursor, and we know how to set the position of a sprite from our previous animation scripts, we can make a sprite follow the cursor around.

Place a graphic on the stage and into sprite channel 1. Use the script in Figure 6-1 as your frame script.

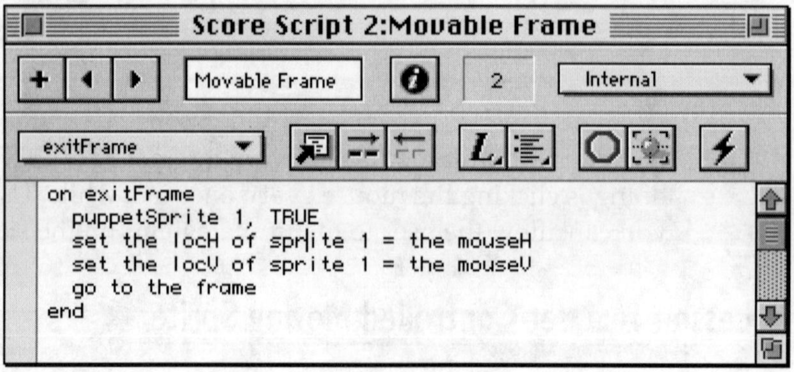

Figure 6-1: *A frame script that makes sprite 1 follow the cursor.*

Every time this script executes, it sets *the locH* of the sprite to the horizontal location of the cursor. It does the same for the vertical position. Note that the exact location of the graphic under the cursor depends upon the registration point of the cast member.

One effect of this script is that it makes the sprite act almost like a cursor—that is, if we didn't already have the real cursor visible on top of it. We can use the *cursor* command to get rid of the real cursor and leave only our traveling sprite around.

cursor is a Director command that accepts one parameter, the number of the cursor you want to display. For instance, if you used the command *cursor(4)*, the watch or the hourglass cursor would be activated, depending upon your system. In this case, we want to use *cursor(200)*—which is an empty cursor—thus making the real cursor invisible but leaving behind our traveling sprite as evidence of where it is on the stage.

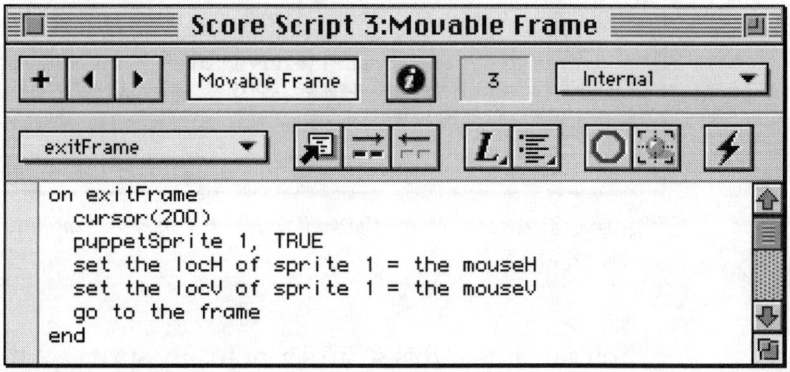

Figure 6-2: *A frame script that makes sprite 1 act as the cursor.*

You could use the script in Figure 6-2 to create custom, colorful, and/or large cursors for your Director movies. You would probably want to use sprite channel 48 instead of 1, however, since you want the cursor to exist on top of other elements in the movie. As this last statement implies, sprites in higher numbered channels appear over the top of those in lower numbered channels.

Let's get away from the cursor idea and return to the idea of just moving sprites around. We can use the same Lingo technique to let the user click and drag elements around the screen. We can even attach such a script to multiple sprites.

In the script in Figure 6-3 we set up a *repeat* loop that lasts until the user releases the mouse button. We need an *updateStage* in the loop, because the *go to the frame* does not happen until all the action is over. Without the *updateStage* command, users would have to wait until they were done dragging to see where the sprite is.

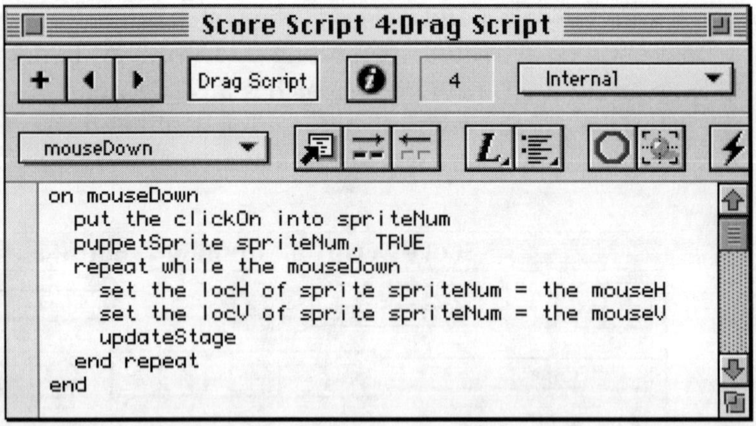

Figure 6-3: *A score script that will allow the user to drag any sprite around the stage.*

You can assign this score script to any sprites in the frame. Remember that you should have at least a basic *go to the frame* script in the *exitFrame* handler of the frame.

If you play with this script enough, you will notice one strange behavior. When you click on a sprite, it immediately jumps to align the registration point of the graphic with your cursor's position. So if you click on the upper right of the graphic, without moving the mouse just yet, the graphic appears to jump.

This makes sense, since we are asking that the graphic be at exactly the location of the cursor from the moment it is clicked on until the time the mouse button is released. We can correct this odd behavior with a little math.

First, we need to find the mouse location at the time of the initial click. We also need to get the sprite location at the time of the click. The difference between the two is called the "offset." We can record this offset and make sure that the cursor position and the sprite position are always that much off. Figure 6-4 shows a script that compensates for such an offset.

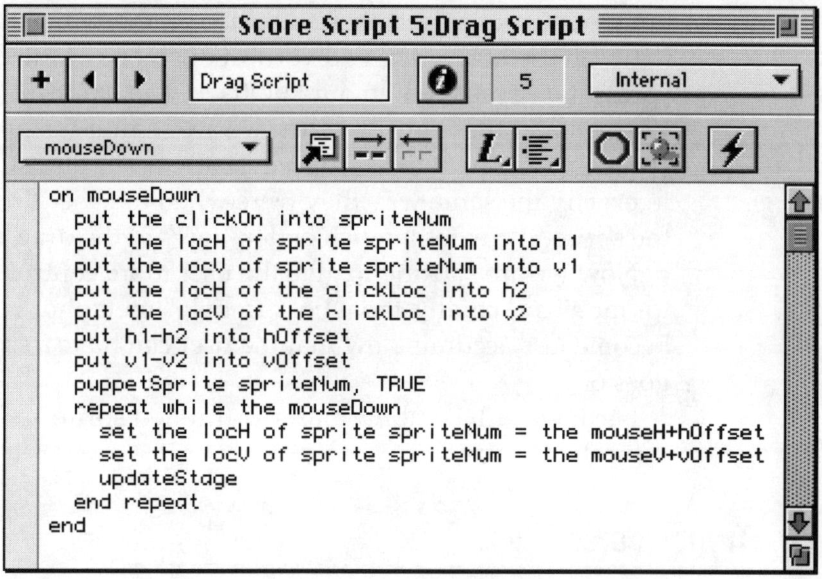

Figure 6-4: *A script that lets the user drag a graphic, remembering exactly where on the graphic they clicked.*

We use the temporary variables "h1," "h2," "v1," and "v2" to gather the information on the mouse location and the sprite location. Instead of using the Director functions *the mouseH* and *the mouseV* to get the initial location of the mouse, we use *the clickLoc*. This returns the point at which the last mouse click occurred, instead of the current location of the mouse, which may have changed since the click happened. Try it in the message window:

```
put the clickLoc
-- point(260,185)
put the locH of the clickLoc
-- 260
put the locV of the clickLoc
-- 185
```

The actual value that *the clickLoc* returns is in the form of a Director data structure called a *point*. It looks just like it does above and is pretty straightforward. We can extract the horizontal and vertical coordinates of that structure by using *the locH* and *the locV*.

Once our script gets these numbers, it then finds the difference between the horizontal and vertical positions of the cursor and the sprite and saves them in our "hOffset" and "vOffset" variables. We then add these offsets when we are setting the position of the sprite in the repeat loop. This keeps the sprite and cursor lined up in exactly the same way they were when the user first clicked on the sprite. It creates a much better "feel" to the drag action.

Now we are starting to give the user more control in our Director movies. Actually, the whole "movie" metaphor is starting to become less accurate now that the user can have a say in what goes on.

Next, we will combine a user-controlled sprite and a Lingo-controlled sprite.

Try It Yourself

Draw or import several small graphics and place them on the stage. Set up your program to allow the user to drag these sprites around and rearrange them. See if you can add a button that returns all of the sprites to their original positions.

Lesson 17: Shall We Play a Game?

Lingo syntax:

```
intersects, alert, the left of sprite, the right of sprite,
and, or
```

By now you have learned enough Lingo to do some pretty complex stuff. Let's learn two new commands and combine them with a bunch of commands we already know so that we can create a game.

The first new Lingo command we need is *intersects*. This simply tells us whether two sprites overlap each other on the stage. Try placing any two graphics on the stage and in sprite channels 1 and 2. Make sure the sprites do not overlap. Try this in the message window:

```
put sprite 1 intersects sprite 2
-- 0
```

Now, move one of the sprites so that it slightly overlaps the other and try again.

```
put sprite 1 intersects sprite 2
-- 1
```

It is easy to see how this can be useful to create simple games. When we have sprites moving around the stage, as they are apt to do in game situations, then we can test to see if any two sprites have collided.

Our simple game will include a baseball and a baseball glove. The ball will drop from a random spot at the top of the stage. The glove will be at the bottom of the stage and its horizontal position will be controlled by the user. The object is to catch the ball in the glove.

Figure 6-5: *A ball and glove to use for our simple game script.*

Create two cast members that resemble a ball and glove, as in Figure 6-5. The script in Figure 6-6 will make the ball fall at a steady rate, while the user controls the horizontal position of the glove with the mouse. When the ball hits the level of the glove, it will figure out whether or not the ball is in the glove. Regardless, it will reset the ball to a random position on the top of the screen to start all over again.

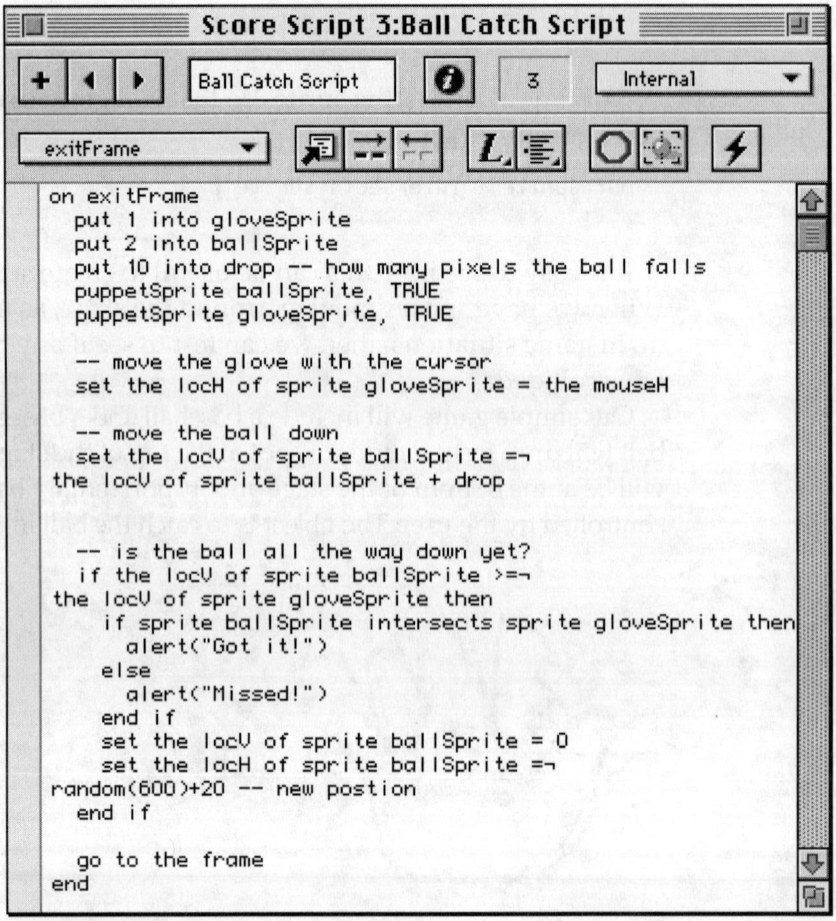

Figure 6-6: *A game-of-catch script.*

The *alert* command here is new but needs little explanation. It simply displays a string in a quick-and-dirty system dialog box. In this case we use it to tell us if the ball was caught or not.

Alerts

The *alert* command is useful for the early testing of scripts like this. We may later replace the *alert* with a more elaborate command, or simply go to another frame.

Alert boxes are a good, simple way to convey messages to the user.

In the script, the ball is moved down 10 pixels every frame loop, and the glove is always horizontally aligned with the cursor. Once the registration point of the ball is equal to or passes the registration point of the glove, the script makes a decision as to whether a catch was made. If the ball and glove sprites intersect at that moment, then the catch was good—otherwise you missed.

The script then resets the ball to the top of the screen but assigns a new horizontal position—a random number between 20 and 620.

This script can be made better by more accurately defining when a good catch was made. The current script only requires that the sprites intersect in any way. This means that the edge of the ball could be in contact with the edge of the glove and it would be counted as a good catch. We want to find a way to make sure that the ball is close to the center of the glove.

Since we know *the locH* of both the ball and the glove, we can just compare the two to see if the ball has hit dead center. But the ball would have to hit exactly in the middle of the glove. Using some math, however, we could see if the ball has hit within 20 or so pixels of dead center.

A better way would be to try to determine if the center of the ball is inside the edges of the glove. To do this we need to determine where the left and right edges of the glove are. We can use the Lingo commands *the left of sprite* and *the right of sprite* to get these numbers. Figure 6-7 shows such a script.

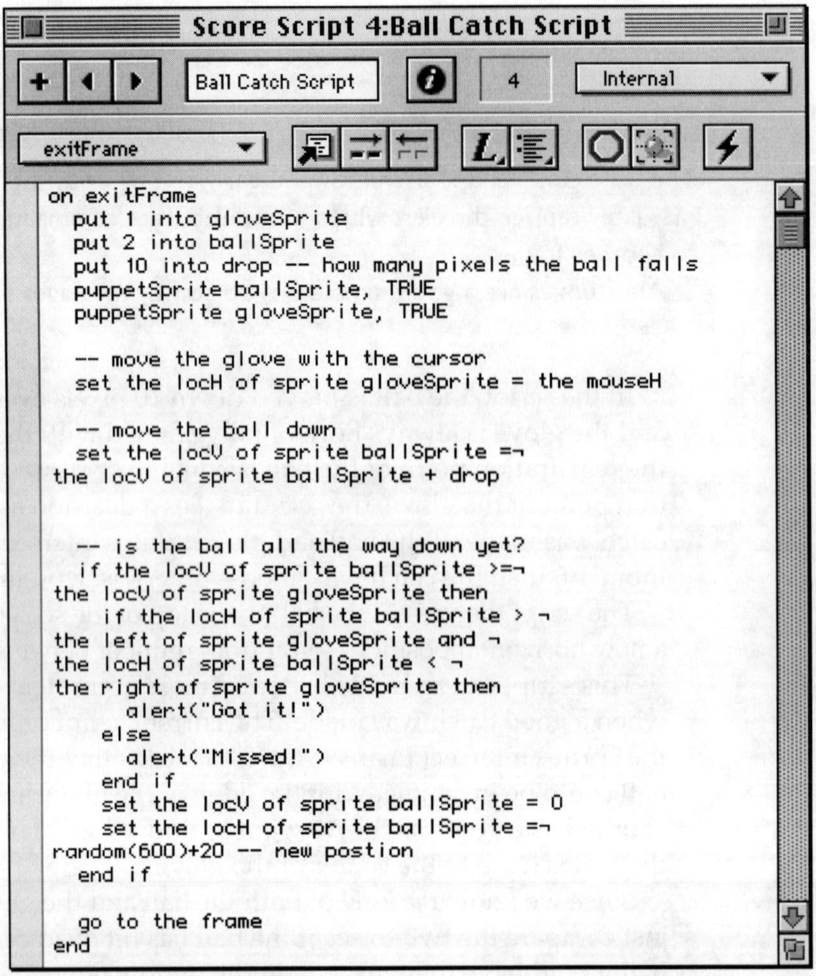


```
on exitFrame
  put 1 into gloveSprite
  put 2 into ballSprite
  put 10 into drop -- how many pixels the ball falls
  puppetSprite ballSprite, TRUE
  puppetSprite gloveSprite, TRUE

  -- move the glove with the cursor
  set the locH of sprite gloveSprite = the mouseH

  -- move the ball down
  set the locV of sprite ballSprite =¬
the locV of sprite ballSprite + drop


  -- is the ball all the way down yet?
  if the locV of sprite ballSprite >=¬
the locV of sprite gloveSprite then
    if the locH of sprite ballSprite > ¬
the left of sprite gloveSprite and ¬
the locH of sprite ballSprite < ¬
the right of sprite gloveSprite then
      alert("Got it!")
    else
      alert("Missed!")
    end if
    set the locV of sprite ballSprite = 0
    set the locH of sprite ballSprite =¬
random(600)+20 -- new postion
  end if

  go to the frame
end
```

Figure 6-7: *A better game-of-catch script.*

This script is identical to the previous one, except that we have replaced the *intersects* command with a statement that tests to see if *the locH* of the ball sprite is within the left and right boundaries of the glove sprite.

Notice that we can use *and* to include more than one element in an *if...then* condition. You can also use *or* in these statements as well as multiple levels of parentheses.

Logical Operators

True and false statements, like the ones we use in *if...then* or *repeat while* commands can contain many elements. Logical operators, such as *and*, *or*, and *not*, will be needed to perform complex tests.

and: Both conditions must be true in order for the entire statement to be true.

or: Only one of the conditions needs to be true for the entire statement to be true.

not: The condition is reversed, a true statement becomes false and a false statement becomes true.

You can combine the logical operators in any way to make complex condition tests. Use parentheses to control the order in which the logical operators are executed, as well as making the syntax easier for you to read.

Now that we have created our first real game, we can start improving it. In the next lesson we will learn how to use global variables, which will allow us to keep score.

Try It Yourself

Build a game-of-catch movie. Try using gloves of different sizes to see how easy or hard you can make the game. Also, change the script to make the ball drop faster.

Lesson 18: Keeping Score

Lingo syntax:

```
global, on startMovie, field
```

So far, all the variables we have created have existed only inside the handlers that use them—things like "spriteNum," "speed," and "h1."

As soon as that handler is done, the variable no longer exists. The next time that handler is called, the variable must be created all over again, by either being passed in as a parameter or set to a value in the code.

This type of variable is called *local*. Local variables only exist locally to our handlers and are not available to any other handlers.

But what if we wanted to keep score? The ball-glove catch game in the previous lesson, for instance, would be a lot more fun if you knew how many times you caught the ball and how many times you missed.

There is another type of variable called a *global* variable. Global variables are basically the same as local variables, but they exist for any handler that is set up to use them. Global variables are sometimes just refered to as "globals."

We need to declare which of our variables are global. This means we simply have to tell Director which globals each handler plans to use. We do this using the *global* command.

Where to Declare Globals

Placing a command like *global myGlobalVariable* inside a handler will make that global available for use inside that one handler as well as any other handlers where you place the same global variable declaration. However, you can make a global available to all of the handlers in one script cast member by placing the same line of script outside of each handler, usually at the top of the script cast member.

One interesting problem that we now have to take care of is how to initialize our globals. Our ball-glove catch script, for instance, is called many times, over and over again very quickly. Each call is a segment of the "action" of the game. We want to be able to set our globals before the action starts, to give the game a real beginning. For example, a variable called "score" should be set to 0.

One way to do this is to use the *on startMovie* handler. This is a standard handler that reacts to the "startMovie" message that Director sends out any time a movie begins. We can initialize our globals there.

The *on startMovie* handler needs to be in a movie script, not a score script. So we need to give it its own cast member, since the ball-glove catch code exists in a score script. Look at Figure 6-8 for an example.

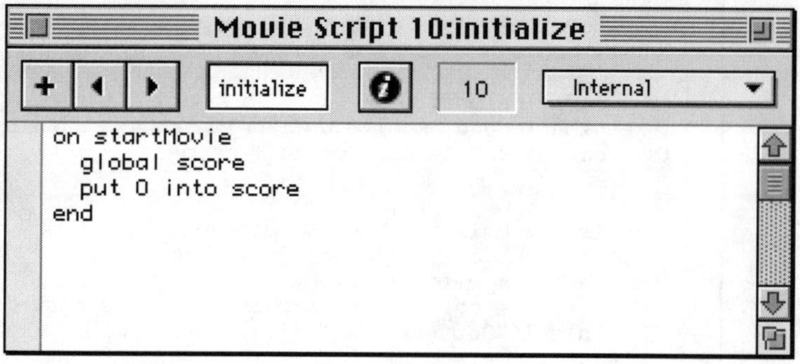

Figure 6-8: *The movie script that initializes the global variable "score."*

The command *global score* tells Director that we want to be able to use the global "score" in the *on startMovie* handler. We then set this variable equal to 0.

We can use the *on startMovie* handler for other things as well. In our game, we'll probably want to display the score somewhere on the stage. To do this, create a text field box on the stage. In the cast window, select the new text box and name it "score display." Now we can also use the *on startMovie* handler to clear that field or, better yet, display a welcome message in that field. The script in Figure 6-9 does this.

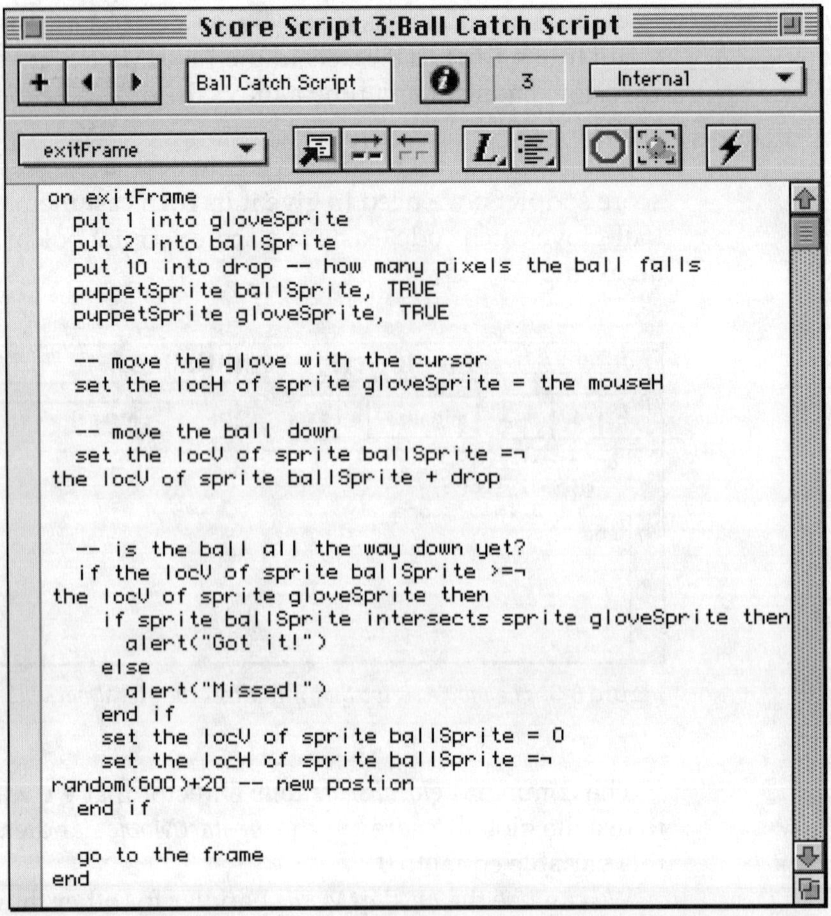

Figure 6-9: *A movie script that sets up our "score" global and clears the score display.*

Now, let's alter our *on exitFrame* script for the game so that it takes advantage of the "score" global and the "score display" field. It should look like Figure 6-10.

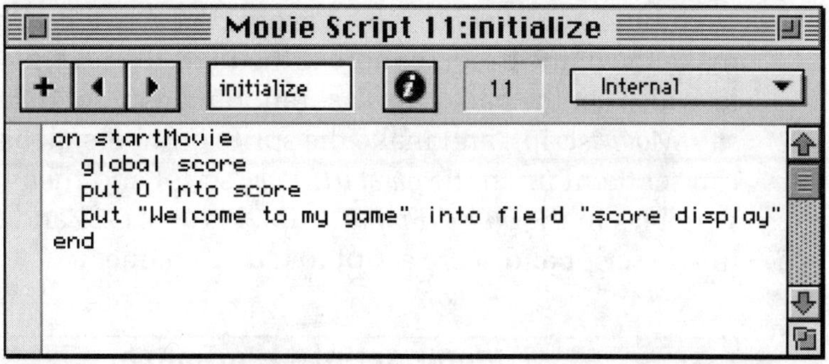

Figure 6-10: *A game script that uses globals and a text field to display the score.*

In the script, we take the opportunity to place a new piece of text in the "score display" field every time the ball reaches the bottom. We can refer to text cast members with the Lingo syntax *field*. The global "score" simply keeps track of how many times the ball was caught.

Fields

Field is just another word for a text cast member. Don't confuse fields with the new Director 5.0 rich text cast members, which are related to bitmaps.

Fields work just like variables, except that they can only hold text and they can be displayed on the stage. They also retain some text attributes like font, size, and style that variables do not.

Fields can also be given a variety of display attributes such as a border, margins, width, and height, and can even be set to appear as scrolling text boxes.

We can do even better. Let's have a global that keeps track of misses. In addition, move the *puppetSprite* commands to our *on startMovie* handler since those commands only need to be executed once. Let's also make "drop" a global and set it to 10 at the beginning but increase it by 2 every time a ball is caught. This will make the game become more difficult as the user plays. Finally, let's also set the ball to its first random position in the *on startMovie* script, and make the sprite numbers globals so that we can set them up in the *on startMovie* script and then use those variables in the *on exitFrame* script. Figures 6-11 and 6-12 show the movie script and score script for such a game.

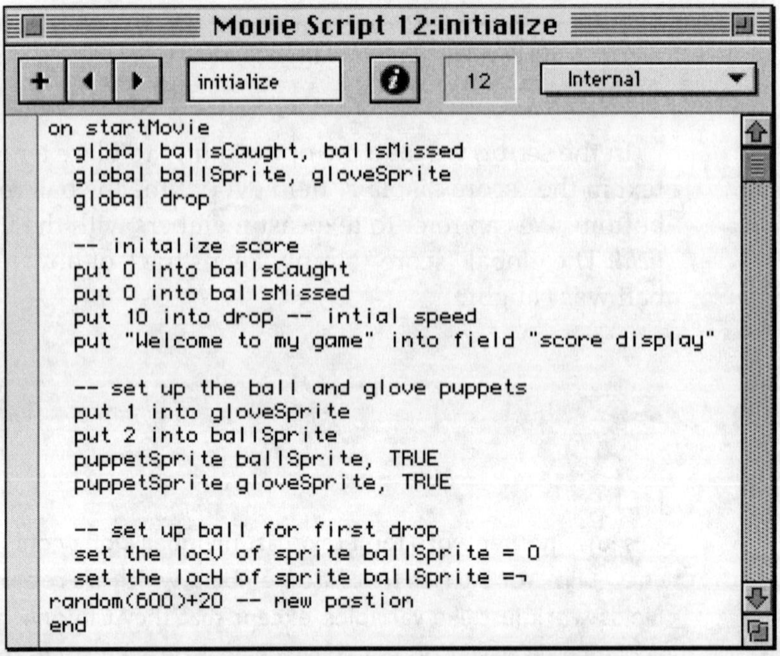


```
on startMovie
  global ballsCaught, ballsMissed
  global ballSprite, gloveSprite
  global drop

  -- initalize score
  put 0 into ballsCaught
  put 0 into ballsMissed
  put 10 into drop -- intial speed
  put "Welcome to my game" into field "score display"

  -- set up the ball and glove puppets
  put 1 into gloveSprite
  put 2 into ballSprite
  puppetSprite ballSprite, TRUE
  puppetSprite gloveSprite, TRUE

  -- set up ball for first drop
  set the locV of sprite ballSprite = 0
  set the locH of sprite ballSprite =¬
random(600)+20 -- new postion
end
```

Figure 6-11: *A movie script that also sets puppetSprites.*

Score Script 6:Ball Catch Script

Ball Catch | 6 | Internal

```
on exitFrame
  global ballsCaught, ballsMissed
  global ballSprite, gloveSprite
  global drop

  -- move the glove with the cursor
  set the locH of sprite gloveSprite = the mouseH

  -- move the ball down
  set the locV of sprite ballSprite =¬
the locV of sprite ballSprite + drop


  -- is the ball all the way down yet?
  if the locV of sprite ballSprite >=¬
the locV of sprite gloveSprite then
    if the locH of sprite ballSprite > ¬
the left of sprite gloveSprite and ¬
the locH of sprite ballSprite < ¬
the right of sprite gloveSprite then
      put ballsCaught+1 into ballsCaught
      put drop+2 into drop
    else
      put ballsMissed+1 into ballsMissed
    end if
    put ballsCaught&&"caught and"&&ballsMissed&&"missed"
into field "score display"

    -- reset ball for next drop
    set the locV of sprite ballSprite = 0
    set the locH of sprite ballSprite =¬
random(600)+20 -- new postion
  end if

  go to the frame
end
```

Figure 6-12: *A new game script that keeps track of catches and misses and gets progressively faster.*

Notice that the *global* command can appear more than once, and that more than one variable can be declared as a global on each line.

We can go even further in our game. There can be another field on the screen that displays the speed of the ball for users to see. We can also find a way to end the game. Maybe it ends when the user has been thrown enough balls. We can do this by testing the sum of the catches and the misses every time these numbers change and seeing if the sum exceeds a certain value. Or maybe we want to only allow the user so many misses—a sort of "see how many you can catch before you miss ten" game. Another way to end the game may be to go to another frame and display a message. You will want to turn off the *puppetSprites* when you do this, or the ball and glove will hang around.

Note that this game needs to be in frame 1 and the play head of the movie needs to be in frame 1 when you press Play. This is because our *on startMovie* handler needs to *puppetSprite* the first and second sprites—and the ball and glove need to be in those sprites in order for things to work properly. Try adding a *go to frame 1* at the beginning of the *on startMovie* handler. This will reset the play head to the first frame any time you start the movie, even if it is not on the first frame at that moment. In turn, this will assure us that the sprites will be puppeted properly.

We can make the program more versatile by placing our initializations in an *exitFrame* script that is in the frame before the game frame, as in Figure 6-13. Figure 6-14 shows how the score may look.

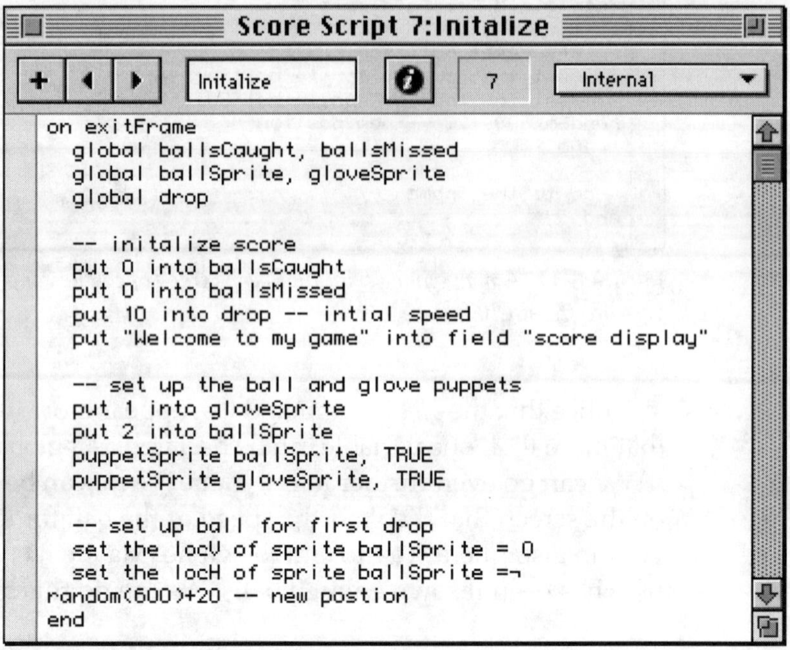

Figure 6-13: *An on exitFrame script that initializes the game.*

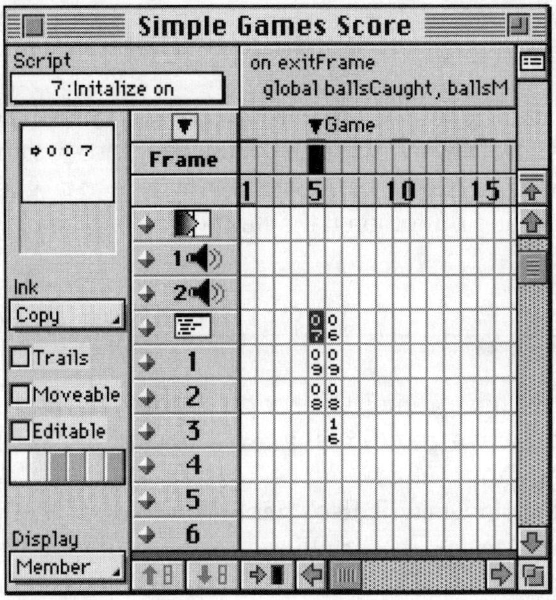

Figure 6-14: *The initialization frame is placed directly before the game frame. In order to play the game, we go to that frame first, which then drops us into the next frame after everything is ready to go.*

Now we can start our game at any time with a *go to frame "game"* command. This will initialize the variables and *puppetSprite* everything for us before proceeding to the frame where the game actually runs. Notice that we placed the ball and glove in the initialization frame so that the *puppetSprite* command can take hold of them. The "score display" field didn't need to be there, since we don't need to *puppetSprite* it.

There is one thing you will have to change if you are developing these scripts in a step-by-step manner in the same movie: our *on startMovie* script must be taken out of the movie script for the previous script to work, since otherwise it will execute and try to *puppetSprite* the ball and glove on frame 1, even though they are not there. You don't need to delete the script to do this, however; just try changing the name of the *on startMovie* handler to *on startMovieX* or something similar, to make the handler stop intercepting "startMovie" messages.

Try It Yourself

Build the game described in this lesson. Add a new field on the stage that will show players the speed of the ball. Also, when the ball has been thrown, say, 20 times, have the movie go to a "game over" frame that has a button on it that allows the user to play again.

Moving On

How far we have come! The scripts in this chapter allow you to create interactive games that go way beyond what is possible in Director without Lingo.

Global variables will also enable you to do many other things. The *on startMovie* handler will be very useful when creating all sorts of projects that need to initialize themselves.

Next, we'll take another look at animation using Lingo.

7

Special Effects

Now that you are able to change sprite properties using the *puppetSprite* functionality, we can explore ways to use Lingo to create wild and interesting effects. You will learn how to shrink and enlarge sprites and change other properties to give them a different appearance.

Lesson 19: Faking 3D

Lingo syntax:

```
the rect, the left, the right, the top, the bottom, the
width, the height, sqrt, float
```

There are many other properties of sprites that you can control in Lingo. We have already looked at changing the cast member and the location of the sprite. We can also change the size of the sprite on the stage.

At this point it is important to revisit the distinction between the cast member and the sprite. The cast member is the actual graphic bitmap stored in the movie. The sprite is an element on the stage. We can tell a sprite to "look like" a cast member—in fact, we can tell more than one sprite to "look like" the same cast member.

Sprites also have other properties. For instance, they have a location on the stage. If you are experienced at using Director's score, you know that a sprite also has an *ink effect*, such as "copy" or "matte." We have also assigned score scripts to certain sprites.

Another property of a sprite is its *rectangle*. This is the invisible "box" that the sprite fills on the stage. It is similar to the location of a sprite but actually refers to the upper left and lower right corners of the sprite rather than to the horizontal and vertical position of the cast member's registration point.

You can see this in action in the message window. Create a bitmap cast member and stick it on the stage and into sprite channel 1.

```
put the rect of sprite 1
-- rect(40,37,245,196)
```

Whatever your numbers turn out to be, they represent the horizontal location of the left side of the sprite, the vertical location of the top edge of the sprite, the horizontal location of the right side of the sprite, and the vertical location of the bottom edge of the sprite.

So far, this gets us nothing new. We already know how to get *the left of sprite* and *the right of sprite*. There are also similar commands: *the top of sprite* and *the bottom of sprite*.

The structure of the value that *the rect* returns is like that of the point structure we saw earlier. In fact, we can extract the individual numbers from any *rect* structure by using *the left*, *the right*, *the top*, and *the bottom*.

```
put the rect of sprite 1 into r
put r
-- rect(40,37,245,196)
put the left of r
-- 40
put the right of r
-- 245
put the top of r
```

```
-- 37
put the bottom of r
-- 196
```

Most important, not only can we capture the value of the *rect* of a sprite, but we can *set* it as well. This means that we can resize the sprite on the screen to shrink or stretch the bitmap to any size we want. Remember, we are not actually changing the cast member, just the sprite's version of that cast member on the stage.

Try this in the message window:

```
set the rect of sprite 1 = rect(60,57,225,176)
updateStage
```

Presto! The bitmap has been resized to fill our rectangle. You can even do odd vertical and horizontal stretches this way.

```
set the rect of sprite 1 = rect(20,40,620,80)
updateStage
set the rect of sprite 1 = rect(200,20,280,440)
updateStage
```

Note that you can only *set the rect* of a sprite. You cannot *set the left* of *the rect* of a sprite or similar properties.

Now we can create some Lingo handlers that do some shrink/enlarge animation for us. Figure 7-1 shows an *on exitFrame* script that shrinks sprite 1 until it is very small.

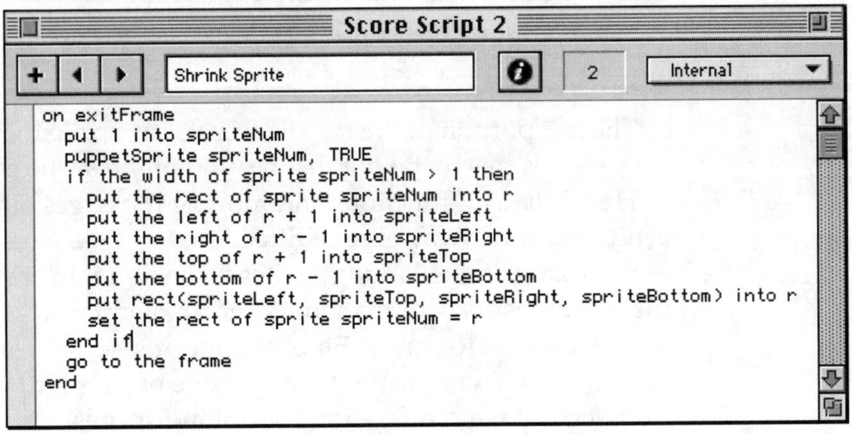

Figure 7-1: *A script that shrinks a sprite.*

In this last script we used *the width of sprite*. This simply returns the number of pixels wide that the sprite is at that moment. A companion function to this is *the height of sprite*.

In addition to finding *the width* and *the height* of sprites, we can also find *the width of cast* and *the height of cast*. This means we can figure out what the original size of the bitmap is, and reset it to that size whenever we want. The script in Figure 7-2 demonstrates this.

Score Script 3:Repeating Shrink Sprite

Repeating Shrink Sprite | 3 | Internal

```
on exitFrame
  put 1 into spriteNum
  puppetSprite spriteNum, TRUE
  if the width of sprite spriteNum > 1 then
    put the rect of sprite spriteNum into r
    put the left of r + 1 into spriteLeft
    put the right of r - 1 into spriteRight
    put the top of r + 1 into spriteTop
    put the bottom of r - 1 into spriteBottom
    put rect(spriteLeft, spriteTop, spriteRight, spriteBottom) into r
    set the rect of sprite spriteNum = r
  else
    put the memberNum of sprite spriteNum into cNum
    put the width of member cNum into w
    put the height of member cNum into h
    put the locH of sprite spriteNum - (w/2) into spriteLeft
    put the locH of sprite spriteNum + (w/2) into spriteRight
    put the locV of sprite spriteNum - (h/2) into spriteTop
    put the locV of sprite spriteNum + (h/2) into spriteBottom
    put rect(spriteLeft, spriteTop, spriteRight, spriteBottom) into r
    set the rect of sprite spriteNum = r
  end if
  go to the frame
end
```

Figure 7-2: *A script that shrinks a sprite over and over again.*

The *else* portion of the handler resets the sprite to its original size. It does this by taking the location of the sprite through *the locH* and *the locV* functions and moving the edges out from that center point halfway in each direction.

Shrinking and enlarging sprites is the secret to creating faked three-dimensional animation. When an object moves away from you, it appears to shrink. Since a computer screen is two-dimensional, we of course cannot really move objects farther away from the user, but we can fake it by shrinking sprites.

The script in Figure 7-3 not only shrinks a sprite but moves it to the right to create the illusion that the graphic is falling back into the screen. To use it, place a decent-sized bitmap in sprite channel 1 and position it on the left side of the screen.

Score Script 4:Moving, Shrinking Sprite

Moving, Shrinking Sprite | 4 | Internal

```
on exitFrame
  put 1 into spriteNum
  puppetSprite spriteNum, TRUE
  if the width of sprite spriteNum > 1 then
    put the rect of sprite spriteNum into r

    --shrink the sprite
    put the left of r + 1 into spriteLeft
    put the right of r - 1 into spriteRight
    put the top of r + 1 into spriteTop
    put the bottom of r - 1 into spriteBottom

    -- move it over 8 pixels
    put spriteLeft + 8 into spriteLeft
    put spriteRight + 8 into spriteRight

    put rect(spriteLeft, spriteTop, spriteRight, spriteBottom) into r
    set the rect of sprite spriteNum = r
  end if
  go to the frame
end
```

Figure 7-3: *A script that fakes three-dimensional movement.*

At this point you can play with some of the numbers in the script to get different speeds and depths.

The next step is to combine this faked three-dimensional movement with our two-dimensional animation used in earlier lessons. Let's go back to the idea of having a character walk across the stage. This time, we will have him walk toward the back of the stage. Figure 7-4 shows the combination of these two scripts.

Score Script 5:Animated, Shrinking Sprite

Animated, Shrinking Sprite | 5 | Internal

```
on exitFrame
  put 1 into spriteNum
  puppetSprite spriteNum, TRUE
  put the memberNum of sprite spriteNum into cNum
  put the name of member cNum into cName
  if the width of sprite spriteNum > 1 then
    put the rect of sprite spriteNum into r

    --shrink the sprite
    put the left of r + 1 into spriteLeft
    put the right of r - 1 into spriteRight
    put the top of r + 1 into spriteTop
    put the bottom of r - 1 into spriteBottom

    -- move it over 16 pixels
    put spriteLeft + 16 into spriteLeft
    put spriteRight + 16 into spriteRight

    put rect(spriteLeft, spriteTop, spriteRight, spriteBottom) into r
    set the rect of sprite spriteNum = r

    -- Animate it, too
    if cName = "MAN1" then
      put "MAN2" into cName
    else
      put "MAN1" into cName
    end if
    put the number of member cName into cNum
    set the castNum of sprite spriteNum = cNum
  end if
  go to the frame
end
```

Figure 7-4: *A script to make a character walk toward the back of the stage.*

Next, let's give the user control of our three-dimensional animation. Let's go back to the idea of just having a single bitmap that shrinks as it moves to the right. In Figure 7-5, we give control of the vertical, the horizontal, and, in turn, the depth positioning of the sprite to the user.

The new rectangle for the sprite first depends on the position of the cursor. We move the edges of this rectangle out a certain width and height from this center point. The width and height are multiplied by a "scale" variable that is related to the horizontal screen position of the cursor. When the cursor is to the left side of the screen, the "scale" variable is close to 0, while it is close to 1 at the other end.

To do the simple division needed to determine the scale, we have to use the *float* function. This converts a number to a decimal, or floating-point number. Lingo keeps everything in integers, or nonfractional numbers, unless you request a change to floating-point. Try this in the message window:

```
put 1/3
-- 0
put 1.0/3
-- 0.3333
put float(1)/3
-- 0.3333
```

Lingo does the second and third lines of this test correctly, because we started the calculation off with a floating-point number. The first test starts with an integer, so the result is rounded to the closest integer, which is 0.

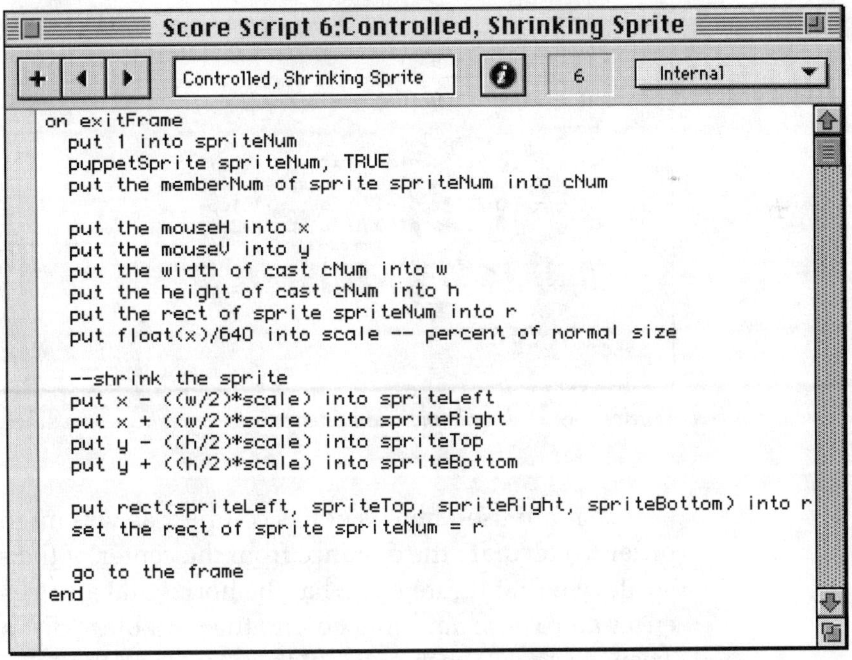

Figure 7-5: *A script that lets the user control a sprite in three dimensions.*

Here is another cool effect we can produce. Using some basic geometry, we can calculate the distance from a sprite to the center of the stage. Then we can take this number and use it to make the sprite appear smaller toward the center of the stage and normal toward the edges. This will create the effect that the sprite is in a sort of "vortex," or that it is the shadow on the wall of a very long hallway. Figure 7-6 shows this script.

Score Script 7:Sprite caught in a vortex

Sprite caught in a vortex | 7 | Internal

```
on exitFrame
  put 1 into spriteNum
  puppetSprite spriteNum, TRUE
  put the memberNum of sprite spriteNum into cNum

  put the mouseH into x
  put the mouseV into y
  put the width of cast cNum into w
  put the height of cast cNum into h
  put the rect of sprite spriteNum into r

  put 320-x into dx
  put 240-y into dy
  put sqrt(dx*dx+dy*dy) into d
  put float(d)/300 into scale

  --shrink the sprite
  put x - ((w/2)*scale) into spriteLeft
  put x + ((w/2)*scale) into spriteRight
  put y - ((h/2)*scale) into spriteTop
  put y + ((h/2)*scale) into spriteBottom

  put rect(spriteLeft, spriteTop, spriteRight, spriteBottom) into r
  set the rect of sprite spriteNum = r

  go to the frame
end
```

Figure 7-6: *A three-dimensional vortex.*

The math used here is not as complex as you might think. In order to calculate the distance from the center of the screen to our sprite, we first figure out what the horizontal and vertical differences are. These amounts go into the variables "dh" and "dv." Then we square each one *(dh*dh, dv*dv)*, add these two numbers together, and take the square root of the result *(sqrt(dh*dh+dv*dv))* and this gives us the desired distance, in pixels.

We use this number to calculate the rectangle of the sprite. If the distance is 300, which is close to the distance from the center to the edge of the stage, then we will display the sprite at 100 percent of its size. That is, the left and right edges of the sprite are each half the total width of the bitmap away from the center. The same for the vertical proportions.

The script figures out what percentage of the normal size of the bitmap should be used at any given moment by dividing the distance to the center of the stage by 300. So when the sprite is at the edge, you will get 300/300, which is 1. When the sprite is halfway toward the center, you will get 150/300 which is .5.

These three-dimensional effects can be used in many ways throughout your projects. Plus, the understanding you now have of sprite rectangles will help you build future scripts that use a lot of sprite movement.

In the next lesson, we look at some other sprite properties that you can control.

Try It Yourself

Create a script that makes a sprite appear to float back into the stage and then come forward again. You can have the sprite shrink as it gets closer to the top of the stage. Then try animating that sprite using two or more cast members.

Lesson 20: Various Special Effects

Lingo syntax:

```
repeat with, the blend, the ink, the palette, the foreColor,
the backColor
```

There are plenty of other sprite properties in addition to the cast member and location that we can manipulate in Lingo. Blends, inks, and colors can be used to change the appearance of a sprite on the stage.

Blends

The property *the blend* can be used to create single-sprite fades. This property determines the visibility of the sprite on the stage. A blend setting of 100 means that the sprite is entirely visible, while a value of 50 means it is halfway faded to the background. You are supposed to only use blend values on sprites that are set to the inks Matte, Blend, Bkgnd Transparent, or Mask in the score. However, in practice the blend property works in other cases too.

Figure 7-7 shows how you can set the blend property of a sprite in the score. We can also take control of *the blend* in lingo.

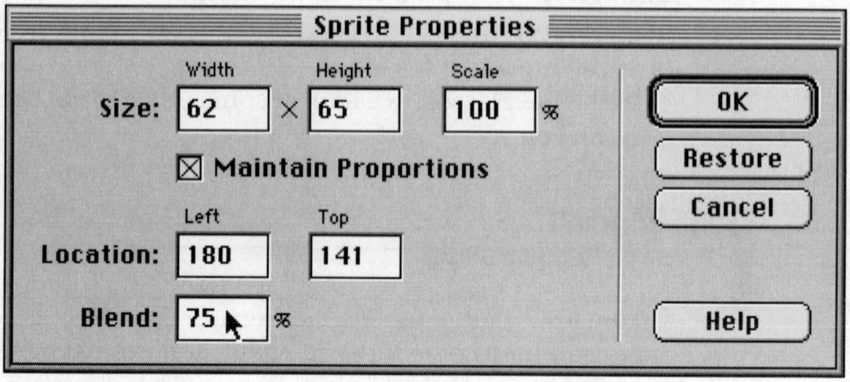

Figure 7-7: *You can set a sprite's blend in the score by selecting the Sprite Properties menu item in the Modify menu.*

Using Lingo, we can not only *puppet* a sprite and assign a new blend value to it, but we can use a *repeat* loop to change the value and create a fade-in or fade-out effect.

Figure 7-8 shows a movie script with two handlers. The first, "fadeOut," takes the sprite number as a parameter. It then uses *the blend of sprite* to take the blend value of that sprite from 100, the maximum value, to 0, the minimum value. The result is that the sprite fades to invisibility.

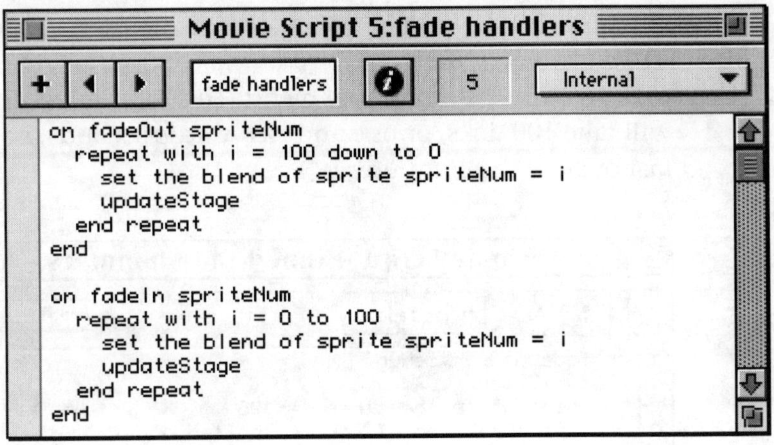


```
on fadeOut spriteNum
  repeat with i = 100 down to 0
    set the blend of sprite spriteNum = i
    updateStage
  end repeat
end

on fadeIn spriteNum
  repeat with i = 0 to 100
    set the blend of sprite spriteNum = i
    updateStage
  end repeat
end
```

Figure 7-8: *A set of fade handlers.*

These handlers use a new kind of *repeat* loop: the *repeat with* loop. These loops are pretty straightforward. Following the *repeat with* command is a variable name. This variable will move between the first and second values that the rest of the *repeat with* statement provides.

The line: *repeat with a = 1 to 20* will loop 20 times, and the value of the variable "a" will change from 1 to 20 during the 20 loops. If we want the *repeat with* loop to count from a higher number to a lower, then we need to use *down to* instead of *to* in the statement.

The *repeat with* loop ends just like a *repeat while* loop, with an *end repeat* statement.

Notice that we don't use *puppetSprites* here. Our fade routines are totally self-contained and don't even let any other action take place until the fade is complete, so we don't need to *puppetSprite* anything. However, because we do not do this, the very next time the movie's frame advances or loops, the sprite will return to its normal state. We could fix that by placing a *puppetSprite spriteNum, TRUE* command at the beginning of both fade handlers, if we wanted to.

Another problem with this handler is that the time it takes for the fade to occur depends on the speed of the computer that's running the movie. If it is a slow machine, it will take a long time for each increment of the fade to draw, and the whole thing could last a while.

Figure 7-9 shows a better set of fade handlers. Instead of using a *repeat with* loop, they use a *repeat while* loop, and rely on *the timer* to determine the amount of blend. This guarantees that the blend will take 100 ticks, or one and two-thirds seconds, no matter how fast or slow the computer is.

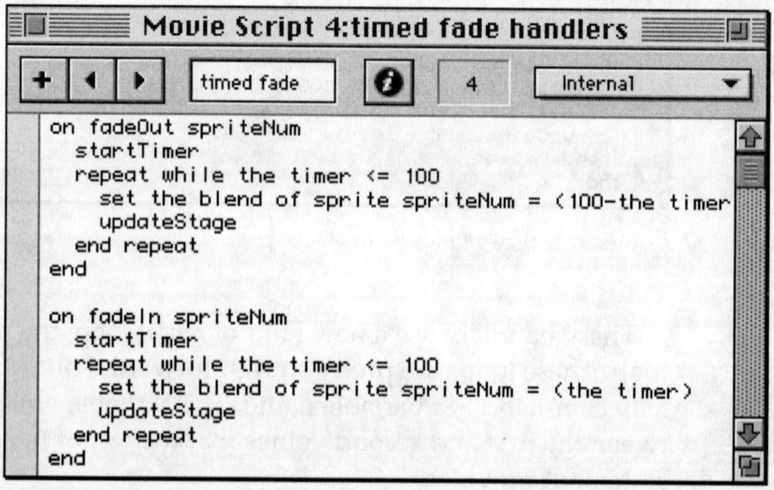

Figure 7-9: *Properly timed fade handlers.*

In cases like this you still lose something when the movie is running on a slow machine: smoothness. A slow machine might only be able to generate a dozen different increments of the blend before the time is up, while a fast machine might get to implement all 100, making it look very smooth. The important thing is that we keep a constant pace when doing animated effects, no matter what the speed of the playback machine is.

Inks

We have mentioned the ink property of a sprite several times previously. As Figure 7-10 shows, there are a number of settings you can choose from for each sprite in the score.

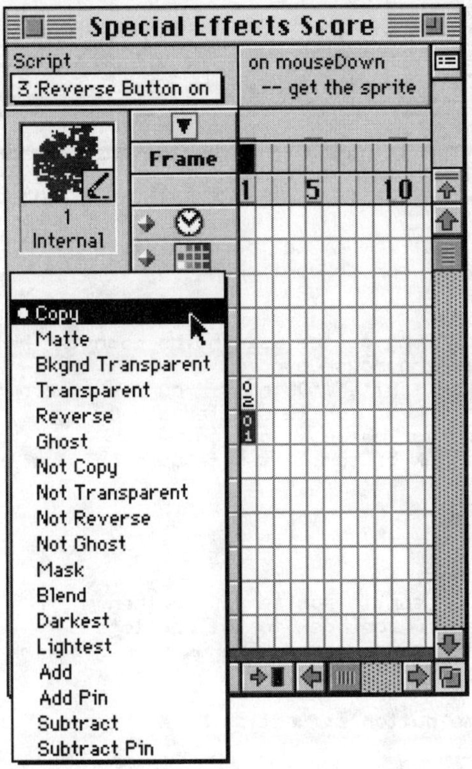

Figure 7-10: *Setting the ink of a sprite in the score.*

Each one of these ink effects changes the way a bitmap is drawn on the stage. There is a complete listing of ink effects, including the numbers that we need to use to refer to them in Lingo. You'll find a listing of them in Appendix C, "Tables & Charts," of this book.

Let's say we wanted to set the ink to something different than what it is set to in the score. A good place for this might be in a button handler. Instead of having a second, down state of the bitmapped button, we could instead change the ink of the bitmap while the user is pressing it. Figure 7-11 shows just such a button handler.

Score Script 3:Reverse Button

Reverse Button | 3 | Internal

```
on mouseDown
  -- get the sprite number and the two cast numbers
  put the clickOn into spriteNum
  put the ink of sprite spriteNum into originalInk

  -- set the cast member to the down state
  set the ink of sprite spriteNum = 6
  updateStage

  -- repeat as long as the user holds down the button
  repeat while the mouseDown
    if rollover(spriteNum) then -- cursor over button
      set the ink of sprite spriteNum = 6
    else -- cursor not over button
      set the ink of sprite spriteNum = originalInk
    end if
    updateStage
  end repeat


  if the ink of sprite spriteNum = 6 then
    -- set the cursor back to the up state
    set the ink of sprite spriteNum = originalInk
    updateStage

    -- add the button's function here

  end if
end
```

Figure 7-11: *A button handler that changes the ink of the sprite when pressed.*

The ink effect we use is number 6, the Not Transparent ink effect. Against a white background, this ink effect will do a sort of color reverse of the original bitmap.

ForeColor & BackColor

The bitmapped cast members we have been using so far have all been full-color graphics. Now, we are going to learn to use 1-bit graphics. There are black-and-white, or two-color, graphics where each pixel is either on or off—no color assignments. While it may seem that two-color graphics hold little potential for spectacular effects, this in not the case.

The two colors of 1-bit graphics are called *the foreColor* and *the backColor*. In other words, the foreground color and the background color. These two colors are often black and white, but they can be green and red if you want them to be.

Create a simple graphic in Director's paint window. A circle will do. Select the Transform menu item from the Modify menu. Figure 7-12 shows how to convert the graphic to 1-bit. You will get a warning that you cannot undo this operation.

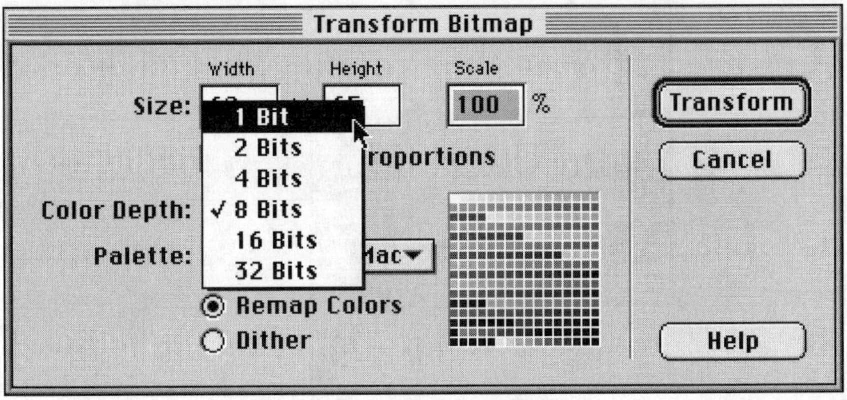

Figure 7-12: *Transforming a cast member to one-bit.*

Now that we have a one-bit cast member, place it on the stage. Bring up Director's tool window and use the color boxes to change the forecolor and the backcolor of the sprites. Figure 7-13 shows a selected 1-bit cast member and its background color being changed.

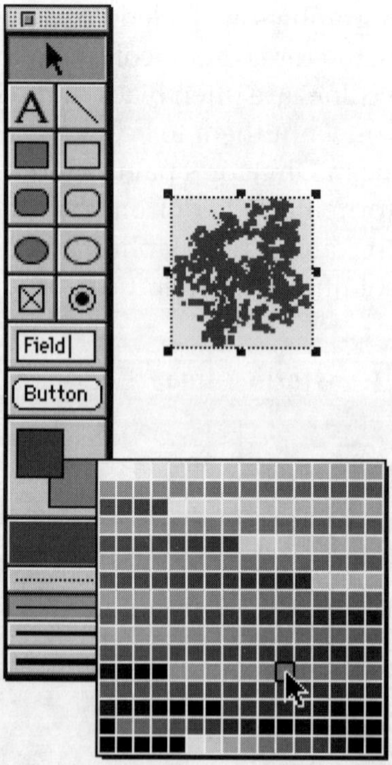

Figure 7-13: *Changing a sprite's* backColor *value.*

You can see that these 1-bit cast members don't have to be black and white at all. You can assign any two colors you want from the current palette. Better still, we can change these colors in Lingo.

In Lingo, we use *the foreColor* and *the backColor* properties of the sprite to set the two colors. For each color we assign a number from 0 to 255, corresponding to the respective number of the color in the palette.

Figure 7-14 shows Director's Color Palettes window, which you find listed under the Windows menu. It shows color 118 selected. You can use this window to find precisely the colors you want and use their numbers in your Lingo handlers.

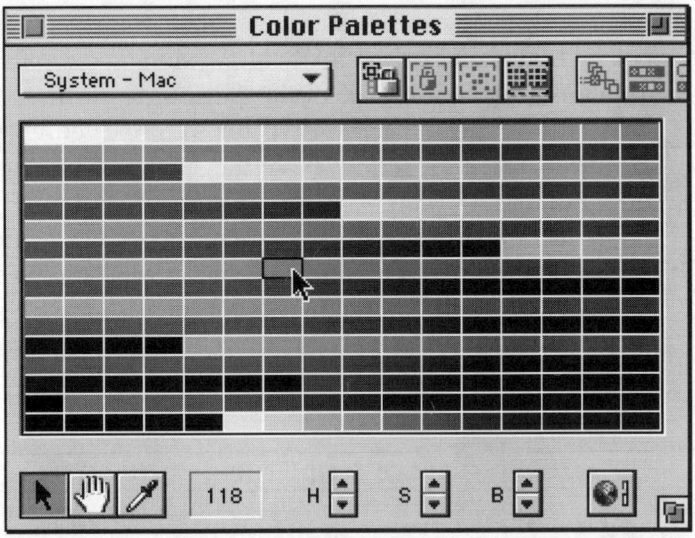

Figure 7-14: *Director's Color Palettes window.*

The script in Figure 7-15 is a simple frame script that *puppetSprites* a sprite and then cycles *the foreColor* between 0 and 255. Make sure you place a 1-bit cast member in that sprite.

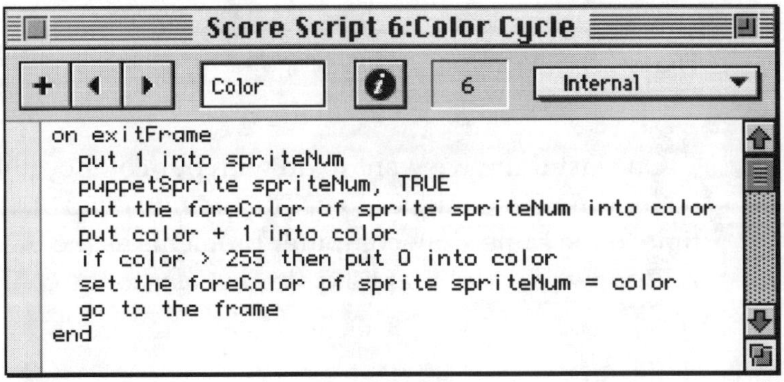

Figure 7-15: *A color-cycling frame script.*

The script causes the sprite to cycle through all 256 colors, which creates an odd cycle of colors, since most palettes aren't set up in an order that makes cycling through all the colors appealing. Those of you familiar with Director's color-cycling functionality know that there's a way to have the sprite only cycle through certain colors. We can do this in our routine too.

Figure 7-16 shows a script that cycles between color numbers 215 and 224, which correspond with several shades of red on the Macintosh system palette. If you are on a Windows machine, you can switch to the Mac palette in the Movie Properties menu item in the Properties menu.

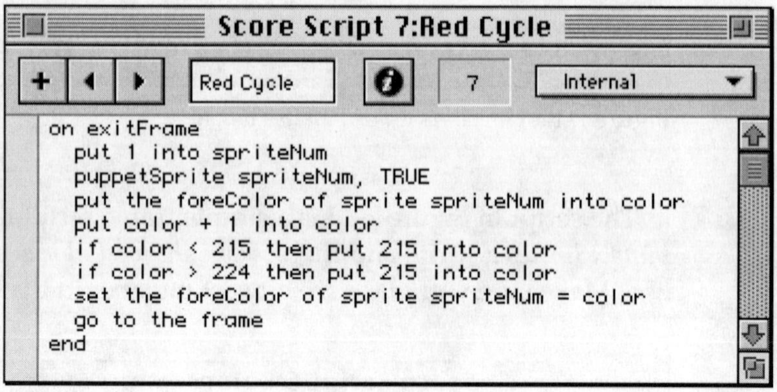

Figure 7-16: *A red color-cycling script.*

One last thing we want to do with our color cycling is to apply better timing techniques to it. The previous two scripts are susceptible to the same slow-computer problems as the blends. Figure 7-17 shows a script that links *the foreColor* to the computer's clock.

Score Script 8:Color Cycle

```
on exitFrame
  put 1 into spriteNum
  puppetSprite spriteNum, TRUE
  put the ticks mod 256 into color
  set the foreColor of sprite spriteNum = color
  go to the frame
end
```

Figure 7-17: *A timed color cycle script.*

Using Special Effects

This small library of special effects can be used in many ways. The fade handlers can be used to make a smooth transition from one bitmap to the next. Just *fadeOut*, switch cast members, and *fadeIn*. Figure 7-18 demonstrates this.

Movie Script 10:Gentle switch

```
on switchWithFade spriteNum, toMember
  fadeOut spriteNum
  put the number of cast toMember into cNum
  set the memberNum of sprite spriteNum = cNum
  fadeIn spriteNum
end
```

Figure 7-18: *A cast member fade-out, change, fade-in transition.*

The ink effects can be used to highlight a sprite on the stage like we did with the sample button script. You could have a sprite change inks when the cursor rolls over it. You will remember the *rollover* function from our button behavior scripts. Figure 7-19 combines that function with our *set the ink of sprite* command to create a highlight effect when the cursor moves over a spot. You could use this to signify that the sprite is "hot"—the user can click there and expect something to happen.

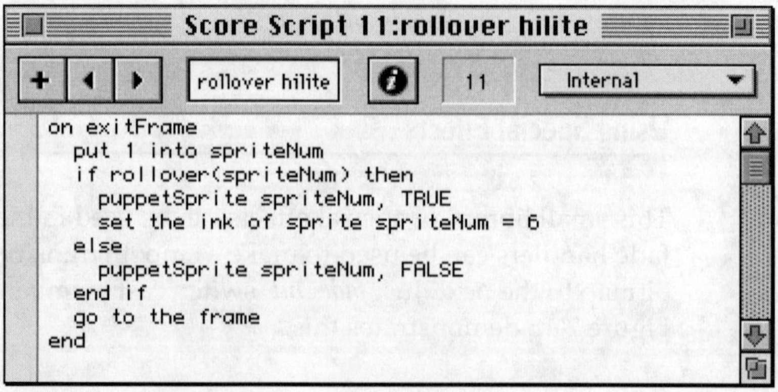

Figure 7-19: *A rollover hilite frame script.*

Notice that we use a *puppetSprite spriteNum, FALSE* when we want the sprite to return to its normal state. This is better than having to remember which ink it was previously and setting it back to that ink. It also means that there are fewer puppeted sprites that we need to turn off before going to another frame that doesn't use them.

The one-bit coloring effects have plenty of applications. One-bit cast members take up 1/8 the space of full graphics, making them perfect for movies that need to fit on a single disk or are delivered over the Internet through Shockwave or stand-alone applications.

Try It Yourself

Create a scene that contains three circles: one that cycles through shades of green, another that cycles through shades of blue, and a third that cycles through shades of red. They should all be cycling at the same time.

Moving On

In this chapter we learned many new sprite properties that can be useful in creating all sorts of effects. Don't forget that you can combine them to create even more unusual things.

In the next chapter, we look at other score elements that we can puppet besides sprites.

8

Multimedia

Up until now, we have mostly been controlling the basic visual aspect of the Director movie with Lingo. We have changed the locations and shapes of graphics. Now, let's explore ways to control sound and other elements of a movie.

Lesson 21: Giving Lingo a Voice

Lingo syntax:

```
puppetSound, soundBusy, sound playFile, sound stop, sound
close, soundEnabled, the volume of sound, sound fadeIn,
sound fadeOut
```

Most Director users know how to add sounds to the score. The two sound channels in the score, shown in Figure 8-1, let you include sounds in frames just as cast members are included in the sprite channels.

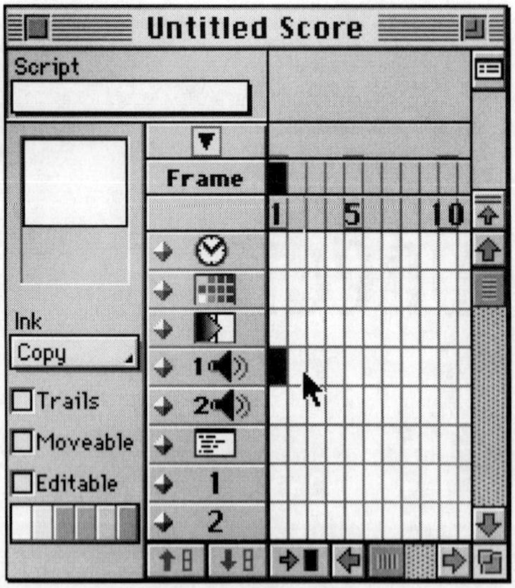

Figure 8-1: *There are two sound channels in the score.*

This method of adding sound to your projects is fine as long as you are not using Lingo. Some of the scripts we have developed so far, such as the button handler and the simple games, could use some sounds, but the sounds need to be played at the right time in the handler. The sound channels in the score will not help us because the sounds don't happen at a score-controlled time.

However, we can puppet the sound channels, just as we puppetSprite channels. The command to do this is *puppetSound*. It takes control of one of the sound channels and lets us play sounds at any time we want. Just as with puppetSprites, we need to use the *updateStage* command to trigger the sound.

Import a sound file into your cast. If you are using a Macintosh, you should be able to record a sound on the fly by using the Media Element menu item of the Insert menu. Rename that cast member "my sound."

Create a simple button on the stage and place the script shown in Figure 8-2 inside it. This script simply executes the *puppetSound* command with the name of the sound cast member as the only parameter. To make this work, we need to place a basic *go to the frame* handler in the frame script.

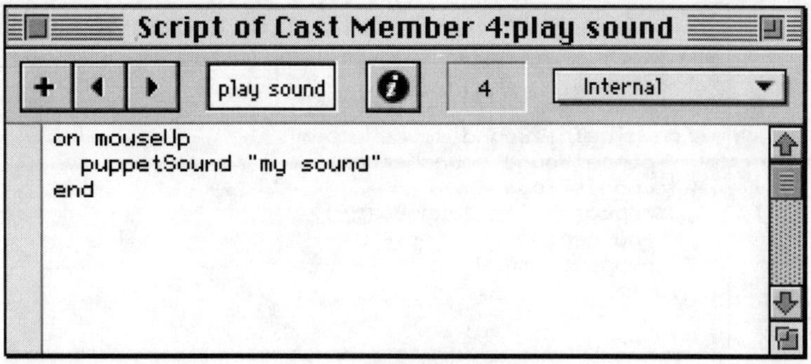

Figure 8-2: *A button script that plays a sound.*

Notice that we don't use an *updateStage* here. We are letting the *go to the frame* line in the *exitFrame* script do that work for us. Notice also that we don't specify which sound channel we are using anywhere in this script. The default is sound channel 1. We will use that for now.

Some things we need to keep in mind: We *do* have to worry about adding *updateStage* if there is any doubt that a *go to the frame* or other *updateStage* is coming up soon. Also, we have to remember that by puppeting sound channel 1 we take control of it away from the score. This means that none of the sounds specified in the score will work any longer until we return control of the channel to the score. We do this by using the *puppetSound 0* command.

A good utility script to have in your movies is a handler that plays a sound using *puppetSound*, waits until that sound is done, and then returns control of the sound channel to the score. We can use a Lingo function called *soundBusy* to determine if a sound is done playing. We'll call our handler "playThisSound." Take a look at Figure 8-3 to see how it works.

Figure 8-3: *A handler that plays a sound, waits until it is done, and returns control of the sound channel to the score.*

The *soundBusy* function takes one parameter: the number of the sound channel. Since *puppetSound* defaults to using sound channel 1, we give *soundBusy* a 1 as its parameter. The *repeat while* loop freezes the movie in that handler until the sound is finished. This can be disastrous if you have a long sound, or the sound is set to "loop" in the sound cast member information box.

It could be useful to modify this script so that there is an escape out of the loop. The user who is flying along in your program should be able to keep moving and not have to wait for sounds to finish. Figure 8-4 shows a modified version of the script that will terminate the loop and the sound if the user clicks the mouse. This same mouse click would also still activate any button or other object the user clicked on.

Figure 8-4: *An improved sound-playing handler that lets the user terminate the sound.*

Another command we can use to play sounds is the *sound playFile* command. This command takes two parameters: the sound channel you wish to use and the name of the sound file. The file must be either an AIFF file or a .WAV file.

When you are done playing a sound using the *sound playFile* command, it is a good idea, but not necessary, to issue a *sound close* command. This stops the sound playing in the sound channel you specify, and closes it. Let's try these in the message window:

```
sound playFile 1, "test.aif"
sound close 1
```

In order for these to work, you must have a sound file with that name in the same folder as the movie. Otherwise, you can specify the full path name of that sound file. If you used a file called "test.wav," then just make the appropriate changes.

Note that you can use sound channels higher than 2, the number available in the score. Try the same script with sound channel 3.

There are several other useful Lingo commands that relate to sound. *the soundEnabled* allows you to turn all of the sound in a movie on or off. This is useful for giving the user the option to turn off the sound in case they are using your project in a situation that requires a quiet working environment. Have you ever been in a classroom with 30 students on 30 computers? It can be quite noisy.

```
set the soundEnabled = FALSE
set the soundEnabled = TRUE
```

You can set the individual volume of each sound channel with *the volume of sound* property. You need to specify the sound channel and also the volume. Volumes range from 0, silence, to 255, the loudest.

```
set the volume of sound 1 to 180
set the volume of sound 2 to 40
```

There are two more sound-related commands: *sound fadeIn* and *sound fadeOut*. You need to pass these two commands the parameters indicating which sound channel you are referring to and how many ticks you want the fade to last. If you leave out the number of ticks, Lingo will make the fade last for 15 frames of the movie.

The fade commands do *not* work inside Lingo repeat loops. They need the score play head to be moving. You can use them when the movie is entering or leaving a sequence of frames that have a looping sound in the sound channel. Just place the command inside an *on exitFrame* script a few frames into or near the end of the sequence.

```
sound fadeIn 1, 180
sound fadeOut 1, 180
```

Timing Animation With Sound

Anyone who has tried to match sound and animation in Director knows that it can be very difficult. You can time the mouth movements of a character with the audio script so that it matches perfectly on your high-end development machine, only to have the animation lag dreadfully behind the sound on a user's slower machine.

Using Lingo, we can fix this. The problem is this: although your movie's frame rate may be at 15 frames per second, the user's machine is only fast enough to play 8 frames a second, or even fewer. I have seen machines that can barely play 3 frames per second when doing even the simplest animation.

Ideally, we want to make the movie smart enough so that if the animation gets behind the sound, the movie skips a frame or two to catch up. While the animation may not be as smooth if this happens, at least the character won't be mouthing the words that the computer's speaker uttered several seconds back.

To do this, we need two scripts. One that starts off a piece of the animation, and another that tracks along with it to make sure the timing is kept. The first one, shown in Figure 8-5, resets the timer and sets a global to the number of ticks each frame should take. Let's use 10 ticks for our example. Since there are 60 ticks per second, this matches 6 frames per second. While animators may be disappointed that they have to make movies to such low frame rates, they have to remember that most users, especially in the consumer market, don't have very fast machines. The script also remembers the frame number that starts off the animation.

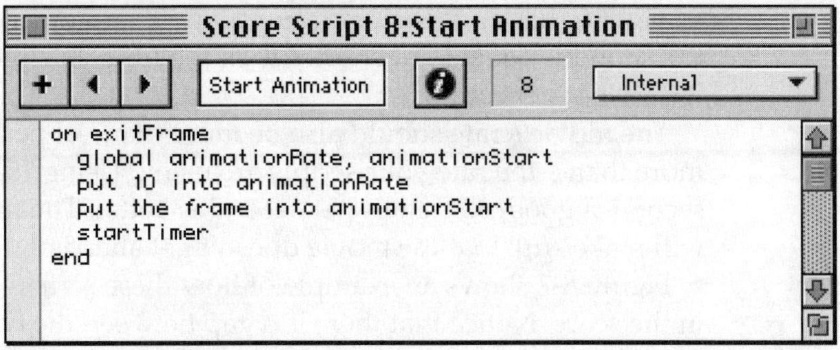

Figure 8-5: *A script that will start a timed animation sequence.*

The second script, shown in Figure 8-6, should be placed in all subsequent frames of that animation piece. It calculates which frame the animation *should* be on by dividing the current time by the rate of the animation and adding the start frame. If the animation is not up to that point yet for some reason, it jumps ahead to the appropriate frame.

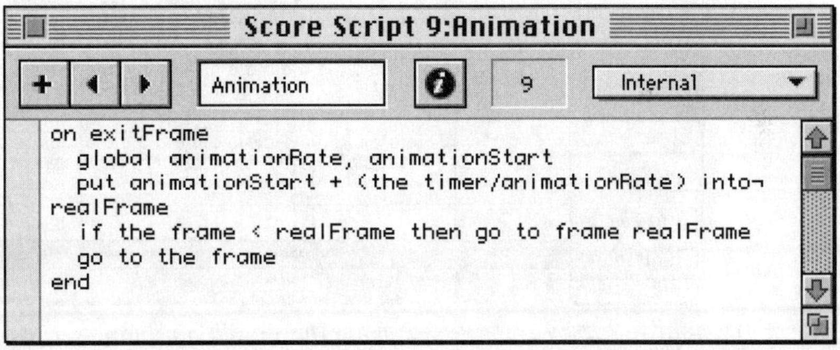

Figure 8-6: *A script that keeps a timed animation sequence at a set pace.*

To use these scripts you should break up your audio script into small pieces—sentence fragments or phrases are best. Then, you should make sure they are precisely timed to fit into the number of frames that you are allocating for them. In our example, we are going with 10 ticks per frame. That is 6 frames per second. So if a sound is 7 seconds long, it should occupy at least 42 frames. It is all right to have a few extra frames, say, 45, as long as the length of the sound is equal to or shorter than the time you allow it so that it does not get cut off.

The movie's rate should also be more than—if possible, much more than—the rate your scripts are using. Using 15 frames per second is good, 30 frames per second is better. The timing scripts will make sure that the movie doesn't get ahead of itself.

Figure 8-7 shows an example of how these scripts can be used in the score. Notice that there is a gap between the two sound pieces. If your sounds are divided well enough, you should be able to have small gaps of silence between them. This will help to ensure that each sound will end before the next one begins. If that is impossible, the scripts will still work.

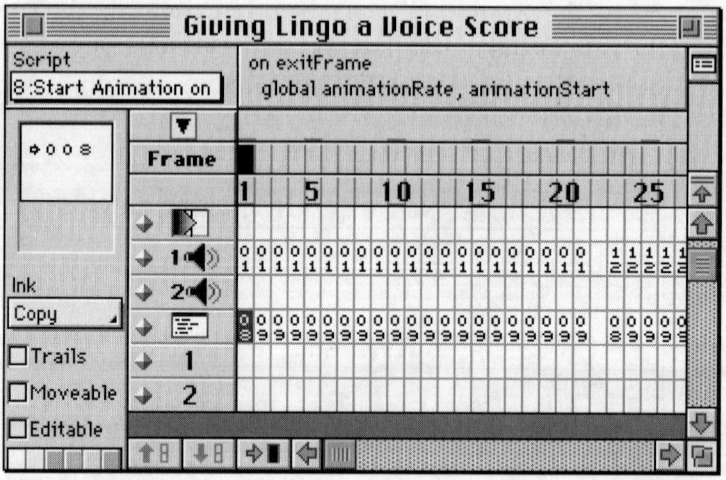

Figure 8-7: *A sample score using the animation timing scripts. Script 8 starts off an animation segment and script 9 makes sure the segment keeps a constant pace no matter how slow or fast the computer.*

Now we are getting into real multimedia—pictures *and* sound. The animation timing scripts may also cure some of your animators' headaches.

In the next lesson we take a look at other things we can control in Lingo, such as transitions, tempo, and the palette.

Try It Yourself

Assign the "playThisSound" handler to several buttons on the stage. Have each button play a different musical sound. Then place a looping sound in sound channel 2 of the score. Make it some sort of musical rhythm. The result should be the creation of your own music machine.

Lesson 22: More Puppets

Lingo syntax:

```
puppetTransition, puppetTempo, puppetPalette
```

There are three control channels at the top of the score that we have not yet dealt with: the transition, tempo, and palette channels. These can also be controlled in your Lingo handlers to create some interesting effects.

Puppet Transitions

The transition channel in the score is an easy way to add pizzazz to your projects. Figure 8-8 shows the dialog box that lets you change the transition in this channel. Director has a wide variety of built-in transitions.

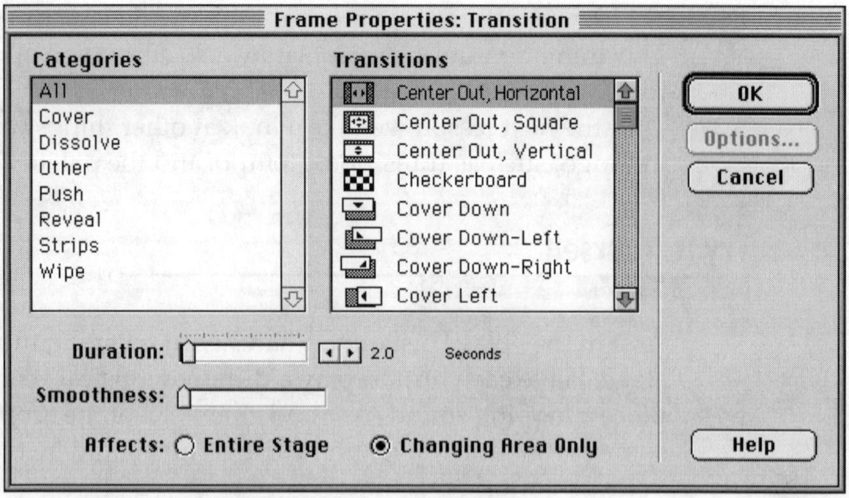

Figure 8-8: *Changing the transition in the score.*

The *puppetTransition* command allows you to control the next transition, which occurs either when the movie enters a frame or when you issue the *updateStage* command. All you need to do is place your *puppetTransition* command just before any command that will create a change—for example, a *go to the frame*, or *go to frame "a."* Figure 8-9 shows a simple button script that uses *puppetTransition*.

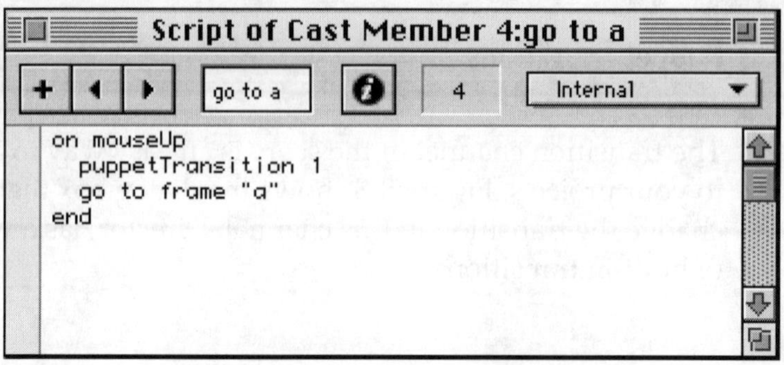

Figure 8-9: *Using a custom transition.*

The *puppetTransition* takes up to four parameters, but only the first one is required. This first parameter is the transition number. There are 52 transitions built into Director. In the case of our example in Figure 8-9, we use transition 1, a wipe to the right. A complete list of all 52 transitions can be found in Appendix C, "Tables & Charts," of this book, and in the Director manuals.

The complete *puppetTransition* command can look as complex as this:

```
puppetTransition 1, 8, 10, TRUE
```

The second parameter is the time it takes, in 1/4-second increments, for the transition to complete. In the above example, the 8 means that we want the transition to last for 2 seconds. This number should be taken with a grain of salt, however, because some effects don't use it and others may take too long on slow computers to make your deadline. It is best to experiment with the transitions you would like to use.

The third parameter is the chunk size of the transition. With each step the transition takes, a certain number of pixels are changed. This value helps determine how many. For instance, with a "wipe right" transition, if the chunk size is set to 10—as it is above—then the wipe to the right will happen 10 pixel lines at a time.

By setting this value higher, you will lose the smoothness of the transition. However, you will also gain some speed. This can help if you absolutely need a transition to finish on time.

The last parameter is a true or false value that determines if the transition will occur in only the portion of the stage that changed. This will create a very different effect for some transitions. A "push right" transition—number 12—will seem to push the entire stage to the right, replacing it with the new stage, if the value is *FALSE*. However, if only a small portion of the stage has changed, and the value is set to *TRUE*, then the push will only happen in a small area of the stage.

The most common problem with *puppetTransition,* and also with normal transitions placed in the score, is that you may wish to place one on a looping frame. If a frame is looping and a transition is also present, that transition will continue to happen over and over again. You may not see it because after the first transition the stage hasn't changed, so the transition is happening from B to B instead of from A to B. But, you will see the effects of this continuous transitioning: response times will be slowed, and cursors on the Macintosh will appear to blink on and off.

You can easily fix this problem by not having score and puppet transitions inside loops. For the score, create another, identical frame just before the looping one and place the transition in there. Then the second frame has the loop. That way, the movie enters the first frame, does its transition, and then loops on the second frame.

In Lingo handlers, you need to avoid placing your *puppetTransition* commands inside of loops. Figure 8-10 shows an example of this.

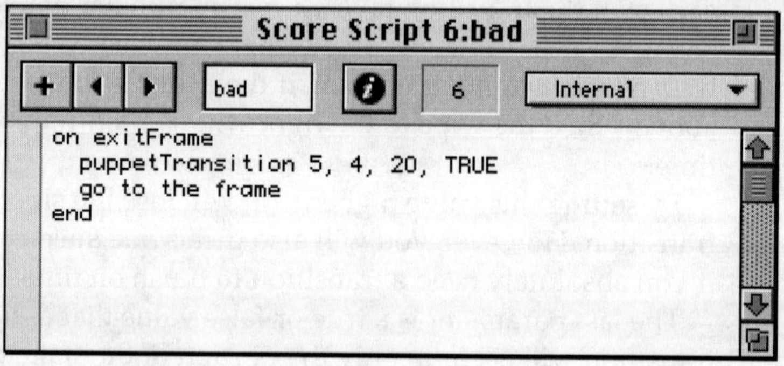

Figure 8-10: *Incorrect implementation of a* puppetTransition. *Don't do this.*

Puppet Tempos

The next control channel to deal with is the tempo channel. This simply controls the flow of the movie from one frame to the next. Figure 8-11 shows the dialog box that let's you control this in the score.

Figure 8-11: *Setting the tempo in the score.*

Mostly, the tempo channel lets you set the frame rate of an individual frame, which overrides the movie's frame rate. This change in the frame rate disappears as soon as the frame is over.

Using the *puppetTempo* command, we can set this value in Lingo. The change will take effect the very next time the play head moves to another frame or to the same frame in the case of a loop. It will stay at the same frame rate until another *puppetTempo* command is issued or the tempo channel in the score changes the tempo.

Puppet Palettes

The last control channel in the score is the palette channel. This allows you to set an individual palette for each frame. This palette choice overrides the movie's palette. Figure 8-12 shows the dialog box that lets you control palettes in the score.

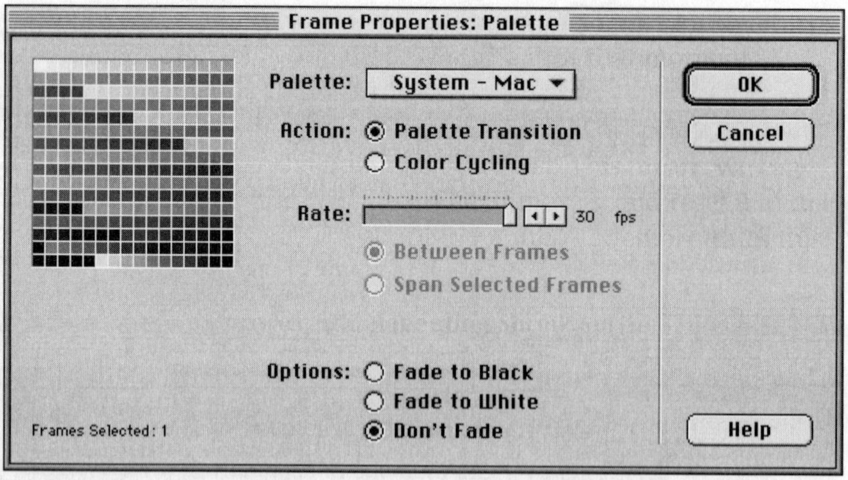

Figure 8-12: *The frame palette dialog box.*

The *puppetPalette* command takes control of the frame palettes in the movie. You can import a new palette as a cast member. Use that cast member's name as the parameter for the *puppetPalette* command.

```
puppetPalette "Gray", 20
```

The second parameter we used in this example is the speed of the transition. With this command, a 1 is the slowest and a 60 is the fastest. Assuming that our palette named "Gray" is a palette with 256 levels of gray, this command would gradually shift the colors on the stage to shades of gray. A very nice effect.

You can also have a third parameter: the number of frames over which you want the change to take place. This means that you can combine the palette change with other changes on your stage as well.

The *puppetPalette* command is like the *puppetSound* command in that control of the palettes will not return to Director until you issue a *puppetPalette 0* command.

Try It Yourself

Make a movie that has two frames with very different colorful graphics in each. Have buttons on each of these frames that allow the user to go back and forth between them. Then use the *random* function with the *puppetTransition* command to do a random transition when moving back and forth.

Moving On

Now we have taken complete control of the score with Lingo. Technically, it is now possible to create entire presentations by using only one frame and lots of puppets. Or, at the very least, you can go beyond what is easily done with traditional score animation by using nonlinear storytelling and adding interactivity to your projects.

Next, we will learn more about handling text. This will make some of the previous techniques much easier to implement.

9 Text

Graphics are only one part of a multimedia experience. Quite possibly the most important medium is pure text. After all, a few words and sentences can convey information that even the coolest graphics, photographs, and sound cannot.

Lesson 23: Playing With Text

Lingo syntax:

```
char, word, line, contains, length, string, value
```

Text can also be a valuable programming tool. We have already used it once—in our button handler script.This script took the name of the cast member of the button's "up" state and appended "down" to it to figure out the name of the cast member that was in the down state.

Lingo has several commands to let you handle text. A piece of text, no matter how big or small, is referred to as a *string*. Any single letter, numeral, punctuation mark, symbol or space is a *character*. Strings can also be broken into *words* and *lines*.

We can place strings into variables and perform functions on these variables. Try this in the message window:

```
put "The quick brown fox jumps." into text
put text
-- "The quick brown fox jumps."
```

Now, let's learn some Lingo text-handling commands. The *word* command will return one or more words in the string.

```
put word 4 of text
-- "fox"
```

We can also use this to find more than one word at a time:

```
put word 2 to 4 of text
--  "quick brown fox"
```

The *char* command will do the same thing at the single-character level:

```
put char 9 of text
-- "k"
put char 7 to 11 of text
-- "ick b"
```

You can even combine the *char* and *word* commands:

```
put char 3 of word 5 of text
-- "m"
```

To go further, we need a longer string. Use the text window to create a text cast member and enter the three lines of text shown in Figure 9-1. Make sure you create a "field" cast member, not a "rich text" cast member. Press Return after each line. Then name the cast member "sample text."

Figure 9-1: *A text field with our sample text.*

Now use the message window again and type the following command line.

```
put field "sample text" into text
```

This puts a copy of the string that was in the cast member into our "text" variable. Now that we have more than one line of text in our variable, we can use the *line* command.

```
put line 2 of text
-- "There is really no reason for this."
put word 4 of line 2 of text
-- "no"
```

You can also access the text directly, without putting it in a variable first.

```
put word 3 of line 3 of field "sample text"
-- "just"
```

Also note that you don't need to use the *line* command to get to words and characters on other lines.

```
put word 10 of field "sample text"
-- "There"
```

Not only can you get text from a field cast member, but you can place text into one as well.

```
put "new text" into field "sample text"
```

The result of this Lingo command would be to have the text in the field "sample text" changed to our new string. Figure 9-2 shows the field's condition after the command has been executed.

Figure 9-2: *A text field after we have used Lingo to place text inside it.*

We can perform tests on strings, just like we do on numbers. For instance, we can compare two strings to see if they are the same.

```
put "quick brown fox" into thisText
put "quick brown fox" into thatText
put "slow brown fox" into otherText
put thisText = thatText
-- 1
put thisText = otherText
-- 0
```

Lingo is smart enough to know if two strings are the same, even if the capitalization doesn't match.

```
put "quick brown fox" into thisText
put "Quick Brown Fox" into thatText
put thisText = thatText
-- 1
```

We can also use the *contains* command to determine if one string is found anywhere inside the other.

```
put thisText contains "fox"
-- 1
put thisText contains "slow"
-- 0
```

Lingo will also let us convert strings to numbers and numbers to strings. The *string* function takes a number and makes it a string, while the *value* function interprets any string as an expression, giving us a number if that is what the string contains. If it is not a string, it returns the value <void>.

```
put "42" into text
put value(text)
-- 42
put string(43)
-- "43"
put value("6*9")
-- 54
```

In the last example, we showed that you can even have math expressions evaluated inside a *value* function.

Finally, we can use *the number of* to count things inside strings. We can count lines, words, and characters. Another way to count characters is to use the *length* function.

```
put the number of lines in field "Sample Text"
-- 3
put the number of words in field "Sample Text"
-- 23
put the number of chars in field "Sample Text"
-- 115
put length(field "Sample Text")
-- 115
```

Using Text to Make Life Easier

Now that we know how to use text functions, we can use them in handlers. For instance, you could have a single script that handles several buttons. The script would figure out the name of the cast member that makes up the button and go to a frame of that same name. Figure 9-3 shows such a script.

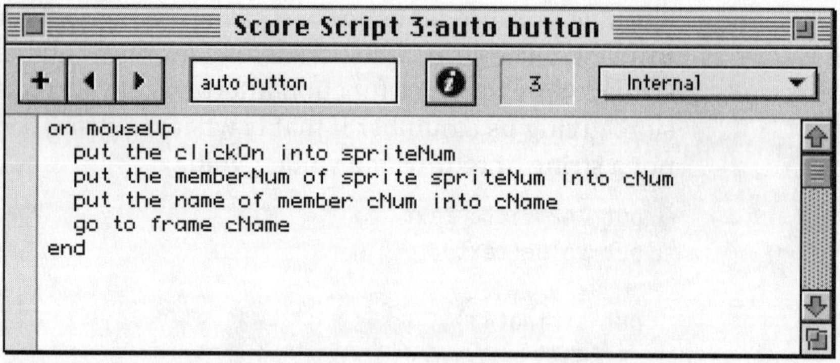

Figure 9-3: *A button script that uses the name of the cast member to decide which frame to go to.*

The beauty of this script is that you can assign it to many buttons in the score throughout your movie, and in each case it would go to a different frame. The frame it goes to depends on the name of the actual cast member in the sprite channel that was clicked.

A more complex way to handle this type of situation would be to give a button a longer name, starting with the word *button*, to distinguish it from a sound or other cast member with the same name. For instance, you might name the button cast member "button one." Then you can include a companion sound, "sound one," in the cast. The script in Figure 9-4 can then be assigned to the same sprite channel as the button. It will grab the name of the button, attach the second word of its name to "sound" to get "sound one," and play that sound. Then it will go to frame "one."

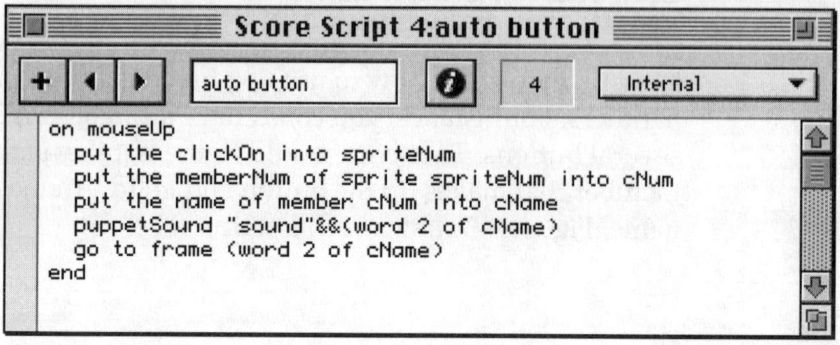

Figure 9-4: *A button script that plays a related sound and goes to a related frame.*

Next, we will use some of these text functions to implement simple hypertext.

Try It Yourself

Create a score script that handles a bitmap button. Have the script figure out the cast member name of the button and derive the name of a sound from that. Then, have it play that sound. Assign the same score script to several bitmaps on the stage so that each plays its own sound.

Lesson 24: Simple Hypertext

Lingo syntax:

```
the mouseCast, the mouseWord, the textStyle, the type of
member
```

Hypertext is often a desirable feature—in anything from small presentations to large CD-ROM and online projects. The term *hypertext* simply means that the user can click on certain pieces of text on the screen to seek more information related to the subject of that text. Usually, hypertext is shown as an underlined or colored piece of text within a text field. World Wide Web browsers, for instance, usually show hypertext in blue and underlined.

Many people, especially Macromedia's competitors, say that Director is not capable of hypertext functionality. This is not true at all. With fairly little scripting, you can put hypertext functionality into your movies.

The quickest way to add hypertext is to simply place an invisible box over a piece of text. Figure 9-5 shows what this might look like on the stage. Then, you can attach a simple *on mouseUp* script to the invisible box that does whatever the hypertext is supposed to do.

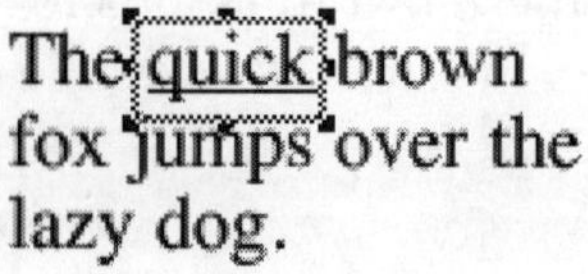

Figure 9-5: *A piece of rich text with an invisible box over a word. The box has been selected so that we can see it.*

Although this is pretty much the only way to do hypertext with rich text cast members or bitmapped text, there are many drawbacks. First, if your text changes, even slightly, you will probably have to realign all the invisible boxes. Second, each box will take up a sprite channel in that frame—this can use up your 48 sprites rather quickly. Last, keeping track of invisible boxes and what they do is a real pain—it can turn what should be simple changes into deadline-breaking nightmares.

A better way to do hypertext is to use field cast members and the Lingo commands that work with strings. Create a text field that looks like the illustration in Figure 9-6. Remember to make it a real text field, not a rich text cast member.

Figure 9-6: *A text field with some sample text.*

Now, we want to make a part of this text hypertext. The first thing we need to do is signify to the user that some of the text is *hot*. Let's just make some words hot by underlining them. You can select the text in its edit window and use the Font menu item in the Modify menu to underline it. Figure 9-7 shows our field as it would be displayed on the screen.

Implementing hypertext in Director 5.0 is not difficult at all. You can use some simple Lingo handlers to accomplish the task.

Figure 9-7: *Our text field with underlined words as it would look on the stage.*

Our hypertext handler will reside in a score script we can then attach to the sprite channel that contains the text field. It will be an *on mouseDown* script, so that when a user clicks on that field on the stage, our script will capture that click and figure out what to do with it.

Figure 9-8 shows the simple hypertext script. First, it gets the number of the cast member that was clicked on. We must be careful to only assign this script to sprites that contain text fields. Next, we use the new function *the mouseWord* to get the number of the word that the cursor is currently over. We take this number and figure out exactly which word it is inside the text field. The *if...then* statement uses the function *the textStyle* to see if the word is underlined. This function will return the string "underline" if the text is underlined. Notice that we use *contains* here instead of =. This is just in case we have a piece of text that is also bold. In that case, *the textStyle* would return "bold, underline."

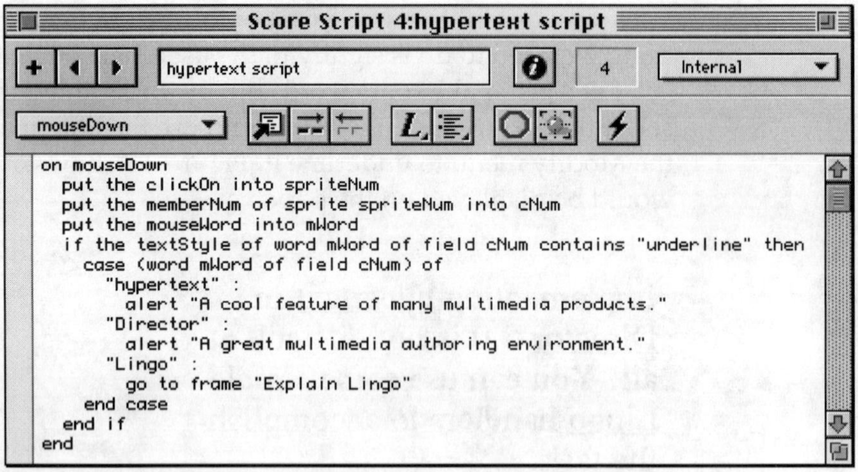

Figure 9-8: *A simple hypertext score script.*

The *case* statement in the script simply lists all the possibilities of hypertext in that field. Since we may want to use this same script with other fields, the list could also contain other words not in the field we are currently dealing with.

The actions that the different cases take can be anything. In this case we use the *alert* command to bring up little tidbits of information. For the word *Lingo* we use a *go to* command. You can also place *puppetSound* functionality here to pronounce words.

Hypertext & Cursors

One more thing you might want to add to a screen with hypertext is a script that changes the cursor when it is over a piece of hot text.

To do this we need to use the *cursor* command, which changes the current system cursor. The script in Figure 9-9 is a frame script that can be placed in any frame that has one of our hypertext fields. It looks to see if the cursor is over a cast member, then checks to see if it is a *field* cast member, and then to see if it is over a piece of underlined text. We use *the mouseCast* to see which cast member the cursor is over. If all that is true, it changes the cursor to a hand, which is cursor number 280.

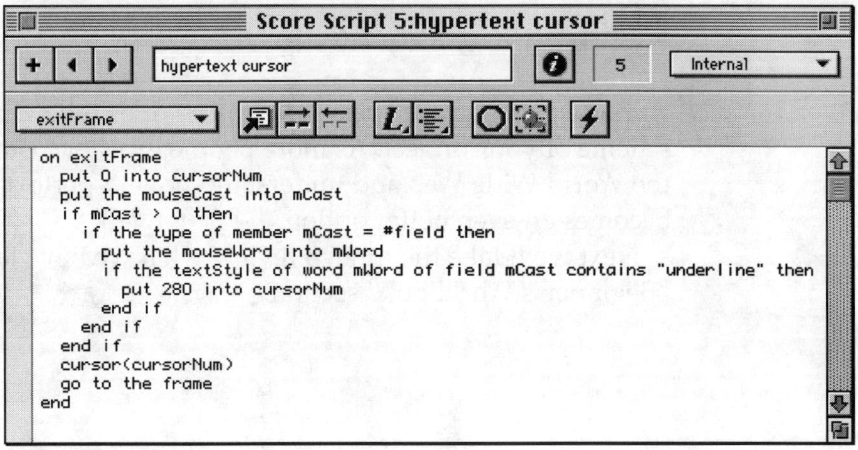

Figure 9-9: *A frame script that changes the cursor to a hand when it is over hypertext.*

A new function, *the type of member*, returns certain values. The one we are interested in right now is the *#field* value that will tell us if the cast member is a text field.

If you are running under Windows, the hand cursor may be available to you only when you're in Director but not in a projector. Cursor number 3, the crosshairs, may be a good alternative. We will be making our own custom cursors in a future chapter.

Try It Yourself

Use our hypertext handler with alert boxes to define difficult words in a large piece of text. Put the text into a scrolling text field so you can make it as long as you want. The text can be a short story, and the definitions can be for school children. Or the text may be a legal document and the definitions for nonlawyers.

Moving On

Hypertext can be used as a side feature or as the main navigation scheme of your project. As more people grow accustomed to using the World Wide Web and understand how hypertext works, it becomes an even better option.

Next we'll take the time to review what we have learned in this "Beginner's Workbook" section.

10 Beginner's Workbook Review

You have now mastered the basics of the Lingo programming language. You should know enough to allow you to fill your Director movies with all sorts of useful Lingo routines.

In addition, you will find at this point that you can look at other Lingo scripts and figure out what they do and how they do it. This is sometimes the best way to learn—by looking at other people's code and learning from it. The Internet and commercial online services have Director and Lingo areas where many examples are posted. The advanced and expert sections of this book are also excellent sources of a variety of scripting examples.

Let's review the Lingo commands and structures we learned in this section.

Frame Scripts

By using the *on exitFrame* handler in the score script of a frame, you can execute commands before moving forward. Using the *go to the frame* command, the movie will continuously loop on that one frame until some other Lingo command tells it to go to another.

Commands that break movies out of these loops are known as navigation commands. Most of them start with *go*. They can be triggered by mouse clicks by being placed inside *on mouseDown* or *on mouseUp* handlers, or they can be triggered via the keyboard with the *on keyDown* handler.

You can build some basic navigation into your movies by taking advantage of the *if...then* structure in Lingo. Frames can also be made to wait for a certain amount of time to pass, using *repeat while* loops and *the ticks*. More complex navigation can be handled using buttons.

Buttons

For simple presentations and prototypes, you can use Director's ready-made buttons, or you can make your own bitmap buttons. These buttons can be made to conform to user interface standards with *on mouseDown* handlers and two graphics: an up state and a down state.

These handlers use *repeat while* loops and the *rollover* command to make the buttons act properly. They also use cast and score functions such as *the memberNum of sprite* and *the clickOn* to allow them to work in more than one specific case.

Button handlers are custom-made functions that can be applied to a variety of buttons in different situations. They allow you to have consistent button behavior throughout your presentation and yet have each button look different and perform different functions. We use the *return* command to tell us whether a button click was valid.

Animation

You can use many different Lingo commands to animate. *The visible of sprite* will make a sprite invisible then visible again. Setting *the memberNum of sprite* will allow you to change which bitmap is on the stage. You can use *if...then* or *case* statements to determine which bitmaps to use. You can use *the timer* to synchronize these animations.

You can also write handlers that perform steps of the animation for you and have them called by another script. That way, you can animate several sprites in the same way.

The *puppetSprite* command allows you to temporarily take control of a sprite away from the score.

User Control

The position of the mouse can be obtained by using *the mouseH* and *the mouseV*. You can apply these numbers to sprites with *the locH* and *the locV* to make them move around the stage, and even let users drag them to wherever they want.

Simple games can be created by combining Lingo animation and user-controlled sprites. An element of randomness can be added using the *random* function. You can also keep score using global variables and display that score in fields.

Special Effects

Three-D animation can be faked in Director using *the rect* property of a sprite. You can shrink or enlarge any bitmap to make it look like it is coming toward or moving away from the viewer.

Other sprite properties, such as *the blend*, *the ink*, *the foreColor*, and *the backColor*, can be used to create all sorts of special effects.

Multimedia

You can use other puppet commands such as *puppetSound*, *puppetTransition*, *puppetTempo*, and *puppetPalette* to take total control of the score and create various effects.

Text

By using a whole set of Lingo commands such as *word, line, char, contains, the number of,* and *field,* you can create handlers that are easy to maintain and reuse.

You can use these same commands to implement hypertext in your movies. Using the *cursor* command will create an even better hypertext environment.

Programming in Lingo

Director offers many tools to help you script in Lingo. Turn on the Script Toolbar option in the View menu when you are using the scripting window. This toolbar appears at the top of a script window and looks like the screen shown in Figure 10-1.

Figure 10-1: *The script window with the script toolbar present.*

The pull-down menu in this toolbar and the button next to it will help you quickly locate handlers you have written. The next two buttons will let you comment or uncomment lines of code.

The button with the "L" and the one next to it will bring up menus listing Lingo commands, in case you forget the exact syntax needed. It will insert the command as well as dummy variables for the parameters needed in functions. The rest of the buttons are for using the debugger, which we will deal with in the advanced section, coming up next.

Other Programming Tips

One of the most common reasons that a script doesn't work is not that there is something wrong with the Lingo programming but that the script has been misplaced.

Check to make sure the script is the proper type: a score script or movie script. Make sure it is assigned to the correct frame or sprite. Check the handler name: is it an *on mouseUp* when it should be an *on mouseDown*?

Be patient and take your time with your scripts to make sure you don't look right past the obvious solution to your problem. And when you do find out what is wrong with a script that didn't work at first, take the time to really understand why it works now. This will help you avoid the same problem in the future.

Moving On

Now we are ready to take on more advanced concepts. The next section, "Advanced Lingo," will explore all sorts of uses for Lingo. Much of this will build upon this first section.

SECTION II

Advanced Lingo

11 Computer Programming & Lingo

Welcome to the "Advanced" section of this book. Don't be intimidated by the word "advanced." This section picks up right where the "Beginner's" section left off. It is not arranged in "lessons," however, but in standard chapters that cover a large topic.

Remember, though, that you are now ready to leave the basics behind and learn some things that can add real power to your Director movies. From now on, you are no longer a Director author who knows some Lingo but a true "Lingo programmer."

Programming Secrets of the Pros

Lingo programmers can be divided into two types: those that have a computer science or engineering background, and those that don't. The former are by far in the minority as most Lingo programmers start off as multimedia artists, designers, or authors and began using Lingo as an extension to their work in Director.

Secretly, computer engineers are jealous of the Lingo programmer. After all, they went through years of college learning about logic circuits, compilers, mathematical algorithms, and operating systems. Some remember carrying around stacks of punch cards and signing up for time on the main frame computer.

Many of these engineers are still programming in languages like C++ or FORTRAN, creating large databases for banks and telecommunications companies. They toil away as part of a team creating a complex program that will only be seen by other people in their corporation. When they are finished with their work, the reaction it gets is usually something like this: "It works."

Meanwhile, Lingo programmers are having fun. With a few quick lines of code they have characters dancing across the computer screen. They play with graphics, sound, and video all day, creating colorful multimedia presentations and games. They are able to work with artists and writers, and perhaps they are artists and writers themselves. When they are finished with their work, the reaction is usually more like "Cool."

On the Shoulders of Giants

Isaac Newton said: "If I have seen farther than others, it is because I was standing on the shoulders of giants." What he meant was that he was able to build his ideas on the ideas of scientists who came before him. He didn't have to start from scratch.

With Director and Lingo, we are doing precisely that. Without it, we would have to write C++ or Pascal programs that were pages long just to get a graphic to display on the screen and move a few pixels to the left.

Fortunately, we don't have to deal with things like C code or operating system toolboxes. Director takes care of all that and makes it possible for us to create our own multimedia products.

The "giants" we are indebted to start with the engineers at Macromedia who wrote Director and added Lingo to it. They are then standing on the shoulders of the systems programmers who put together the Macintosh and Windows operating systems. In turn, they were able to do their work because of the engineers at Motorola and Intel who made the microprocessors. You can even follow the path back to the early scientists who pioneered computers, computer languages, and operating systems. All the work they did helps us now to do ours.

Solving Problems

Computer programming is really nothing more than problem solving. In Director, the problem usually concerns presenting a certain visual effect or providing an interactive environment.

It is important when trying to program that you clearly define the problem. Do you want to have a sprite move across the stage? In that case, define the problem further: Which sprite? From where to where? How fast? Once, or multiple times?

Once defined, problems can be broken into smaller problems, which can then be broken into still smaller problems, and so on. If you are trying to do something in Lingo and can't quite figure out how, it is a sign that you should break the problem up into smaller pieces, rather than attempt to figure it all out at once.

An odd characteristic of programming is that there is usually more than one solution to a problem. The solutions are simply different ways to accomplish the same task.

Writing a Program

Whether you are attacking a programming problem that may take weeks, or you are writing a quick piece of code, it is pretty much the same process. A program is just a series of instructions that perform a task. These instructions must be part of the computer's vocabulary, so that it can understand what to do.

The first step in writing a program, as was just mentioned, is to define the problem clearly. Then you'll know what you are dealing with and what your goal is.

The second step is to figure out how you will go about writing a program to solve this problem. Many people prefer to do this on paper before they ever touch the computer keyboard. You don't necessarily have to write actual Lingo at this point, however. An outline, sketch, or flowchart may be enough for you. Sometimes, just planning in your head is enough.

Next, we try writing the Lingo handler or handlers to do the desired task. Don't be afraid of writing code that you may not be sure works. The computer will not criticize your program. Use the message window and half-finished handlers to test out things you are not sure of. If a program can be broken into steps, try getting just the first step to work before you tackle the second.

TIP

Don't try to re-invent the wheel. Stealing small pieces of code, like the scripts found in this book, is an accepted practice in computer programming. However, it is a good practice to credit the source of larger segments of code.

You will probably have to write, rewrite, and edit even simple handlers before they work properly. This is a normal part of the development process. It is nearly impossible to sit down and write a handler that works right the first time. Be patient, and also be confident that the program will eventually work given enough effort. Also, comment your code!

The process of fixing errors in your programs is called *debugging*. There are two types of debugging you need to do. One is to fix Lingo errors in your scripts. The program will not run, and will often not even compile, with these bugs. Compiling usually takes place when you close a script window. At that point, Director looks at your code and checks for errors.

The second type of debugging is done when you try to fix the functionality of your scripts. This happens when the Lingo is actually all correct but the program does not do exactly what you want it to do. Say you want a sprite to move clockwise around the screen but it moves counterclockwise.

Once a script works the way you want it to, you should go back through your code, clean it up, and add more comments if needed. Cleaning it up may be as simple as renaming variables with descriptive names or reorganizing the script to make it easier to work with in the future.

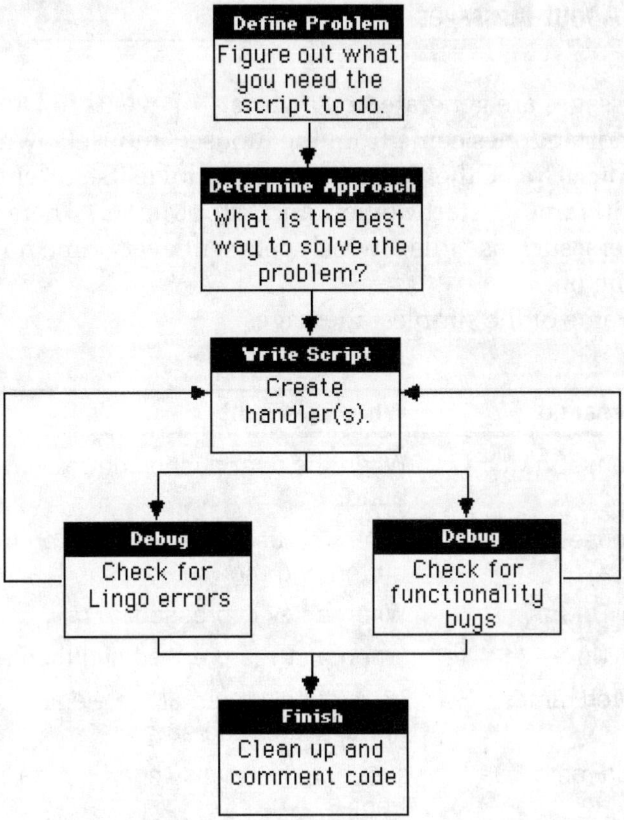

Figure 11-1: *One way to approach writing a Lingo program.*

How Lingo Works

In the "Beginner's Workbook" section, we discussed a little bit about how Lingo works: events trigger messages, and messages trigger handlers. Handlers can then call other handlers. The events and messages are taken care of by Director. We have to supply the handlers. These handlers can be placed in movie scripts, score scripts, or cast member scripts. Let's take a closer look at what is actually happening.

All About Messages

Messages are generated by a variety of events in Director. Two important ones come from the mouse: "mouseDown" and "mouseUp." Others come from the movie itself: "enterFrame," "exitFrame," "startMovie," and "stopMovie." There are plenty of others, such as "idle," which gets sent every time nothing else is going on.

Some of the simplest messages:

Message	When it is sent
mouseDown	When the user pushes down on the mouse button.
mouseUp	When the user pushes down on the mouse button and then releases.
keyDown	When a key is pressed.
keyUp	When a key is pressed and then released.
enterFrame	Immediately after all the elements of a frame are drawn on the stage.
exitFrame	Just before the play head moves on to the next frame.
idle	Is sent at least once, more if time allows, between the "enterFrame" and "exitFrame" messages.
startMovie	When "play" is hit or a new movie is loaded and run.
stopMovie	When "stop" is hit or a movie finishes.

We can write handlers to intercept any of these messages. The handler just has to be named the same as the message it is supposed to intercept. For instance: "on mouseUp," "on exitFrame," or "on idle."

But where to put these messages? If we want an "on mouseUp" handler, for example, we could place it in the cast member script of a bitmap, in the score script assigned to the same sprite as the bitmap, in the score script assigned to the frame, or we could put it in a movie script.

A message follows a certain order when hunting for a handler. "mouseUp" and "mouseDown" messages first look in the sprite score script for that sprite. Then they look in the cast member for a handler. After that, they look for a corresponding handler in the frame score script. If no handler is found up to this point, they will look in all of the movie scripts. If a handler is found, all of its Lingo code is executed and the message goes no further.

All messages follow the same route but may not start at the same place. exitFrame, for instance, has no relationship to a specific sprite or cast member, so it skips to the frame score script to find its handler. Figure 11-2 shows the search path of some messages.

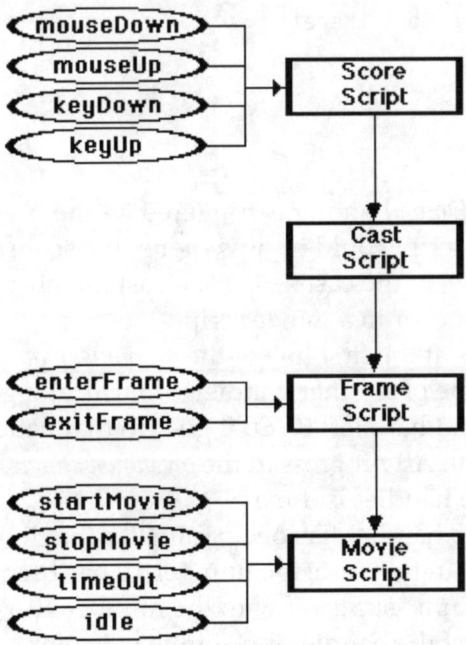

Figure 11-2: *How messages find handlers.*

Thinking Lingo

Once a message finds a handler, it begins to execute the code inside the handler. It starts at the top, of course, and tries to work its way down. In between, it may jump all around, depending on what is in the handler.

Consider this script:

```
on mouseDown
  countTo(10)
  alert "All done!"
end

on countTo num
  put "Now starting to count to"&&num
  repeat with i = 1 to num
    put i
    if i = num-1 then
      alert "Almost there!"
    end if
  end repeat
  put "Done."
end
```

The *on mouseDown* handler is triggered by the user clicking on the mouse. The script could be anywhere: in a score script assigned to a sprite, in the cast script of a cast member, in the score script of the frame, or in a movie script.

Director looks at the first line of the *on mouseDown* handler. It contains the name of another handler, *countTo*, along with a single parameter for that handler, 10. So it goes to that handler and begins running it. All progress in the *on mouseDown* handler stops until the *countTo* handler is done.

The *on countTo* handler has one parameter that it needs: the variable "num." In this case, the number 10 has been provided. The local variable "num" starts off with the number 10 assigned to it.

The first line of the handler is a simple *put* command. Since there is no *into* part of the *put* command, the output goes to the message window. The output in this case is the text *"Now starting to count to"* plus a space and the variable "num."

Next, a *repeat with* loop begins. The first line of code inside the loop just sends the current value of "i" to the message window. The first time through the loop, the value will be "1." The next time, the value will be "2." And so on . . . .

The *if...then* statement checks to see if the value of "i" is equal to one less than the value of "num." In other words, if the loop is in its next-to-last time through. If it is, the *alert* statement will put the message *"Almost there!"* in a dialog box that waits for the user to click "OK."

The loop ends when the value of "i" reaches the value of "num." It executes one last time, and then moves on.

There is one more line after the *end repeat* statement. The word *"Done."* is placed in the message window. The handler is now finished and we now go back to the handler that called it, the *on mouseDown* handler.

There is one last line in this handler as well. The *alert* command is used to signal that the count is over.

Exploring a simple script like this in this much detail may seem tedious. However, the point is to always remember to think like the computer when writing scripts. This will make scripting easier, faster, and more bug-free.

TIP

One of the best ways to learn computer programming is to take script examples, like the ones in this book, and walk through them command by command. Look up any commands you are unfamiliar with. Then try the script on the computer and see if the result was what you expected.

Writing Lingo

There is a process to writing Lingo scripts. Eventually, this process will seem like second nature to you. However, it is useful to examine the procedure step by step.

The process follows the same rules that apply to all types of programing, as outlined earlier. We will skip these generalizations and discuss the specifics as they apply to Lingo programming.

The first step is to determine what type of script we want. If we want a stage element to react to a mouse click, for example, then we want a score script we can assign to a sprite. If we want something to happen over time, we probably want a score script to assign to a frame.

Next, we have to figure out what message will trigger this script. A mouse click means an *on mouseDown* or *on mouseUp* handler. Something happening in a frame usually means an *on exitFrame* handler.

The beginning of the handler sets up as much of what is to come as possible. Are we using a certain sprite channel? Then place that channel number in a variable: *put 7 into spriteNum.*

Now the actual programming happens. There is no formula here; you just need to organize your thoughts and make it happen. Call other handlers whenever you think you may need to use the same chunk of Lingo in several places in your script instead of placing all of the code inside the main handler. Comment your code while going along, as well as when you are all finished.

TIP

You can color your scripts by using the Tools palette in conjunction with the script window. This is useful for highlighting important variables or coloring all comments to make the code easier to browse. You can also use bold, underline, and italics styles.

If the program doesn't work, don't be afraid to go all the way back to step 1 and examine what you have done. For instance, a long handler may be perfectly programmed but not working because it is assigned to the wrong sprite or frame.

Setting Up Your Movie

In almost every Lingo project, you will find some of the same basic scripts. It is typical for a Lingo programmer to start off by placing these scripts in the cast.

Frame Scripts

The first is the frame script. This can be your basic *on exitFrame* score script that can be used on any frame that needs to loop and has no special functions. We can call this a "normal frame script." It looks like this:

```
on exitFrame
  go to the frame
end
```

You may later find other things to add to this script. A normal frame script that also changes the cursor to a "hand" when over any cast member that has the word *hot* in its name would look like this:

```
on exitFrame
  put the mouseCast into num
  put 0 into cursorNum
  if num > 0 then
    put the name of member num into name
    if name contains "hot" then put 280 into cursorNum
  end if
  cursor(cursorNum)
  go to the frame
end
```

You can use both of the previous scripts in the same movie. Call the first one "normal frame script" and the second one "hot cursor frame script." Then, you can use the second one where you want the cursor to change over hot sprites, and the first one in frames where you don't.

Other handlers can be placed in these script cast members along with the *on exitFrame* handler to give your movies more functionality on certain frames. An *on keyDown* handler, for instance, can allow users to seek help by typing a "?"—but only in certain frames. Check out this script:

```
on exitFrame
  go to the frame
end

on keyDown
```

```
global goBackFrame
if the key = "?" then
   put the frame into goBackFrame
     go to frame "help"
  end if
end
```

The *on keyDown* script will look for a "?" as the key that was pressed. If it was a "?," it would store the number of the current frame in a global variable and go to a general help frame labeled "help." We can call this script the "normal frame script w/help."

The reason for storing the current frame number in a global is so that the user can then go back to the original frame after referring to the help frame. A button handler to do that would look like this:

```
on mouseUp
  global goBackFrame
  go to frame goBackFrame
end
```

There are many other types of frame scripts you will find useful in your movies. After programming for a while, you will have developed your own set and will start off each project by adding them to the cast.

TIP *You can combine several of your* on exitFrame *handlers into one, and use* if the frameLabel = *statements to distinguish which functions are performed on which frames.*

Button Handlers

Several lessons in the "Beginner's Workbook" section of this book were dedicated to button handlers. These scripts take bitmapped images and make them behave as buttons, complete with up and down states.

The standard button handler shown in Chapter 4 is a must for most Director movies. It should be a handler in a movie script so that it can be called by various sprite and cast scripts throughout your movie.

You may want to create other button handlers that live in score scripts and perform automatic functions as well as proper button behavior. For instance, you may want to have a handler that jumps to a frame with the same label as the name of the button's cast member.

The handler might look like this:

```
on mouseDown
  -- get the sprite number
  -- and the two cast numbers
  put the clickOn into spriteNum
  put the memberNum of sprite spriteNum into upNum
  put the name of member upNum into upName
  put (upName&&"down") into downName
  put the number of member downName into downNum

  -- set the cast member to the down state
  set the memberNum of sprite spriteNum = downNum
  updateStage

  -- repeat as long as button is down
  repeat while the mouseDown
    if rollover(spriteNum) then -- cursor is over button
      set the memberNum of sprite spriteNum = downNum
    else - cursor not over button
      set the memberNum of sprite spriteNum = upNum
    end if
    updateStage
  end repeat

  if the memberNum of sprite spriteNum = downNum then
    -- set the cursor back to the up state
```

```
        set the memberNum of sprite spriteNum = upNum
        updateStage

        go to frame upName

    end if
  end
```

It is the *go to frame upName* that actually performs the function of going to a frame with the same label as the button's cast member. This is a handy script to have sitting around, waiting to be attached to any sprite you need.

Other ideas for automatic button scripts might include a handler that plays a movie with the same name as the button cast member; a handler that plays a sound with a name similar to that of the button cast member; or a handler that calls a Lingo handler with the same name as the button.

The code you will need to implement the last of these ideas is the *do* command. This command simply executes a piece of text as Lingo. The line *do "myHandler"* is the same as saying *myHandler*. All the *do* command gets you is the ability to run a handler that is determined while the movie is playing instead of while you are programming. Taking the above script and substituting the line *do upName* for *go to frame upName* will accomplish this.

This last script is important. It gives you the ability to create many buttons that all use the same script but do different things. If a button uses cast member "processData," then that button will call handler "processData" when it is pressed. Another button named "quitMyMovie" will run the handler "quitMyMovie" when it is pressed. The uses for such a versatile button script are limitless.

Other Standard Handlers

Chapter 8 shows a basic *on playThisSound* script. This is another handler you will want to have in many of your movie cast members. It takes the name of any sound cast member and plays that sound. It waits until the sound is done before moving on. This is to ensure that the *puppetSound* is turned off so that future sounds work properly. The handler also accepts a mouse click as a way for the sound to terminate.

A "wait" handler is another good one to have around. It takes one parameter, the number of ticks to pause, and stops everything until that time has elapsed. The movie script handler would look like this:

```
on wait waitTime
  put the ticks + waitTime into endTime
  repeat while the ticks < endTime
  end repeat
end
```

The *on wait* handler can be called from inside other scripts to slow things down. Since it uses the clock to time its wait, the pause will be the same length no matter what the speed of the user's machine.

Some people use hypertext in all their projects. If that is the case for your users, then you would want to have a hypertext script in your movies. The "Beginner's Workbook" showed a simple example of implementing hypertext. This section will show a better, more detailed system.

Other handlers depend on your needs. Look back through the "Beginner's Workbook" section and pick out scripts you think you may need to use often. Then, as you move forward through the book, make a note of useful scripts that could be included in your standard movie template.

on startMovie

The *on startMovie* handler will become a standard part of your movies. Use it to initalize global variables, jump to the start frame if it is not frame 1, and perform other miscellaneous tasks.

A typical handler might look like this:

```
on startMovie
  global pointerSprite, sliderSprite, animatedSprite,→
gameScore
```

```
    put 5 into pointerSprite
    put 9 into sliderSprite
    put 45 into animatedSprite
    put 0 into gameScore
end
```

This *on startMovie* handler just sets a bunch of globals that we can use in other scripts in the movie. The example shows three globals that are probably going to be used to refer to sprites for different functions. Another global initializes some kind of game score variable.

This is also a good place to set the line spacing in some of your field cast members. Director allows you to change the overall line spacing in a single field with *the fontHeight* property. However, when this property is set, and the movie is saved and reloaded, Director forgets it and defaults back to the normal line spacing. We can fix this by just setting all the fields that need setting in the *on startMovie* handler.

```
on startMovie
    set the fontHeight of field "instructions" = 18
    set the fontHeight of field "text display"= 22
end
```

Setting *the textHeight* is also a good idea for cross-platform projects. Director tends to set a different default line spacing for the Mac than it does for Windows, but by setting this property you can make them identical.

TIP

It is better to create one or several "on init" handlers that are called by the on startMovie *handler. This way, you can call the "on init" handler at other times when you want to re-initialize some variables.*

Moving On

This chapter reviewed some of the basics of computer science, Lingo, and setting up your movies. Now it is time to move on to some more advanced techniques.

12 Advanced Hypertext

In the "Beginner's Workbook" section we looked at a simple way to implement hypertext in Director movies. This method, however, did not have much flexibility. It would be very hard to implement for anything more than a few paragraphs of text.

We need a more robust system that can expand as our projects grow more complete. A good hypertext system should allow us to link hundreds of words as easily as a few words and allow us to define what these words link to without much hassle.

We'll keep one idea around from our previous script: hypertext words are underlined in the text. This allows us to quickly identify if a hypertext word has been clicked on, and it gives us the power to have the cursor change when it's over hypertext.

The Hypertext Phrase

To begin with, we want to add the ability to define multiple words, not just a single word, as hypertext. We can't do that with the script used in Chapter 9. That script simply looks at the word clicked on and uses that word to look up its hypertext function. It doesn't care whether the previous or next words are also part of a greater phrase.

For instance, we might want to have the phrase "Macromedia Director" linked to something. The old script would allow us to link each word, "Macromedia" and "Director," individually but not both as part of a single link. If you look at most hyperlinks on the World Wide Web or other hypertext applications, you will see more multiword links than single-word links.

TIP

When underlining a chunk of text, try to use the field editing window instead of highlighting and changing the text directly on the stage. The latter sometimes doesn't work properly and will revert to the way the text looked before you tried to underline it.

The smart way to grab an entire piece of linked text, called a hyperlink, is to look at it character by character, not as an entire word. When the mouse clicks on an underlined piece of text, we can search backward to find the first underlined character in the phrase, and then forward to find the last. These characters and everything in between will give us the whole phrase. Figure 12-1 describes this function.

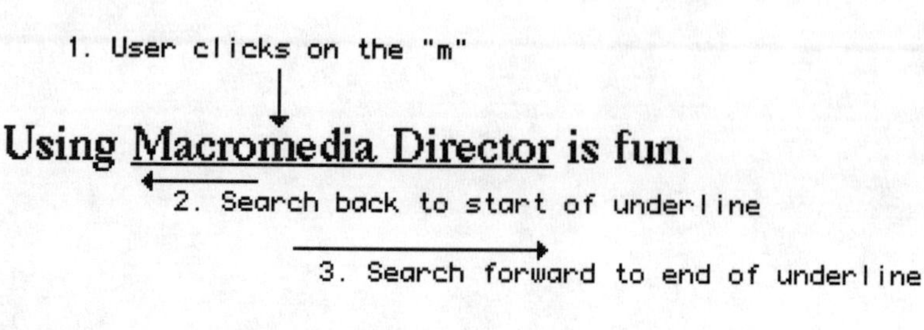

Figure 12-1: *How we want to grab the text of a hyperlink.*

Let's put the code we need to build our hypertext phrase into a handler called "buildPhrase." The first thing our handler needs to do is determine which cast member and which character were clicked on. We will use the *mouseCast* and *mouseChar* functions to do this. We can assume that the cast member that was clicked on is a text field, since we will only assign our hypertext scripts to these kinds of sprites. Otherwise, we would first have to test the type of the cast member before going further.

```
put the mouseCast into fieldNum
put the mouseChar into charClicked
```

A safer way to determine which field was clicked is to use *the clickOn* function instead of *the mouseCast* function. The problem with *the mouseCast* function is that it returns the number of the cast member that the mouse is currently hovering over. If users are quick enough, they can click the mouse, and before the Lingo handler has a chance to check *the mouseCast*, the cursor moves off that cast member and on to another—or, worse, over no cast member at all. This can cause error messages.

By using *the clickOn* command to get the sprite number of what was clicked, and then looking up the cast member in that sprite, we have a much more solid handler.

The same danger of an erroneous reading is there for *the mouseChar* command as well, but it is less serious since it can only result in the user missing the word they wanted to click on and not big, fat error messages or undesired results.

```
put the mouseChar into charClicked
put the clickOn into spriteNum
put the memberNum of sprite spriteNum into fieldNum
```

After we know which character was clicked on, we check to see if it is underlined. If not, we will just return a null string, or *EMPTY*, to signify this. When we use the *return* command before the last line of a handler like this, the rest of the handler does not execute at all.

```
if not (the textStyle of char charClicked of field→
fieldNum contains "underline") then return EMPTY
```

If the handler is still going, we know that we have at least a one-character underlined phrase. Since the user could have clicked anywhere in the phrase, from the first character to the last, we need to look in both directions to find the beginning and the end of the phrase.

We'll start by going backward to find the beginning. For this, we use the *repeat with* loop and look at each character, moving backward from the one that was clicked. When we find a character that is not underlined, we have figured out where the beginning is.

```
put 1 into firstChar
repeat with x = charClicked down to 1
  if the textStyle of char x of field fieldNum contains→
"underline" then
    put x into firstChar
  else
    exit repeat
  end if
end repeat
```

In this last piece of code, we needed to initialize the variable "firstChar" with 1. This is in case the *repeat* loop ends without ever finding the beginning of the phrase. The only case where that could happen is if the phrase extends all the way back to the first character of the field.

When this piece of code is done executing, the variable "firstChar" will contain the character number of the beginning of our phrase. Now, lets go after the last character of our phrase.

```
put length(field fieldNum) into lastChar
repeat with x = charClicked to length(field fieldNum)
  if the textStyle of char x of field fieldNum contains→
"underline" then
    put x into lastChar
  else
    exit repeat
  end if
end repeat
```

In this piece of the script, we initialized the variable "lastChar" with the total length of the whole text field—in other words, the last character that the phrase could possibly go to. The *repeat* loop then looks forward though the field until it finds a character not underlined.

TIP

If you want to use underlining for other purposes, you can modify the hypertext scripts to look for the "bold" style, or both "underline" and "bold." You can even add the foreColor *of the character to the mix.*

Now we have both the first and the last character of the phrase. The only thing left for our "makePhrase" handler to do is to get the actual phrase and return this string to the handler that called it.

```
put char firstChar to lastChar of field fieldNum into phrase
return phrase
```

Remember that we returned an *EMPTY* string if the user did not click on an underlined word to begin with; otherwise we return the entire underlined phrase. The complete handler looks like this:

```
on makePhrase
  put the mouseChar into charClicked
  put the clickOn into spriteNum
  put the memberNum of sprite spriteNum into fieldNum
  if not (the textStyle of char charClicked of field→
fieldNum contains "underline") then return EMPTY

  put 1 into firstChar
  repeat with x = charClicked down to 1
    if the textStyle of char x of field→
fieldNum contains "underline" then
      put x into firstChar
    else
```

```
      exit repeat
    end if
  end repeat

  put length(field fieldNum) into lastChar
  repeat with x = charClicked to length(field fieldNum)
    if the textStyle of char x of field fieldNum contains→
"underline" then
      put x into lastChar
    else
      exit repeat
    end if
  end repeat

  put char firstChar to lastChar of field fieldNum into phrase
  return phrase
end
```

Advanced programmers should look into the *locToCharPos*, the *locVtoLinePos*, and *the clickLoc* functions if something beyond this current script is needed.

You can use the same cursor-handling routine from Chapter 9 with this hypertext environment.

The Hypertext Action

Now that we can figure out what hyperlinked text was clicked on, we need to make it possible for the movie to figure out what to do with it. We have two pieces of information: what the phrase was, and what cast member it is a part of.

What we need is a list of hyperlinks and the actions they should perform. We could make this a part of a Lingo handler, as we did for the simple hypertext script earlier. There, we used a long *case* statement to handle all the options.

But what if there were dozens, or even hundreds, of links? There is an easier way to handle this: we create a text field cast member that holds all of this information, and write a handler to match the hyperlink with its function. Let's call this field "hyperlinks."

For instance, if the phrase "Macromedia Director" should perform the function of jumping the movie to a frame named "Director Info," then we would create a line in our "hyperlinks" field that looked like this:

```
Macromedia Director/go to frame "Director Info"
```

We separate the two items in the line with a "/". We can add several other lines to this same field:

```
Macromedia Director/go to frame "Director Info"
Lingo/playThisSound "fanfare"
other multimedia authoring tools/go to frame "other tools"
```

This field can get as long as we want, but at an expense of taking longer to process the match. What we need to do now is write a handler that matches the hypertext phrase to a line in this field. We'll call this handler "findPhrase." It should take one parameter: the phrase itself.

```
on findPhrase phrase
  set the itemDelimiter = "/"
  repeat with i = 1 to the number of lines in→
field "hyperlinks"
    if item 1 of line i of field "hyperlinks" = phrase then
      return item 2 of line i of field "hyperlinks"
    end if
  end repeat
  return EMPTY
end
```

One new piece of Lingo here is *the itemDelimiter*. This is a Lingo variable you can set that determines what you mean when you use the *item* instruction to specify a piece of text. Here, we set it to a slash, so that each item is separated by slashes. If we had used something else, say, a comma or a colon, then the slash would be ignored by the item instruction. The *itemDelimiter* is preset to be a comma by Director, so we need to set it in a handler like this to fit our needs. The reason we don't use a comma instead of a slash is that we may have a comma in the "hyperlinks" list as either part of the hypertext term or the function it performs.

Our "findPhrase" handler will return the second item of the line where the first item matches the phrase we were looking for. If the entire field was searched and a match was not found, an *EMPTY* is returned.

But what if the same word is used twice? It could appear twice in our list, but our search routine would only find the first one, regardless of which one we really wanted.

We can make a more specific list by including the cast member name of the field that was clicked. That way, we can have two phrases that are exactly the same (but in different cast members) perform different functions. All we would need to do is alter our previous script slightly.

```
on findPhrase phrase
  put the clickOn into spriteNum
  put the memberNum of sprite spriteNum into fieldNum

  set the itemDelimiter = "/"
  repeat with i = 1 to the number of lines in field "hyperlinks"
    if (item 1 of line i of field "hyperlinks" = phrase) and→
(item 2 of line i of field "hyperlinks" = fieldName) then
      return item 3 of line i of field "hyperlinks"
    end if
  end repeat
  return EMPTY
end
```

The handler is about the same, but we have another parameter: the name of the field clicked. We use this as another criterion for matching the phrase with a line in the field. It is important to remember to name these fields now, since this handler will only work if it can find the field by name.

Since this takes up another item in each line, the actual function of each hyperlink is now stored in the third item of each line. A "hyperlinks" field may now look like this:

```
Macromedia Director/text1/go to frame "Director Info"
Lingo/text1/playThisSound "fanfare"
other multimedia authoring tools/caption1/go to frame "other→
tools"
```

So now we have allowed the use of the same phrase twice, as long as it appears in different field cast members. But what about using the same phrase more than once in one field?

This problem has many solutions, but all are so difficult to implement that it is not worth it. One way would be to record the position of each phrase in the field, so that each occurrence of the phrase could be uniquely identified. This would work but would force you to retype all of these positions every time you edited the text and changed them by even one character. Another way to do this would be to identify each phrase as the first, second, third, etc., occurrence of that phrase. However, it would mean that our hypertext routine would have to search through that field for multiple occurrences every time the user clicked.

A Complete Hypertext Script

The "makePhrase" and "findPhrase" handlers are the two pieces we need to put together a hypertext script like we discussed at the beginning of this chapter. The script will just call these two handlers.

```
on hyperText
  put makePhrase() into phrase
  if phrase <> EMPTY then
    put findPhrase(phrase) into whatToDo
```

```
    if whatToDo <> EMPTY then
      do whatToDo
    end if
  end if
end
```

This script simply calls "makePhrase" to get the entire phrase that was clicked on. It makes sure that hypertext actually was clicked on and then proceeds to look it up in the "hyperlinks" field. If a match is found, it executes that match with the *do* command.

All three of these handlers can be placed in a movie script cast member. Then this score script can be assigned to any sprite that holds a text field.

```
on mouseDown
  hyperText()
end
```

Alternatively, you could place all three of the handlers in the score script and rename the "hyperText" script to *on mouseDown*.

More About Hypertext Actions

These handlers perform their functions well. But the real strength of hypertext is being able to *do* things when the user clicks. In the above example of three hyperlinks, two of them go to a new frame and another calls our own "playThisSound" handler.

A good strategy here is to make a set of small handlers that perform any action a hyperlink might need. Then, we can just list these handlers where needed in the "hyperlinks" field.

The "playThisSound" reference already works this way. We should also change the *go to frame* references to call a handler. This handler can simply perform the *go to frame* command but can also include other things like a *puppetTransition*.

```
on goFrame frameName
  puppetTransition 3
  go to frame frameName
end
```

Other handlers could bring up *alert* boxes, kick off animations, play other movies, or *puppetSprite* and swap the cast member of a sprite on the stage. Check out this handler:

```
on swapMember spriteNum, memberName
  puppetSprite spriteNum, TRUE
  put the number of member memberName into memberNum
  set the memberNum of sprite spriteNum = memberNum
  updateStage
end
```

This handler can be used to change a picture on the stage depending on what hyperlink the user clicked. For instance, if a piece of text lists several animals: "kangaroo, koala bear, crocodile." Each is an individual hyperlink. In the "hyperlinks" field, each one calls "swapMember" to change a picture on the stage to a picture of that animal. Assuming the field cast member that contains this text is named "animals," the "hyperlinks" field would look like this:

```
kangaroo/animals/swapMember 16, "kangaroo pict"
koala bear/animals/swapMember 16, "koala pict"
crocodile/animals/swapMember 16, "crocodile pict"
```

Suppose we don't want to go as far as allowing our hyperlinks to do just anything at all but would rather restrict them to having only one function. For instance, all hyperlinks would just go to another frame. Or perhaps all the hyperlinks would just play a sound.

This would shorten our "hyperlink" field. In the case where every link just goes to another frame, we would just use the third item in the list to store the name of the frame. Then our "hyperText" handler would execute a *go to frame whatToDo* instead of using the *do* command.

We could do the same thing if all hyperlinks were to play sounds. Just put only the name of the sound in the third item of each line of the list, and call our "playThisSound"" handler with that item in the "hyperText" list.

Moving On

Hypertext is just one way to allow the user to make choices. Buttons are another way. Actually, there are many different ways to use buttons that we have not yet discussed. The next chapter presents some of these ideas.

13 Advanced Button Input

In addition to working with hypertext, you will want to provide other ways for users to navigate through your movies. If you think about it, navigation is the same as asking the user the question "Where do you want to go next?" Their response, whether it is clicking on a button or something else, is the answer to the question.

Button Lists

We can use Lingo to build interfaces that ask users questions like this. The simplest way is to provide them with a list of options and allow them to select the one they want.

These options can be displayed as a group of buttons on the stage. They don't necessarily have to look like traditional buttons. In fact, they don't have to be visible at all.

You could have several photographs and ask the user to click on one to find out more about it. These photographs can be bitmaps with an *on mouseUp* handler, or our more advanced button handler, attached.

The pictures can highlight when clicked, or even before—for instance, when the user moves the mouse over them. We can even have invisible boxes positioned over a larger picture and have those boxes act as the buttons.

These buttons can react to one another: when one is pushed down, it stays down. Then, when another is pushed down, the button that was previously down will rise up, similar to the way preset buttons on car radios used to work. This is called a button list.

Let's look at some useful types of button lists.

Standard Button List

The simplest type of button list is just a collection of bitmaps that have *on mouseDown* scripts attached to them. Figure 13-1 shows a menulike collection of buttons that are actually bitmaps. We could also have photos, drawings, or just use Director's default buttons.

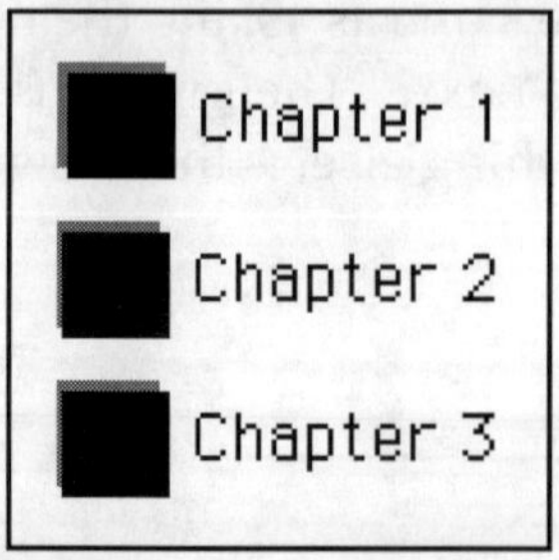

Figure 13-1: *A simple collection of buttons that make up a menu.*

Each of these can have its own script attached as either a score script assigned to the same sprite as the cast member, or the cast script stored inside the cast member. The script could look something like this:

```
on mouseUp
  go to frame "chapter 1"
end
```

We could also call our button handler, "buttonClicked," from the "Beginner's Workbook" section.

```
on mouseDown
  if buttonClicked() then
    put the clickOn into c
    put the memberNum of sprite c into mNum
    put the name of member mNum into name
    go to frame name -- the function
  end if
end
```

Instead of just going to a frame, we can call handlers that we used in our hypertext scripting. For instance, we can use the "playThisSound" handler or the "swapMember" handler.

So far, there is nothing new here. The buttons are performing basically the same way they did way back in Chapter 4.

TIP

Use Director 5.0's ability to use Photoshop filters as a quick way to make unique custom buttons. Some of Kai's Power Tools are perfect for this task.

Related Button List

Additional functionality can be added to a button list by having the buttons react to one another. When we have a group of buttons that are in some way attached in function or form, we can say that these buttons are *related*.

A simple way to make buttons related to each other is to have them act as one big button but with multiple parts. The user can click on any button, hold down the mouse, and roll the cursor over any button in the list. The button that the mouse is currently over will show its down state, while the other buttons are in the up state. After users decide which one to activate, they lift the mouse button.

The Lingo code for this is actually a frame script. It uses the *rollover* command we first saw in Chapter 4.

```
on exitFrame
  go to the frame
end

on mouseDown
  put relatedButtons() into buttonClicked
  if buttonClicked <> "" then
    go to frame buttonClicked -- the function
  end if
end

on relatedButtons
  repeat while the mouseDown
    repeat with spriteNum = 1 to 3
      if rollover(spriteNum) then
        put the memberNum of sprite spriteNum into mNum
        put the name of member mNum into mName
        put mName&&"down" into downName
        put the number of member downName into downNum
        set the memberNum of sprite spriteNum = downNum
        updateStage
        repeat while rollover(spriteNum)
          if the mouseUp then return mName
        end repeat
        set the memberNum of sprite spriteNum = mNum
      end if
    end repeat
  end repeat
  return EMPTY
end
```

The “relatedButtons” handler returns the name of the button the user was over when the user released the mouse. It returns an empty string if it is not over any button.

The handler works by looping while the mouse button is held down then looping from 1 to 3—which assumes that our three related buttons are in sprites 1, 2, and 3. If we need more buttons, or we need to have them in other channels, we must adjust this number. We also need to include an appropriately named down state of each button. So the button named "chapter1" needs a down state named "chapter1 down."

If the handler detects that the cursor is over one of these sprites, it changes that sprite to its down state then loops until either the cursor has been moved from that sprite or the mouse button has been released. In the second case, it returns the name of the button. Otherwise, it just loops through the sprites again and again.

Back in the *on mouseDown* handler, the script takes nonempty returned values of "relatedButtons" and jumps to that frame. Figures 13-2 and 13-3 show what the screen may look like when the user is clicking on a button and then moves the cursor, without lifting, to another button.

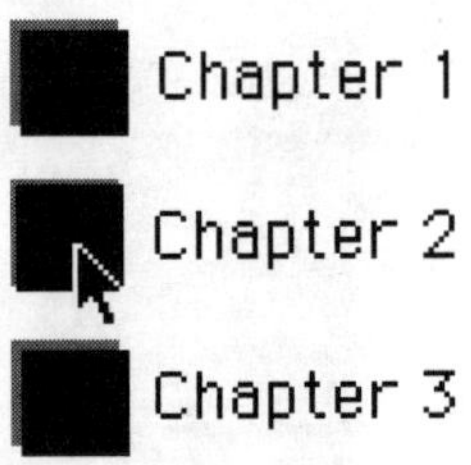

Figure 13-2: *The user clicks on one button in a related button set.*

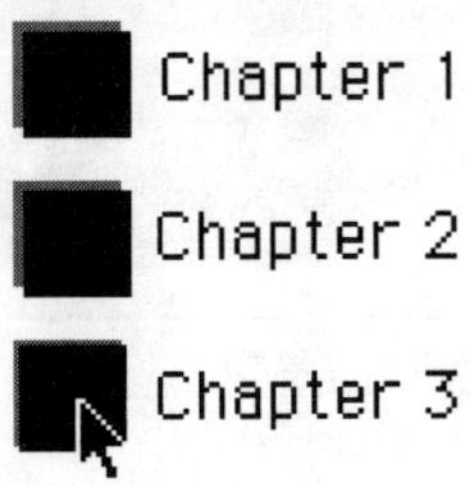

Figure 13-3: *The user moves to another button before releasing.*

A second way to make buttons related is to have them act like a set: only one can be pushed down at a time. This is the way car radios used to work. Their preset station buttons could be pushed one at a time, and each time you pushed a new button, the one previously selected returned to its normal state.

We could do this with no special scripting at all. Suppose you had five buttons that were to work together in this way. You could make six frames. The first frame showed all of the buttons in their normal state. Each of the five remaining frames had a different single button depressed. Then you would attach scripts to the buttons on all the frames so that when the user selected a button, the movie would move to the frame where the button was shown as depressed. In addition to showing the button depressed, the movie could also display different content on each frame depending on the function of the buttons. Figure 13-4 shows an example. The third button is depressed and appears to stay down. It is actually that way on that frame of the movie.

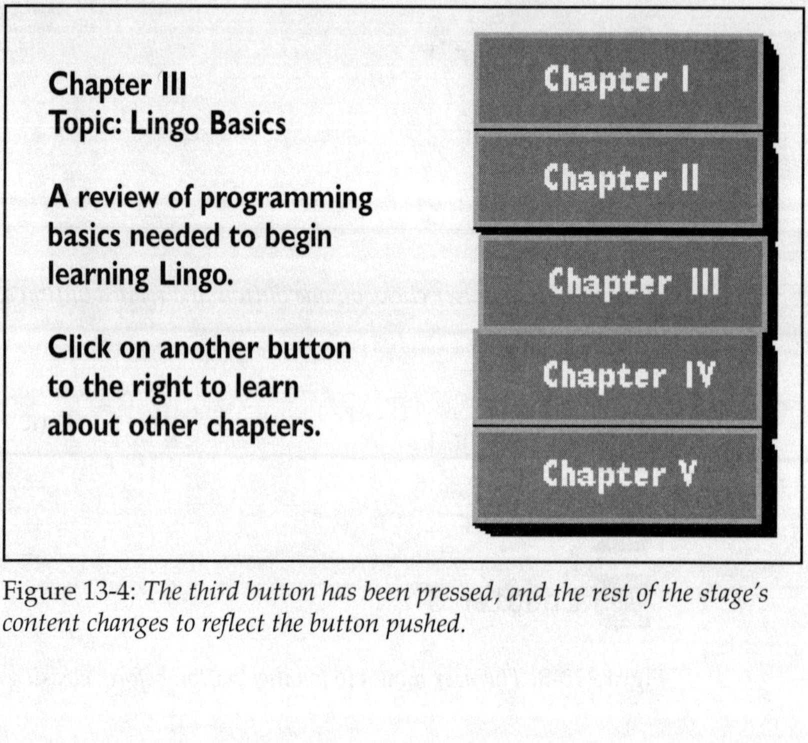

Figure 13-4: *The third button has been pressed, and the rest of the stage's content changes to reflect the button pushed.*

A script can be written to do this, however, keeping it all in one frame. Just puppetSprite the button that was pressed so that it stays down, and, at the same time, use the "swapMember" script we created earlier to change the text or picture on another sprite on the screen.

Rollover-Sensitive Button List

A popular effect in multimedia is the rollover. This simply means that something on the stage changes—not because of a user click but simply because the cursor moved over that element.

Rollovers can make buttons highlight when the user moves over them. This effect can be used to invite users to select a button. Figure 13-5 shows the desired effect.

Figure 13-5: *The cursor is positioned over a button and the button visibly reacts even though the mouse button is not down.*

Our handler will again be a frame script. We will call a "hiliteButtons" handler from the *on exitFrame* handler every time the frame loops. Like the related button script, we will loop through each of the sprites: 1, 2, and 3. This time, however, we do not need to include any *repeat while the mouseDown*, since our highlight effect will only require that the user be over the sprite.

If the script detects that the cursor is over a sprite, it gets the name of the cast member there and attaches the word *hilite* to it. It uses this new name to find the highlight state cast member of that sprite and then displays it. If the button was already in the highlight state, the new name would have "hilite" in it twice—for instance, "chapter1 hilite hilite." That cast member does not exist. So we must check to make sure the new name is a valid cast member. We do this by asking for *the number of member hiliteName* below. It will be –1 if there is no cast member of that name.

```
on exitFrame
  hiliteButtons()
  go to the frame
end

on hiliteButtons
  repeat with spriteNum = 1 to 3
    if rollover(spriteNum) then
      put the memberNum of sprite spriteNum into mNum
      put the name of member mNum into mName
      put mName&&"hilite" into hiliteName
      put the number of member hiliteName into hiliteNum
      if hiliteNum > 0 then
        puppetSprite spriteNum, TRUE
        set the memberNum of sprite spriteNum = hiliteNum
      end if
      if the mouseDown then
        go to frame (word 1 of mName)
      end if
    else
      puppetSprite spriteNum, FALSE
    end if
  end repeat
end
```

The "hiliteButtons" script will also allow each button to react to mouse clicks by checking *the mouseDown*. In this case we just go to a frame with the same name as the first word of the button. You could also make it do other things.

Invisible Button List

We have spent a lot of time worrying about how buttons look. Instead of using the standard Director buttons, we learned how to use bitmap images as buttons. We have up states and down states, and even highlight states.

However, sometimes the button you really need is one that has no appearance at all: an invisible button. The most common use of this is when you have a large picture and wish to allow the user to click on parts of it to go to other places.

Invisible buttons can be made using the nonfilled rectangle or oval shape tools in Director. The shapes you create should have zero-width line borders as well. Figure 13-6 shows a picture with several of these invisible buttons over it.

Figure 13-6: *A picture with three invisible boxes positioned over it. All of these boxes are selected so that they can be seen.*

Scripts can be attached to these boxes by either including them in the cast members or by assigning score scripts to the sprites. You could use simple *on mouseUp* and *on mouseDown* handlers in them, or you could call one of the handlers that we used for other buttons or hypertext. You can even name these cast members and use the names, as we do above, to determine the function of each.

The invisible buttons could have down states. You could use inks and the forecolor and backcolor properties to temporarily highlight the area when the user presses down.

Another way to do invisible buttons is to cut out a piece of a picture and make a bitmap button out of it. Then position that piece directly over the main picture so it matches seamlessly. When the user clicks on it, it could have a down state that highlights or perhaps distorts that portion of the picture.

When the buttons are invisible, changing cursors might be a good way to let the user know where to click. We could use a simple script that works as long as each button has the word *button* in its name.

```
on exitFrame
  put 0 into cursorNum
  put the mouseCast into mc
  if mc > 0 then
    if the name of member mc contains "button" then
      put 280 into cursorNum
    end if
  end if
  cursor(cursorNum)
end
```

Invisible buttons can also take advantage of the rollover method of highlighting when the cursor moves over them. However, if you are using invisible boxes, you may want to consider using ink, blend, and color effects rather than swapping out cast members.

Getting Creative With Button Lists

The examples of button lists in this chapter are intentionally simple so they can demonstrate the techniques involved. However, your programs don't have to be simple.

Consider how you could arrange a related button set on the screen. The buttons could be in a "toolbar" section of the stage. They could be used as interactive labels for a photograph. They could be placed inside the metaphor of some machine or spaceship control panel.

It is important to consider the possibility of having buttons that don't look like buttons at all. There is certainly nothing in Director or Lingo that forces you to limit the appearance of your buttons.

Check Boxes

There are two other types of buttons we haven't talked about yet: check boxes and radio buttons. Figure 13-7 shows check box-type buttons. You probably recognize this type from other computer programs.

Figure 13-7: *Check boxes.*

The purpose of check boxes is to allow the user to select none, one, some, or all of the buttons. This is different from radio buttons, which we get to later, that allow the user to select only one of the buttons.

It is important to remember these rules. Both Macintosh's and Windows's interface guidelines insist on them, and your users can be confused or turned off if you use the wrong button type in the wrong situation.

These button types work best when the buttons are part of a related button list. The buttons act together to perform one function, depending on which one or ones are selected.

Let's use Figure 13-7 as an example. The question being posed could be "Which fruits did you eat this week?" The check box button type is the correct one to use since the user could choose none, one, some, or all of the options.

The command we need to learn in order to get the state of the button is *the hilite of member* function. This will return a TRUE or a FALSE depending on whether the user has checked the button.

The actual functionality of a check box button requires no Lingo scripting at all. While a check box button is present on the stage, the user can click on it and it will react automatically by toggling its state, checked to unchecked, or vice-versa. The only programming we really have to do is to check the states of the buttons at the right time.

To check the buttons, we need to refer to the cast member, not the sprite. The name of the cast member is not necessarily the same as the text placed inside the cast member. In this case, let's use the names "fruit 1," "fruit 2," and "fruit 3" as the names of the check box cast members. A simple script to do this would look like this:

```
on examineBoxes
  global apples, oranges, bananas
  put the hilite of member "fruit 1" into apples
  put the hilite of member "fruit 2" into oranges
  put the hilite of member "fruit 3" into bananas
end
```

This handler simply determines *the hilite* of each cast member and puts its TRUE or FALSE state into its corresponding variable—fruit 2, for example. These variables are declared as globals so that other handlers can access them.

The "examineBoxes" routine can be called from an *on exitFrame* script, or it can be called from an *on mouseUp* script attached to the buttons themselves.

You cannot call "examineBoxes" in an *on mouseDown* script, because the actual change of the button state happens between the "mouseDown" and "mouseUp" messages. Examining *the hilite* of a button in an *on mouseDown* handler will not take into account the change that is about to happen.

You may only need to call "examineBoxes" once. For instance, there could be another button that when clicked evaluates check box buttons. When Web pages use check box buttons in this manner, there is usually a "Submit" button below them on the screen. We could have a button labeled "Submit answer," or something more colorful, after these check boxes. This button would then call "examineBoxes" or it might just use the same Lingo code inside itself.

A utility routine that could be useful is a handler that sets up the check boxes, making sure they are empty to begin with. In this specific case, it would look like this:

```
on resetBoxes
  set the hilite of member "fruit 1" = FALSE
  set the hilite of member "fruit 2" = FALSE
  set the hilite of member "fruit 3" = FALSE
end
```

We can get fancier and use some text manipulation routines to make a handler that can reset a larger number of similar check boxes. This next handler will reset check boxes "fruit 1" to "fruit 8."

```
on resetBoxes
  repeat with i = 1 to 8
    put "fruit"&&i into mName
    set the hilite of member mName = FALSE
  end repeat
end
```

You may have to put some thought into where to call "resetBoxes." You can call it when the user is finished making a selection, so that it is cleared out and fresh the next time the same boxes are used. Or you could call it just before every time you show those buttons.

Radio Buttons

Radio buttons are also a familiar sight in many computer applications. Figure 13-8 shows an example.

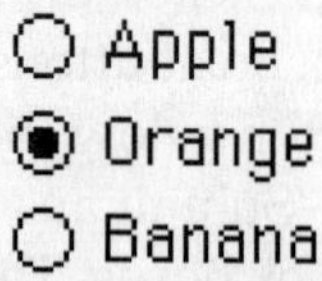

Figure 13-8: *Radio buttons.*

Radio buttons are much harder to implement in Lingo than check boxes. This is because of their very nature: only one can be selected at a time. When the user selects a radio button then selects another related button, the first one needs to be reset. In addition, there should never be a time when all of the buttons are off. So one of the buttons must be chosen as the default and start off in the highlighted state.

The question that could be associated with Figure 13-7 was "Which fruits did you eat this week?" The question associated with Figure 13-8 could be "What was the last fruit that you ate?" This is a question that demands one and only one selection from the button list.

Despite the harder implementation for radio buttons, the basic Lingo functionality is the same as for check boxes. We use *the hilite of member* function to get or set the state of each button.

However, we now have work to do every time the user selects a radio button. We need to check to see which button was previously selected, and turn that one off. In addition, if the user for some reason clicks on the button that is already selected, we don't want to turn that one off but rather leave it on.

```
on mouseUp
  put "radio" into familyName
  put the clickOn into spriteNum -- get sprite number
  put the memberNum of sprite spriteNum into mNum
  put the name of member mNum into mName -- get name
  repeat with i = 1 to 3
    put familyName&&i into rName
    if rName = mName then
      set the hilite of member rName = TRUE -- turn this one on
    else
      set the hilite of member rName = FALSE -- turn other
off
    end if
  end repeat
end
```

This *on mouseUp* handler should be a score script assigned to each of the related radio buttons. We should name these buttons "radio 1," "radio 2," and "radio 3." We signify that all the button names start with the word "radio" by placing it in the variable "familyName." We then loop through the three buttons. We turn on the one we clicked on; we turn off the others.

Note that we are ignoring the fact that Director is already toggling the buttons for us before Lingo gets into the play. We set *the hilite* of the button to what we need it to be anyway. This will avoid allowing the user to turn off all the radio buttons.

We could use the same "resetBoxes" handler to initialize the radio boxes, however we have to add one line of code to turn on the default radio button.

```
on resetRadioButtons
  repeat with i = 1 to 3
    put "radio"&&i into mName
    set the hilite of member mName = FALSE
  end repeat
  set the hilite of member "radio 1" = TRUE
end
```

To detect which button has been selected we can have a simpler handler than the check boxes. This is because we know that one and only one radio button can be on at a time.

```
on examineRadioButtons
  repeat with i = 1 to 3
    put "radio"&&i into mName
    if the hilite of member mName then return mName
  end repeat
end
```

The "examineRadioButtons" handler is a function that returns the name of the button that was selected.

TIP

Check boxes and radio buttons are examples of standard interface design. You don't need to get a degree in this subject to adhere to good interface design. Just observe how other computer applications look and operate.

Uses for Check Boxes & Radio Buttons

The above examples are pretty basic. Remember that you could have anywhere from 1 to 48 (the number of sprites) buttons in a check box or radio button list. In the case of radio buttons, however, it would make no sense to have only one radio button.

You could, however, have just one check box. This could be useful for letting the user choose options in your program. For instance, a check box button labeled "sound off" could have the following script:

```
on mouseUp
  put the clickOn into spriteNum
  put the memberNum of sprite spriteNum into mNum
  set the soundEnabled = not the hilite of member mNum
end
```

This would be a simple way to let the user turn off the sound in your movie. You could put this check box in every frame of your movie, positioned in a corner of the stage.

Check box button lists can be used for a variety of things. Figure 13-9 shows a short quiz where the user is asked to select the statements that are true. Figure 13-10 shows how they can be used to ask surveylike questions.

☒ Jupiter is the largest planet.

☐ Saturn is the only planet with rings.

☒ Venus is the closest planet to Earth.

☐ The asteroid belt lies between Jupiter and Saturn.

Figure 13-9: *A short true-false quiz.*

Which do you have:

☒ CD-ROM Drive
☒ Printer
☐ Scanner
☐ MIDI Device
☒ External Speakers

Figure 13-10: *A peripherals survey.*

Radio buttons can be used in cases when one and only one answer is needed. Figure 13-11 shows a multiple-choice question using radio buttons. Figure 13-12 shows how radio buttons can be used to set playback options in your movies.

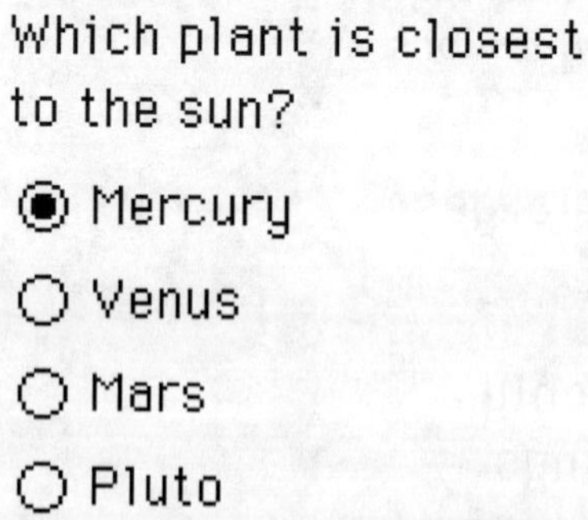

Figure 13-11: *A multiple-choice quiz.*

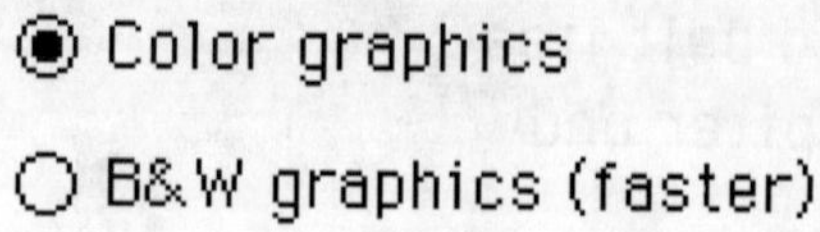

Figure 13-12: *Giving the user options.*

Custom Check Boxes & Radio Buttons

Just as with normal push buttons, there is no need to stick with Director's standard button types. You could create the same functionality with your own bitmap image buttons.

With push buttons, we had two states: an up state and a down state. We later added a highlight state for rollovers. With check boxes and push buttons we can have two states: on and off. Figure 13-13 gives some examples of both states.

Figure 13-13: *Some bitmap images that could be used as check boxes or radio buttons.*

If you are going to use your own bitmaps as check boxes or radio buttons, you need to replace the Lingo function *the hilite of member* with some handlers of your own. Here is a routine that toggles a bitmap like a check box button. The check box bitmap images should have names that match the first word of the name and have *on* and *off* as the second word of the name. For instance: *select on* and *select off*.

```
on toggleHilite spriteNum
  put the memberNum of sprite spriteNum into mNum
  put the name of member mNum into mName -- old name
  if word 2 of mName = "on" then
    put "off" into state
  else
    put "on" into state
  end if
  put ((word 1 of mName)&&state) into newName -- new name
  put the number of member newName into newNum
  puppetSprite spriteNum, TRUE
  set the memberNum of sprite spriteNum = newNum
end
```

Notice that we are now worried about the sprite number, not the cast member. This sets our bitmap check boxes apart from the Director-style ones.

To get the value of a bitmap check box controlled by the above script, you only need to check the name of the cast member:

```
on checkHilite spriteNum
  put the memberNum of sprite spriteNum into mNum
  put the name of member mNum into mName
  return (word 2 of mName = "on")
end
```

Bitmapped versions of radio buttons need different scripts. Instead of toggling these buttons, we need to be able to set them. We will pass our handler a second parameter that will be true or false, depending on whether we want the button to turn on or off.

```
on setHilite spriteNum, setTo

  put the memberNum of sprite spriteNum into mNum
  put the name of member mNum into mName --old name
  if setTo then
    put "on" into state
  else
    put "off" into state
  end if
  put ((word 1 of mName)&&state) into newName --new name
  put the number of member newName into newNum
  puppetSprite spriteNum, TRUE
  set the memberNum of sprite spriteNum = newNum
end
```

Sliders

Until now, we have mostly been adding click functionality to our movies. In earlier chapters we played with moving objects around the stage, but we were mostly just moving them to move them, not to act as user input devices.

A slider is a neat little device allowing you to get user input that can span a range of values, rather then just be on or off. This method is often better than buttons for some types of input.

For instance, you may want to allow the user to set the audio volume level. The Lingo command *the volume of sound* can take numbers from 0 to 255. So you can give the user 256 buttons to press, or just a few buttons representing "off," "low," "mid," and "high," and have them set the volume to certain levels. However, with a slider the user can get very specific about how loud the volume should be.

Figure 13-14 shows a slider that allows the user to set the volume. The left end of the line represents silence, while the right end represents the loudest setting. The slider in the middle can be grabbed with the mouse and moved in either direction.

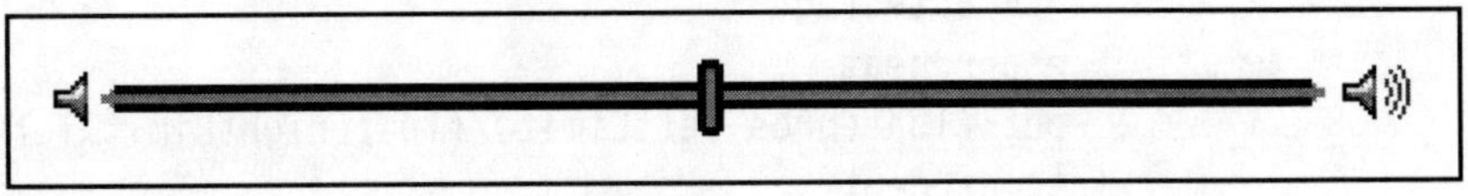

Figure 13-14: *A volume-setting slider.*

The slider itself actually has two graphic elements: the bar and the slider itself. The bar doesn't do much except tell us where the boundaries for the slider are and give the slider a visual background. In this case we want the boundaries to be about 20 or 30 pixels in from the left and right sides of the bar. The slider can then be dragged freely along the bar between these limits.

The script for the slider should be an *on mouseDown* script attached to the sprite in the score. We'll have it call a "slider" handler that will take care of the actual sliding and return the value corresponding to the position in which the slider was left. This value will be a number between 0 and 1, with 0 being all the way to the left and 1 being all the way to the right.

```
on mouseDown
  put slider() into percent
  put integer(percent*255) into vol
  set the volume of sound 1 = vol
  put vol -- for testing purposes
end

on slider
  put the clickOn into spriteNum
  puppetSprite spriteNum, TRUE
  put the rect of sprite (spriteNum-1) into limitRect
  put the left of limitRect + 20 into leftLimit
  put the right of limitRect - 29 into rightLimit
```

```
    repeat while the mouseDown
      put the mouseH into hPos
      put max(leftLimit,hPos) into hPos
      put min(rightLimit,hPos) into hPos
      set the locH of sprite spriteNum = hPos
      updateStage
    end repeat
    put float(hPos-leftLimit)/float(rightLimit-leftLimit)→
  into percent
    return percent
  end
```

Our "slider" handler gets the rectangle of the bar, which it assumes is in the previous sprite channel. It uses the left and right sides of this rectangle, with a slight offset to compensate for how this specific bar looks, to set the limits for the slider. The *repeat* loop just keeps the slider aligned with the cursor while the user is dragging. We puppetSprited the sprite so that the slider remains there when the handler is done.

We use two Lingo functions to constrain the slider to the bar: *min* and *max*. These functions just return the highest or lowest value among a sequence of numbers. In this case we use the *max* function to get the highest value between the slider position and the leftmost value it should have. If the user attempts to push the slider past the left side of the bar, the *max* function will substitute the leftmost value for the actual value of the horizontal position of the cursor—thus making the slider stop. The same happens in reverse for the rightmost value using the *min* command. This might seem confusing at first—using the *max* command to restrict the minimum value of the slider, and using the *min* command to restrict the maximum value of the slider.

The "slider" handler finishes by doing some math to determine where the slider is along the bar, and returns that value. Our *on mouseDown* handler converts this 0-to-1 value to a 0-to-255 value so that we can set the volume.

This same slider could have been done in a vertical format. Figure 13-15 shows what it would look like. We use the same style for the bar and the slider, with a vertical instead of a horizontal orientation.

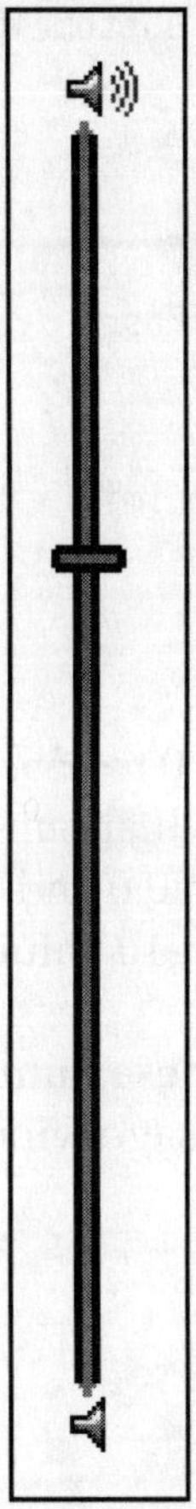

Figure 13-15: *A vertical slider.*

The only changes needed in the Lingo are to refer to *the mouseV* instead of *the mouseH, the top* and *the bottom* of the bar's rectangle instead of *the left* and *the right*, and to set *the locV of sprite* instead of *the locH of sprite*. The script would then look like this:

```
on slider
  put the clickOn into spriteNum
  puppetSprite spriteNum, TRUE
  put the rect of sprite (spriteNum-1) into limitRect
  put the top of limitRect + 20 into topLimit
```

```
  put the bottom of limitRect - 29 into bottomLimit
  repeat while the mouseDown
    put the mouseV into vPos
    put max(topLimit,vPos) into vPos
    put min(bottomLimit,vPos) into vPos
    set the locV of sprite spriteNum = vPos
    updateStage
  end repeat
  put float(vPos- topLimit)/float(bottomLimit - topLimit)→
into percent
  return percent
end
```

While our example is going for a value of 0 to 255, we could use sliders for a more limited range, say, 1 to 10. Just remember that the "slider" handler returns a value between 0.0 and 1.0. This means that if we want to translate it to a 1-to-10 value, we have to do some rounding.

If we use the *integer* command to round these numbers, we get an interesting side effect. Try this in the message window:

```
put integer(.04*10)
-- 0
put integer(.06*10)
-- 1
put integer(.44*10)
-- 4
put integer(.46*10)
-- 5
put integer(.54*10)
-- 5
put integer(.94*10)
-- 9
put integer(.96*10)
-- 10
```

The (rounded) product of each multiplication could be the value returned by the "slider" handler. The numbers round properly, which gives us the actual option of having numbers from 0 to 10, not 1 to 10. Another problem is that the numbers 0 and 10 only have half the range of the other numbers. The number 10, for instance, will come only from a value of .95 or higher.

We can solve this problem by adding .05 to each value returned by the "slider." That means that the minimum value returned will be .05, which translates to 1. The highest value, however, would be 1.05, which would translate to 11. This would only happen in the extreme case, since the value of 1.04999 would translate to a 10. We can compensate for this by using the *min* function: *min(10,num)*. Here is an *on mouseDown* script that does all this.

```
on mouseDown
  put slider() into percent
  put integer((percent+.05)*10) into num
  put min(10,num) into num
  put num -- to message window
end
```

Since the slider is puppeted, all you'd need to do is include the bar on several frames and you could use the slider as a method of navigation. The value returned by sliding it would cause the movie to jump to one of ten frames, and the user could then use the same slider to go back or to another frame. Figure 13-16 shows an example of what a slider that does this might look like. Notice that the slider is a little more unconventional than the previous example—it has a big gap for the bar to show though.

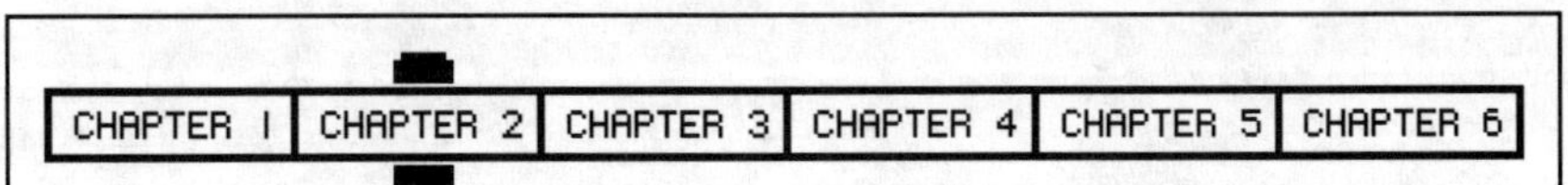

Figure 13-16: *A navigation slider.*

Moving On

Using a group of buttons is a great way to control navigation or ask the user questions. Sliders allow us to offer a different navigational choice to the user.

Next, we look at using text lists as another way for the user to interact with your movies.

14

Text Input

Button lists are useful when you want to ask the user a question and you have a predefined, stable set of answers. If there are four answers to a question, you could make four buttons, and that would get the job done. But what if there are dozens or hundreds of possible answers? Or what if the possible answers change as your project evolves—so often that it would be a pain to keep making new buttons and throwing away unused ones?

Selecting From a Text List

A good way to get user input in these situations is to provide users with a list of answers in text format. You see this consistently in other computer programs. For instance, whenever you want to open a new file, you are given a list of what is on the disk drive to choose from.

Figure 14-1 shows an example of a list of text in Director using the text field cast member type. This could be a query for the type of product a computer store customer is interested in. We make the list a scrolling text type, so if we want to add more items later, we won't interfere with the rest of the screen design.

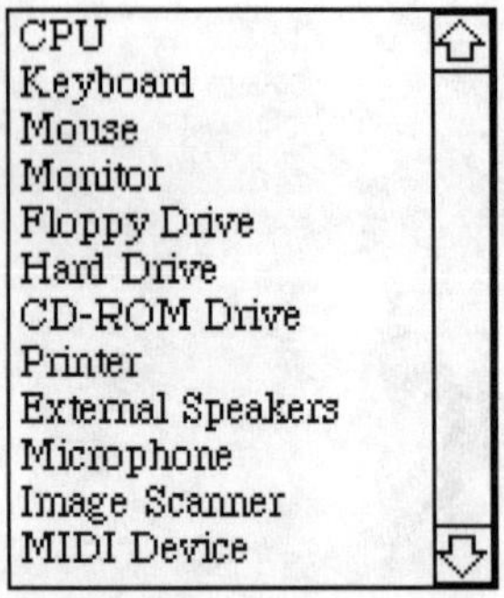

Figure 14-1: *A text list.*

Single Selection List

In the chapters dealing with hypertext, you've already learned how to get the word and character that the user clicked on and to translate that to some action. Now we can use *the mouseLine* to get the line that the mouse was over when it was clicked. We can use the line number or the actual contents of that line to decide what action to perform.

```
on mouseDown
  put the clickOn into spriteNum
  put the memberNum of sprite spriteNum into mNum
  put the mouseLine into mLine
  if mLine < 1 then exit
  alert (line mLine of field mNum)
end
```

This handler could be a score script assigned to the same sprite as the text field, or it could be the cast script for that text field. It uses some familiar Lingo to get the name of the field and then *the mouseLine* to get the line that was clicked. If some other part of the field, like the scrolling bar, is clicked, a –1 is returned as *the mouseLine*. We place the Lingo command *exit* in there to quit the entire handler if that is the case. Otherwise we just use the *alert* command to signify our selection. You would want to place a *go to frame* or our "playThisSound" handler in there depending on what you want the list to do.

But what if you wanted the list to act more like a group of radio buttons? You would want the user to be able to select one of the items in the list but not necessarily react to the choice immediately. The following handler uses *the foreColor property* to set a portion of the text a different color than black.

```
on mouseDown
  put the clickOn into spriteNum
  put the memberNum of sprite spriteNum into mNum
  put the name of member mNum into mName
  put the mouseLine into mLine
  if mLine < 1 then exit
  set the foreColor of field mName = 255
  set the foreColor of line mLine of field mName = 35
end
```

The handler first sets the color of the entire field to black, which is color 255. This way it will erase the user's last choice. It then sets the color of the line that was clicked to 35, which should be red if you are using the Macintosh system palette.

This handler will allow the user to choose a line in the list without an immediate action taking place. At some point, however, we will need a way to figure out what the user has selected. We could take the easy route and introduce a global variable to the handler above that gets set to "mLine" every time the user clicks. Then, when we wanted to know which line it was, we could just look at that global.

```
on mouseDown
  global lineSelected
  put the clickOn into spriteNum
  put the memberNum of sprite spriteNum into mNum
  put the name of member mNum into mName
  put the mouseLine into mLine
  if mLine < 1 then exit
  set the foreColor of field mName = 255
  set the foreColor of line mLine of field mName = 35
  put mLine into lineSelected
end
```

The global "lineSelected" could also be set to the contents of that line, rather than the number itself, if you prefer. We do need to find a way, however, to preset this global to 0 or an empty string, so that it has a valid value when we want it—even if the user never selects something from the list.

Another way to find out what the user selected would be to examine the text field and find out which line is red.

```
on getSelection whichField
  repeat with i = 1 to the number of lines in field→
whichField
    if the foreColor of line i of field whichField = 35→
then return i
  end repeat
  return 0
end
```

We pass into this custom handler the name of the field we are interested in. Then it just loops through the lines until it finds the red line and returns its number. If no red line is found, it returns 0.

Some Useful Colors

Here are the Macintosh system palette number equivalents for some popular colors:

red	35, 215
blue	235
light blue	186
green	225
yellow	5
medium gray	249

You can pick your own colors from whatever palette you are using with Director's Color Palettes window. It will display the number of any color at the bottom of the window.

Instead of turning the selected line a color, we could use the Lingo command *hilite* to give it the operating system's natural highlight effect. The handler would look like this:

```
on mouseDown
  put the clickOn into spriteNum
  put the memberNum of sprite spriteNum into mNum
  put the name of member mNum into mName
  put the mouseLine into mLine
  if mLine < 1 then exit
  hilite line mLine of field mName
end
```

The *hilite* command is sometimes difficult to work with, however. It never seems to highlight precisely what you want and can't be used in multiple selection lists or to select single items in several lists.

There is another method that provides a smoother way for the user to select an item. With the previous script, the mouse click just grabs the line under it and makes that the selection. But by altering the script a bit, we can make the selection behavior a little more friendly to the user.

```
on mouseDown
  put the clickOn into spriteNum
  put the memberNum of sprite spriteNum into mNum
  put the name of member mNum into mName
  put 0 into lastLine
  repeat while the mouseDown
    put the mouseLine into mLine
    if mLine < 1 then next repeat
    if mLine = lastLine then next repeat
set the foreColor of field mName = 255
    set the foreColor of line mLine of field mName = 35
    put mLine into lastLine
  end repeat
end
```

This handler contains a *repeat* loop that keeps the handler going as long as the mouse is pressed. It then changes the selected line as the user rolls over the field. It uses the variable "lastLine" to remember which line is currently selected, so that it doesn't keep updating the selection until there is a real change.

Multiple Selection Lists

The next type of selection list behaves much like a group of check boxes. It will allow the user to select none, one, some, or all of the lines.

The handler to do this will be very different from the one above. For one thing, it cannot reset the field every time the user clicks. It must instead add to the selections already made. The handler also needs to recognize that the user is clicking on an item that is already selected, and react by deselecting it.

```
on mouseDown
  put the clickOn into spriteNum
  put the memberNum of sprite spriteNum into mNum
  put the name of member mNum into mName
  put the mouseLine into mLine
  if mLine < 1 then exit
  if the foreColor of line mLine of field mName = 35 then
    set the foreColor of line mLine of field mName = 255
  else
    set the foreColor of line mLine of field mName = 35
  end if
end
```

Now that we have this handler in place to make the multiple selection list behave properly, we will need a way to read the list to find out what is selected. There are two handlers we could use: one that returns a true or false if we feed it the field name and line number, and one that returns a whole list of the lines that are selected.

```
on isSelected whichField, lineNum
  if the foreColor of line lineNum of field whichField = 35→
then return TRUE
```

```
    else return 0
end

on allLinesSelected whichField
    put "" into list
    repeat with i = 1 to the number of lines in field whichField
        if the foreColor of line i of field whichField = 35 then→
put string(i)&" " after list
    end repeat
    return list
end
```

The first handler, "isSelected," will return a TRUE or a FALSE depending on whether the line, "lineNum," of field "whichField" is red. The second handler returns a text string with a list of all the lines in field "whichField" that are red. The string may look like this: "3 6 13 22."

Asking for Text Input

For the most basic user input, Director makes things very easy for us. All we need to do is place a text field cast member on the stage and set it to Editable in the field cast member properties box shown in Figure 14-2.

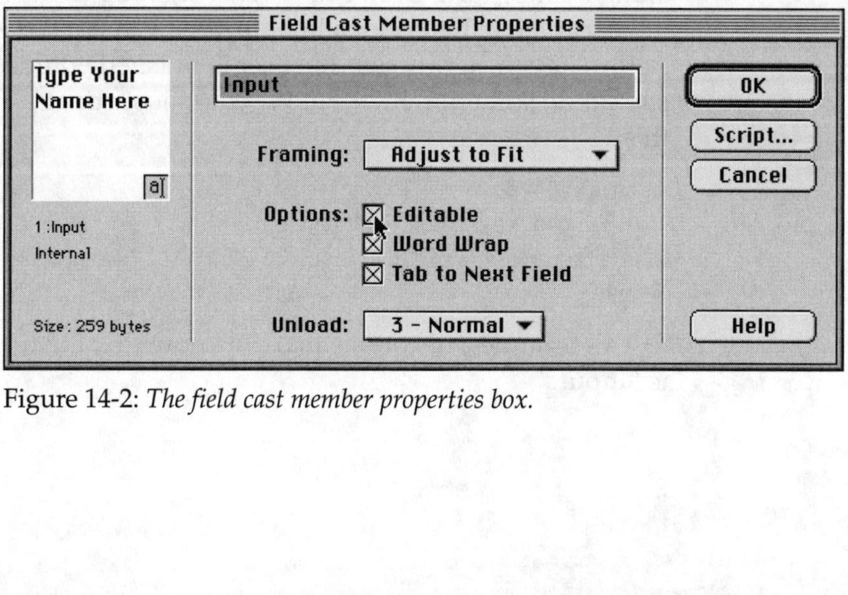

Figure 14-2: *The field cast member properties box.*

Now, when the movie is on that frame, users can type whatever they want into that text box. If there is more than one field on the stage, the user can use the Tab key to quickly move between fields, as long as we have the Tab to Next Field property turned on.

TIP

When you have more than one editable text field on the stage at a time, Director will start the user off by setting the cursor into the text field that is in the lowest numbered sprite channel.

This method of text input requires no scripting to begin with, but it has several flaws. First, users tend to press the Return key when they are done entering something. This will have no effect here, except to create a new line in the field in which they are currently typing. If the field is of a set size, the new line may extend beyond that size and therefore not be visible to the user.

We can fix this problem by attaching a simple script to the sprite channel or cast member.

```
on keyDown
  if the key <> RETURN then pass
end
```

The *pass* command allows a message, like "keyDown," to continue past the current handler. In this case we check to see if the key pressed was a Return. Only if it isn't a Return do we pass along the key for Director to process and add to the field.

We can take this script a little further. What if we wanted the Return key to signify that the user is finished entering text and we should do something with it. We could just change the script like this:

```
on keyDown
  if the key <> RETURN then pass
  else alert (field "input")
end
```

This assumes, of course, that we know that the text field's name is "input."

A more useful action than just using the *alert* command would be to store the field in a global variable and go to another frame. This way, you could ask a succession of questions one at a time.

You could also ask a bunch of questions on the same screen. Just have each field place its contents in a different variable when the Return key is pressed. Or you could just leave the text in the fields and refer to them later instead of using globals.

Another script that might be useful is one that restricts the number of lines the user can add to a field. For instance, you might be asking the user for an address and want to restrict the size of the address to only three lines:

```
on keyDown
  if the key = RETURN then
    if the number of lines in field "input" < 3 then
      pass
    end if
  else pass
end
```

This handler would allow Returns to pass only if there are no more than three lines in the field. All other characters could pass freely.

We can use this same idea to impose other restrictions on characters. You might want to allow only numbers and nothing else. The handler below will only allow characters associated with numbers to pass.

```
on keyDown
  if "0123456789." contains the key then
    pass
  else if the key = RETURN then
    -- do something with the data here
  end if
end
```

The little text string "0123456789." represents valid characters, in this case the numbers 1 to 10 and the decimal point. We might want to add a "$" or something else to the list. A similar list might just be the 26 letters of the alphabet, if we wanted to restrict the user's input to letters only.

Text Selection

Lingo gives us a few commands to determine what text the user has selected in an editable text box.

The function *the selection* simply returns the text of whatever the user has selected. So if the user highlights the word *apple* in an editable text field, the Lingo function *the selection* would return *"apple."*

Note that you cannot do this in the message window. By typing in the message window, you are deselecting whatever you may have selected in another box.

Two other commands, *the selStart* and *the selEnd*, will give you the first and last character positions of the selection. If nothing is selected, these functions will return 0's, or possibly the same number if the user is currently typing.

Notice that there is no way to determine what field we are dealing with. This could present a problem if you are trying to figure out what the user has selected and there are several editable text fields on the stage. The one way to get around this is to set a global variable, say, "currentField," every time the user clicks in, or types in, an editable text field.

Moving On

Text lists and text input are additional ways for the user to provide input to your movies. Now we have a whole arsenal of options to get user input: single mouse clicks (Chapter 3), single buttons (Chapter 4), hypertext (Chapters 9 and 12), button lists (Chapter 13), check boxes and radio buttons (Chapter 13), and selection lists and text input (Chapter 14).

Lets' go on to explore some other Lingo features: lists.

15

Lists

Previously, we have only dealt with simple variables: numbers and text. Lingo has another variable type that is necessary for going beyond simple scripting: the list.

A list is a collection of elements: numbers, text, or a combination of both. These elements are surrounded by brackets and each item in the list is separated by a comma.

The best way to introduce the list is to play around in the message window.

```
put [3,8,1]
-- [3,8,1]
```

We can have as many or as few elements in a list as we want.

```
put [3]
-- [3]
put [3,8,1,4,9,4,7,6,3,8,34,56,2,9,0,2,-6]
-- [3,8,1,4,9,4,7,6,3,8,34,56,2,9,0,2,-6]
put []
-- []
```

What Lists Can Do

Lists can also store text, and can combine numbers and text without any problem.

```
put ["apples", "oranges", "bananas"]
-- ["apples", "oranges", "bananas"]
put ["apples", 5, 7, "oranges", 8]
-- ["apples", 5, 7, "oranges", 8]
```

We can store a list in a variable just as we store a single number or text string.

```
put [3,8,1,4,9] into numberList
put numberList
-- [3,8,1,4,9]
```

To extract a single element from a list, use the *getAt* function. The first parameter is a list and the second is the number element of the list you want to "get."

```
put getAt([3,8,1,4,9],2)
-- 8
put getAt([3,8,1,4,9],5)
-- 9
put getAt(numberList,1)
-- 3
```

To change only one element in the list, without re-creating the whole list, use the *setAt* function.

```
put numberList
-- [3,8,1,4,9]
setAt(numberList,3,42)
put numberList
-- [3,8,42,4,9]
```

The second parameter in *setAt* is the number of the element you wish to change. The third parameter is the value you wish to change it to.

We can add to a list using either the *add* or the *append* command. There's an important difference between these commands, which we will discuss later.

```
put [3,8,1,4,9] into numberList
put numberList
-- [3,8,1,4,9]
add(numberList,7)
put numberList
-- [3,8,1,4,9,7]
append(numberList,6)
put numberList
-- [3,8,1,4,9,7,6]
```

We can insert an element in a list by using the *addAt* command. The second parameter of this command is the position to insert and the third parameter is the value to insert.

```
put [3,8,1,4,9] into numberList
put numberList
-- [3,8,1,4,9]
addAt(numberList,3,7)
put numberList
-- [3,8,7,1,4,9]
```

The *setAt* command would be used to replace an element in the list. We also have a *deleteAt* command to remove an element from a list.

```
put [3,8,1,4,9] into numberList
put numberList
-- [3,8,1,4,9]
deleteAt(numberList,3)
put numberList
-- [3,8,4,9]
```

A useful piece of Lingo is the *count* function. This will return the number of items in a list.

```
put [3,8,1] into numberList
put count(numberList)
-- 3
put [3,8,1,4,9] into numberList
put count(numberList)
-- 5
put [] into numberList
put count(numberList)
-- 0
```

Two functions: *getOne* and *getPos* will help you find elements in the list. They both return the position of the element in the list. If an element is there more than once, it returns the earliest position. If the value is not there at all, it will return a zero. We will talk about the differences between these two functions later.

```
put [3,8,1,4,9] into numberList
put getOne(numberList,8)
-- 2
```

The *getLast* function will return the last item in a list. Note that we can always get the first item of a list with the *getAt* function.

```
put [3,8,1,4,9] into numberList
put getLast(numberList)
-- 9
put getAt(numberList,1)
-- 3
```

Using the very powerful *sort* command, we can order the list.

```
put [3,8,1,4,9] into numberList
put numberList
-- [3,8,1,4,9]
sort(numberList)
put numberList
-- [1,3,4,8,9]
```

Once you have sorted a list, the whole nature of the list changes. If you use the *add* command now, the new value will automatically be placed in the proper sorted position. The *append* command, however, still adds to the end of the list.

```
add(numberList, 5)
put numberList
-- [1,3,4,5,8,9]
```

If you use the *append* or the *addAt* command on a sorted list, it loses its ability to sort itself automatically with an *add* command until you perform the *sort* again.

```
append(numberlist,0)
put numberlist
-- [1, 3, 4, 5, 8, 9, 0]
```

```
add(numberlist,6)
put numberlist
-- [1, 3, 4, 5, 8, 9, 0, 6]
```

We can use the function *listP* to determine if a variable contains a list. This is useful, because if we try to perform one of the above list commands on a variable that is not a list, we get a big fat error message.

```
put [3,8,1] into numberList
put listP(numberList)
-- 1
put [] into numberList
put listP(numberList)
-- 1
put 5 into numberList
put listP(numberList)
-- 0
put "hello" into numberList
put listP(numberList)
-- 0
```

Property Lists

The type of list we have been dealing with so far is called a *linear list*. A second type of list is available in Director: the *property list*.

Property lists are different from linear lists because you can label the elements of the list. Here is an example:

```
[#name: "Gary", #city: "Denver", #state: "Colorado", #acct:
555]
```

The words with the "#" in front of them are called *symbols*. These identify each item in the list. We could use normal numbers or text strings as symbols, but the "#" structure is specially designed to be faster when referring to lists. However, the following are valid:

```
["name": "Gary", "city": "Denver", "state": "Colorado",
"acct": 555]
[1: "Gary", 2: "Denver", 3: "Colorado", 4: 555]
```

Go ahead and use the message window to put this sample list into a variable.

```
put [#name: "Gary", #city: "Denver", #state: "Colorado",
#acct: 555] into list
put list
-- [#name: "Gary", #city: "Denver", #state: "Colorado",
#acct: 555]
```

Our usual set of list commands works with property lists too.

```
put getAt(list,2)
-- "Denver"
```

Property lists also have a whole set of functions to get things based on their symbols. The *getProp* function will return the value that matches the symbol you supply.

```
put getProp(list,#state)
-- "Colorado"
```

The *getAProp* function works exactly the same way, except that if for some reason the property is not there, it will not throw up an error message; it just returns a *<void>*.

```
put getProp(list,#country)
put getAProp(list,#country)
-- <Void>
```

The first line above would cause an error message; the second line would not.

TIP *You can test for a value being <void> with the* voidP *function. For example:* if not voidP(myVariable) then...

To change a property list, we can still use the *setAt* command if we know exactly where something in the list is.

```
setAt(list,2,"Fairbanks")
put getProp(list,#city)
-- "Fairbanks"
```

However, we would normally want to use the *setProp* and the *setAProp* commands when dealing with property lists. The *setProp* command will change the value of an element in the list but show an error message if the property we specify doesn't exist. The *setAProp* command does the same thing, but instead of producing an error message when a property can't be found, it just adds that property and its value to the list.

```
setProp(list,#city,"Philadelphia")
put getProp(list,#city)
-- "Philadelphia"
setAProp(list,#country,"U.S.A.")
put getProp(list,#country)
-- "U.S.A."
```

TIP

If you want to create an empty property list so that you can add to it later, you must create a list like this: [:].

We can use the *sort* command with property lists too. What it does for them is sort the list by property. Let's try this out with a new list.

```
put [#Colorado: 3, #Ohio: 10, #Delaware: 1, #California: 30,
#Texas: 17] into list
put list
-- [#Colorado: 3, #Ohio: 10, #Delaware: 1, #California: 30,
#Texas: 17]
sort list
put list
-- [#California: 30, #Colorado: 3, #Delaware: 1, #Ohio: 10,
#Texas: 17]
```

Now that we have sorted the list, we can use the *addProp* command to insert another property into the list. It will put itself in the proper position.

```
addProp(list, #Maryland, 5)
put list
-- [#California: 30, #Colorado: 3, #Delaware: 1, #Maryland:
5, #Ohio: 10, #Texas: 17]
```

Two other things that can be used once a property list has been sorted are the *findPos* function and the *findPosNear* function. The first will return the position of the property you are looking for in the list. It will, however, return a <void> if the property is not in the list at all. The *findPosNear* function will work the same way, but it will return the position a missing item would take if it were present.

```
put findPos(list,#Colorado)
-- 2
put findPos(list,#Maine)
-- <Void>
put findPosNear(list,#Maine)
-- 4
```

You can use the *deleteAt* function to remove items from a property list, but you can also use the *deleteProp* function to delete an item by its property name. It would be used like this:

```
deleteProp(list,#Maine).
```

We can also use the *getOne* and *getPos* functions on property lists. However, they do different things here. The *getPos* function will return the position number of the element we are looking for. The *getOne* function will return the property of the element we are looking for.

```
put list
-- [#California: 30, #Colorado: 3, #Delaware: 1, #Maryland:
5, #Ohio: 10, #Texas: 17]
put getPos(list,10)
-- 5
put getOne(list,10)
-- #Ohio
```

The *getLast* and *count* functions also work with property lists. Let's review all of the list-related functions.

Function Name	Example	Linear Lists	Property Lists
getAt	put getAt(list,3)	Gets the third item in the list.	Gets the third item in the list.
setAt	setAt(list,3,42)	Puts 42 into the third item of the list.	Puts 42 into the third item of the list.
append	append(list,99)	Adds 99 as the last item in the list.	Will not work.
add	add(list,88)	Adds 88 as the last item in the list. If the list has been sorted, then it adds 88 in the proper spot in the list.	Will not work.
addAt	addAt(list,2,36)	Inserts 36 as the second item in the list.	Will not work.
deleteAt	deleteAt(list,3)	Removes the third item in the list.	Removes the third symbol and its value from the list.
count	put count(list)	Returns the number of items in the list.	Returns the number of items in the list.
getPos	put getPos(list,7)	Returns the position of the first 7 in the list. The list must be sorted first.	Returns the position of the first 7 in the list. The list must be sorted first.
getOne	put getOne(list,7)	Returns the position of the first 7 in the list. The list must be sorted first.	Returns the property name of the first 7 in the list. The list must be sorted first.
getLast	put getLast(list)	Returns the last item in the list.	Returns the last item in the list.
sort	sort list	Sorts the list in alphanumeric order by item.	Sorts the list in alphanumeric order by property.
listP	put listP(list)	Returns the value,“true,” if the variable is a list.	Returns the value, “true,” if the variable is a list.

Function Name	Example	Linear Lists	Property Lists
getProp	put getProp (list,#name)	Will not work.	Returns the item with the property #name. Error message if it is not there.
getAProp	put getAProp (list,#name)	Will not work	Returns the item with the property #name. <void> if it is not there.
setProp	setProp(list, #name,"Gary")	Will not work.	Sets the property #name to "Gary." Error message if the property is not there.
setAProp	setAProp(list, #name,"Gary")	Will not work.	Sets the property #name to "Gary." Creates the property if it is not there.
addProp	addProp(list, #name,"Gary")	Will not work.	Adds a new item with the property #name and the value "Gary" to the list. If it is a sorted list, it will place it properly.
deleteProp	deleteProp (list,#name)	Will not work.	Removes an item from the list that matches the property name.
findPos	put findPos (list,#Maine)	For a sorted list, it returns the position of the requested item.	For a sorted list, it returns the position of the requested property.
findPosNear		For a sorted list, it returns the position of the requested item, or the closest position if not there.	For a sorted list, it returns the position of the requested property, or the closest position if not there.

Creating a Simple Database

Let's use our knowledge about lists to create some simple databases. Say we have a set of questions that we want to ask the user. We could put these in a list and use scripts to ask them in order.

Here is a sample list of questions:

```
["What is your name?", "What is your age?", "Do you own a
multimedia computer?", "Do you work in the multimedia
industry?"]
```

We could place this list in a variable using the put command:

```
put ["What is your name?", "What is your age?", "Do you own a
multimedia computer?", "Do you work in the multimedia
industry?"] into list
```

A better way to do this would be to place the list as a piece of text inside a text field cast member as shown in Figure 15-1. This way, you won't clutter up your code with long list declarations, and the list is easier to edit when it has its own cast member. Then we can use the *value* function to convert this text field to a real list.

Figure 15-1: *A text string that is ready to be converted to a list.*

While this information is stored in a text field it is just a string of characters and has no list functionality. Once we convert it using the *value* function and place it in a variable, we have a real list that we can work with.

```
put value(field "list data") into list
put list
-- ["What is your name?", "What is your age?", "Do you own a
multimedia computer?", "Do you work in the multimedia
industry?"]
```

We can write a simple Lingo handler than displays any question in the list on the stage in another field named "question."

```
on showQuestion n
  put value(field "list data") into list
  put getAt(list,n) into field "question"
end
```

The handler assumes that the parameter "n" will not be more than the number of items in the list.

The conversion of a text field to a list is a time-consuming one. With only four items, as we have here, it isn't so bad. However, we will usually place the list in a global variable, possibly in the *on startMovie* handler, so that it doesn't have to be converted each time the "showQuestion" handler runs.

```
on startMovie
  global list
  put value(field "list data") into list
end
on showQuestion n
  global list
  put getAt(list,n) into field "question"
end
```

Let's take this example further. Now that we have a list of questions, let's ask the user to answer them. To create this movie, just place two fields on the stage: a "question" field and an "answer" field. The "answer" field should have its Editable and Tab to Next Field properties turned on. The following movie script contains most of what you need to get this working:

```
on startMovie
  global questionList, answerList, questionNum
  put value(field "list data") into questionList
```

```
  put [] into answerList
  put 1 into questionNum
  showQuestion
end

on showQuestion
  global questionList, questionNum
  put getAt(questionList,questionNum) into
field "question"
  put EMPTY into field "answer"
end

on recordAnswer
  global answerList, questionNum
  setAt(answerList,questionNum,field "answer")
end

on nextQuestion
  global questionList, questionNum
  put questionNum+1 into questionNum
  if questionNum > count(questionList) then
    go to frame "survey done"
  else
    showQuestion
  end if
end
```

The *on startMovie* handler initializes three globals. The first is the "questionList." The handler places the list-translated contents of the "list data" field into it. The second global is the "answerList." We just start that off with an empty list. The third global is the current question number, called "questionNum." Then the *on startMovie* handler kicks things off by showing the first question.

The "showQuestion" handler takes the "questionList" list global and the current "questionNum" and places the proper question into the "question" field. It also resets the "answer" field to be blank.

At this point, it is up to the user to do something. The frame should be looping with a *go to the frame* in the *on exitFrame* handler. Since the "answers" field has been set up as editable, the user should be able to type the answer there. The stage should look something like Figure 15-2.

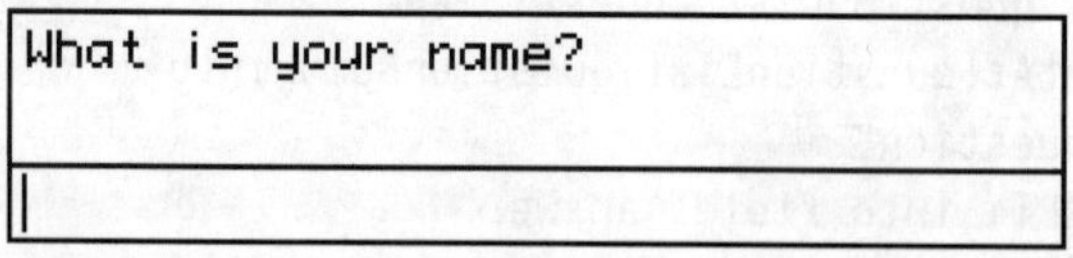

Figure 15-2: *The "question" and "answer" fields. Notice that they have been given a 1-pixel border so we can see them better.*

We want to place a script in the "answer" field so that it detects a Return and kicks off the "recordAnswer" and "nextQuestion" handlers.

```
on keyDown
  if the key = RETURN then
    recordAnswer()
    nextquestion()
  else
    pass
  end if
end
```

The "recordAnswer" handler places the contents of the "answer" field into the "answerList" list. Since we use the variable "questionNum" to place this item, the questions in the "questionList" and the answers in the "answerList" will match each other item for item.

The "nextQuestion" handler increments the "questionNum" by one and then checks to see if it has gone past the end of the "questionList." If it has, it jumps to another frame, otherwise it calls "showQuestion."

Let's add another level of complexity to our database. Suppose we want to give a multiple-choice test. The data we would need for each question would be not just the question text itself but also the possible answers.

So each question actually has several parts: a question and some answers. The entire quiz will consist of several of these question/answer sets. Let's make each question/answer set a list. It could look like this:

```
["What is the capital of Nebraska?", "Omaha", "Lincoln",
"Oklahoma City"]
```

In this case, we need to remember that the first item in the list is the question, and the rest of the items are possible answers. Maybe we want to add one more item to the list: the number of the right answer.

```
["What is the capital of Nebraska?", 2, "Omaha", "Lincoln",
"Oklahoma City"]
```

The number 2 in the second item of the list tells us that the second answer is the correct one. We could make this list easier to decipher if we used a property list instead of a linear list.

```
[#question: "What is the capital of Nebraska?", #correct:
#answer2, #answer1: "Omaha", #answer2: "Lincoln", #answer3:
"Oklahoma City"]
```

Now we can refer to the item we need in the list by symbol, instead of remembering its specific position. The symbol "#correct" has the value of the symbol that corresponds to the correct answer. We could get the correct answer with the following bit of Lingo:

```
getProp(list,getProp(list,#correct))
```

The middle part of this statement, *getProp(list,#correct)*, gives us the value "#answer2." We then look for this property in the list which gives us "Lincoln."

But what if there are more or less than three answers in the list? It is not a good idea to use symbols like "#answer1," "#answer2," and "#answer3." After all, don't these three items deserve to have a list all by themselves? Fortunately, we can have lists living inside of lists. Look at this structure for the same data:

```
[#question: "What is the capital of Nebraska?", #correct: 2,
#answers: ["Omaha", "Lincoln", "Oklahoma City"]]
```

This list only has three items: the question, the number of the correct answer, and a list of possible answers. The third item is itself a list.

We can get to any answer in the list pretty easily. Say we wanted the third possible answer:, this is all we need to ask for:

```
getAt(getProp(list,#answers),3)
```

The inner part of the command, *getProp(list,#answers)*, returns the full list of answers. The outer part of the command gives us the third item in the list.

We can now take this nested list idea one step further. If we want to have more than one question in the quiz, we can make a large list that contains all the questions we need. A list with two questions might look like this:

```
[[#question: "What is the capital of Nebraska?", #correct: 2,
#answers: ["Omaha", "Lincoln", "Oklahoma City"]], [#question:
"What is the capital of California?", #correct: 1, #answers:
["Sacramento", "San Francisco", "Fresno", "Oklahoma City"]]]
```

At this point it is getting hard for us humans to keep track of the brackets. The computer keeps good track of them, however, and won't tolerate it if even one is missing. Don't get frustrated if you run into trouble trying to get brackets in lists to match. Even the most advanced Lingo programmers spend a good deal of time searching for the missing bracket in a list here and there.

We could use a list like this to ask a series of multiple-choice questions in a single text field. The following handler will present a question, assuming the list is stored in a global variable named "list."

```
on showQuestion n
  global list, answerNum
  put getAt(list,n) into questionList
  put getProp(questionList,#question) into field "question"
  repeat with i = 1 to count(getProp(questionList,#answers))
    put getAt(getProp(questionList,#answers),i)& RETURN→
after field "question"
  end repeat
  put getProp(questionList,#correct) into answerNum
end
```

The handler takes the "n"th question from the list and puts it in the local variable "questionList." It then places the question in the text field, followed by each of the answers. It stores the number of the correct answer in the global "answerNum."

You could use this handler, in conjunction with the text selection list scripts, to create a simple multiple-choice quiz. Stealing some of the score-keeping code from our simple games script in the "Beginner's Workbook" section of this book will allow you to keep track of right and wrong answers.

TIP *While lists may be harder to read than in plain text strings with item delimiters, they are much faster for Lingo to process. Using symbols instead of numbers or strings will also improve performance.*

Using Lists to Make Life Easier

Now that we feel comfortable using lists, we can look at ways in which they can make some of our scripts better.

Repeat Loops & Lists

One way to use lists is in *repeat with* loops, to set a variable equal to each item in the list. Try this test handler:

```
on testRepeat
  repeat with state in ["Colorado", "Alaska",
"North Carolina", "Pennsylvania"]
    put state
  end repeat
end
```

Test it out with the message window:

```
testRepeat
-- "Colorado"
-- "Alaska"
-- "North Carolina"
-- "Pennsylvania"
```

This special type of *repeat with* loop takes the variable we name, in this case "state," and assigns each value in the list to it. We could use numbers, text, other lists, or any combination.

Alternating Sprites

Going way back to the chapters that dealt with alternating cast members in sprite channels, we could use lists to make those scripts better. Remember the alternating sprite script in Chapter 3 that made a cartoon hand wave? Consider this handler:

```
on exitFrame
   put ["hand1", "hand2", "hand3"] into list
   put the clickOn into spriteNum
   put the memberNum of sprite spriteNum into mNum
   put the name of member mNum into mName
   put getOne(list,mName) into n
   put n+1 into n
   if n > count(list) then put 1 into n
   put getAt(list,n) into mName
   put the number of member mName into mNum
   puppetSprite spriteNum, TRUE
   set the memberNum of sprite spriteNum = mNum
end
```

The beauty of this script is that we can change the list on the first line to any cast member names we want. We can even use any number of cast members. There is nothing in this script that says you have to have 3—you can have 2, 7, 88, or any number of items in the list.

The problem with this, and it is a problem with the original alternating sprite script as well, is that you can't have a cast member listed more than once. If we put "hand2" as the fourth item in the list, so that the hand would appear to wave back and forth, it wouldn't work. What would happen is the handler would take the sprite from "hand1" to "hand2" to "hand3" and then to "hand2" and then to "hand3" again. The reason is that because the second and fourth items in the list are the same (both are "hand2"), Lingo will continue from the second item, since it comes before the fourth item.

An easy way to get around this would be to duplicate "hand2" and call the copy "hand4." Then our list would be as follows:

```
["hand1", "hand2", "hand3", "hand4"]
```

This works, but you would have two copies of the same cast member in your movie.

A better way to do this would be to have a global that keeps track of which item in the list is currently shown.

```
on exitFrame
  global graphicNum
  put ["hand1", "hand2", "hand3", "hand2"] into list
  put graphicNum +1 into graphicNum
  if graphicNum > count(list) then put 1 into graphicNum
  put getAt(list, graphicNum) into mName
  put the number of member mName into mNum
  puppetSprite spriteNum, TRUE
  set the memberNum of sprite spriteNum = mNum
end
```

This script assumes that the global "graphicNum" is set to a valid number, like 1, before the handler runs the first time. This could be done in an *on startMovie* handler. You may want to take the *puppetSprite* line out of this handler and stick it in the same place as well.

Navigation

Suppose you have a whole bunch of buttons and they each take the movie to a different frame when pressed. You could use the method described in Chapter 4 to connect the name of the button with the name of the frame. Or you could make a lookup list that connects the button and frame. Consider this list:

```
["button1": "chapter27", "button2": "chapter3", "button3":
"chapter15"]
```

Store this list in a text field and then have your movie place it in a global variable called, say, "navList." Notice that we are not using symbols here as properties but rather as text strings.

An *on mouseUp* handler could use this list to match the button pressed with the frame it should go to.

```
on mouseUp
  global navList
  put the clickOn into spriteNum
  put the memberNum of sprite spriteNum into mNum
  put the name of member mNum into mName
  put getProp(navList,mName) into fName
  go to frame fName
end
```

This method may not seem to save you so much work at first, but you can extend this list to include other information about the action each button is supposed to perform. For instance, you could include the type of action: go to a frame, play a sound, or execute some Lingo script. Check out this list:

```
["button1": [#type: #goto, #frame: "chapter27"], "button2":
[#type: #sound, #member: "chapter3"], "button3": [#type:
#lingo, #command: "quit"]]
```

Each item in this list is itself a list. Inside each list is the property "#type" that we will use to figure out what the button is supposed to do. The rest of the list provides the information we need to accomplish the task. Here is a handler that deals with this type of list.

```
on mouseUp
  global navList
  put the clickOn into spriteNum
  put the memberNum of sprite spriteNum into mNum
  put the name of member mNum into mName
  put getProp(navList,mName) into miniList
  put getProp(miniList,#type) into actionType
  case actionType of
    #goto :
      put getProp(miniList,#frame) into fName
      go to frame fName
    #sound :
      put getProp(miniList,#member) into sName
      puppetSound sName
      updateStage
```

```
    #lingo :
      put getProp(miniList,#command) into command
      do command
  end case
end
```

This type of approach to button functionality is incredibly flexible. You can add other actions besides navigation, sound, and raw Lingo. Each item in the list can also include much more than just one piece of information about the action. For instance, the "#goto" action could also have a "#transitionNum" property.

Hypertext

The scripts we developed for advanced hypertext included a text field that defined which words linked to which functions. We could easily take this field and make it into a real list.

A sample hypertext list might look something like this:

```
[[#word: "macromedia", #field: "text 22", #function: #goto,
#frame: "macromedia info"], [#word: "Lingo", #field: "caption
4", #function: #alertbox, #data: "A cool programming
language!"]]
```

The new hypertext handler would simply have to look through the list until it found an item in the list that matched the word and field of the hyperlink that was clicked. The rest of the list would provide all the information it would need to figure out what to do with it.

Moving On

Lists inside of lists inside of lists—this is what is behind some of the more advanced Lingo scripting. Getting to know lists very well is the secret to becoming an advanced Lingo programmer.

Now that you know about some of the uses of lists, try to use them everywhere. There is hardly a Lingo script longer than a few lines that cannot be made better, smaller, and easier to write with the use of lists.

Now, let's take a look at reading and saving files.

Hypertext

16 File Input & Output

While Director 5.0 has the ability to import text files into rich text cast members, there is no simple way to bring text files into text field members or variables. This is a shame, since reading and writing text files is a necessary part of many multimedia applications.

We can read and write files, however, with the use of the fileIO Xobject. An Xobject is an extension to Director that provides extra functionality not usually available in Lingo. The fileIO Xobject is one of the most commonly used one of these and provides all sorts of file functionality.

If you are working on a Macintosh, the fileIO Xobject is included in the Director application as a resource—it is invisible to you and the user. When you make a projector, the Xobject is automatically included.

On a Windows machine, however, the Xobject is included as the file fileio.dll. You must include this file with your projector if you are making a Windows projector. Furthermore, you must include the lingo.ini file that has a command in it to load the fileio.dll when your projector runs.

TIP

Use the command fileIO(mDescribe) *in the message window to see the engineer's description of the Xobject. You can use similar commands with any other Xobject as well.*

Reading Files

For every file you want to deal with, you must create a variable that points to that file. When we create this variable, we have to tell Director what we plan to do with the file: read from it or write to it. If we want to read from a file, it should be one that already exists. If we want to write to a file, it can be one that already exists or we can create a new one.

The command to create a pointer to a file looks like this:

```
set myFile = fileIO(mNew, "read", "myfile.txt")
```

This will open the file named myfile.txt for reading and set the variable "myFile" to point to it. From now on, when we want to refer to this file, we just need to use the variable "myFile."

Once a file is open, we can perform actions on it by using the variable that points to it as a Lingo function. We pass parameters to this function that tell the file what action we want to take. To read the entire contents of the file into a text variable, we will use the "mReadFile" parameter.

```
put myFile(mReadFile) into fileText
```

When we are done with the file, we have to close it. This is done by disposing of the pointer we were using. This only closes the link from the Director movie to the file. The file is not deleted from your hard drive. The command looks like this:

```
myFile(mDispose)
```

We have to remember to always do this, because Director can open only so many files at one time. By disposing of this pointer and closing the file, we can continue on our way without worrying about any memory or system resources that the open file was using.

A short handler that can do all this work for us would look like this:

```
on readFile fileName
  set myFile = fileIO(mNew, "read", fileName)
  put myFile(mReadFile) into fileText
  myFile(mDispose)
  return fileText
end
```

It is a good idea to check to make sure the file was found and could be opened before you start performing functions on it. You can do this by checking to see if the variable pointer is a valid file pointer after you try to open the file. The *objectP* command will do this for you.

```
on readFile fileName
  set myFile = fileIO(mNew, "read", fileName)
  if not objectP(myFile) then return EMPTY
  put myFile(mReadFile) into fileText
  myFile(mDispose)
  return fileText
end
```

Since we are only using a filename, not a full path name, in this handler, Director expects the file to be in the same place as the movie. We can specify other locations by including the full path name of the file.

Windows users are used to seeing path names. On a Windows machine, a typical path name for a file might be: c:\director\project2\myfile.txt. For Macintosh users, path names are something the operating system does not trouble the user with. However, now that you are doing some serious programming, you will have to use them. A typical path name for our file might be Macintosh HD:Director 5.0:Project Number 2:myText.txt.

TIP

You may want to include a standard error message whenever the "readFile" handler returns an empty string. You can use the alert *command to notify the user of the problem.*

There are other fileIO commands that allow you to do various things when reading files. For instance, you could use the "mReadLine," "mReadWord," or "mReadChar" parameters to read only one line, word, or character from the file at a time.

You could use this functionality to search through a long text file for the right line. Here is a handler that looks for a line that contains a given word or phrase:

```
on getLineOfFile filename, phrase
  set myFile = fileIO(mNew, "read", fileName)
  if not objectP(myFile) then return EMPTY
  repeat while TRUE
    put myFile (mReadLine) into fileText
    if fileText contains phrase then return fileText
  end repeat
  myFile(mDispose)
  return EMPTY
end
```

The "mReadLine" parameter not only reads a line in the file, but it also remembers what it has already read, so that the next time "mReadLine" is used, it reads the next line, not the same one over and over again.

There are a bunch of utility commands that we can use in handlers like this as well. When you are progressively reading a file you can use the "mGetPosition" parameter to get the current character position in the file you are reading from. The command would look like this:

```
put myFile(mGetPosition) into filePosition.
```

A companion command to the "mGetPosition" is the "mSetPosition" parameter. You could use this when you know exactly where the data you are looking for resides in the file. The command might look like this if for some reason you wanted to jump to character 374:

```
myFile(mSetPosition,374).
```

If you need to know how long the file is, you can use the "mGetLength" function. It would look like this:

```
myFile(mGetLength).
```

It returns the number of characters in the file.

We can also read from the file using the "mReadToken" command. We need to have two more parameters after the "mReadToken." The first is a string that contains any characters you want skipped, and the second is a string that contains any characters that should signal the end of the read. The Lingo line *put myFile(mReadToken, TAB&"/\", RETURN&"]") into text* will read from a file, skipping all tabs and forward and backward slashes, and stopping the first time it hits a Return or a right bracket.

One more important feature of file reading is the ability to prompt the user for the file to be read. We can do this by substituting a "?read" for the "read" when we open the file. The following handler reads a file specified by the user.

```
on readFile
  set myFile = fileIO(mNew, "?read", "TEXT")
  if not objectP(file) then return EMPTY
  put myFile(mReadFile) into fileText
  myFile(mDispose)
  return fileText
end
```

Not only do we use a "?read" parameter instead of a "read," but we must place the type of file we want to read in the next parameter. In this case, we use "TEXT," which corresponds to the Macintosh text type of file. If you are on a Windows machine, you should use "txt" to correspond to the three-letter file extension of the type of file you are looking for. You can use any Macintosh type or Windows extension.

When we prompt the user for a file to read, we may want to get not only the text in that file but also the name of the file the user selected. The command *myFile(mFileName)* will return this value.

One of the most common problems with reading text files is that Windows applications usually insist that every line end with two characters: a Return and a line feed. On the Macintosh platform, only a Return is needed. Director, originally a Mac-only application, sticks with the Return-only lines. This means that when you read a windows-formatted text file, odd little boxes that are the remnants of the line feeds infest your text. The following handler reads in a text file and gets rid of these pests.

```
on getFile filename
  set myFile = fileIO(mNew, "read", fileName)
  if not objectP(myFile) then return EMPTY
  put EMPTY into fullText
  repeat while TRUE
    put myFile(mReadLine) into fileText
    if fileText = EMPTY then exit repeat
    if char 1 of fileText = numtochar(10) then
      delete char 1 of fileText
    end if
    put fileText after fullText
  end repeat
  myFile(mDispose)
  return fullText
end
```

The new "getFile" handler will read in a file one line at a time. Since the Return character comes before the line feed character, Director thinks that the line feed is actually the first character of the next line. So we check each line to see if there is a line feed at the beginning. If there is, we delete it. Then we add that line to our growing "fullText" variable. When the "mReadLine" returns an EMPTY string, we know we have reached the end of the file.

We use the *numtochar* command here to get a text character from its character code number, sometimes called the ASCII code. In this case, the code 10 translates to the line feed character.

Writing Files

The fileIO Xobject also gives us the power to create and write to files. Using a "write" parameter with the *mNew* function, we can create a file or overwrite an existing file. The command would look like this:

```
set myFile = fileIO(mNew, "write", fileName).
```

To actually write out text to a file once it has been opened, we can use the *mWriteString* command. The full command goes like this:

```
myFile(mWriteString,myText).
```

We could also write to the file one character at a time with the *mWriteChar* command: *myFile(mWriteChar,myChar).*

Remember that in order to write to a file, we need to have opened it with a "write" not a "read." Here is a handler that writes out a file:

```
on writeFile fileName, myText
  set myFile = fileIO(mNew, "write", fileName)
  if not objectP(myFile) then return FALSE
  myFile(mWriteString,myText)
  myFile(mDispose)
  return TRUE
end
```

This handler returns TRUE if it was successful, and FALSE otherwise. Reasons why it could have failed are numerous: the disk could be write-protected or full, there could already be another file of the same name and that file is locked, or the filename may not be valid.

Just as with the "read" function, we can have the user decide the name of the file and where it goes. Using a "?write" instead of a "write" parameter will bring up the standard system dialog box for saving a file. The third parameter in the "mNew" function is the name you wish to suggest to the user for the file.

Here is a save handler that prompts the user for the filename and location.

```
on writeFile myText
  set myFile = fileIO(mNew, "?write", "myfile.txt")
  if not objectP(myFile) then return FALSE
  myFile(mWriteString,myText)
  myFile(mDispose)
  return TRUE
end
```

On the Macintosh, the file is automatically given the type "TEXT" and the creator "????" These are the properties that determine what type of icon the file is given on the desktop. You can use a command like *myFile(mSetFinderInfo, "TEXT", "ttxt")* to customize these settings. In that example, the "TEXT" and the "ttxt" will make it a Teach Text or Simple Text file type. There is also a command, *myFile(mGetFinderInfo)*, that will return this information if you need it.

Deleting Files

There is one last command in our fileIO arsenal: *mDelete*. This allows us to delete a file. Needless to say, you should be careful when using it. Here is a handler than deletes a file.

```
on deleteFile fileName
  set myFile = fileIO(mNew, "write", fileName)
  if not objectP(myFile) then return FALSE
  myFile(mDelete)
  return TRUE
end
```

Notice that we didn't use the *mDispose* command here. That function is done automatically when you use *mDelete*.

Error Codes

Most of the fileIO commands have the ability to return an error code if something goes wrong. The *mWriteChar*, *mWriteString*, *mSetPosition*, and *mDelete* commands will return a number if you call them as functions. For instance:

```
put myFile(mDelete) into errorCode
```

You can translate this error code into a real piece of text with the *mError* function of fileIO. This saves you the trouble of remembering which codes correspond to which error. Besides, these codes change with different operating systems. To use it, we have it call the fileIO Xobject directly and include the number of the error code.

```
alert fileIO(mError,errorCode)
```

TIP

Make sure you give the user options when a file command fails. For instance, when they are trying to save data and it fails because the disk is full, or a disk is locked, don't just throw away the data. Let the user try again after he or she has switched to the finder or file manager and corrected the problem.

Importing Pictures

Director's fileIO function also gives you the power to import PICT files. Although this is a Macintosh file format, even the Windows .dll has the capability. Many of the more advanced graphics programs on Windows can save PICT files (extension .PCT) nowadays.

Here is a handler that uses the *mReadPICT* function of fileIO. It takes the file and then sets *the picture* of an existing cast member to that of the newly opened PICT file.

```
on importPICT fileName, memberName
  set myFile = fileIO(mNew, "read", fileName)
  if not objectP(myFile) then exit
  put myFile(mReadPICT) into myPICT
  set the picture of member memberName = myPICT
  myFile(mDispose)
end
```

Command Summary

Pseudo-Command	Example	Description
mNew, "read"	set myFile = fileIO(mNew, "read", filename)	Opens the file *filename* for reading. Sets the variable "myFile" to point to that file.
mNew, "?read"	set myFile = fileIO(mNew, "?read", fileType)	Lets the user pick which file to read. Sets the variable "myFile" to point to that file.
mNew, "write"	set myFile = fileIO(mNew, "write", filename)	Creates or overwrites the file *filename*. Sets the variable "myFile" to point to that file.
mNew, "?write"	set myFile = fileIO(mNew, "?write", filename)	Lets the user pick which *file-name* to create or overwrite. Sets the variable "myFile" to point to that file.
mNew, "append"	set myFile = fileIO(mNew, "append", filename)	Opens the file *filename* to add to the end of it. Sets the variable "myFile" to point to that file.
mNew, "?append"	set myFile = fileIO(mNew, "?append", filename)	Lets the user pick a file. So you can add to the end of it. Sets the variable "myFile" to point to that file.
mReadChar	myFile(mReadChar)	Gets one character from a file.
mReadWord	myFile(mReadWord)	Gets one word from a file.
mReadLine	myFile(mReadLine)	Gets one line from a file.

Pseudo-Command	Example	Description
mReadFile	myFile(mReadFile)	Gets the entire contents of a file.
mReadToken	myFile(mReadToken, skipString, breakString)	Gets the contents of a file. Stops on skipString and skip breakString.
mWriteChar	myFile(mWriteChar,c)	Writes a single character, c, to a file.
mWriteString	myFile(mWriteString,s)	Writes a whole text string, s, to a file.
mGetPosition	put myFile(GetPosition) into pos	Gets the current position within the file you are reading.
mSetPosition	myFile(SetPosition,n)	Sets the current position within the file you are reading to character *n*.
mGetLength	put myFile(mGetLength) into len	Returns the lenh of the file.
mGetFinderInfo	put myFile(mGetFinderInfo)	Returns the Macintosh file type and creator of a file. Not available on Windows.
mSetFinderInfo	myFile(mSetFinderInfo, type,creator)	Sets the Macintosh file type and creator of a file. Not available on Windows.
mFileName	put myFile(mFileName) into name	Returns the name of the file.
mDelete	myFile(mDelete)	Deletes the file and disposes of the "myFile" pointer.
mDispose	myFile(mDispose)	Disposes of the pointer "myFile" and closes the file.
mError	fileIO(mError,code)	Translates a file error code to a definition.

Importing Databases

One of the features of advanced multimedia that's requested often is the ability to import small databases. Since most spreadsheet and database programs allow the user to export the data as a text file, we should be able to use our file functionality to import them into our movies.

Let's say we have a small database in a spreadsheet format. The first row in the spreadsheet has the column headings. The leftmost column in the spreadsheet has the row names. The database could look something like this:

	Apples	Oranges	Bananas
Store 1	300	500	100
Store 2	200	200	50
Store 3	600	800	500
Warehouse 1	1000	1400	500
Warehouse 2	800	1200	400

Using the database program's ability to export the data as a text file, we save it as a comma-separated variable text file, or CSV file. This means that every row is on a line, and every column is separated by a comma. It would look like this:

```
, Apples, Oranges, Bananas
Store 1, 300, 500, 100
Store 2, 200, 200, 50
Store 3, 600, 800, 500
Warehouse 1, 1000, 1400, 500
Warehouse 2, 800, 1200, 400
```

We could also save it as straight text, which usually means that tab characters, not commas, separate the columns.

Once it is in this format, we can use these handlers to import the database into a Lingo list.

```
on importDatabase fileName
  put "," into columnSep
  put RETURN into rowSep

  -- get text file
  put readFile(fileName) into text
  if text = EMPTY then
    alert "Unable to read database."
    return FALSE
  end if

  -- get the column headings
  put [] into headingList
  set the itemDelimiter = columnSep
  put line 1 of text into colHead
  repeat with i = 2 to the number of items in colHead
    setAt(headingList,i-1,item i of colHead)
  end repeat
  put count(headingList) into numCols

  -- build list
   set list = [:]
   repeat with i = 2 to the number of lines→
   in text
     put item 1 of line i of text into rowName
set tempList = [:]
repeat with j = 2 to numCols+1
      setAProp(tempList,getAt(headingList,→
j-1),item j of line i of text)
   end repeat
   addProp(list,rowName,tempList)
  end repeat
return list
end

on readFile fileName
  set file = fileIO(mNew,"read",fileName)
  if not objectP(file) then return EMPTY
  put EMPTY into text
  repeat while TRUE
```

```
      put file(mReadLine) into textLine
      if textLine = EMPTY then exit repeat
      if char 1 of textLine = numtochar(10) then
        delete char 1 of textLine
      end if
      put textLine after text
    end repeat
    file(mDispose)
    return text
  end
```

The "importDatabase" handler calls the "readFile" handler to get the text file and put it into the variable "text." Notice that the "readFile" handler will strip out line feed characters that may be caused by a Windows or DOS formatted file.

Once the file has been placed in the field "text," we take the first line and process it as the line that holds the column headings. We skip the first item there and record all the others in a list called "headingList."

Then we count the number of items in this "headingList" to see how many columns we can expect from the rest of the database.

The main loop of the handler goes through the rest of the lines of the text. It takes the first item in each line and uses it as the property; the rest of the line is the data list for that row. Each item in the row then gets assigned a property from the "headingList" and places it in "tempList." This "tempList" then gets added to the overall "list" variable, which will eventually contain all the data.

Notice that we have to initialize each property list with a [:]. If we initalized it with just a [], then Director would think we wanted a linear list and not allow us to add properties.

The handler also initializes two important variables at the top. The "columnSep" and the "rowSep" are used to determine what divides columns and rows in the text file. It is very possible, for instance, that you would want columns to be separated by tabs rather than commas. It all depends on how the file was created.

When these handlers are used on our example above, the result is a list that looks like this:

```
-- ["Store 1": ["Apples": "300", "Oranges": "500", "Bananas":
"100"], "Store 2": ["Apples": "200", "Oranges": "200",→
"Bananas": "50"], "Store 3": ["Apples": "600", "Oranges":
"800", "Bananas": "500"], "Warehouse 1": ["Apples": "1000",→
"Oranges": "1400", "Bananas": "500"], "Warehouse 2":
["Apples": "800", "Oranges": "1200", "Bananas": "400"]]
```

The numbers stored in the list are treated as strings. We could have fixed this in the "importText" handler by converting each value to a real number by using the *value* or *integer* functions. However, it may be dangerous to assume that the values are going to be numbers in all cases. You can always convert the text to numbers later, in the handlers that use the data.

We can use simple list functions to get the data now that it is in the list. For instance, we can find out how many oranges are in store 2 with the command *integer(getProp(getProp(list,"Store 2"),"Oranges"))*.

Moving On

Using this technique, you can import a wide range of data into your movies. For instance, if you are presenting a quiz, the actual questions and correct answers can be read in from a database. This database can be made by someone who doesn't know the first thing about Director or Lingo. They just use a spreadsheet or something to create the text file, and your Lingo program reads it in when it is run.

Next, we will begin to explore Lingo control of the user interface: menus, cursors, and timeouts.

17

The User Interface: Menu Bars, Cursors & Timeouts

Director projectors and movies typically don't look like real computer applications. The stage, for one, is either a big block in the middle of the screen, or it encompasses the whole screen. Other applications usually appear in one or more windows and have a standard feature of Macintosh and Windows programs—the menu bar.

We'll deal with the stage versus in-a-window issue later. Right now, let's look at how to add menu bars to our Director movies.

Menu Bars

We create a menu bar by making a text field cast member that describes what the bar should look like. This description must follow a rigid format. Here is an example:

```
menu: File
Open.../O|myOpenHandler()
(-
Quit/Q|quit
menu: Edit
```

```
Copy/C(|myCopyHandler()
Paste/P(|myPasteHandler()
menu: Navigation
Main Menu/0|go to frame "menu"
Chapter 1/1|go to frame "ch1"
Chapter 2/2|go to frame "ch2"
Chapter 3/3|go to frame "ch3"
```

Each individual menu starts with the word *menu:*, followed by the name of the menu. This can be one or several words in length.

The next line contains the first menu item. It starts with the name of the menu item. Next comes a slash and the shortcut key for that item. If you don't want a shortcut key, just leave the slash out.

Then comes the vertical bar, or "or" symbol. This can usually be found above the backslash on most keyboards. After this symbol comes the Lingo code that will be executed when this item is selected.

The next lines follow the same format until all the menu items of that menu have been included. You can then end the field or start the next menu.

The above field describes a three-menu menu bar: File, Edit, and Navigation. The File menu has two items: Open and Quit. Between these two items is a line, signified by the (–. The Open menu item has an "O" as its shortcut key, and the Quit has a "Q" as its shortcut key. When a user selects Open, the handler "myOpenHandler" will run. When the user selects Quit, the Lingo command *quit* will execute. Figure 17-1 shows this menu in action.

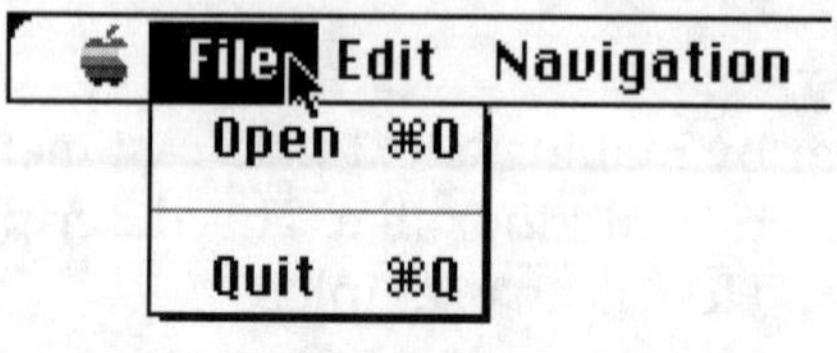

Figure 17-1: *Our custom menu bar.*

Each menu item in the field can also have various symbols that modify that item. The second menu has two items: Copy and Paste. These items are modified by the symbol (. This means that they will appear in the menu as inactive—or grayed-out. We will look at other symbols later.

Once the menu field has been created, it is easy to activate the menu. The *installMenu* command will take a menu field and use it. In order for it to work, the movie must be playing. Here is an example:

```
installMenu 4
```

The number is the number of the cast member that contains the menu field. If you wish to clear away the menu bar, just use the number 0.

If the *installMenu* command doesn't seem to work, your first suspect is the menu field. Make sure that it follows the proper format perfectly.

TIP *Always keep the File and Edit menus as the first and second in your custom menu. Even if none of the functions of the Edit menu are used by your movie, it is accepted interface design practice to keep it there. Just gray out all the menu items.*

Controlling the Menu Bar

Once a menu has been created, there are a bunch of Lingo commands that can be used to modify it. The function *the name of menu* will return the name of any menu, specified by its number. For instance, *the name of menu 1*, will return "File" if used after our example menu has been installed.

This function is good for determining if an *installMenu* command has actually worked. For instance, you could compare *the name of menu 3* to "Navigation." Since Navigation is not typically the name of the third menu item, we can determine whether it is our menu up there or not.

In addition, you can find out the name of any menu item in a menu. The function *the name of menuItem 3 of menu 1* will return "Quit" according to our example. We can also say *the name of menuItem 3 of menu "file."* Item 2 is the line that divides "Open…" and "Quit."

While *the name of menu* cannot be set in Lingo, we do have the power to set *the name of menuItem*. We would just create a piece of code like *set the name of menuItem 3 of menu "file" = "exit."*

A good utility function when dealing with menu items is *the number of menuItems of menu* function. It will return the total number of menu items currently in a menu. For example: *put the number of menuItems of menu "navigation."*

An important part of menu bar functionality is that a menu bar item may be disabled when its function is not currently possible. For instance, if text is not selected, you may want to disable the Copy menu item.

We can do this using *the enabled of menuItem*. For example, to disable the Copy menu item, we would use the command *set the enabled of menuItem "Copy" of menu "Edit" = FALSE*. We could enable the menu item by setting its enabled property to *TRUE*.

We can do the same with the checkmarks that sometimes appear next to a menu item. We can make these appear and disappear with *the checkMark of menuItem*. To place a checkmark next to an item, use a command like this: *set the checkMark of menuItem "Chapter 1" of menu "Navigation" = TRUE*.

Checkmarks can be used for a variety of purposes. In the above example, we use checkmarks to signify what chapters the user has already been to by placing a checkmark next to them in the menu.

We could also use a checkmark to signify a toggle switch. For instance, a menu item named Sound could have a checkmark next to it when sound is on, and none when sound is off. Logically, choosing this menu item would toggle the sound property. Checkmarks can be used to signify the on or off state of a whole menu list of options in your movie.

The last Lingo command that deals with menus is *the script of menuItem*. This will allow us to get and set the Lingo command that has been assigned to a menu item. We could use this to change what an item is supposed to do. For instance: *set the script of menuItem "Paste" of menu "Edit" = "otherPasteHandler()."*

There are also more options that you can assign to each menu item at the time you create the menu. They are symbols like the (symbol that disables an item.

The symbol ! places a single character next to the item. For instance, to get a checkmark next to an item, use Option-V on the Macintosh. Here are some examples:

```
Chapter 1!Ã|go to frame "one"
Chapter 2!*|go to frame "two"
Chapter 3!?|go to frame "three"
```

Using a < followed by a B, I, U, O, or S will give the name of the menu item a text style: bold, italic, underline, outline, and shadow. Some of these, outline and shadow, are not available in Windows.

Remember that there are two different ways to alter your menus. The first happens when you initially create the menu, and the second is by using the Lingo commands described above.

On Macintoshes, use the @ symbol in your menu description to signify that you want Director to include the standard Mac apple menu from the system. Put this menu first, just like it appears normally.

Here is a complete list of the Lingo menu commands:

Command	Example	Description
installMenu	installMenu the number of member "myMenu"	Creates the menu bar based on the menu bar's description in a field.
the name of menu	put the name of menu 3	Gets the name of the third menu.
the name of of menuItem	set the name of menuItem 4 of menu "File"	Gets or sets the name an item in a menu.
the number of menuItems	put the number of menuItems of menu "File"	Gets the number of items in a menu.
the enabled of menuItem	set the enabled of menuItem "Close" of menu "File"	Grays out a menu item when set to FALSE.

Command	Example	Description
the checkmark of menuItem	set the checkmark of menuItem "Chapter 1" of menu "Navigation" = TRUE	Gets or sets the check-mark next to an item.
the script of menuItem	set the script of menuItem "Restart" of menu "Navigation" = "go to frame 1"	Gets or sets the Lingo command associated with a menu item.

Menu Bar Oddities

There are some strange things about how the menu bar in Director movies works. On the surface, it seems to work fine, but with repeated usage the system is less than perfect.

First of all, the menu disappears completely when you *play* or *go to* another movie. This means that when you have a multiple-movie product, you have to re-create the menu bar every time you change movies.

This is harder than it sounds. Since you need to have the menu stored in a field cast member, you cannot just have that field in the internal cast of one movie. You need to have it either in every movie or in a shared cast file.

Even if you are able to get access to the same field in every movie, and you manage to remember to re-create the menu with each movie switch, there will still be the appearance of a menu bar "flash" to the user as it is re-created.

Developers have reported many problems with custom menus. In both Director 4 and Director 5, using the *installMenu* command many times will cause the menu items to cease functioning properly on Windows machines.

Custom Cursors

The primary tool you use to manipulate your movies is the cursor. Typically an arrow pointing up and to the left, the cursor can at times become other icons. We know, for instance, that when a program is asking us to wait, the cursor changes to a watch or an hourglass icon.

We can change the cursor to any of a small variety of icons with the *cursor* command. We can also use this command to change the cursor to our own custom icons.

One way to use the *cursor* command is to feed it a number that corresponds to a standard cursor. Cursor number 4, for instance, is the watch cursor on a Macintosh and the hourglass cursor on a Windows machine. The command would look like this:

```
cursor 4
```

To get the cursor back to normal, use the command *cursor 0*.

Figure 17-2 shows a short list of the standard cursors available on the Macintosh. The Windows set is basically the same, but the watch cursor is the Windows standard hourglass cursor instead.

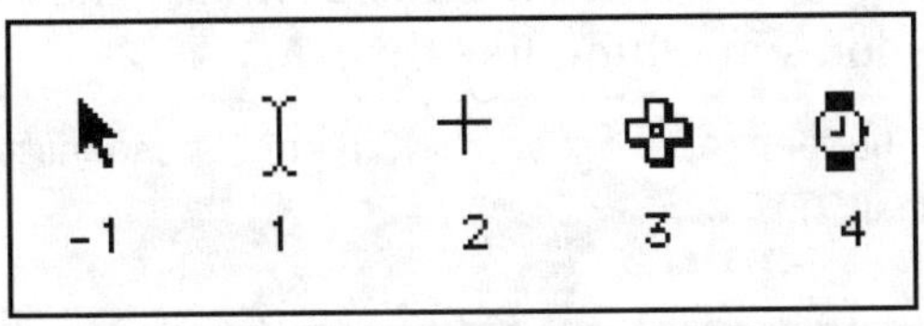

Figure 17-2: *A list of possible cursors.*

These standard cursors are stored in the Director application or the Projector. They are called *resources*. On the Macintosh, it is easy to import new cursor resources using a program like ResEdit. However, we don't need to do that since we can use cast members as cursors.

To make a custom cursor, draw it or import it into a bitmap cast member. Ideally, the bitmap should be 16 pixels across and down. If it is larger, Director will crop it. The cast member must be set to 1-bit or black and white only. Figure 17-3 shows an example of a custom cursor.

Figure 17-3: *A custom hand cursor.*

Once you have a cast member ready, name it "myCursor." You can change its cursor by using the cursor command this way:

```
cursor [the number of member "myCursor"]
```

The cursor will display the black pixels of our bitmap as black, and the other pixels will act as if they are transparent. We can create a *mask* for this cursor so that some of the pixels appear as white. Think of a mask as a small white layer over the screen. The black pixels in a mask bitmap will appear white. Then, the black pixels in the cursor bitmap lay over that. Figure 17-4 shows an example.

Figure 17-4: *An example of a cursor and mask bitmap.*

To use both the mask and the cursor bitmap, the Lingo command should look something like this:

```
cursor [the number of member "myCursor", the number of member
"myCursor mask"]
```

TIP

When you use a custom cursor, the hot spot *for the cursor is the same as the bitmap's registration point.*

Another thing we can do with the cursor command is turn the cursor off completely. For some reason, this is cursor number 200. The command *cursor 200* will make the cursor disappear. Use *cursor 0* to get it back.

Like the menu controls in Lingo, the cursor controls are less than perfect. If another system process wants to take control of the cursor while you are using it in your program, it will.

What's worse is that Director will have no idea that the cursor has changed. Even if you suspect it has changed, trying to set it immediately back to the original cursor will not work. Instead, you need to set the cursor to something else entirely, say, cursor 200, and then back to what you really wanted.

Another Lingo cursor command is *the cursor of sprite*. Once you execute this command, it sets up the movie so that whenever the cursor is over a particular sprite, it changes to a predesignated icon. It would look like this:

```
set the cursor of sprite 7 = [the number of member
"myCursor", the number of member "myCursor mask"]
```

You could also use one of the standard cursor numbers instead of your own custom cursor.

However, there are many flaws to *the cursor of sprite*. First, it changes the cursor based on the rectangle of the sprite, even if the sprite contains a nonrectangular item, such as an oval or a shaped bitmap.

Furthermore, *the cursor of sprite* remains in effect even after we alter the sprite by puppeting it. This can cause the cursor to change based on a "ghost" of the sprite.

We can do much better than this Lingo command. Here is a handler that changes the cursor based on the cast member found under it.

```
on exitFrame
  put the mouseCast into mNum
  if mNum > 0 then
    put the name of cast mNum into mName
    case mName of
      "button1":
        put 3 into newCursor
      "button7":
        put [the number of cast "myCursor"]→
```

```
into newCursor
        otherwise
            put 0 into newCursor
      end case
      cursor newCursor
    end if
end
```

This handler uses *the mouseCast* to figure out which cast member is currently under the cursor. If the sprites are set to ink "Matte," then the cursor will actually change only when it is over the shape of the cast member on the stage, not its rectangle box.

We could make a similar handler using *rollover*, but it would still refer to the rectangle of the sprite, not specifically to the cast shape.

Animated Cursor

By turning off the cursor with the *cursor(200)* command, and using a sprite in its place, we can have cursors that are any size and in full color. We can go one step further and animate these cursors, changing them among a series of bitmaps.

```
on exitFrame
  put 48 into cursorSprite
  put 6 into firstCursorMember
  put 12 into lastCursorMember
  cursor(200)
  puppetSprite cursorSprite, TRUE
  put the memberNum of sprite cursorSprite into cnum
  put cnum +  1 into cnum
  if cnum > lastCursorMember then
    put firstCursorMember into cnum
  end if
  set the memberNum of sprite cursorSprite = cnum
  set the locH of sprite cursorSprite = the mouseH
  set the locV of sprite cursorSprite = the mouseV
end
```

This frame script will take sprite number 48 and loop it through cast members 6 to 12. You could place a rotating globe in these members, a pulsating arrow, a flaming ball, or whatever you like.

Detecting Inaction

Director is a very popular tool for creating multimedia kiosks. Lingo can add some important functionality to these products, such as the ability to go back to start screens and attract loops when a user has walked away from the kiosk. Attract loops are those sometimes interesting, sometimes annoying animations that attempt to lure people at trade shows to walk up to kiosks and play with them.

There are many Lingo commands that allow you to do this. They can be divided into two sets. The first set includes *lastClick*, *lastRoll*, *lastKey*, and *lastEvent*.

These functions will return the time, in ticks, since the last mouse click, mouse movement, and key press. *The lastEvent* will give the time since the most recent of these events.

These commands can be used in a frame script like this:

```
on exitFrame
  if the lastEvent > (2*60*60) then go to frame "Start"
  else go to the frame
end
```

This frame script will continue to test the amount of time that has elapsed since the last user-generated event. If no one has touched the computer in two minutes (2 minutes * 60 seconds per minute * 60 ticks per second), it jumps to the frame labeled "Start."

If you need to reset the time elapsed function without any user input, you can use the *startTimer* command. This command not only resets *the timer* function in Director, as we had used it earlier, but it also resets the *lastClick*, *lastRoll*, *lastKey*, and *lastEvent* commands. This is useful for kiosk-type applications where the user generates no events for several minutes while watching a Director movie.

This type of script will only work on the frame that it has been assigned to. This way you can specify the areas that respond to inaction. You could also put the script in a movie script cast member that will be active throughout the movie.

The second set of Lingo elements that deal with inaction start with *on timeOut*. This is a handler that is called, if it exists, when no user action has taken place for three minutes. It needs to be placed in a movie script. Here's an example:

```
on timeOut
  go to frame "Start"
end
```

This is different than our last script because it stays in effect as long as the handler is available, not just on the frame we specify. So it typically works over the life of the whole movie.

We can set the amount of time before the *on timeOut* handler kicks off by using *the timeOutLength*. This takes a number in ticks.

```
set the timeOutLength = 5*60*60
```

Now there will need to be five minutes of inaction before the "timeout" message is sent and the *on timeOut* handler runs. We can also change the handler that gets executed from the *on timeOut* handler to our own custom script. We just need to set *the timeOutScript* property to our own Lingo command.

```
set the timeOutScript = "myHandler()"
set the timeOutScript = "go to frame 1"
```

Director will actually call both of your Lingo handlers, set with *the timeOutScript*, and the *on timeOut* handler, if they are both present. It will run the *on timeOut* last.

TIP

If you need to set a variable to a Lingo command that includes quotes , use the QUOTE Lingo function set the timeOutScript = "go to frame"&&QUOTE&"Start"&QUOTE.

There are a few Lingo properties that alter the timeout functionality. Setting *the timeOutMouse* determines whether or not mouse clicks will reset the timer. Setting *the timeOutPlay* determines whether playing a new movie will reset the timer.

We can also get the current value of the timer with *the timer* function. When a "timeOut" message is sent because *the timer* has reached *the timeOutLength*, the timer is not reset. However, we can get the time that has passed since the last "timeOut" message with *the timeOutLapsed* function.

Here is a standard set of movie script handlers that demonstrate timeout functionality.

```
on startMovie
  set the timeOutLength = 10*60 -- 10 secs
  set the timeOutScript = "myTimeOut"
end

on myTimeOut
  alert "My timeOut handler"
end

on timeOut
  alert "Standard timeOut handler"
end
```

There is usually no reason to have both your own custom handler and *the timeOut* handler in the same movie. You could, however, use *the timeOutScript* property to switch around which handler gets called depending on the movie's state.

You can test what is actually happening with these timeouts by creating two fields and placing them on the stage: "timer" and "timeout."

```
on exitFrame
  put the timer into field "timer"
  put the timeOutLength into field "timeOut"
  go to the frame
end
```

This handler will place the current value of *the timer* into one field and the value of *the timeOutLength* into another. When you run this movie, you will see that *the timer* does not reset when you click the mouse, or when a timeout occurs. However, *the timeOutLength* does.

Your custom handler and the *on timeOut* handler will be called again and again every time *the timeOutLength* ticks, as long as there is no user action. There are several ways to prevent multiple timeouts: use *startTimer*, change *the timeOutLength*, change *the timeOutScript*, or check the frame in your handler so that it doesn't function during the attract loop.

In many ways, *the lastEvent* is a better way to go as long as you are willing to do some extra coding. One advantage is that it takes into account mouse movement, not just clicks and key presses. It also allows you to selectively place the scripting that activates it only in frames where you want it.

Moving On

Menus, cursors, and timeouts go a long way toward turning "amateur" multimedia projects into real CD-ROM and kiosk products. Getting good at using them is the key to creating professional, finished multimedia.

Now lets get back to using Lingo for some cool animation effects.

18

Drawing With Trails

The sprite and cast member model of multimedia authoring seems to leave out the possibility of on-the-fly creation of graphics by the user. All the bitmaps must be present in the internal or an external cast library, and of course the paint window is not available in a projector.

Actually, there is no way, short of importing a picture from a file, to change the graphics in a movie once the product authoring has been completed.

We can, however, allow the user to draw directly on the stage. We do this by turning on the trails property of a sprite. Figure 18-1 shows how to do this in the score.

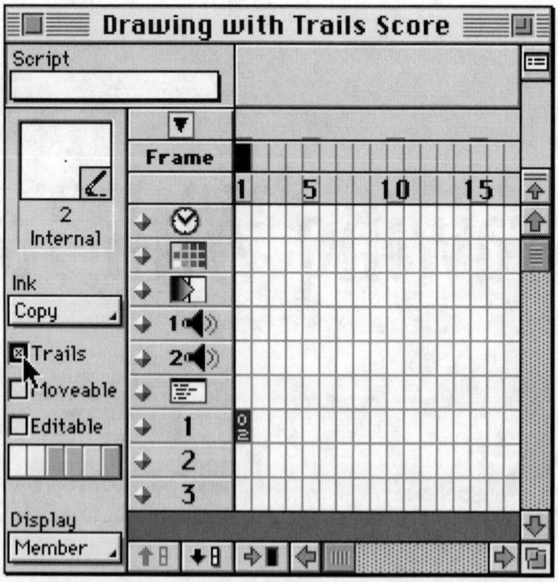

Figure 18-1: *Check the Trails box after selecting a sprite in the score to turn this property on.*

You can also check the Moveable and Editable check boxes of this sprite to test out both of these properties. Put a small bitmap in the sprite and a simple *go to the frame* script in the script channel, and see how you can drag the sprite around and draw with it. Figure 18-2 shows what you might see.

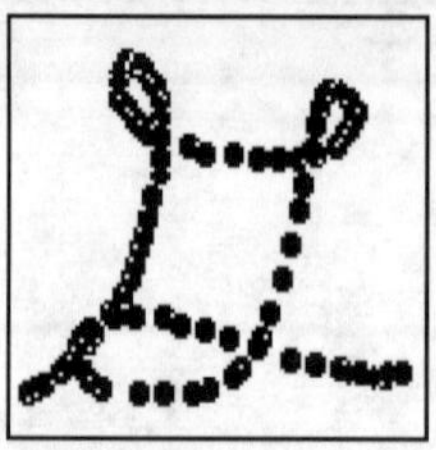

Figure 18-2: *Drawing using trails.*

We can also use Lingo to control the sprite that is leaving the trails. Using *the locH of sprite* and *the locV of sprite* commands, we can change the position of the sprite. We can even turn on and off trails using *the trails of sprite* command.

Make a cast member that is a bitmap of a single black pixel. Set this cast member to 1-bit by using the "Transform Bitmap" menu item, and place it in sprite channel 1. A simple handler that draws a diagonal line with this bitmap would look like this:

```
on drawLine
  set the trails of sprite 1 = TRUE
  repeat with i = 1 to 300
    set the locH of sprite 1 = i
    set the locV of sprite 1 = i

    updateStage
  end repeat
end
```

By setting *the trails of sprite 1,* we enable this sprite to draw on the stage. Then we just change its location during the loop to show it where to draw. The real drawing happens with the *updateStage* command. Since we are doing all the drawing inside the handler's loop, we don't need to puppetSprite anything.

The problem with trails is that they are not permanent. All you need to do is pass another sprite or window in front of them and they disappear. This is simply a way to put temporary information on the stage—like a chalkboard or whiteboard.

TIP

Inks and blends don't work with the graphics left on the stage using trails, since the trail is just an artifact and not really seen by Director.

You can even place text information on the stage with trails. Place a field named "text" into sprite 1 and try this script. Figure 18-3 shows the result.

```
on drawText
  put "This is a test of text with trails" into text
  put text into field "text"
  set the trails of sprite 1 = TRUE
  put the number of words in text into n --how many→
words in text?
```

```
  repeat with i = 1 to n
    set the locV of sprite 1 = 100+i*20
    set the locH of sprite 1 = 100+i*20
    updateStage
  end repeat
end
```

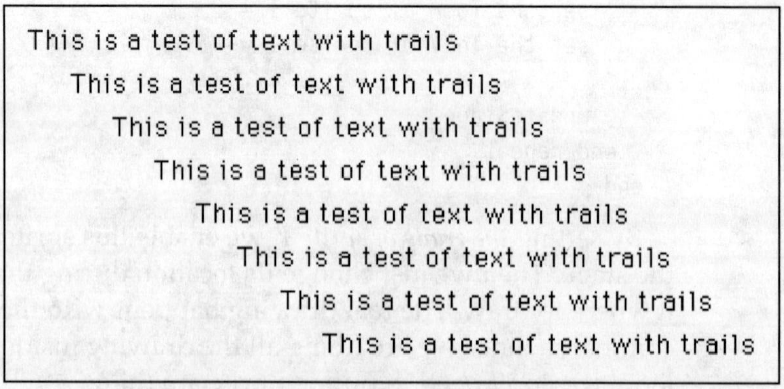

Figure 18-3: *Using trails with text.*

This test should place the same line of text on the stage several times. Ideally, we should be able to place different pieces of text on the screen and save some sprite usage. Here is an example:

```
on drawText
  put "This is a test of trails" into text
  set the trails of sprite 1 = TRUE
  put the number of words in text into n
  repeat with i = 1 to n
    put word i of text into field "text"
    set the locH of sprite 1 = 100+i*20
    set the locV of sprite 1 = 100+i*20
    updateStage
  end repeat
end
```

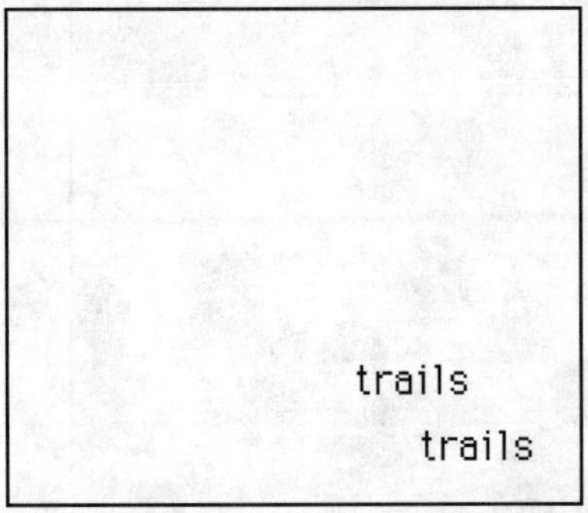

Figure 18-4: *Using trails with text doesn't always work.*

Figure 18-4 shows the result of this example on a typical Macintosh version of Director. This test should write the sentence in a diagonal line across the screen. Does it work? No. Why? That's unclear. Director seems not to handle cases like this correctly. You will need to experiment with drawing text using trails to see if you can perform the tasks you need. Don't rely on it until you have tested your technique and have seen it work.

We can, however, use our arsenal of special effects like colors, inks, and blends. When you leave a trail behind, it is a copy of the original appearance of the sprite. So, by changing the color of a 1-bit bitmap or simple shape as you leave its trails, you can create some pretty neat effects.

This next script will create a random pattern of colored objects. Place a Director circle in sprite 1, set its trails property to TRUE, and use the following frame script. Figure 18-5 shows one possible result.

```
on exitFrame
  set the locH of sprite 1 = random(640)
  set the locV of sprite 1 = random(480)
  set the forecolor of sprite 1 = random(255)
  go to the frame
end
```

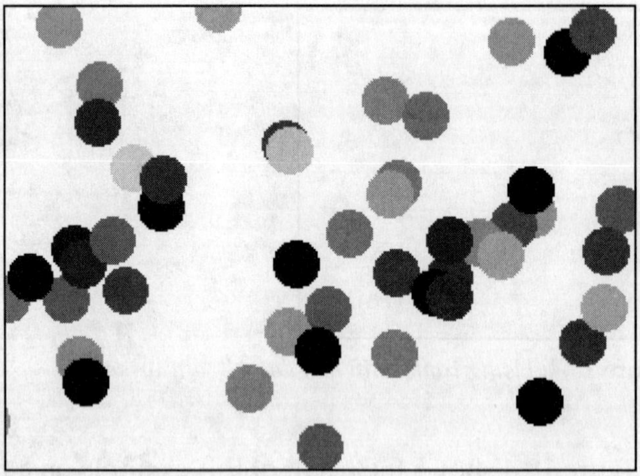

Figure 18-5: *One possible outcome of our script using colors and trails.*

TIP

Using colors works best with 1-bit bitmaps because you can reliably set the forecolor and backcolor. Higher-depth graphics don't work on the same principle.

Using the blend function works the same way. With the same circle, set its ink to Matte and run this movie script by typing its name in the message window. Figure 18-6 shows the result.

```
on drawNeat
  set the trails of sprite 1 = TRUE
  repeat with i = 0 to 100
     set the locH of sprite 1 = 100+i
    set the locV of sprite 1 = 100+i
    set the blend of sprite 1 = i
    updateStage
  end repeat
end
```

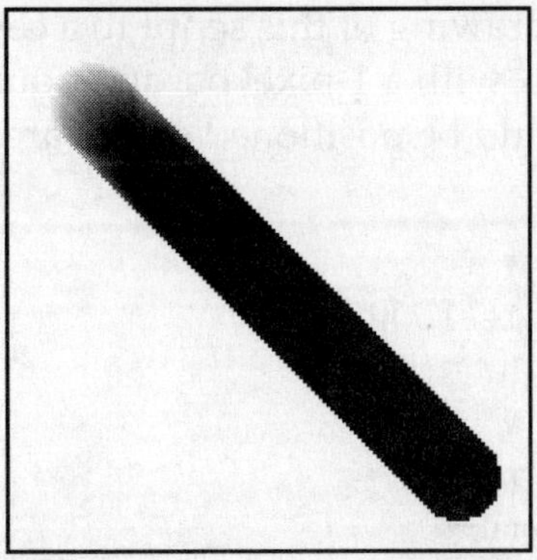

Figure 18-6: *Using blend values with trails.*

We can give control of the sprite being drawn back to the user, just like the effect of having the Trails setting and the Moveable setting turned on for a sprite. The handler we would need to do this would be basically the same as that of our user-controlled sprite scripts from the "Beginner's Workbook" section.

First we need a script to initalize the sprite. We'll put this in an *on startMovie* handler for our example, but you can make it your own custom handler and call it some other time.

```
on startMovie
  puppetSprite 10, TRUE
  set the trails of sprite 10 = TRUE
  cursor(200) - turn off cursor
end
```

Then we will use an *on exitFrame* handler in the frame to control the movement of our sprite. Place a 1-bit bitmap of a dot in sprite channel 1.

```
on exitFrame
  set the locH of sprite 10 = the mouseH
  set the locV of sprite 10 = the mouseV
end
```

This simple script will just make the first sprite follow the location of the cursor. Since the trails property of that sprite is on, it will draw wherever the user moves.

We can constrain the drawing of this script to a certain area pretty easily. Create a box with a 1-pixel border around it and place it in sprite 1. It should be positioned on the area where you want the user to draw.

```
on exitFrame
  put the rect of sprite 1 into r
  put the mouseH into h
  put the mouseV into v
  if (h > the left of r) and→
(h < the right of r) and→
(v > the top of r) and
(v < the bottom of r) then
    cursor(200)
    set the locH of sprite 10 = h
    set the locV of sprite 10 = v
  else
    set the locH of sprite 10 = -1
    set the locV of sprite 10 = -1
    cursor(0)
  end if
  go to the frame
end
```

Now we have a handler that only draws in the area that we specify. When the user moves out of the box, the cursor reappears and the drawing sprite moves harmlessly off the corner of the stage.

The reason we used that long *if...then* statement instead of an *intersects* function you might be familiar with is that the *intersects* function only registers *after* the sprite has appeared on the stage in the current location. We would constantly draw a little out of the box.

The next step would be to combine the ability to give the user control of the sprite and the ability to control the color of the sprite. Place three colored circles on the stage outside of our drawing box. Use the Director Tools palette to make these circles different colors: red, green, and blue. Place this handler in a script and assign it to the three circles:

```
on mouseDown
  set the foreColor of sprite 10 = the foreColor of sprite→
the clickOn
end
```

Now, when a user leaves the drawing area, goes to one of the circles, and clicks it, the color of the drawing sprite changes to be the color of the circle.

You can go on to create other painting tools for a little mini-paint program. For instance, you could have a bunch of different brushes by having various sprites outside of the drawing box. When the user clicks on one of these sprites, it changes *the memberNum of sprite* of our drawing sprite to be equal to the sprite that was clicked.

Moving On

The main disadvantage of trails is that they cannot be saved in any way. At least not without an Xobject to help. They do, however, provide an extra level of interactivity that has many uses.

Next, lets take a look at the powerful mathematics functions that are a part of Lingo.

19

Lingo & Math

There are a whole bunch of standard mathematical functions built into Lingo. Understanding them is the key to creating handlers that do anything from simple drawings to advanced animation.

Types of Numbers

Let's start by looking at how Lingo deals with numbers. There are two types of numbers in Lingo: integers and floating-point numbers.

Integers are nonfractional numbers, both positive and negative. For example: 3, 7, 42, 59364, 0, –3, –8762. We use these numbers mostly to count objects or determine screen positions.

Floating-point numbers can be anything: integers or decimal numbers. For example: 3, 3.5, 0.4, 0.00003, 7.87, 76389.29, 0, –0.3, –7334.3. We will use these numbers to compute complex math functions and figure out percentages.

Unfortunately, Lingo does not automatically convert between integers and floating-point numbers. For instance, if you try to divide two integers, the result will be an integer. This means that 4/3 will equal 1.

```
put 4/3
-- 1
```

In order to get the correct result, we need to divide two floating-point numbers, or at least start off with a floating-point number.

```
put 4.0/3
-- 1.3333
```

You could also use the *float* command to convert an integer to a floating-point number. You will notice that Lingo likes to place a ".0" after a floating-point number that has no decimal component.

```
put float(4)
-- 4.0
put float(4)/3
-- 1.3333
```

The companion to the *float* function is the *integer* function. This will convert a floating-point number to an integer, rounding in the process.

Fortunately, Lingo will allow you to compare integers and floating-point numbers. Try this out:

```
put 4.0 = 4
-- 1
put float(4) = 4
-- 1
put 4.000001 = 4
-- 0
```

Number Limits

Both integers and floating-point numbers have their limits. The largest integer you can use is 2147483647. If you try to add one to this number, this is what you get:

```
put 2147483647+1
-- -2147483648
```

You also have the same limits on the other side of zero. Lingo does give you one more negative integer, but it doesn't work in math functions.

```
put -2147483647-1
-- -2147483648
put -2147483647-2
-- 2147483647
```

There is a Lingo function, *maxInteger()* that will return 2147483647 so you don't have to remember that number.

```
put the maxInteger
-- 2147483647
```

Unfortunately, Lingo has no way of telling us when a math operation has caused it to return a bad number because of this limit. Other programming languages have an overflow flag that signals us when this happens. We'll just have to make sure we stay far away from the upper and lower limits of integers.

Floating-point numbers can go much higher and lower than integers. However, they sacrifice accuracy as they grow.

```
put 100000000000000000.0+27
-- 100000000000000032.0
```

Precision corresponds to the number of decimal places a number is given. The default in Lingo is 4. You can set the precision of all floating-point numbers with the Lingo command *the floatPrecision*.

```
set the floatPrecision to 4
put 47.0123456789
-- 47.0123
set the floatPrecision to 6
put 47.0123456789
-- 47.012346
```

Notice how the last number was rounded up by Director because it only had size decimal places to work with.

Lingo will automatically convert integers that exceed the maxInteger range to floating-point numbers. This conversion does not happen in calculations, but it does happen when you just give a number.

```
put 2147483648
-- 2147483648.0
put -2147483648
-- -2147483648.0
```

Simple Math

We have already used simple math in many of our scripts. The basic math functions—addition, subtraction, multiplication, and division—work for both integers and floating-point numbers.

```
put 3+4
-- 7
put 3-4
-- -1
put 3*4
-- 12
put 20/4
-- 5
```

Order of precedence is the math term for determining which simple math operations happen first. Lingo follows the accepted standards of performing all multiplication and division before doing addition and subtraction.

```
put 3+4*9
-- 39
```

The result is 39 because Lingo multiplies the 4 and the 9 together before adding them to 3. We can override the order of precedence by using parentheses.

```
put (3+4)*9
-- 63
```

You can nest parentheses in just about as many levels as you wish.

Functions

The following is a collection of math Lingo functions. They are pretty standard functions found in most programming languages. They can be used for everything from business applications to drawing graphics.

Absolute Value

There will be times when you need to throw away the positive or negative aspect of a number. Without a positive or negative aspect, you have what is known as the *absolute value* of the number. The *abs* function in Lingo will return this value.

```
put abs(7)
-- 7
put abs(-7)
-- 7
```

Square Root

The square root is a function found on even basic calculators. In Lingo, the *sqrt* function takes care of this for us. However, you need to pass it a floating-point number if you expect a floating-point number in return.

```
put sqrt(16)
-- 4
put sqrt(7)
-- 3
put sqrt(7.0)
-- 2.6458
```

Power

We can figure out squares, cubes, and numbers to any power by using the *power* function. We can even use this function to determine powers less than 1 as well.

```
put power(7,2)
-- 49.0
put power(7,.5)
-- 2.6458
```

We can also determine powers with negative exponents:

```
put power(7,-2)
-- 0.0204
put power(7,-.5)
-- 0.3780
```

Trigonometry

Trigonometric functions in Lingo include sine, cosine, tangent and arctangent. These functions all relate to the ratios between the angles and the lengths of the sides of triangles. We will mostly be using these to help us with graphics and animations where circles or circular motion are needed. We'll leave the explanation of trigonometry to the math text books.

pi

Pi is a useful number for graphics and animation. Since all of our trigonometric functions expect parameters of radians, not degrees, having pi readily available is necessary to using these functions.

Understanding radians is easy. In a circle, there are 360 degrees. If we use radians instead of degrees, we get about 6.28 radians around a circle. This is pi, times two. So 180 degrees is equal to 3.14 radians, or pi.

The Lingo function *pi()* will return the number to as many decimal places as *the floatPrecision* is set to.

```
put pi()
-- 3.1416
```

sine, cosine, tangent

These three functions are all represented in Lingo, and each accepts radians as its parameter. Figures 19-1 to 19-3 show the simple graphs of the three functions y=sin(x), y=cos(x), and y=tan(x) for reference.

```
put sin(pi()/4)
-- 0.707107
put cos(pi()/4)
-- 0.707107
put tan(pi()/4)
-- 1.0
```

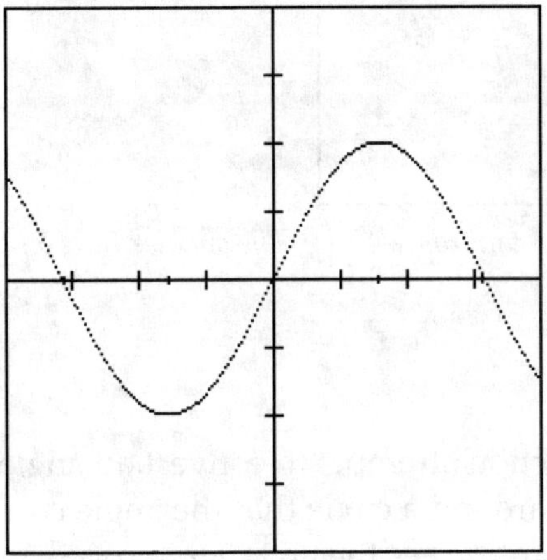

Figure 19-1: *A graph of sin from –4 to 4. The smaller ticks on the x-axis represent pi/2 and pi.*

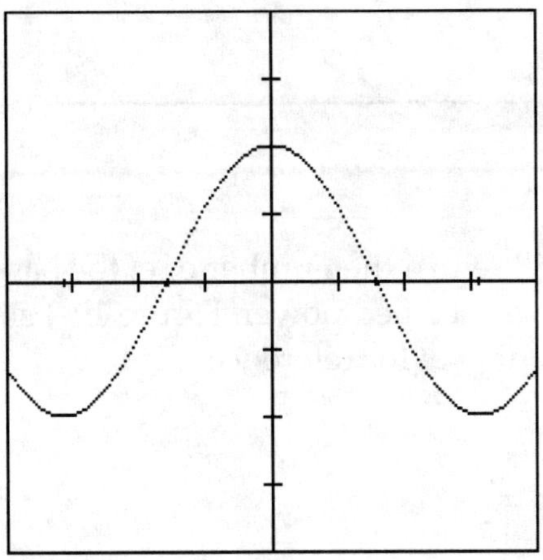

Figure 19-2: *A graph of cos from –4 to 4. The smaller ticks on the x-axis represent pi/2 and pi.*

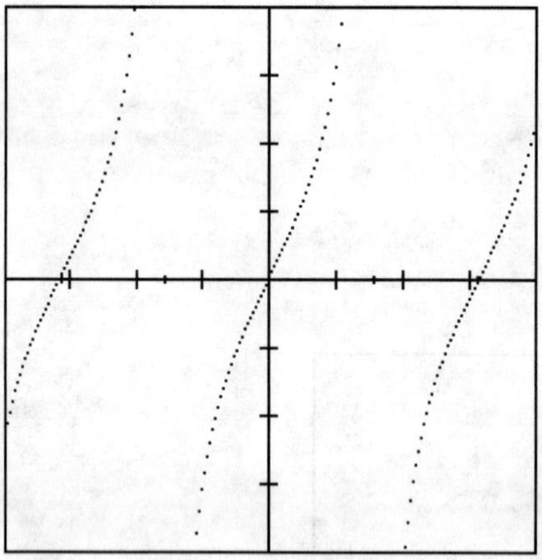

Figure 19-3: *A graph of tan from –4 to 4. The smaller ticks on the x-axis represent pi/2 and pi.*

arctangent

The arctangent function attempts to convert an angle back to a number of radians around a circle that the angle corresponds to. The following example gives the arctangent of a diagonal line: line with a slope of 1.0. The result, .7854, is pi/4, or 45 degrees.

```
put atan(1.0)
-- 0.7854"
```

Natural Logarithms

e

The *exp* function will return the number of e, the base natural logarithm, raised to a specified power. Figure 19-4 shows the graph of the function, $y=e^x$ for reference.

```
put exp(7)
-- 1096.633158
```

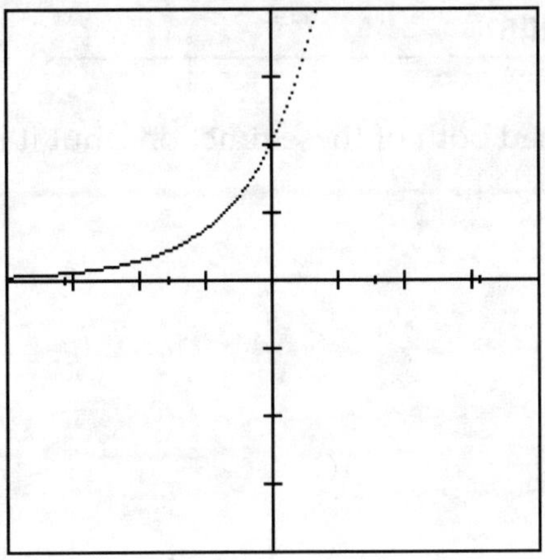

Figure 19-4: *A graph of the exp function.*

log

Lingo also lets you compute the natural logarithm of a number with the *log* function. Figure 19-5 shows the graph of the function y = ln(x) for reference (where ln means natural logarithm). You can demonstrate the *exp* function and the *log* function by converting numbers back and forth.

```
put log(3.5)
-- 1.2528
put exp(1.2528)
-- 3.5001
```

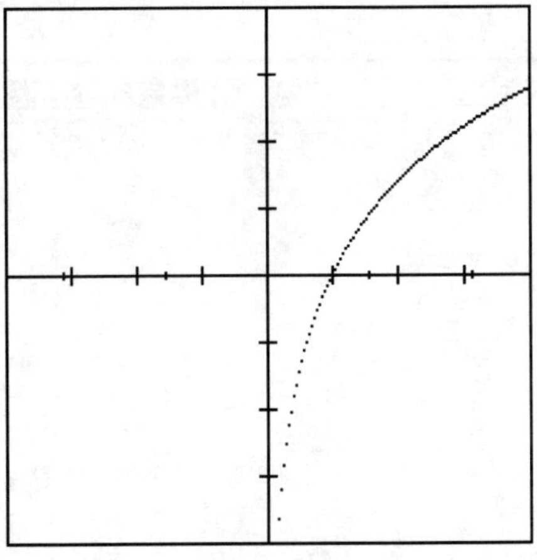

Figure 19-5: *A graph of the log function.*

Maximum & Minimum

We have already used both of these functions, but it is useful to include them in this list.

```
put max(4,7)
-- 7
put min(4,7)
-- 4
put max(4,7,5,9)
-- 9
```

Random Numbers

We have also already used random numbers with the *random* function. All this function is doing is using a very complex formula which returns a number that "seems" random to us humans. An important part of this function is a number called the *seed*. If you set the seed to be something specific, you can make the *random* function return the same numbers over and over again. Try this:

```
set the randomSeed = 5
put random(10)
-- 2
put random(10)
-- 3
set the randomSeed = 5
put random(10)
-- 2
put random(10)
-- 3
set the randomSeed = 5
put random(10)
-- 2
put random(10)
-- 3
```

On the other hand, you can break this predictability by using the semirandom number *the ticks* as the seed. Or you can just not set *the randomSeed* at all and the function will do a good job of seeming totally random.

Using Math in Animation

In all of our previous animations we have made objects move in straight lines, either horizontally or vertically. By using math, we can make objects move along diagonal lines, accelerate and decelerate, and move in curves and circles.

Diagonal Lines

A line can be defined with two points. In the case of movement, one would be the start point, and the other the end point. With a simple handler we can make a sprite move from one point to the next.

```
on lineMove spriteNum, x1, y1, x2, y2, numSteps
  repeat with i = 1 to numSteps
    put float(i)/numSteps into p2
    put 1.0-p2 into p1
    put x1*p1+x2*p2 into x
    put y1*p1+y2*p2 into y
    set the locH of sprite spriteNum = x
    set the locV of sprite spriteNum = y
    updateStage
  end repeat
end
```

This script takes six parameters, starting with the number of the sprite you want to move. The next four are the x and y positions of the starting and ending positions of the sprite. The last is the number of steps that the handler should take in moving the sprite from one point to the next.

The handler relies on two key variables: "p1" and "p2." The "p1" variable is set to 1.0 the first time through the loop and the "p2" variable is set to "0.0." As the loop continues, "p1" decreases and "p2" increases. The two variables are used to determine how close the object is to the starting and ending positions of the sprite.

The above script would be more useful if you didn't have to have the last parameter. If you use a number like 100 as the number of steps, it will make movement between two nearby points seem slow and movement between two far away points seem too fast. This is because we are doing both movements in the same number of steps, despite the fact that they are different distances.

A simple handler could be used to figure out exactly how many pixels two points are from each other and that could be used as the number of steps.

```
on distance x1, y1, x2, y2
  return sqrt(power(x2-x1,2)+power(y2-y1,2))
end
```

This formula can be found in any trigonometry book (see hypotenuse of right triangle). It just returns the distance between two points. Now we can feed this into our "lineMove" handler.

```
on lineMove spriteNum, x1, y1, x2, y2
  put distance(x1,y1,x2,y2) into numSteps
  repeat with i = 1 to numSteps
    put float(i)/numSteps into p2
    put 1.0-p2 into p1
    put x1*p1+x2*p2 into x
    put y1*p1+y2*p2 into y
    set the locH of sprite spriteNum = x
    set the locV of sprite spriteNum = y
    updateStage
  end repeat
end
```

We can do exactly the same movement, but in an *on exitFrame* script. The advantage of this is that other things, including mouse events, are allowed to take place while the movement occurs.

```
on setUpMove
  global moveStatus
  put 0 into moveStatus
  puppetSprite 1, TRUE
end

on exitFrame
  global moveStatus
  put 1 into spriteNum
  put 100 into x1
  put 100 into y1
  put 300 into x2
  put 250 into y2
  put distance(x1,y1,x2,y2) into numSteps
  if moveStatus < numSteps then
    put float(moveStatus)/numSteps into p2
    put 1.0-p2 into p1
    put x1*p1+x2*p2 into x
    put y1*p1+y2*p2 into y
    set the locH of sprite spriteNum = x
    set the locV of sprite spriteNum = y
    updateStage
    put moveStatus+1 into moveStatus
   go to the frame
  else
     puppetSprite 1, FALSE
    go to the frame + 1
  end if
end
```

The first handler, "setUpMove," should be in a movie script and called before the frame with the *on exitFrame* script is reached. It uses the variable "moveStatus" to replace the "i" in the previous handler. Every time the *on exitFrame* handler is called, it gets incremented by one until the movement is done. Don't forget to have the "distance" handler available as well.

You could also have this animation start over again by placing an *else* clause in the handler to reset the movement. The script below does that and even includes a new global to control the direction of the movement. It will make the object seem to move back and forth between the two points.

```
on setUpMove
  global moveStatus, moveDirection
  put 0 into moveStatus
  put 1 into moveDirection
  puppetSprite 1, TRUE
end

on exitFrame
  global moveStatus, moveDirection
  put 1 into spriteNum
  put 100 into x1
  put 100 into y1
  put 300 into x2
  put 250 into y2
  put distance(x1,y1,x2,y2) into numSteps
  if moveStatus < numSteps then
    put float(moveStatus)/numSteps into p2
    put 1.0-p2 into p1
    if moveDirection = 1 then -- forward
      put x1*p1+x2*p2 into x
      put y1*p1+y2*p2 into y
    else -- backward
      put x1*p2+x2*p1 into x
      put y1*p2+y2*p1 into y
    end if
    set the locH of sprite spriteNum = x
    set the locV of sprite spriteNum = y
    updateStage
    put moveStatus+1 into moveStatus
  else -- switch direction
    put -1*moveDirection into moveDirection
    put 0 into moveStatus
  end if
  go to the frame
end
```

Circular Movement

Using the *sin* and *cos* functions, we can make a sprite move in a circular path.

```
on circleMove spriteNum, x0, y0, r, numSteps
  repeat with i = 0 to numSteps
    put float(i)/numSteps into p
    put p*2*pi() into a
    put x0+r*cos(a) into x
    put y0+r*sin(a) into y
    set the locH of sprite spriteNum = x
    set the locV of sprite spriteNum = y
    updateStage
  end repeat
end
```

The "x0" and "y0" variables refer to the center, or origin, of the circle, and "r" is the radius of the circle.

This handler can work in a counterclockwise directon by changing the *repeat* loop: *repeat with i = numSteps down to 0.*

You can also have the handler only go from one point in the circle to another. Let's make this handler work with degrees instead of radians.

```
on partCircleMove spriteNum, x0, y0, r, d1, d2
  put abs(d2-d1) into dist
  repeat with i = 0 to dist
    put (float(i)/360)+float(min(d1,d2))/360→
into p
    put p*2*pi() into a
    put x0+r*cos(a) into x
    put y0+r*sin(a) into y
    set the locH of sprite spriteNum = x
    set the locV of sprite spriteNum = y
    updateStage
  end repeat
end
```

The parameter "d1" is the start position, in degrees, of the path. The parameter "d2" is the end position. If the two parameters were set to 90 and 270, for instance, the object would move along the bottom half of the circle.

More Fun With Trails

Using some of the above techniques, we can turn on our trail property of a sprite and get some fun results. Place a 1-pixel bitmap into sprite 1 and try out some of these scripts. They use the "distance" handler that we wrote earlier.

```
on starBurst x1, y1
  set the trails of sprite 1 = TRUE
  repeat with n = 1 to 30
    put random(200) into x2
    put random(200) into y2
    put distance(x1,y1,x2,y2) into numSteps
    repeat with i = 1 to numSteps
      put float(i)/numSteps into p2
      put 1.0-p2 into p1
      put x1*p1+x2*p2 into x
      put y1*p1+y2*p2 into y
      set the locH of sprite 1 = x
      set the locV of sprite 1 = y
      updateStage
    end repeat
  end repeat
end
```

The "starBurst" handler draws random lines emanating from a single point. The "gradualStarBurst" handler uses *the blend* property of the sprite to make the lines darker the farther away from the center they are.

```
on gradualStarBurst x1, y1
  set the trails of sprite 1 = TRUE
  repeat with n = 1 to 30
    put random(200) into x2
    put random(200) into y2
```

```
    put distance(x1,y1,x2,y2) into numSteps
    repeat with i = 1 to numSteps
      put float(i)/numSteps into p2
      put 1.0-p2 into p1
      put x1*p1+x2*p2 into x
      put y1*p1+y2*p2 into y
      set the locH of sprite 1 = x
      set the locV of sprite 1 = y
      set the blend of sprite 1 =→
min(100,distance(x1,y1,x,y))
      updateStage
    end repeat
  end repeat
end
```

The "spiral" handler will create a spiral emanating from a point. The radius of each iteration of the spiral is based upon "r" and the number of spirals is indicated by "numSpirals."

```
on spiral x0, y0, r, numSpirals, numSteps
  set the trails of sprite 1 = TRUE
  repeat with i = 0 to numSteps*numSpirals
    put float(i)/numSteps into p
    put p*2*pi() into a
    put x0+(r*p)*cos(a) into x
    put y0+(r*p)*sin(a) into y
    set the locH of sprite 1 = x
    set the locV of sprite 1 = y
    updateStage
  end repeat
end
```

The “colorSpiral” handler cycles through colors in the palette while drawing.

```
on colorSpiral x0, y0, r, numSpirals, numSteps
  set the trails of sprite 1 = TRUE
  repeat with i = 0 to numSteps*numSpirals
    put float(i)/numSteps into p
    put p*2*pi() into a
    put x0+(r*p)*cos(a) into x
```

```
    put y0+(r*p)*sin(a) into y
    set the locH of sprite 1 = x
    set the locV of sprite 1 = y
    set the foreColor of sprite 1 =→
min(255,distance(x0,y0,x,y))
    updateStage
  end repeat
end
```

Moving On

This chapter showed a lot of special effects that required some of Lingo's math functions. Next, let's look at more multimedia effects that Lingo can help us with.

20 More Special Effects

While Lingo gives you the power to deal with data and user interface issues, it is more commonly used to create various graphic effects that are difficult to produce with just the score. Let's take a look at other handlers that create some of these effects.

Times Square Marquee

The effect of having text scroll across the screen is very common. The obvious examples would be stock prices or news headlines in Times Square. On the practical side, it is a decent way to present a piece of information in a limited space.

Our first handler we'll create only has two lines. It simply takes the first character from the field and puts it at the end of the field. Then it deletes the character from the first position. This creates the desired horizontal scrolling effect.

```
-- A simple handler to make a field act like a
--   Times Square display
-- Field should be set with "Word Wrap" turned off
```

```
-- You should insert some extra spaces at
--   the beginning or end of field
on tickerTape fieldName
  put char 1 of field fieldName after field fieldName
  delete char 1 of field fieldName
end
```

We could take this concept a little further by having the field move across the screen as the text rotates. The example that comes to mind is that of an advertising blimp: it moves across the sky while displaying its message. Figure 20-1 shows what this might look like. You could also use an airplane trailing an electronic display or a boat in the water.

Figure 20-1: *A display blimp.*

We will use two sprites for this. The first will be the graphic component of the blimp, and the second will be the text field.

```
-- Uses the "tickerTape" handler, plus another
--   sprite and moves them both across the screen
-- Use the "speed" variable to change the speed
on travellingTickerTape fieldName, blimp, text
  puppetSprite blimp, TRUE
  puppetSprite text, TRUE
  put 5 into speed

  -- move forward
  set the locH of sprite blimp = the locH→
of sprite blimp + speed
  set the locH of sprite text = the locH→
of sprite text + speed
```

```
  -- check to see if at end of stage
  if the left of sprite blimp > 640 then
    set the locH of sprite blimp = the locH of→
sprite blimp - 700
    set the locH of sprite text = the locH of→
sprite text -700
  end if

  -- Advance the text
  tickerTape fieldName
end
```

Getting back to the stationary display, it would be nice to be able to scroll other objects across the stage in addition to text. You can scroll any graphic cast member, including rich text, with the following handler. It simply puts the cast member on the stage in two different sprites. The second one follows the first, so that when the graphic reaches the edge of the stage you can see the end of the graphic on one side of the stage and the beginning of the graphic on the other side at the same time it wraps around and reappears on the opposite side of the stage. You need to make sure that the actual bitmap cast member is wider than the stage or the illusion will be broken.

```
-- Uses a bitmap or rich text cast member to
--    create the Times Square display. Places the
--    same cast member in two sprites, so that both the
--    end and the beginning of the graphic can be
--    displayed at the same time
-- Uses "step" to speed up or slow down the
--    movement
on graphicTicker sprite1, sprite2, whichMember
  put 0 into leftSide
  put 5 into step
  puppetSprite sprite1, TRUE
  puppetSprite sprite2, TRUE

  -- Set the sprites to the right cast member
  set the memberNum of sprite sprite1 =→
```

```
the number of member whichMember
  set the memberNum of sprite sprite2 =→
the number of member whichMember

  -- If at the end, then swap the two sprites
  if the right of the rect of→
sprite sprite1 < 0 then
    set the locH of sprite sprite1 =→
the locH of sprite sprite2
    set the locH of sprite sprite2 =→
the locH of sprite sprite1 + the width of→
member whichMember
  end if

  -- move forward
  set the locH of sprite sprite1 =→
the locH of sprite sprite1 - step
  set the locH of sprite sprite2 =→
the locH of sprite sprite1 + the width of→
member whichMember
end
```

This last handler can be used for much more than just text. You can have scenery, like mountains or clouds, scrolling by. You can even make the variable "step" into a parameter and have the mountains and clouds scrolling independently of each other, at different speeds.

Bouncing

The problem with animation on computers is that real-world physics, like Newton's laws, do not apply unless you actually implement them yourself. Things like gravity and friction need to be programmed—you can't take them for granted.

The handler below will take a sprite, with a forward motion, and "drop" it. This just means that we create gravity—a force that accelerates the object toward the bottom of the stage. When the object hits the bottom, we obey Newton's law of action and reaction and have the object's downward speed reflected up. In addition, we acknowledge that some of the object's speed is lost due to a less-than-perfect world and the bounce isn't quite as high as the original altitude of the ball. Figure 20-2 shows the action of the handler with the trails turned on so that it traces the path of the ball.

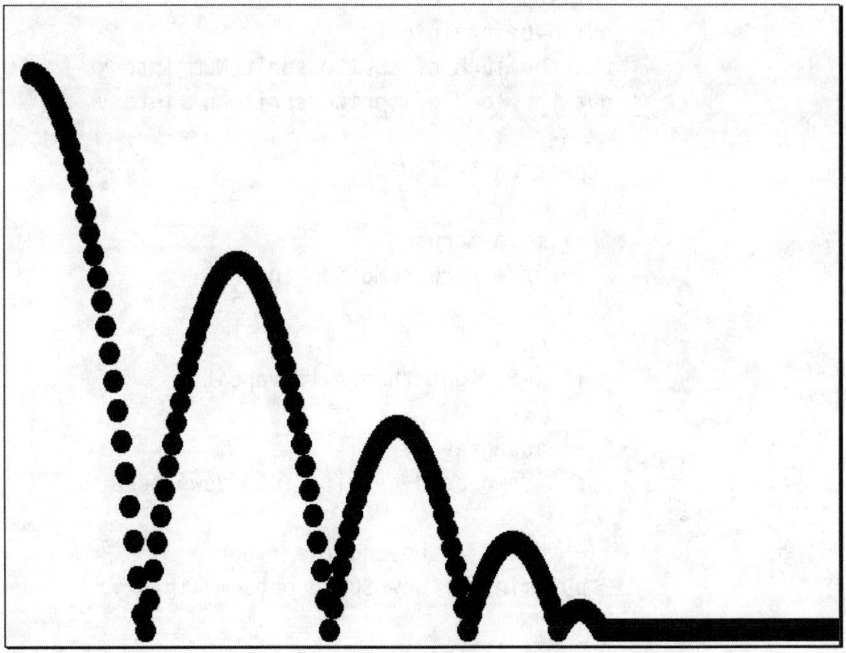

Figure 20-2: *What our "bounce" handler does to a simple circle.*

```
-- Takes a sprite and drops it, with a real bounce
--   when it hits bottom.
-- "gravity" is the acceleration due to gravity
-- "forwardMotion" is the ball's horizontal speed
-- "friction" is the amount of speed removed
--   with every bounce
on bounce spriteNum
  -- remove the two preceding dashes before the next line to
leave trails
  -- set the trails of sprite spriteNum = TRUE
```

```
    -- set these variables as you like
    put 1 into gravity
    put 3 into forwardMotion
    put 5 into friction

    -- initialize other variables
    put 0 into downSpeed
    put 460 into bottom
    put 640 into right
    put the locH of sprite spriteNum into x
    put the locV of sprite spriteNum into y

    repeat while TRUE

      -- move forward
      put x + forwardMotion into x

      -- done?
      if x > right then exit repeat

      -- add gravity
      put downSpeed+gravity into downSpeed

      -- don't go beyond the floor
      put min(y + downSpeed,bottom) into y

      -- if at the floor, bounce
      if y >= bottom then

        -- slow down, due to friction
        put downSpeed-friction into downSpeed

        -- bounce!
        put -downSpeed into downSpeed
      end if

      set the locH of sprite spriteNum = x
      set the locV of sprite spriteNum = y
      updateStage
    end repeat
  end
```

The problem with this script is that it all takes place inside the handler, freezing the rest of the movie while it does its thing. We can take this script and change it into something that can be called from an *on exitFrame* handler, so that it happens while the frame loops.

The first handler, "setFrameBounce," will initialize some globals and puppet the sprite. It needs to be called from the *on startMovie* handler or some other handler played only once before the bounce animation occurs.

The second handler can be called from inside an *on exitFrame* handler. It performs the same bounce as the above script, and then does nothing after the sequence is over.

```
-- Initializes the "frameBounce" handler
-- The sprite "bounceSprite" must be available to
--   puppet
on setFrameBounce spriteNum
  global bounceSprite, forwardMotion,→
downSpeed, gravity, friction, bounceBottom,→
bounceRight
  put spriteNum into bounceSprite
  puppetSprite bounceSprite, TRUE

  -- uncomment the next line to leave trails
  -- set the trails of sprite bounceSprite = TRUE

  -- set these variables as you like
  put 1 into gravity
  put 3 into forwardMotion
  put 5 into friction

  -- initialize other variables
  put 0 into downSpeed
  put 460 into bounceBottom
  put 640 into bounceRight
end

-- Call from an "exitFrame" handler
-- Must use "setFrameBounce" first
```

```
on frameBounce
  global bounceSprite, forwardMotion,→
downSpeed, gravity, friction, bounceBottom,→
bounceRight
  put the locH of sprite bounceSprite into x
  put the locV of sprite bounceSprite into y

  -- done
  if x > bounceRight then exit

  -- move forward
  put x + forwardMotion into x

  -- add gravity
  put downSpeed+gravity into downSpeed

  -- don't go beyond the floor
  put min(y + downSpeed,460) into y

  -- hit floor
  if y >= 460 then

    -- slow down, due to friction
    put downSpeed-friction into downSpeed

    -- bounce!
    put -downSpeed into downSpeed
  end if

  set the locH of sprite bounceSprite = x
  set the locV of sprite bounceSprite = y
end
```

Planet Rotation

We already know how to get an object to move in a circle. It is no big feat to place another object in the center of this circle and make one object appear as if it is orbiting the other.

This script takes this idea one step further. We have a third object that orbits the second object that is orbiting the first. In other words, we get a stationary sun, the Earth orbiting it, and the moon orbiting the Earth.

The "setCheapRotate" handler must be called before the sequence begins. The "cheapRotate" handler is then called from an *on exitFrame* script.

```
-- Sets up "cheapRotate"
on setCheapRotate
  global speed, progress1, progress2
  puppetSprite 1, TRUE
  puppetSprite 2, TRUE
  puppetSprite 3, TRUE
  put 0.0 into progress1
  put 0.0 into progress2
end

-- Call from an "exitFrame" handler
-- Rotates one object around a stationary one, and
--   a second object around the first
-- Called "cheap" because it doesn't really use
--   any physics formulas
-- Must call "setCheapRotate" first
on cheapRotate
  global progress1, progress2

  -- Sprites involved
  put 1 into sun
  put 2 into earth
  put 3 into moon

  -- Distances of objects
  put 100 into distanceEarth
  put 20 into distanceMoon

  -- Speed of objects
  put .05 into speedEarth
  put .1 into speedMoon
```

```
  -- Move each object forward
  put progress1+speedEarth into progress1
  put progress2+speedMoon into progress2

  -- Get location of stationary object
  put the locH of sprite sun into xSun
  put the locV of sprite sun into ySun

  -- Figure new location of second object
  put cos(progress1)*distanceEarth+xSun→
into xEarth
  put sin(progress1)*distanceEarth+ySun→
into yEarth

  -- Figure new location of third object
  put cos(progress2)*distanceMoon+xEarth→
into xMoon
  put sin(progress2)*distanceMoon+yEarth→
into yMoon

  -- Set the sprites to match locations
  set the locH of sprite earth = xEarth
  set the locV of sprite earth = yEarth
  set the locH of sprite moon = xMoon
  set the locV of sprite moon = yMoon
end
```

Compass

This next script demonstrates the use of lines in Director. We'll make a simple script that uses lines to create a sort of compass. This has many uses, but for now we'll just make it spin around.

There are actually two types of lines available in Director: one that draws from the bottom left to the top right and one that draws from the top left to the bottom right. Figure 20-3 shows these two types in the cast window.

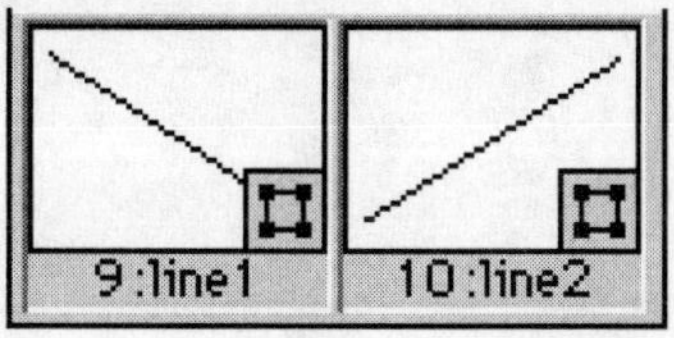

Figure 20-3: *The two types of lines.*

Director will not automatically switch from one to the other for you when you are animating a line. You have to keep track of which line you want, and change *the memberNum* of that sprite. In this script we create the two types of lines first by drawing them on the stage and then deleting them in the score. They still exist as cast members and we label them "line1" and "line2."

Which one we use will depend on which way we want the line to point. Luckily, since there are only two types of lines, we don't have to get frustrated trying to get this type of thing to work. After all, if it doesn't work one way, you have just mixed them up. Just switch them and it will work.

The script below will draw a line at an angle emanating from a point. We use degrees for the angle, although the handler converts this to radians.

```
-- Will draw a line of length "length" from point
--   x0, y0 going out at angle "angle"
-- Requires the cast members "line1" and "line2"
--   which should be the two types of Director
--   lines on compass spriteNum, angle, length, x0, y0
  puppetSprite spriteNum, TRUE

  -- Make 0 degrees point up, not to side
  put angle-90 into angle

  -- Convert from degrees to percentage
  put float(angle)/360 into a

  -- Convert from percentage to radians
  put a*2*pi() into a
```

```
   -- Get the base x and y
   put cos(a)*length into x
   put sin(a)*length into y

   -- Make the rectangle
   put rect(x0,y0,x+x0,y+y0) into r

   -- Figure out if this should be a diagonal left
   -- line or a diagonal right line
   if ((x < 0) and (y > 0)) or→
((x > 0) and (y < 0)) then
     set the memberNum of sprite spriteNum =→
the number of member "line2"
   else
     set the memberNum of sprite spriteNum =→
the number of member "line1"
   end if

   -- Position the new line
   set the rect of sprite spriteNum = r
   updateStage
end
```

This small handler tests out the "compass" handler by making the line spin around once.

```
-- Tests the "compass" handler with a quick spin
on compasstest
   repeat with i = 0 to 360
     compass 1,i,40,100,100
   end repeat
end
```

Moving On

Take these scripts, modify them to fit your needs, and start building your own library of special effects. You will find that you can combine them with scripts from earlier chapters to exponentially expand your library.

Next, lets look at some Lingo functions that give us information about the movie's environment.

21 System Variables

Lingo gives you the ability to check on certain system variables, such as the date, the time, and the type of computer the movie is currently running on. You could use these variables as "window dressing" in fields of your movie, or bring them into play when making navigation or user interface decisions.

Date & Time

The Lingo command *the date* will return the current date. It gets this from the operating system the computer is running on, so whether or not it is correct depends on whether the user has correctly set it.

```
put the date
-- "3/9/96"
```

You could have the date returned to you in two other formats as well:

```
put the abbr date
-- "Sat, Mar 9, 1996"
put the long date
-- "Saturday, March 9, 1996"
```

Technically, there is another format, *the short date*, but that just returns the same value as *the date*. These formats are totally dependent on the system settings in your computer. For instance, if your system is set up to display dates in a European format, then you might see this:

```
put the date
-- "9/3/96"
```

We can use some clever string manipulation to extract individual elements out of *the date*. For instance, we can get the month, day and year from *the date* like this:

```
on getDate
  global month, day, year
  set the itemDelimiter = "/"
  put value(item 1 of the date) into month
  put value(item 2 of the date) into day
  put value(item 3 of the date) into year
end
```

We could also get information from *the long date* in a similar way.

```
on getDate
  global dayOfWeek, month, day, year
  set the itemDelimiter = ","
  put the long date into text
  put item 1 of text into dayOfWeek
  put word 1 of item 2 of text into month
  put value(word 2 of item 2 of text) into day
  put value(item 3 of text) into year
end
```

The system variable *the time* works in the same way as *the date.* It relies on whatever the system clock has been set to, and what time format the user has set.

It also has three formats, but *the time* and *the abbr time* are usually identical.

```
put the time
-- "3:41 PM"
```

The third format is *the long time*. This is basically the same but returns the seconds as well as the minutes and hours.

```
put the long time
-- "3:41:23 PM"
```

We can write a handler to extract the components of *the time.*

```
on getTime
  global hours, minutes, seconds, isPM
  put the long time into text
  set the itemDelimiter = ":"
  put value(item 1 of text) into hours
  put value(item 2 of text) into minutes
  put value(word 1 of item 3 of text) into seconds
  put word 2 of item 3 of text into ampm
  put (ampm = "PM") into isPM
end
```

Kiosk projects can use the date and time as window dressing—just up in one corner of the stage for a visual effect. You can also grab these elements to keep a record of each time the kiosk is used.

The following handler will append a date and time to a text file. A tab will be used as an item delimiter so that the file can later be read in by a spreadsheet program.

```
on recordTime
  set myFile = fileIO(mNew, "append",→
"timefile.txt")
  if not objectP(myFile) then exit
  myFile(mWriteString,(the date&TAB&the time))
  myFile(mDispose)
end
```

Type of Computer

Lingo has quite a few variables to let you determine what type of computer your movie is running on. The most basic is *the machineType*. This function returns a number. If it is 255, then you are running under Windows. All of the other numbers represent some type of Macintosh computer. See the user documentation of Director for an up-to-date list. Here is what you get on a Power Macintosh 8500:

```
put the machineType
-- 67
```

You can use this function only to determine if the movie is running on a Mac or a PC, or the specific type of Mac. The following handler sets a global that you can use throughout the rest of the movie:

```
on whatComputer
  global isMac
  if the machineType = 255 then put FALSE→
into isMac
  else put TRUE into isMac
end
```

Once you know what computer the movie is running on, the next most useful item is learning what the monitor is capable of. The system function *the colorDepth* will return the number of bits of color that the monitor is set to. For optimum Director performance, it should be 8, standing for 8-bit or 256-color mode. Other values might be 16, for thousands of colors, and 32, for millions of colors. Monochrome monitors will return a value of 1.

```
put the colorDepth
-- 8
```

In the case of multiple Macintosh monitors, the value returned is the one that applies to the monitor where the Director stage is. If the stage crosses over monitors, the number returned is the greatest depth.

You can set *the colorDepth* as well. If, for instance, you want the monitor set to 8-bit color, and you find out that it is 16-bit at present, you can change it on the fly. This only works properly for Macintoshes. Windows machines are dependent on their video cards for such changes and often have to be restarted to change the depth. You also may want to save the original color depth in a global so that you can reset it when you are done.

```
set the colorDepth = 8
```

TIP

If the monitor's depth is not set to 8-bit, then color palette references, like those you would use to set the forecolor *of a bitmap or text, will not give you the desired result.*

You can also check to see if a Macintosh has color QuickDraw installed with *the colorQD* function. Otherwise, you may be running on an old black-and-white Macintosh. You can test for QuickTime on both platforms with *the quickTimePresent*. Also, the function *the multiSound* will tell you if more than one sound channel can be played at the same time. This may affect how you want your movie to behave.

The Lingo function, *the deskTopRectList*, will return a list of rectangles that correspond to the desktop positions of each monitor.

```
put the desktoprectlist
-- [rect(0, 0, 832, 624)]
```

Finally, *version* will tell you what version of Macromedia Director the movie is running under. In the case of a projector, it returns the version of Director the projector was made from.

```
put version
-- "5.0"
```

Keyboard Variables

There are several important keyboard system variables that can be accessed in Director. These all correspond to keys with Shift-like functionality.

The function *the shiftDown* will return a true or false depending on whether the Shift key is being held down at the moment. There are three companion functions: *the optionDown*, *the controlDown*, and *the commandDown*. These correspond to the Option, Control, and Command keys on the Macintosh.

On Windows machines, *the optionDown* corresponds to the Alt key, and both *the controlDown* and *the commandDown* correspond to the Ctrl key.

One way to use these variables is to allow the user to have some "expert" control over the movie. For instance, this score script handler could be used to speed up a movie when the user holds down the shift key.

```
on exitFrame
  if the shiftDown then puppetTempo 60
  else puppetTempo 0
end
```

You could also use these variables in combination. This next script allows you, the author, a way to test one of your critical variables while a movie is playing as a projector. If the shift and control keys are both held down, an *alert* box will display the contents of a global.

```
on exitFrame
  global importantVariable
  if the shiftDown and the controlDown then
    alert string(importantVariable)
  end if
end
```

The obvious use for these variables is to use them in conjunction with *on keyDown* and *on keyUp* handlers. This way, you can check for Command key or Option key commands.

```
on keyDown
  if the key = "G" and the commandDown then
    go to frame "whatever"
  else
    pass
  end if
end
```

TIP

The function the key *is a good one for getting the result that we want. However, the function* the keyCode *is faster and will enable us to more easily capture keys like the arrows.*

The Clipboard

Lingo has two commands that allow you to access and control the system clipboard.

PasteClipBoardInto will take the current contents of the clipboard and put them into a cast member. The clipboard must contain some data that Director can understand, and you should be placing it in an existing member that is already set up for this type of data. For instance, pasting text into a text cast member or a PICT into a bitmap cast member. Note that text loses its formatting in this process.

```
pasteClipBoardInto member "readyToGetClipboard"
```

CopyToClipBoard will take the contents of a cast member and copy them to the clipboard, erasing whatever was previously there. You can only do this with cast members, so in order to place a piece of text into the clipboard, use a handler like this:

```
on copyText text
  put text into field "readyForClipboard"
  copyToClipBoard member "readyForClipboard"
end
```

Movie File Information

Lingo also gives us access to file information about our movie. The function *the pathName*, returns the path of the current movie.

```
put the pathname
-- "Macintosh HD:Director 5.0:"
put the pathname
-- "c:\director\"
```

The Lingo function *the movie* will return the filename of the current movie.

```
put the movie
-- "mymovie.dir"
```

Lingo also gives us two commands for controlling where it looks for movies when you issue a *play* command. The property *the searchCurrentFolder* determines if Director looks in the current movie's folder. The second command, *the searchPath,* is a Lingo list of as many pathnames as you want to provide. It will use all of these paths to search for movies as well as linked media.

Quitting

There are several Lingo commands that allow a projector to quit. Both the *quit* and the *halt* commands perform the same action in projectors. Try to use only the *halt* command, since it only stops the play head when you are editing the movie in Director, while the *quit* command will try to exit Director.

Two more powerful commands, *shutDown* and *restart*, allow you to quit the projector; they also affect the operating system. *Restart* only works on Macintosh.

If you have ever created a projector that gets a lot of use, you may have experienced problems with users hitting Command+period, Escape, or Command+w. The projector just quits.

The function *the exitLock* can be turned on to avoid these quick exits. However, it has many side effects. For one, sounds seem to experience some problems on Windows machines.

Use *the exitLock* with caution. If unusual things are happening in your project that can't easily be explained, and you have set *the exitLock*, it should be the first thing you suspect.

Moving On

This chapter has provided a quick overview of the system variables available to you in Lingo. Their real power comes when you start to use them in your handlers.

Next, let's look at ways to control Director's use of memory.

22

Memory Management

Have you ever tried playing a looping movie and noticed that the first time it played, the movie went slowly then speeded up and maintained its speed the rest of the time? This is because the first time it played, it needed to load all of the cast members into memory as they were needed. The second and subsequent times, it already had them in memory.

With Lingo, we can load cast members into memory before they are used, so that the movie plays smoothly the first time through. Before we look at Lingo commands, however, lets look at some movie settings that can help.

Figure 22-1 shows the Cast Properties dialog. There are three options for loading in cast members: When Needed, After Frame One, and Before Frame One.

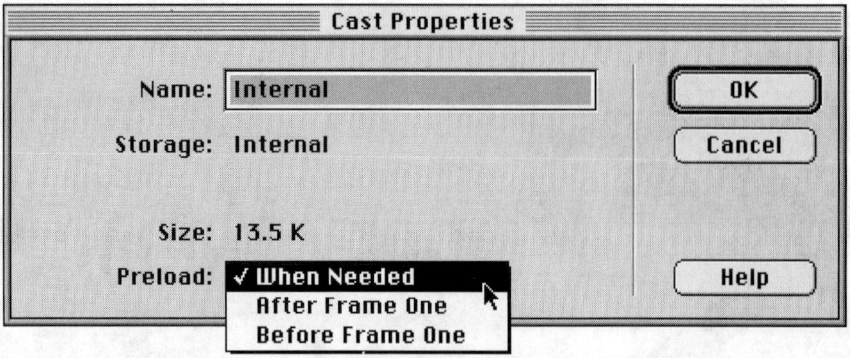

Figure 22-1: *The Cast Properties dialog box offers several options for loading in cast members.*

The options do exactly what their names imply. The first one is the least effective when it comes to animation performance. The other two are more effective and are basically the same, except that the After Frame One will display the first frame and then pause to load all other cast members. This is fine if you don't mind a long wait between the first and second frames.

The After Frame One and Before Frame One settings will delay the start of large, and even medium-sized, movies for a noticeable period of time. They will most likely not cause too much of a delay if you have a lot of cast members—as memory can only hold so many.

As a matter of fact, when Director cannot store all of the cast members in memory, it has to constantly swap cast members in and out of memory. This is the number one reason for poor performance in movies.

Each cast member has a setting, shown in Figure 22-2, that determines when it can get swapped out for a new cast member. No cast member will be swapped out if it is still visible on the stage.

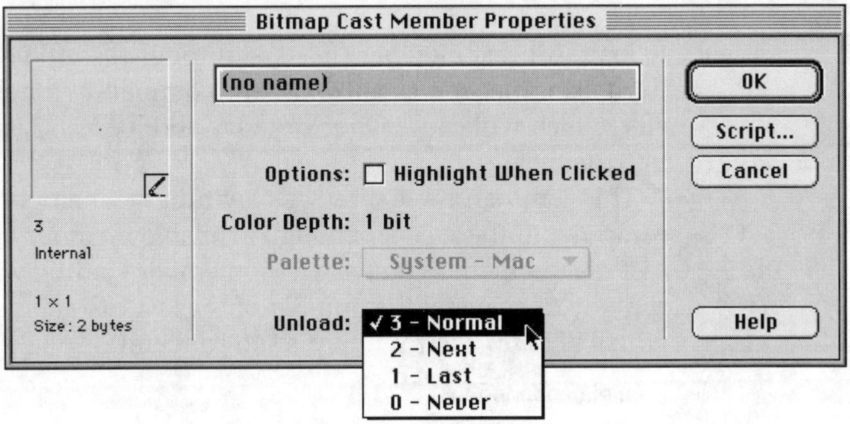

Figure 22-2: *Setting the cast member's Unload property.*

The Normal setting should be used in almost all cases. It means that it is up to Director to determine when the cast member is swapped out. The Next setting means that a cast member will be removed from memory very soon after it disappears from the stage. The Last setting means that the cast member will only disappear as a last resort, when no other memory is available.

The Never setting is not recommended. It creates the potential for running out of memory even on computers with lots of RAM. You should use the Last setting for cast members that need to remain loaded throughout the movie.

With Lingo, you have the power to tell Director to load a single cast member into memory, several consecutive cast members, or a frame or several frames containing cast members.

To load a cast member into memory, simply use the *preLoadMember* command. This command will accept the member number of one cast member or of a range of cast members. For example:

```
preLoadMember 47
preLoadMember the number of member "big picture"
preLoadMember 34, 38
preLoadMember the number of member "big picture", the number→
of member "big picture"+5
```

The third and fourth examples indicate a range of cast members to load. All cast members from 34 through 38 will be loaded in the third example. You can also use the command without any parameter, which will cause Director to try and load all cast members into memory.

This command will only work within the memory limits of the computer. If there is not enough available memory to load all the cast members that you wish, cast member loading will be interrupted. You can get the number of the last cast member loaded with *preLoadMember* with *the result* function.

```
preLoadMember 34, 38
put the result
-- 36
```

In this example, only cast members 34, 35, and 36 were loaded. You can also use *loaded of member* function to see if an individual cast member has already been brought into memory. This function returns a true or false value.

The *preLoad* command performs a similar function, except by specifying the frame number, or range of frames, to load. What it does is simply look in the sprite and sound channels of the frame for the cast members it needs.

If you are jumping to a new movie with the *play* or *go to* commands, you can *preLoadMovie* in advance. This will just load the cast members needed in the first frame of the new movie.

The function *the preLoadEventAbort* may come in handy if you want to attempt to preload cast members or frames but don't want to cause the computer to seem "frozen" to users. By setting it to *TRUE*, you can allow the user to stop the preload by clicking the mouse or a key.

We also have several commands for determining how much memory is available to your movie. The function *the memorySize* returns the number of bytes available to the program. The function *the freeBytes* returns the number of these bytes that are available. The function *the freeBlock* returns the size of the largest available contiguous block of memory. In order to load a large cast member, you must have a similarly large block of contiguous memory available.

You can see the size of any cast member by looking at its information box. Figure 22-3 shows a cast member that is 104 pixels by 150 pixels and takes up 15.2K. This information is in the lower left side of the information box.

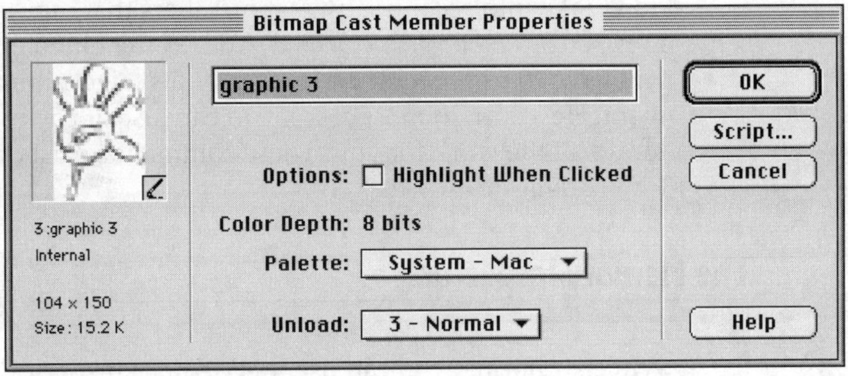

Figure 22-3: *A cast member's information box.*

If you select several cast members in the cast and click on the information button, you will get a summary like the one shown in Figure 22-4. This summary includes the total file size. It even works when you select members of different types.

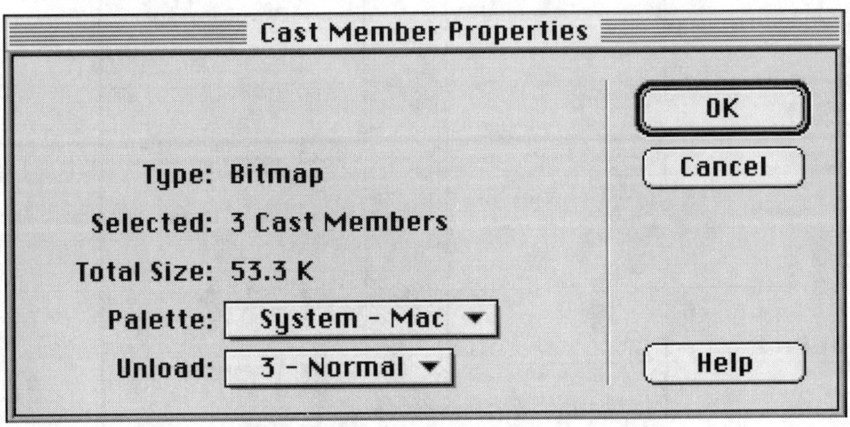

Figure 22-4: *A summary box of several cast members.*

With Lingo, you can use *the size of member* to determine how much memory any one cast member needs. You can also use *ramNeeded* to determine how much memory Director thinks a frame or range of frames might need.

The problem with all of these memory commands is that they don't take into account any cast members that may be needed due to *puppetSprites* or *puppetSounds*. You, as the Lingo programmer, will have to use specific *preLoadCast* calls to get a jump on loading them. However, in most cases, you can just sit back and let Director do all the work for you. These commands exist only for fine-tuning delicate movies.

The Memory Inspector

While authoring, you can use the Memory Inspector tool to check conditions on your computer. Figure 22-5 shows an example. You get the Memory Inspector by going to the Inspectors menu item in the Window menu.

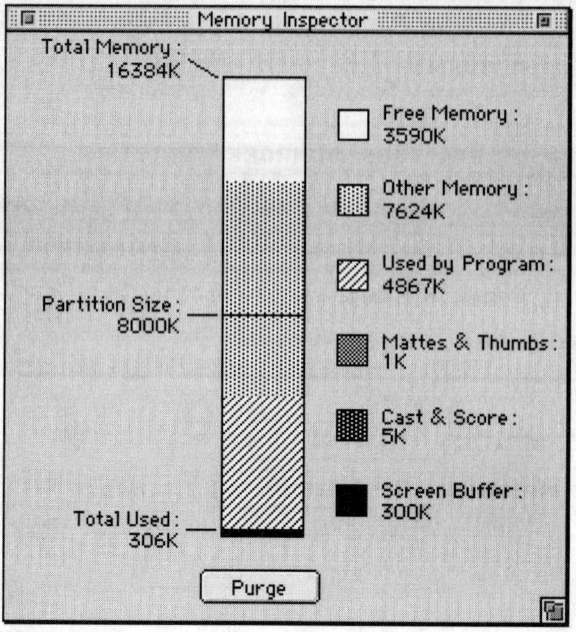

Figure 22-5: *The Memory Inspector window.*

The Total Memory line signifies the total amount available to Director. There would also be a Physical Memory line if you were using virtual memory. The Partition Size is the amount of memory allocated specifically to Director. The amount of memory available and the amount allocated are different, as Director also accesses other parts of memory.

The bar is filled with different patterns to represent different uses of memory. Note that the patterns and the lines don't necessarily correspond. Think of them as separate elements.

Free Memory is memory available to Director but not currently used. Other Memory is memory used by the system and other programs. Used by Program shows how much Director has in use at the moment.

Mattes & Thumbs shows how much memory is being used for any "matte" inked sprites and how much is being used to present the thumbnail images in the cast window. Cast & Score is mostly the amount taken by cast members loaded into memory. The Screen Buffer is used to map each pixel of the stage. Total Used combines these last three items.

The Purge button will unload all cast members that it can in an attempt to reclaim memory.

This Memory Inspector is not as useful as it looks, especially on Windows machines. For instance, when you get a Windows memory error, there is probably no way to fix the problem except by restarting Windows.

Moving On

Many Lingo programmers spend too much time worrying about which cast members are loaded into memory and when. They are also disappointed when the abundant use of the preload commands do not get them great results. The fact is that if you are developing products for low-end machines, they will always run much slower than on our high-end development computers.

Next, we will look at one of the most useful features added to Director 5.0: the debugger.

23

Debugging

The process of debugging in Director used to be very unpleasant. All you could do to follow lines of code was to turn the *trace* function on and every line would be spit out to the message window. This would create a huge dump of text that was all but useless. To examine local variables, you needed to have small *put* commands in your handlers that would clutter up the message window even more. It was a slow, painful process to chase down that one odd bug.

However, Director 5.0 introduced a full-featured debugger. Complete with a variable watcher window, Lingo has the debugging power of languages like C and Pascal.

Using the debug window is easy. For instance, when you get a Lingo error, you are given the option of going right to the debugger to see if you can identify the problem. Figure 23-1 shows what happens when you get an error.

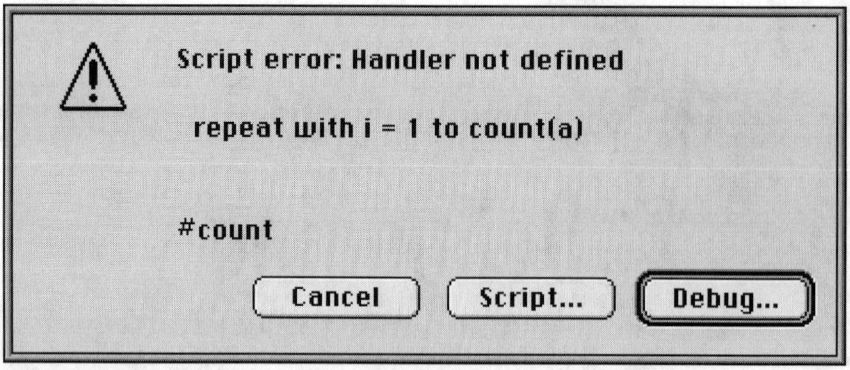

Figure 23-1: *Director's error message box gives you the chance to go right to the debugger.*

Once in the debugger, you can use one of the three information windows to figure out where the bug is. Figure 23-2 shows the debug window. The area in the upper left shows the handler that is currently running and the handlers that were called up to this point. The area on the upper right shows all of the local and global variables and their values used by the handler. The main area shows the script itself, and an arrow points to where the error occurred.

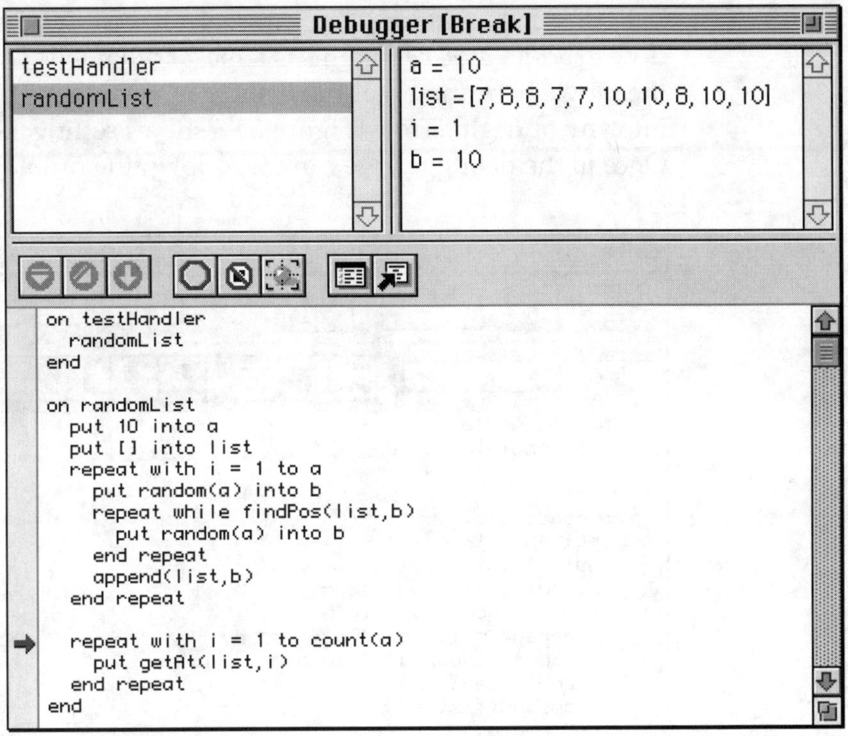

Figure 23-2: *The debug window.*

The small set of buttons in the middle of the window provides a variety of important functions for us. The only one we can really use in this situation is the last button on the right. This button will take us to the scripting window so that we can correct the problem. You cannot change the script in the debug window.

In this case, the error is that we are trying to use the *count* function on a number. The correct usage would be on the "list" variable. So we go to the script window and make the change.

Now the handler runs without any errors. However, it doesn't produce the desired effect. We want it to be able to generate a list of random numbers but without repeating any. This handler returns a list that often repeats numbers. What's wrong? We can use the debugger to find out.

In the script window, you can click on the left side of the window to add a *breakpoint*. This is a marker that tells Director to stop the movie here and enter the debugger, even though it hasn't run into any outright errors. Figure 23-3 shows setting a breakpoint. Once in the debugger, we can track down the problem ourselves.

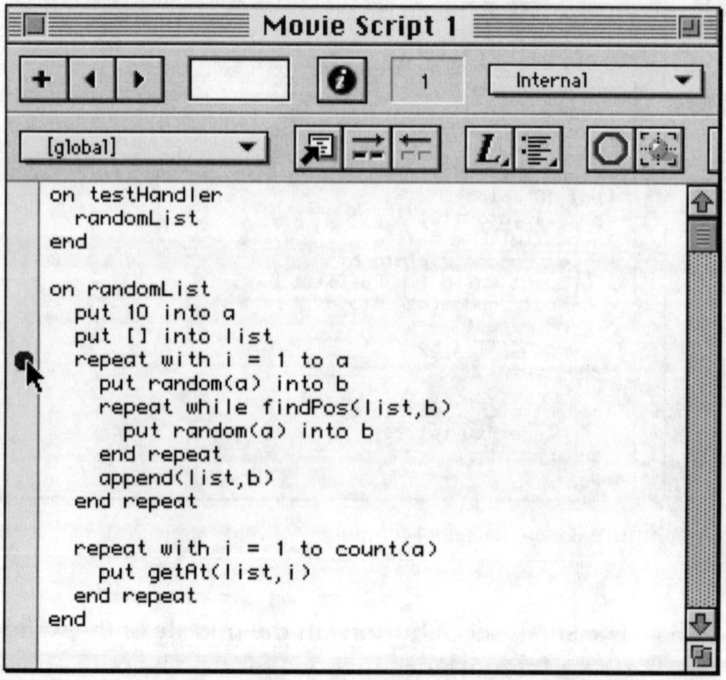

Figure 23-3: *Click on the left side of the script window to set a breakpoint.*

Now, when we run the handler, it stops at the line where we set the breakpoint. Figure 23-4 shows the debugger in this state. We can now use the buttons in the debug window to identify our problem.

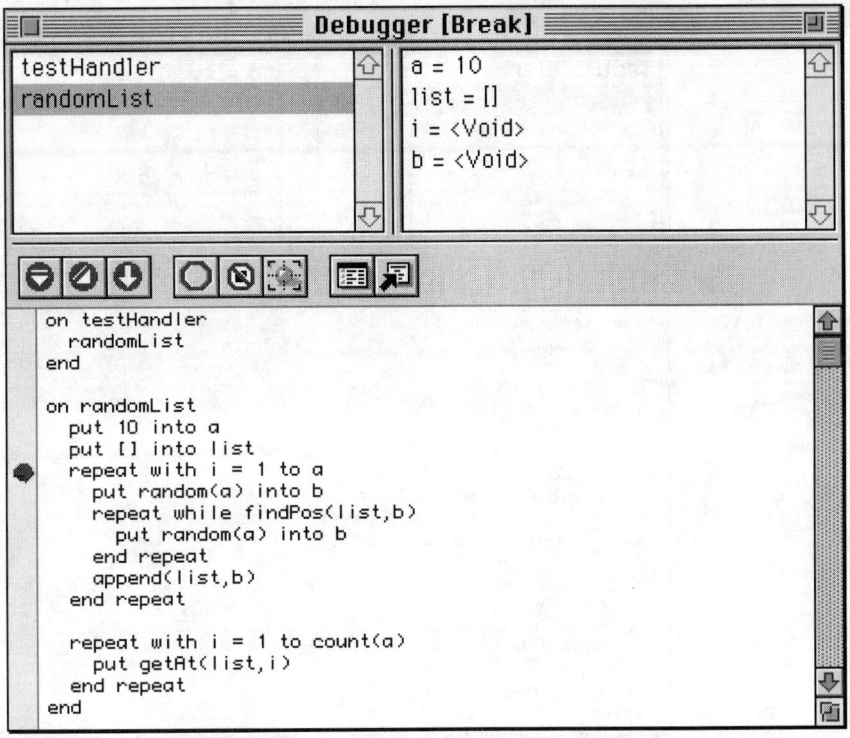

Figure 23-4: *The debug window comes up automatically when it hits the breakpoint.*

Notice that both the breakpoint dot and the arrow appear at the same place. The arrow points to the line currently being executed. Also, notice that both "i" and "b" are shown as "<void>" since neither has been used yet.

We can now step, line by line, through the handler using the first button on the left, the one that looks like a downward-pointed triangle with a line above it. If you step through two more lines by clicking this button twice, the window should look like Figure 23-5.

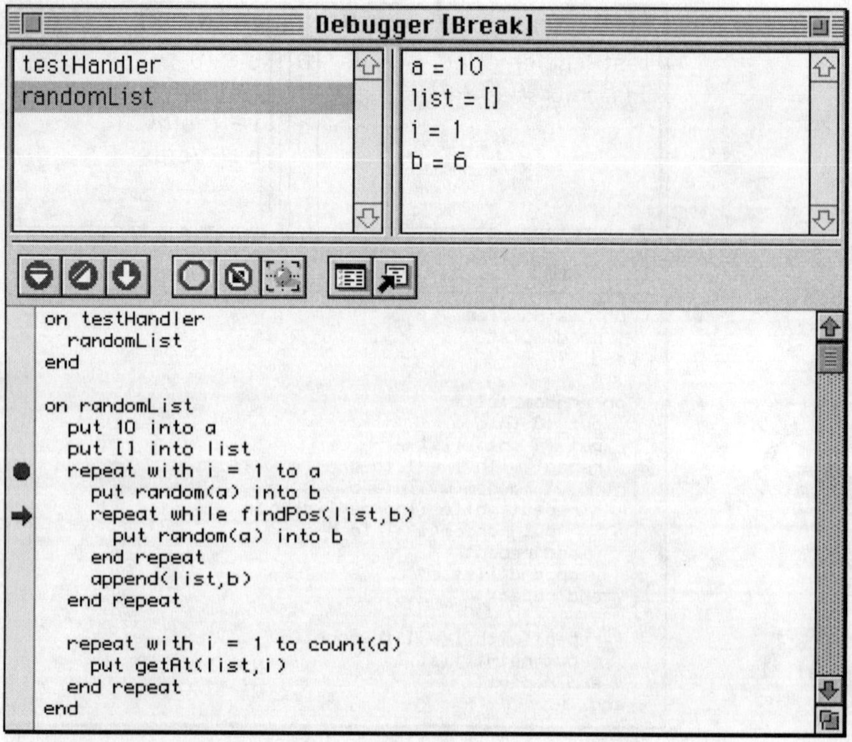

Figure 23-5: *Stepping through the handler.*

Now variables "i" and "b" have both been set. Everything seems to be working fine, so far. If we take a few more steps, the loop will complete, and our "list" variable will contain the first number. If we step through the second time, the "list" variable will contain a second number.

At this point, we want to figure out what it is we are looking for. Our handler is supposed to generate a list of numbers, with none repeated. So, when the variable "b" is generated each time through the loop, we check it to make sure it is not already in the list. If it is already in the list, we do a little mini-loop and keep trying numbers until we find a number that is not yet in the list.

Now that we understand how the handler should behave, let's use the step button to see if it does behave that way. In fact, it doesn't. We can quickly see that it enters our mini-loop even if the number is a new one. From this we can deduce that there must be something wrong with our *repeat while findPos(list,a)* line. If it was working properly, this is the line that should prevent the handler from looping here in the first place.

A quick check of the *findPos* command shows that this function only works on property lists and that we should be using the *getPos* function instead. Once the change is made, the function works perfectly.

The other buttons in the debugger have very useful functions. The second button, the one that points to the right and down, will step through the handler and automatically take you into any handlers that the current handler calls.

The Down arrow button will stop the stepping process and let the script run. It will still respond to any future breakpoints it encounters. This is especially useful if you have a long *repeat* loop that you only need to check a few lines of. You can place a breakpoint where you need to, examine a few lines around that area, and then click this button to continue until the handler loops and hits that point again.

The two red "stop sign" buttons allow you to set or remove breakpoints while debugging. The "target" button will let you add variables or expressions to the Watcher window. The first "window" button will bring up the Watcher.

The Watcher is another window that lets you look at variables while the program is running. You can use it with the debugger or without it. Figure 23-6 shows this window.

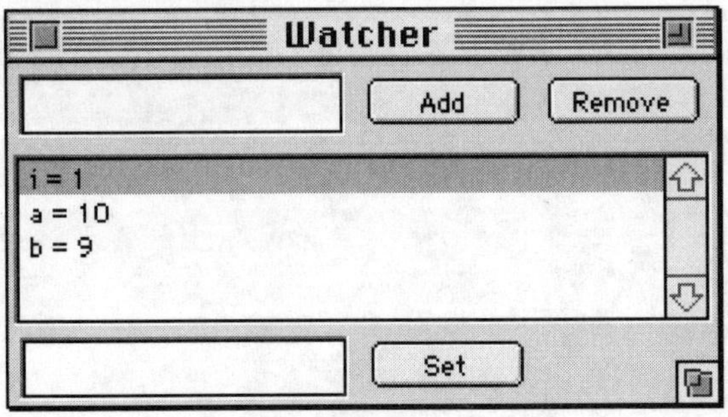

Figure 23-6: *The Watcher window.*

You can add variables to the window and even set their values. When showing a local variable, the value corresponds to the value of the variable within the currently executing handler.

Before the Watcher window, Lingo programmers had to litter their code with *put* commands to the message window or *alert* boxes. Now you can just watch the variable contents change and hopefully spot the problems in your scripts with ease.

The old-fashion style of Lingo debugging hasn't gone completely away, however. There will still be the need for using *alert* boxes and small fields on the stage that show bits of information. You will need these when problems occur that are not present while in Director but exist in projectors or Shockwave movies. Things like changes in path names and different computer environments may require you to see what is happening after you leave Director and are running a projector.

Moving On

The debugger is an immense time-saver. It is improbable that even the best programmers can write bug-free code without a little debugging. Plus, debugging in this manner often leads to a better understanding of how the computer thinks, and helps you crawl up the learning curve faster.

SECTION III

Expert Lingo

24

Scrolling Areas

Sometimes your stage just isn't large enough to fit all of the information you would like to display. Scrolling text fields provide a good way to fit large amounts of information into a small screen space. You can also use Lingo to create scrolling graphics spaces.

Scrolling Graphics

You can make bitmaps into scrolling areas. There is no ready-made Director tool to do this type of function, however. You will need to create your own scrolling environment, complete with scroll bar graphical elements.

Vertical Scrolling Image

Let's examine the pieces of a scroll bar. There are four graphical elements: the up arrow, the down arrow, the bar between the arrows, and the box that moves up and down the bar. The arrows need up and down states, as does the box. The box is the only element that moves. Figure 24-1 shows these elements.

Figure 24-1: *The scroll bar.*

There are different types of actions that users must be able to perform with the scroll bar. When they click on the arrows, the content of the scrolling area moves up or down one line. When they drag the box along the bar, they should be able to position the content anywhere in its acceptable range. When they click on the bar, the content should page up or down, depending on whether they clicked above or below the box.

The box also acts as a signal to the user to indicate the current position within the content. So it must react to both arrow element clicks and bar clicks.

To begin with, we need the basic elements all placed in cast members and named appropriately. Figure 24-2 shows the cast window with some sample elements. The names of these elements should be "scroll bar," "scroll box," "scroll box 2," "scroll up," "scroll up 2," "scroll down," and "scroll down 2." You could substitute any graphics you want for these in order to customize your movie.

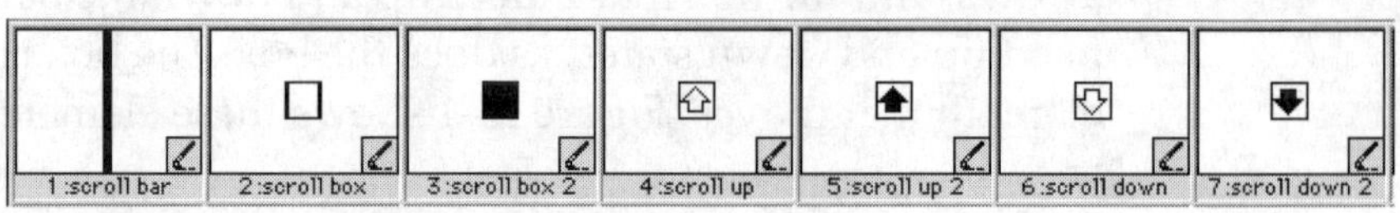

Figure 24-2: *The elements of a scroll bar as cast members.*

In addition to these elements, we also need the bitmap that contains the content. Figure 24-3 shows some content that obviously lends itself to scrolling because its height is greater than our stage.

Figure 24-3: *A vertical picture that can be used as content in a scrolling field.*

The script we need to control the scroll bar elements and the content are somewhat based on the "slider" script described in Chapter 13. The first piece is the initialization routine, which we will put in an *on startMovie* handler. Notice that it assumes that the arrows and the box are the same height.

```
on startMovie
  put 1 into scrollPos
  put 10 into scrollLineSize
  put 50 into scrollPageSize
  put 2 into contentSprite
  put 3 into barSprite
  put 4 into boxSprite
  put (the top of sprite barSprite) - (the→
height of member "scroll up") + 1 into topOfScroll
  put (the bottom of sprite barSprite) + (the→
height of member "scroll down") into botOfScroll
  put the height of cast (the memberNum of→
sprite contentSprite) into totalScroll
  put totalScroll-(botOfScroll-topOfScroll) into maxScroll
  put (the height of sprite boxSprite)/2 into a
  put the bottom of sprite barSprite - a into botBoxPos
  put the top of sprite barSprite + a into topBoxPos
  puppetSprite contentSprite, TRUE
  puppetSprite boxSprite, TRUE
  setScrollBox
end
```

In this handler, we introduce all of the global variables we will need. Instead of declaring them as globals in this one handler, we place them at the top of the movie script cast, right above the *on startMovie* handler, so that other handlers in the movie script can access the global variable values.

```
global scrollPos, scrollLineSize,→
scrollPageSize, barSprite, boxSprite,→
contentSprite, maxScroll, list,→
topOfScroll, botOfScroll, totalScroll→
topBoxPos, botBoxPos
```

The variable "scrollPos" will remember the current position of the content in the scrolling box. The two variables "scrollLineSize" and "scrollPageSize" are the number of pixels the image moves when you click the arrows or the bar. The next three variables hold the sprite numbers of the important elements. The "topOfScroll" and "botOfScroll" variables are set to the very top and very bottom of the scroll bar area. The variable "totalScroll" is set to the real height of the image, and the variable "maxScroll" is the same but minus the total height of the scrolling area. The "topBoxPos" and "botBoxPos" variables store the maximum top and bottom positions that the box can travel.

Finally, our initialization handler puppets the two sprites that move. It finishes by calling our handler that sets up both the scroll bar box and the position of the image.

```
on setScrollBox
  put float(scrollPos)/maxScroll into p

  set the locV of sprite boxSprite =→
float(botBoxPos-topBoxPos)*p+topBoxPos
  set the locV of sprite contentSprite =→
topOfScroll+(totalScroll/2)-scrollPos
  updateStage
end
```

This handler first figures out the position, as a percentage, of the image. This number goes into "p." Then it calculates the position of the box along the bar and places that into "v." It sets the location of the box to that vertical position. Next it figures out the vertical location of the image and sets that.

Now we need to create the handlers that deal with the arrow buttons. These handlers should scroll the image up or down one line.

```
on scrollDownArrow
  put scrollPos+scrollLineSize into scrollPos
  if scrollPos > maxScroll then put maxScroll into scrollPos
  setScrollBox
end
```

```
on scrollUpArrow
  put scrollPos-scrollLineSize into scrollPos
  if scrollPos < 1 then put 1 into scrollPos
  setScrollBox
end
```

These two routines should be as much a part of the same movie script as the rest of the code, so that they have access to the global variables we set up at the top of the cast member. Each routine adds one line of pixels to the "scrollPos." It checks to make sure that the number doesn't go beyond the top or bottom of the image. Then it calls our "setScrollBox" handler.

These two handlers need to be called from scripts assigned to the cast members or sprites of the two arrow buttons.

```
on mouseDown
  put the clickOn into c
  set the castNum of sprite c = the number of→
member "scroll down 2"
  updateStage
  scrollDownArrow
  repeat while the mouseDown
    scrollDownArrow
  end repeat
end

on mouseDown
  put the clickOn into c
  set the castNum of sprite c = the number of member→
"scroll up 2"
  updateStage
  scrollUpArrow
  repeat while the mouseDown
    scrollUpArrow
  end repeat
end
```

The first handler should be assigned to the down button. It swaps out the cast member and then calls our "scrollDownArrow" handler once. If the user continues to hold down the mouse, it will call it again and again. The second *on mouseDown* script above will do the same thing but for the up arrow.

Now we need some scripts to handle the box. This little element can be dragged up and down the bar. When the user is done dragging, the image should position itself appropriately.

```
on posBox
  set the memberNum of sprite boxSprite = the→
number of member "scroll box 2"
  updateStage
  repeat while the mouseDown
    put the mouseV into v
    put min(v,botBoxPos) into v
    put max(v,topBoxPos) into v
    set the locV of sprite boxSprite = v
    updateStage
  end repeat
  set the memberNum of sprite boxSprite = the→
number of member "scroll box"
  updateStage
  put float(v-topBoxPos)/float(botBoxPos-→
topBoxPos) into p
  put integer(p*maxScroll+.5) into scrollPos
  setScrollBox
end
```

The "posBox" handler will change the box to its down state. It then repeats while the user is still holding down the mouse. The current vertical location of the mouse is placed into "v." The *min* and *max* functions are used to make sure that the box doesn't go outside of the bar.

When the user releases the mouse button, the box is returned to its up state. Then the position of the box is calculated by first determining its position down the bar as a percentage, and then converting it to a pixel position. The *+.5* is used to make sure it rounds in the direction we want it to. We finish off by calling "setScrollBox" so that the image changes to match the new box position.

We need to link this script to the actual box element. All we need to do this is a simple *on mouseDown* handler.

```
on mouseDown
  posBox
end
```

The last script we need is the one that attaches to the bar. This one has to page the image up if the user clicks on the bar above the box, or page the image down if the user clicks on the bar below the box.

```
on clickOnBar
  put the mouseV into v
  if v < the locV of sprite boxSprite then
    repeat while the mouseDown
      put scrollPos-scrollPageSize into scrollPos
      if scrollPos < 1 then put 1 into scrollPos
      setScrollBox
      if the locV of sprite boxSprite < v then exit repeat
      if not rollover(barSprite) then  exit repeat
    end repeat
  else
    repeat while the mouseDown
      put scrollPos+scrollPageSize into scrollPos
      if scrollPos > maxScroll then set scrollPos = maxScroll
      setScrollBox
      if the locV of sprite boxSprite > v then exit repeat
      if not rollover(barSprite) then  exit repeat
    end repeat
  end if
end
```

The "clickOnBar" handler first figures out which of the two cases is true. Each case then executes a *repeat* loop until the user lifts up the mouse. The "scrollPos" variable changes by one "scrollPageSize," and the "setScrollBox" handler is called. Then we do two checks: one to see if the box has moved all the way up or down to the position of the mouse, and the other to see if the user has moved the cursor from over the bar. Either one will result in halting the paging process.

This script also needs to be linked to the bar sprite with a simple handler.

```
on mouseDown
  clickOnBar
end
```

This set of scripts is now complete. All you need to do is set up your sprites correctly, make sure that the *on mouseDown* scripts are assigned to the right sprites or cast members, and place the rest of the scripts into one large script cast member with the *global* declaration at the top.

We also need a way to mask the top and bottom portions of the content as it scrolls up and down the screen. One way to do it is to create a "frame" bitmap with a rectangular hole in the middle of it for the content to show through. The hole can become transparent by using the "Background transparent" ink. This frame must cover the space above and below the allowed scrolling area. A collection of several Director boxes can also be used to mask this area. (A "Director box" is one created from the drawing tools, sometimes referred to as a "box shape.")

You can also use a technique that works in the opposite way. If you place a black Director box under the allowed scrolling area and set the stage color to white, you can then set the ink of the scrolling image to "Lightest." This means that when it is over the box, the image will show, because it is lighter than the black box. The portion of the image above or below the black box will be on the white background of the stage and therefore be invisible.

Horizontal Scrolling Image

This same technique can be applied to make an image scroll horizontally. Figure 24-4 shows an image that would lend itself to such a thing.

Figure 24-4: *A horizontal image good for scrolling.*

The script for this is almost identical to the vertical scrolling scripts. You just need to make sure that all references to **"top," "bottom," and *the locV*** are changed to **"left," "right" and *the locH***. Figure 24-5 shows a sample set of cast members to use for horizontal scrolling.

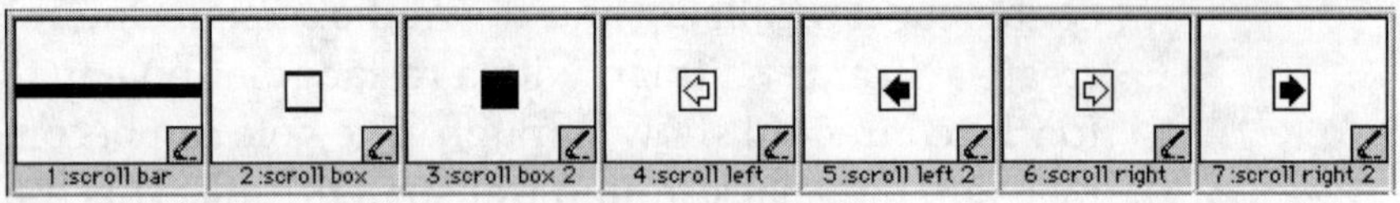

Figure 24-5: *The elements of a horizontal scroll bar.*

This is the main script for the scroll bar. The smaller scripts, like the ones attached to the arrow sprites and the bar and box, need to be changed to reflect the new cast member names and the new handler names.

```
global scrollPos, scrollLineSize,→
scrollPageSize, barSprite, boxSprite,→
contentSprite, maxScroll, list,→
leftOfScroll, rightOfScroll, totalScroll,→
rightBoxPos, leftBoxPos

on startMovie
   put 1 into scrollPos
   put 10 into scrollLineSize
   put 50 into scrollPageSize
   put 2 into contentSprite
   put 3 into barSprite
   put 4 into boxSprite
   put (the left of sprite barSprite) - (the width→
of member "scroll left") + 1 into leftOfScroll
   put (the right of sprite barSprite) + (the width→
of member "scroll right") into rightOfScroll
   put the width of cast (the memberNum of→
sprite contentSprite) into totalScroll
```

```
  put totalScroll-(rightOfScroll-leftOfScroll) into maxScroll
  put (the width of sprite boxSprite)/2 into a
  put the right of sprite barSprite - a into rightBoxPos
  put the left of sprite barSprite + a into leftBoxPos
  puppetSprite contentSprite, TRUE
  puppetSprite boxSprite, TRUE
  setScrollBox
end

on scrollRightArrow
  put scrollPos+scrollLineSize into scrollPos
  if scrollPos > maxScroll then put maxScroll into scrollPos
  setScrollBox
end

on scrollLeftArrow
  put scrollPos-scrollLineSize into scrollPos
  if scrollPos < 1 then put 1 into scrollPos
  setScrollBox
end

on posBox
  set the memberNum of sprite boxSprite = the→
number of member "scroll box 2"
  updateStage
  repeat while the mouseDown
    put the mouseH into h
    put min(h,rightBoxPos) into h
    put max(h,leftBoxPos) into h
    set the locH of sprite boxSprite = h
    updateStage
  end repeat
  set the memberNum of sprite boxSprite = the→
number of member "scroll box"
  updateStage
```

```
  put float(h-leftBoxPos)/float(rightBoxPos-leftBoxPos) into p
  put integer(p*maxScroll+.5) into scrollPos
  setScrollBox
end

on clickOnBar
  put the mouseH into h
  if h < the locH of sprite boxSprite then
    repeat while the mouseDown
      put scrollPos-scrollPageSize into scrollPos
      if scrollPos < 1 then put 1 into scrollPos
      setScrollBox
      if the locH of sprite boxSprite < h then exit repeat
      if not rollover(barSprite) then exit repeat
    end repeat
  else
    repeat while the mouseDown
      put scrollPos+scrollPageSize into scrollPos
      if scrollPos > maxScroll then set scrollPos = maxScroll
      setScrollBox
      if the locH of sprite boxSprite > h then
exit repeat
      if not rollover(barSprite) then exit repeat
    end repeat
  end if
end

on setScrollBox
  put float(scrollPos)/maxScroll into p
  put float(rightBoxPos-leftBoxPos)*p+leftBoxPos into h
  set the locH of sprite boxSprite = h
  set the locH of sprite contentSprite =→
leftOfScroll+(totalScroll/2)-scrollPos
  updateStage
end
```

Scrolling Text

There are yet better ways to handle scrolling text with Lingo. Although the ability to have scrolling text in Director seems not to need Lingo at all, you can improve or modify its performance and behavior.

Scrolling Text Fields

Any text field can be made into a standard scrolling box by changing its properties in the field's information box, as shown in Figure 24-6. This will attach a standard scroll bar to the right of the text window that automatically responds to user clicks correctly.

Figure 24-6: *Setting a text field to make it scrollable.*

There are three Lingo commands that can be used to control scrolling fields. The *scrollByPage* and *scrollByLine* fields are simple commands to move the viewable area of the field up or down.

```
scrollByPage member "text", 1
scrollByLine member "text", 1
```

Both commands take two parameters: a cast member with a name or number, and the number of lines or pages to move. This number can be either positive or negative, depending on the direction in which you want to scroll.

The other property you can use is *scrollTop*. With this property, you can specify the pixel position of the top of the viewable area.

```
set the scrollTop of member "text" = 1
set the scrollTop of member "text" = 200
```

The first line above resets the scrolling field to the top. The second will move it down 200 pixels.

The best thing about these three functions is that they don't require that the text field be set as a "scrolling" field. You could set the field up as a "fixed" type and use them. Here are scripts that can be attached to two simple buttons to make a "fixed" type text field scroll:

```
on mouseUp
  scrollByLine member "text", 1
end

on mouseUp
  scrollByLine member "text", -1
end
```

You could use numbers other than 1 or –1, or use the *scrollByPage* command. You could also use *scrollTop* in these situations. You would need to make sure that the user didn't scroll past the last pixel in the cast member. You can figure out what this maximum is by using *the lineHeight*, *the lineCount*, and *the pageHeight*.

```
on mouseDown
  repeat while the mouseDown
    put the scrollTop of member "Text" - 1 into v
    if v < 1 then put 1 into v
    set the scrollTop of member "Text" = v
  end repeat
end

on mouseDown
  put (the lineHeight of member "Text")*
(the lineCount of member "Text")-→
(the pageHeight of member "Text") into maxV
```

```
  repeat while the mouseDown
    put the scrollTop of member "Text" + 1 into v
    if v > maxV then put maxV into v
    set the scrollTop of member "Text" = v
  end repeat
end
```

The first handler should be attached to an "up" button. It automatically stops when the scrolling field is at the top. The second handler should be attached to a "down" button. This handler stops when the field is at the bottom. The first line does the calculation to determine the maximum value corresponding to the bottom.

Remember that *the lineCount* doesn't return the number of lines signified by Return characters but rather the number of lines according to word wraps. This means that this number will adjust itself properly if you change the width of your field on the stage.

If we wanted to add a full custom scroll bar to control this text field, it would be no problem. We would just need to use the same scripts from the vertical bitmap scroll bar but with different initialization and "setScrollBox" handlers. These would have to account for the new way to calculate the maximum scroll position and use *the scrollTop* function to set the location. We would not have to worry about any sprites to mask the nonvisible portions, however.

Scrolling Rich Text

Rich text cast members can be set to type "scrolling" the same way text fields can. Once set this way, you can use *scrollTop* to set the visible area. However, *scrollByLine* and *scrollByPage* do not work.

We can also set the type of the rich text cast member to "cropped." This will get rid of the scroll bar but still allow us to use *scrollTop* to change the viewable area.

Moving On

Scrolling areas are like little windows in your screen. Keep in mind that just because you *can* make text and bitmaps scrollable, it isn't always the best strategy for presenting information.

Next, let's look at some advanced game programming techniques.

25

Complex Games

More often than not, multimedia is meant to be entertaining. Even educational or training products need to be fun in order to accomplish their goals.

Let's take a look at three games. Each one demonstrates a few expert Lingo techniques. None of them are totally "finished." It is up to you to decide what you would like to do, if anything, with the basic functionality provided.

The Matching Game

First, we will look at the often-requested game of matching, sometimes known as "Concentration." It is a game that tests your memory.

You have 36 cards lying face down. There are actually 18 pairs of matching cards. You can turn over two cards at a time. If they match, the cards are removed. If they don't match, the cards are turned back over and you get to guess again.

To start with, we need some cards. Figure 25-1 shows a few sample cards. For this example we use some simple symbols, but you could use other shapes, colors, or pictures.

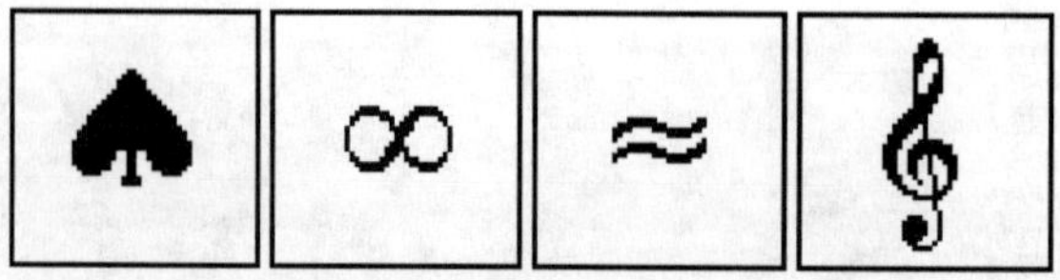

Figure 25-1: *Four of the 18 cards for our game.*

We only need to have each card in the cast once, since we can duplicate it by placing it in two sprite channels in the score. For this game, we will place the 18 cards in cast members 1 to 18 and refer to them by number, not by name.

Another cast member we need is the back of the cards. Only one cast member will represent all 36 cards at the beginning of the game. Let's just take a standard card and fill it with a pattern for this. Figure 25-2 shows an example.

Figure 25-2: *The cast member that represents the back of the cards.*

Now, let's fill frame 1 of the score with 36 cards. Use sprite channels 1 to 36 and place the card back cast member in each one. Arrange them in a square, with six cards across and six cards down. They don't necessarily have to touch if you don't want them to.

Now we need some scripting to make the game work. Start off by placing a looping frame script in the score on that frame:

```
on exitFrame
  go to the frame
end
```

Create a separate movie cast member to hold most of the handlers. Start off by declaring some global variables. We'll need to maintain a list that tells us where the cards are. Let's just call this global "list." When a player selects the first card, we need to know which card it is and what symbol or picture is on it. Let's use "firstNum" and "matchNum" as these globals.

```
global list, firstNum, matchNum
```

To start things off, we need to randomize the placement of the cards. We'll take care of that in the *on startMovie* handler. However, we will simply have the *on startMovie* handler call our own "shuffle" handler. By taking this code and placing it in our own handler, rather than in the *on startMovie* handler, we can call it from other places if we need to.

```
on startMovie
  shuffle
end
```

Our "shuffle" handler needs to do some clever things. First, it clears out the current "list" and creates a local variable: "templist." Then it populates "templist" with one pair of each card, in a straightforward order. We then have an ordered list of cards.

The rest of the "shuffle" will take this ordered list and randomly pick cards from it. The cards are placed in the "list" global. When all the cards are picked, the shuffle is done. We end up with a random list of cards.

```
on shuffle
  put [] into list
  put [] into templist

  -- Create ordered list
  repeat with i = 1 to 18
    append(templist,i)
    append(templist,i)
  end repeat

  -- Shuffle into random list
  repeat while count(tempList) > 0
    put random(count(tempList)) into r
    append(list,getAt(tempList,r))
    deleteAt(tempList,r)
  end repeat
end
```

The next handler will handle the user's clicking on the first card. Since we know that no other card has been turned over, we just have to swap the cast member on the stage and set some variables. We place the cast member number of the card into "matchNum" and the sprite number of the card into "firstNum."

```
-- Turn over a card, put its value into "matchNum"
on turnOverFirst num
  put num into firstNum
  put getAt(list,num) into matchNum
  puppetSprite num, TRUE
  set the memberNum of sprite num = matchNum
  updateStage
end
```

The last major handler deals with the user's clicking on the second card. First, we show that card and wait one second. Then we compare the cast member number of this card to the number we stored in "matchNum." If they match, we want to remove both cards from the stage. Otherwise, we turn both cards back over and reset "matchNum" and "firstNum." The global "firstNum" is used to remember which other sprite (the first card the user turned over) to return to the original state (with the back of the card visible).

```
-- Turn over another card, compare to "matchNum"
on turnOverSecond num
  set the memberNum of sprite num = getAt(list,num)
  updateStage

  -- wait one second
  startTimer
  repeat while the timer < 60
  end repeat

  -- compare
  if getAt(list,num) = matchNum then
    -- make both go away
    puppetSprite num, TRUE
    set the memberNum of sprite num = 0
    set the memberNum of sprite firstNum = 0
```

```
    else
      -- no match, turn back over
      puppetSprite firstNum, FALSE
    end if
    put 0 into matchNum
  end if
```

Finally, we need a handler to place in a score script and be assigned to the 36 sprite channels containing the cards. This handler needs to decide, based on whether "matchNum" is set, if the player is clicking on the first or the second card for that round of play.

```
on mouseDown
  global matchNum
  put the clickOn into c
  if c > 0 and c < 37 then
    if matchNum = 0 then turnOverFirst c
    else turnOverSecond c
  end if
end
```

The final result is a quick and easy matching game. You could easily make the game less than six by six. If you want to go seven by seven, you run into the limitation of only having 48 sprites. You could get around this by using "trails" to paint the cards on the screen.

To finish off this game, you would want to add some sort of payoff when all the cards are matched. You could also add a running tally of how many attempts the player has made at a match. Also, if the member numbers corresponding to the cards were moved farther down the score, you could place a picture in a sprite with a lower number so that it reveals itself as the player finishes the game.

Blackjack

The game of blackjack is one of the most basic and well-known card games. We can make such a game, BlackJack, with Lingo, but it is a little more complex than the previous matching game.

First, we need a deck of cards. There are 52 cards in a deck, divided into four suits: clubs, spades, hearts, and diamonds. Each suit has the cards numbered 2 to 10, plus a jack, a queen, a king, and an ace. Figure 25-3 shows a few sample cards. You can make your cards as simple or as lavish as you want. For this deck, let's make them all 1-bit black-and-white cards. We can change the appropriate cards to red using *the foreColor* property.

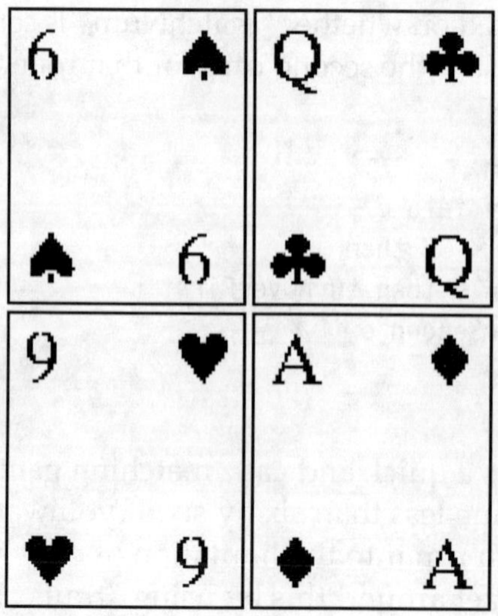

Figure 25-3: *A few cards from our deck.*

The names of these cast members should make sense—if we start with the face value of the card, using the numbers 2 to 10 and the letters "j," "q," "k," and "a," then follow with a "c," "s," "h," and "d" to represent the four suits. This means that the cards in Figure 25-3 should be named: "6s," "qc," "9h," and "ad."

Now, let's define the globals we will need for our main movie script. We'll put a deck of shuffled cards in a list called "deck." Every time we want to display a card, we'll assign it to the next available sprite, called "nextCardSprite." The two hands will be short lists called "dealer" and "player"" Last, the amount of cash that the player has will be stored as a number in "cash."

```
global deck, nextCardSprite, dealer, player, cash
```

The *on startMovie* handler will call our "shuffle" handler and reset the player's cash to 100. We also need to create two fields on the stage to display some information. The first field will hold all sorts of things on different lines and we will call it "display." In this handler, we place the total cash available on the first line. The second field will be one that the user can edit. We'll call this one "bet." It will contain the amount of the current bet. We'll set it to five dollars.

This initialization handler also jumps to the "bet" frame, which will be one of two frames used in this movie. The "bet" frame will be where the player can change the value of the "bet" field. Another item on the "bet" frame is a button that tells the computer to deal the cards. Figure 25-4 shows the "bet" frame right after the initialization.

```
-- Shuffles Deck, resets cash
on startMovie
  shuffle
  put 100 into cash
  put "Cash:"&&cash into field "display"
  put "5" into field "bet"
  go to frame "Bet"
end
```

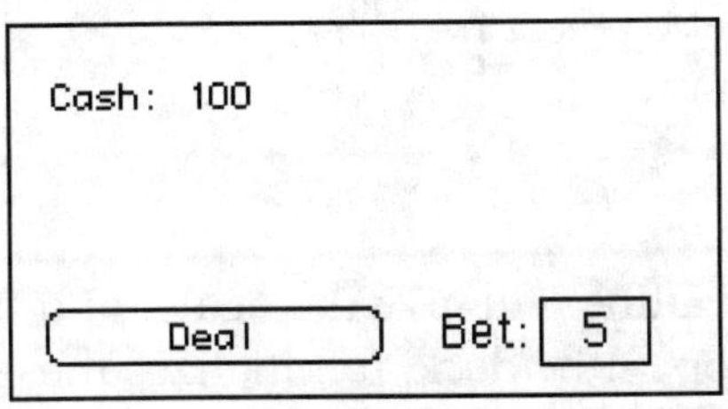

Figure 25-4: *The initial "bet" frame contains the "display" field (shown with the amount of cash the user currently has), "bet" fields, and a "deal" button.*

The "deal" button contains a simple *on mouseUp* script that just calls our "dealHand" handler. The frame itself has only a simple *go to the frame* script in the score.

The "shuffle" handler works in a way similar to the "shuffle" of the matching game above. It places an ordered deck into a local list and then deals it out in a random order to the "deck" global list. We use two short lists to translate the card and suit numbers to their actual values.

```
-- Set up deck list
on shuffle
  put [] into deck
  put [] into tempList
  put ["c","s","h","d"] into suit
  put
["2","3","4","5","6","7","8","9","10","J","Q","K","A"]→
into number

  -- create an ordered deck
  repeat with s = 1 to 4
    repeat with n = 1 to 13
      put getAt(number,n)&getAt(suit,s) into card
      append(tempList,card)
    end repeat
  end repeat

  -- randomly pick cards from tempList and put in the deck
  repeat while count(tempList) > 0
    put random(count(tempList)) into r
    append(deck,getAt(tempList,r))
    deleteAt(tempList,r)
  end repeat
end
```

The "dealHand" routine will give the dealer and player each two cards from the top of the deck. It initializes the "nextCardSprite" variable to use sprite channel 10 (the graphic of the back of the card). Then it makes sure that every sprite from that one on is clear.

The two hands, globals "dealer" and "player," are emptied, and two cards are dealt to each. The first card to the dealer is assigned *TRUE* as its second parameter—to signify that the card should be displayed face down for now.

Then the handler subtracts the player's bet from the "cash" variable. It writes a bunch of things to the "display" field: the amount of cash the player has left, the current bet, and the current value of the player's hand. It also takes the movie to the "play" frame where the "deal" button and "bet" field will be replaced with two buttons: "hit" and "stay." Figure 25-5 shows what the stage should look like now.

Finally, the "dealHand" handler will check to see if the player has 21, in which case the player instantly wins back his or her bet, plus 50 percent.

```
-- Clears screen and deals initial hand
on dealHand
  put 10 into nextCardSprite
  repeat with i = 10 to 48
    puppetSprite i, FALSE
  end repeat
  updateStage
  put [] into dealer
  put [] into player

  -- initial deal
  dealCard #dealer,TRUE
  dealCard #player
  dealCard #dealer
  dealCard #player

  put cash-value(field "bet") into cash
  put "Cash:"&&cash into field "display"
  put "Bet:"&&value(field "bet") into line 2 of field "display"
  put figureHand(player) into playerVal
  put "You Have:"&&displayVal(playerVal) into
line 3 of field "display"
  go to frame "Play"

  -- Check for initial Blackjack
  if getLast(figureHand(player)) = 21 then
    put "BlackJack!" into line 5 of field "display"
    put 2.5*value(field "bet")+cash into cash
    put "Cash:"&&cash into line 1 of field "display"
    go to frame "bet"
  end if
end
```

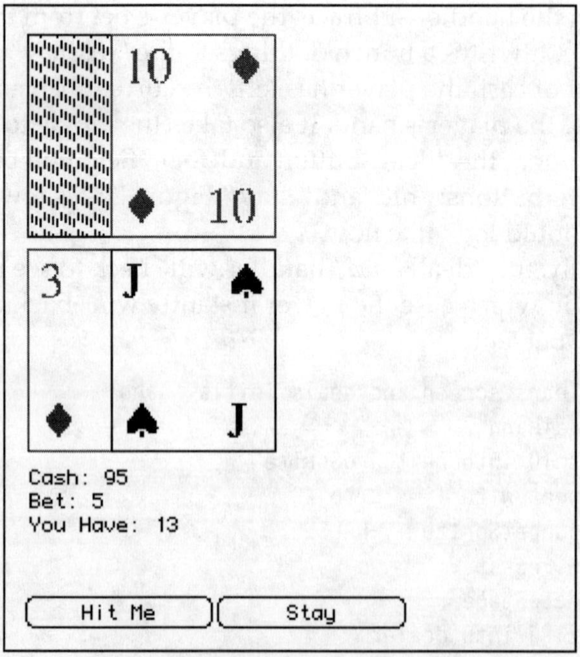

Figure 25-5: *The stage after the initial deal.*

The "dealHand" handler calls the routine "dealCard" several times. This handler takes two parameters: "toWho" and "faceDown." It gets the next card from the top of the "deck" and then adds it to either the "dealer" list or the "player" list. This is determined by the value of "toWho." We use our own custom symbols "#player" and "#dealer" as the values of "toWho."

TIP

Making your own symbols by placing a "#" in front of words is a good way to pass information into handlers or store it in globals.

```
-- Pick the next card off the deck
on dealCard toWho, faceDown
  put getAt(deck,1) into c
  deleteAt(deck,1)
```

```
    if toWho = #dealer then
      append(dealer,c)
      drawCard(60,count(dealer),c,faceDown)
    else
      append(player,c)
      drawCard(160,count(player),c,faceDown)
    end if
  end
```

The handler "drawCard" is used to place the image of the card on the stage. The first parameter represents the vertical position of the card. Throughout the program, we pass either a 60 or a 160 as this parameter, depending on whether it is the dealer's card or the player's card.

The second parameter is the card number in that hand. This will be translated into the horizontal position of the card.

The third parameter is the card's value. This should be directly translatable into the cast member name of the card.

The last parameter is a true or false value indicating whether the back of the card should be shown instead of the card itself. Most of the time, we pass in nothing for this parameter. This nothing is then read as a <void> value and translated to false.

TIP

Place true or false parameters that are usually false at the end of the parameter list for a handler, so that you can just leave the value out entirely unless you want it to be true.

The "drawCard" handler uses an unusual technique to change a sprite to show the desired card. Instead of already having a cast member in the sprite channel and then changing it, we start with no cast member present at all.

You can still puppetSprite an empty sprite. However, if you do this you have to set all the sprite properties: *the memberNum*, *the ink*, *the blend*, *the foreColor*, *the locH*, and *the locV*. In this case we set the color to black if it is a club or spade card; we set the color to red if it is a heart or diamond. If the card is face down, we just set it to black.

```
-- Draw the card on the stage
on drawCard y,n,card,faceDown
  puppetSprite nextCardSprite, TRUE
  set the locV of sprite nextCardSprite = y
  set the locH of sprite nextCardSprite = n*40+10

  -- Card up or down
  if not faceDown then
    set the memberNum of sprite nextCardSprite→
= the number of member card
  else
    set the memberNum of sprite nextCardSprite→
= the number of member "back"
  end if

  -- Need to make the sprite visible
  set the ink of sprite nextCardSprite = 0
  set the blend of sprite nextCardSprite = 100

  -- Color black if down, black or red if up
  if faceDown then

    set the forecolor of sprite nextCardSprite = 255
  else if card contains "s" or card contains "c" then
    set the forecolor of sprite nextCardSprite = 255
  else
    set the forecolor of sprite nextCardSprite = 35
  end if

  put nextCardSprite+1 into nextCardSprite
  go to the frame

  -- Delay a bit
  startTimer
  repeat while the timer < 15
  end repeat
end
```

The "figureHand" handler takes a list of cards as a parameter and determines the total value of the cards. If a hand contains an ace, it could have two possible values, since an ace can be worth either 1 or 11. If the higher value is greater than 21, however, then the ace can only be worth 1. We only need to worry about the first ace, since the second ace can only be worth 1 if the first ace is worth 11.

This handler will return a list. If there is only one possible value for the hand, the list will contain one element: that value. Otherwise, the list will contain both possible values of the hand.

```
-- Calculate the value of a hand and return a list
on figureHand list
  put 0 into total

  -- Loop through hand and add up cards
  repeat with card in list
    if "1JQK" contains char 1 of card then
      put total+10 into total
    else if char 1 of card = "A" then
      put total+1 into total
      put TRUE into haveAce
    else
      put value(char 1 of card)+total into total
    end if
  end repeat

  -- If an ace there are 2 possible values for the hand
  if haveAce then
    if total+10 > 21 then return [total]
    else return [total,total+10]
  else
    return [total]
  end if
end
```

The "displayVal" handler takes the returned value of "figureHand" and translates it into something that can be placed into the "display" field.

```
-- Take the returned value list and display it in English
on displayVal val
  if count(val) = 1 then return string(getAt(val,1))
  else return→
string(getAt(val,1))&&"or"&&string(getAt(val,2))
end
```

The "hitMe" handler should be called from the "hit" button on the "play" frame. It deals the player another card and then displays the new value of the hand in the "display" field.

If the lowest possible value of the hand is greater than 21, then the player busts and the "dealerWins" handler is called.

```
-- Give the player another card
on hitMe
  dealCard #player
  put figureHand(player) into playerVal
  if getAt(playerVal,1) > 21 then
    put "Bust." into line 3 of field "Display"
    dealerWins
  else
    put "You Have:"&&displayVal(playerVal)→
into line 3 of field "display"
  end if
end
```

The "doDealer" handler is called when the "stay" button is pressed. It first turns over the face-down card of the dealer so the player can see it. Then, it deals out cards to the dealer until they total 17 or greater. At this point, the "decideWhoWins" handler is called.

```
-- Dealer hits until 17 or above
on doDealer
  -- Show face down card first
  put getAt(dealer,1) into card
  set the memberNum of sprite 10 = the number of member card
  if card contains "s" or card contains "c" then
    set the forecolor of sprite 10 = 255
  else
    set the forecolor of sprite 10 = 35
  end if
  updateStage

  -- wait a second
  startTimer
  repeat while the timer < 60
  end repeat

  -- Keep adding cards
  repeat while TRUE
    put figureHand(dealer) into dealerVal
```

```
    -- See if dealer is done
    -- Dealer stands on a soft 17 in this version
if (getAt(dealerVal,1) > 16) or ((getLast(dealerVal) > 16)→
and (getLast(dealerVal) < 22)) then
      put "Dealer Has:"&&displayVal(dealerVal)→
into line 4 of field "display"
      updateStage
      decideWhoWins
      exit repeat
    else
      dealCard #dealer
    end if

    -- wait a second
    repeat while the timer < 60
    end repeat
  end repeat
end
```

The "decideWhoWins" handler just compares the two hands and determines the winner. If the dealer has more than 21, then the player wins. If the two hands are equal, then the dealer wins. The "playerWins" or "dealerWins" handler is called to handle the cash.

```
-- Figure out who has highest valid hand
on decideWhoWins
  -- Get hand values
  put figureHand(dealer) into dealerVal
  put figureHand(player) into playerVal

  -- Dealer busts
  if (getAt(dealerVal,1) > 21) then
    put "Dealer busts. You Win." into line 5 of field "Display"
    playerWins

    -- Dealer and player have valid hands
  else
    -- Decide highest hand, given aces present
    if (getLast(dealerVal) < 22) then put→
getLast(dealerVal) into dval
    else put getAt(dealerVal,1) into dval
    if (getLast(playerVal) < 22) then put→
getLast(playerVal) into pval
    else put getAt(playerVal,1) into pval
```

```
    -- Who wins
    if pval > dval then
      put "You Win." into line 5 of field "Display"
      playerWins
    else
      put "You Lose." into line 5 of field "Display"
      dealerWins
    end if
  end if
end
```

The last two handlers in the movie script deal with the two outcomes. If the player wins, the player gets twice his or her money back. Either way, the new "cash" value is placed in the "display" field and the game returns to the "bet" frame. The cards will remain on the stage until the next deal.

```
-- Double money back
on playerWins
  put 2*value(field "bet")+cash into cash
  put "Cash:"&&cash into line 1 of field "display"
  go to frame "bet"
end

-- No money back
on dealerWins
  put "Cash:"&&cash into line 1 of field "display"
  go to frame "bet"
end
```

One last useful script in this game is a validity check on the "bet" field. This will make sure that the user can only enter numbers in this field and that the number never exceeds the cash available.

```
on keyDown
  if "0123456789" contains the key then
    pass
  end if
end
```

```
on keyUp
  global cash
  if value(field "bet") > cash then
    put string(cash) into field "bet"
  end if
end
```

To finish this game, you might want to add a "walk away" button for those with a strong will. You should also deal with the case of the player running out of money. Maybe an animation of the player getting kicked out of the casino? There are also different rules, such as the dealer staying on a 16, or the player winning when there is a tie. BlackJack also includes the option to "double down" when you start with a pair of matching cards and the option to split pairs into two independent hands.

This game is played with only one deck. You could easily alter it to have more in the initial shuffle. You also need to deal with what happens when the deck is finished. As is, the game doesn't handle that case at all.

You could even use a card-counting system and have the computer display the count values. This would be a good way to learn how to count cards in BlackJack, although I cannot recommend doing it in real life.

For programmers who are up for a real challenge, you can program a computer player that accurately counts cards and plays alongside the human player. See who does better.

Puzzle Game

Let's take a picture, cut it into pieces, and let the user reassemble it. The trick to doing this is using registration points to line up the pieces with each other.

Take a picture and make 16 copies of it in the cast window. Then erase most of each of these cast members so that each member has a unique piece of the entire picture. Figure 25-6 shows the 16 broken pieces of a sample picture in the cast window.

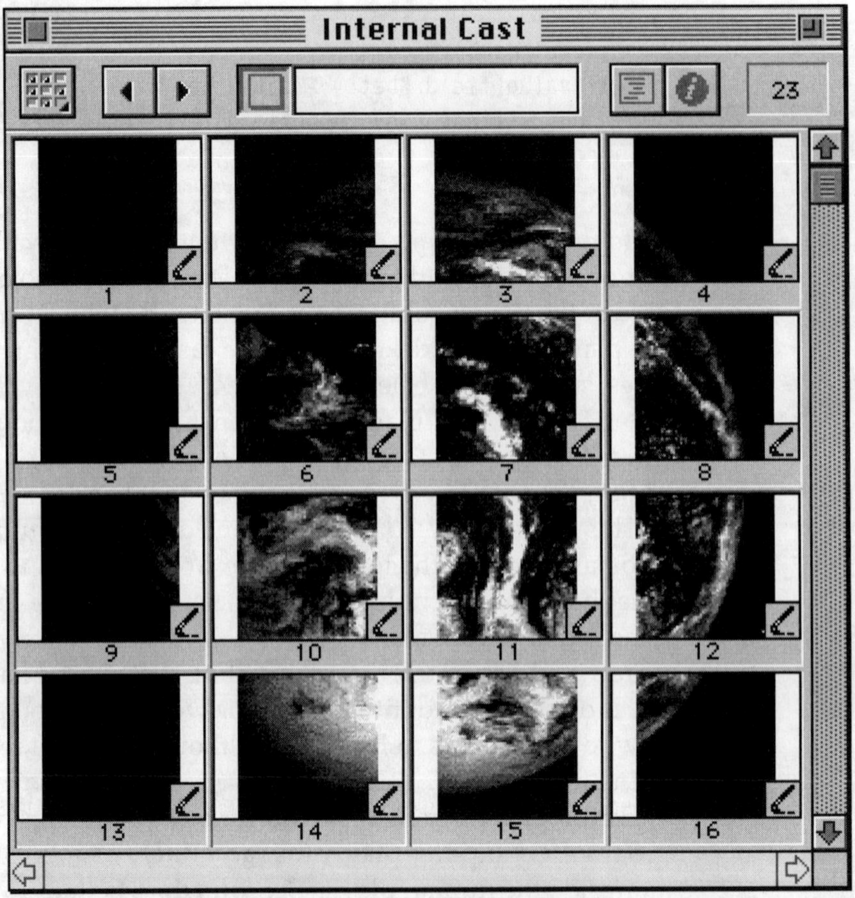

Figure 25-6: *Puzzle pieces made from a single picture.*

Make sure that when you cut out the pieces, you don't disturb the original registration point. Figure 25-7 shows the piece that goes in the bottom right corner of the puzzle. Notice that the registration point is still where the middle of the picture was before the rest of it was removed.

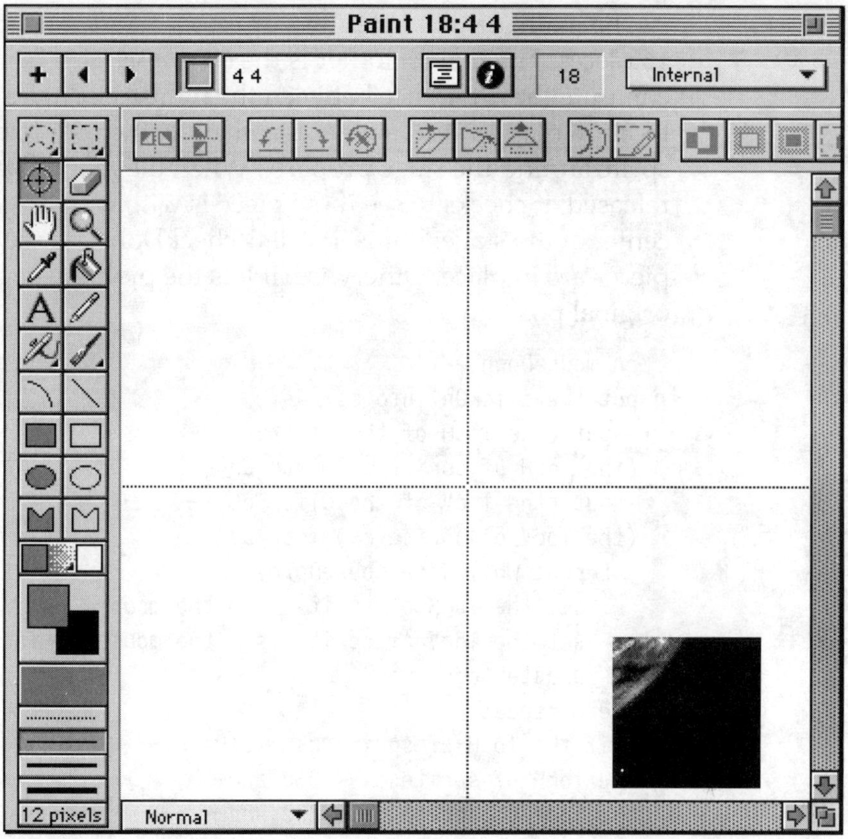

Figure 25-7: *The bottom right puzzle piece.*

Now, arrange the pieces on the stage around a rectangle that has been sized so that it perfectly houses the finished puzzle. The rectangle should be exactly centered on a stage that is 640 by 480.

The scripting for this game is actually not very complex at all. It expects the player to position each piece so that *the locH* and *the locV* of each piece are within 10 pixels of the center of the screen. Since *the locH* and *the locV* refer to the registration points of the cast members, each piece is properly placed when it is "centered" on the stage this way. In other words, if the registration point of every puzzle piece were aligned, the puzzle would be solved.

The main script is actually a score script assigned to each of the 16 pieces. The main handler is the *on mouseDown* handler. It will compute the difference between the mouse click location and the location of the sprite, so that it can allow the user to drag the sprite around the stage properly. When the mouse button is released, it checks to see if the piece is within 10 pixels of the center of the stage. If it is, it calls "checkDone" to see if all the pieces are in place. Otherwise, it lets the piece fly back to its original position.

```
on mouseDown
put the clickOn into cs
  put (the locH of the clickLoc)-→
(the locH of sprite cs) into dh
  put (the locV of the clickLoc)-→
(the locV of sprite cs) into dv
  repeat while the mouseDown
    set the locH of sprite cs = the mouseH - dh
    set the locV of sprite cs = the mouseV - dv
    updateStage
  end repeat
  if the locH of sprite cs > 310 and→
the locH of sprite cs < 330 and→
the locV of sprite cs > 230 and→
the locV of sprite cs < 250 then
puppetSprite cs, TRUE

    set the loc of sprite cs = point(320,240)
    updateStage
    if checkDone() then alert "You got it!"
  else
    puppetSprite cs, FALSE
  end if
end
```

The "checkDone" handler will loop through all 16 sprites and see if any are not in place. We use sprites 2 to 17 for this example, so that we can place the box that frames the whole puzzle in sprite 1.

```
on checkDone
  repeat with i = 2 to 17
    if the locH of sprite i <> 320 or→
the locV of sprite i <> 240 then
      return FALSE
    end if
  end repeat
  return TRUE
end
```

Of course a *go to the frame* command has to be placed in the *on exitFrame* script for this game to work.

This script can be easily altered to deal with more pieces—up to Director's limit of 48 sprite channels. Experts may be able to use trails to have a puzzle with even more pieces.

Variations on this puzzle game would have the pieces staying put rather than snapping back to their original positions when placed incorrectly. You could also use puppetSprites to randomize where the pieces begin at the start of the game. There's no reason for them to be so neat, either. You could have all the pieces in a pile, some on top of others.

There is no reason to use square pieces either. You could use advanced graphics programs to create jigsaw puzzle pieces, or even scan in a real jigsaw puzzle for cast members.

Sliding Puzzle Game

Another type of puzzle is the traditional sliding puzzle game. This is where one piece is not present, and you use that blank spot to slide adjacent pieces around until the puzzle is in order. A game like this usually comes as a "desk accessory" with Macintosh computers. Figure 25-8 gives you an idea of what we mean.

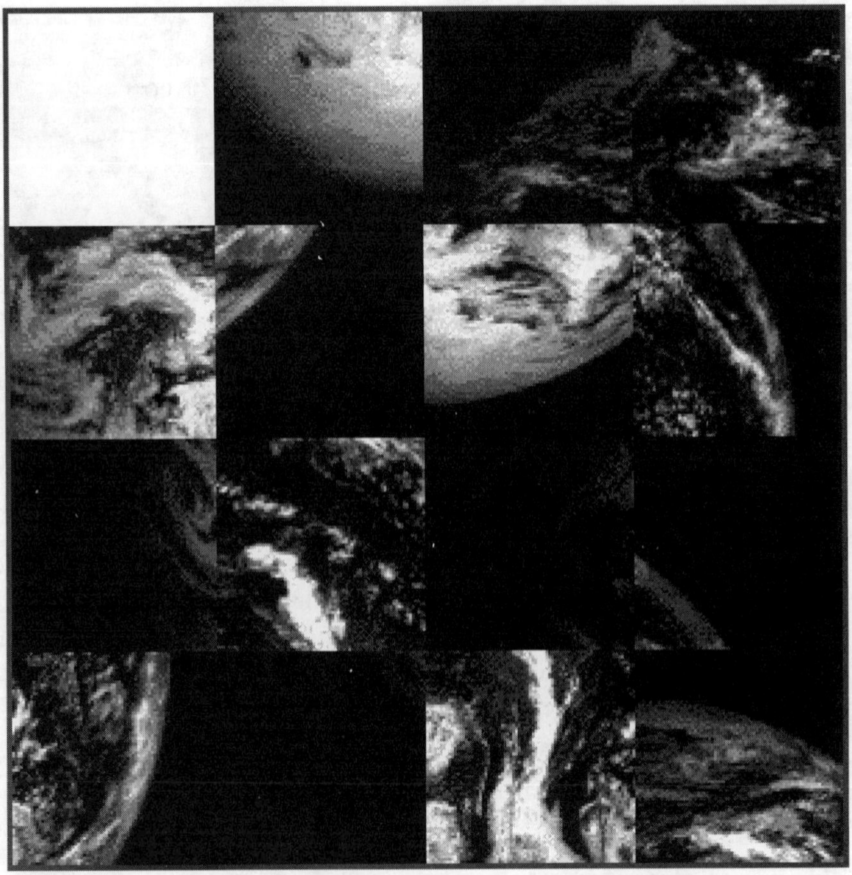

Figure 25-8: *A puzzle ready for the user to solve by sliding pieces into the empty spot.*

We can use the same puzzle pieces and frame used in the previous game to create this game. Just go into each cast member and reset the registration point to be centered on each piece. You can do this by double-clicking on the registration point tool in the paint window.

Now, name these cast members with two numbers, the x and y order (not coordinates) of the piece. For instance, the second piece in the third row should be "2 3," the fourth piece in the forth row should be "4 4." We will not use the first piece in the first row. Instead, this will be the blank spot.

We start by initializing the two globals that we need: "openSpotX" and "openSpotY." These simply hold the x and y position of the blank spot. We also puppetSprite everything and call our handler "scramble."

```
global openSpotX, openSpotY

on startMovie
  put 1 into openSpotX
  put 1 into openSpotY
  repeat with i = 3 to 17
    puppetSprite i, TRUE
  end repeat
  scramble
end
```

The "scramble" handler will pick two random pieces and swap their positions. It does this 100 times. Not only does this mix the puzzle up, but it looks kind of neat.

```
on scramble
  repeat with i = 1 to 100
    put random(15)+2 into s1
    put random(15)+2 into s2
    put the loc of sprite s1 into tempLoc
set the loc of sprite s1 = the loc of sprite s2
    set the loc of sprite s2 = tempLoc<alan>
    updateStage
  end repeat
end
```

The "clickOnPiece" handler should be called from an *on mouseDown* handler assigned to the puzzle pieces. It needs to be passed *the clickOn* from this handler.

The script takes the location of the sprite that was clicked on and performs some math to figure out which column and row the piece is currently in. Then it looks in each direction to see if the blank spot is next to it. If it finds the blank spot there, it calls "slide" to move the piece.

```
on clickOnPiece spriteNum
  put the locH of sprite spriteNum into h
```

```
  put the locV of sprite spriteNum into v
  put (h-170)/75+1 into h
  put (v-90)/75+1 into v

  -- check all surrounding spots
  if (openSpotX = h-1) and (openSpotY = v) then
    slide(spriteNum,-1,0)
  else if (openSpotX = h+1) and (openSpotY = v) then
    slide(spriteNum,1,0)
  else if (openSpotX = h) and (openSpotY = v-1) then
    slide(spriteNum,0,-1)
  else if (openSpotX = h) and (openSpotY = v+1) then
    slide(spriteNum,0,1)
  end if
end
```

The "slide" handler takes the sprite number and two variables that represent the direction in which the piece should move. It assumes that the pieces are 75 pixels in width and height. The 90 and 170 that appear in the code above represent the location of the upper left corner of sprite 1.

It then just eases the piece into the new location. It also resets the globals to show that the blank spot in the puzzle has moved.

```
on slide spriteNum, dx, dy
  put 20 into step
  put the locH of sprite spriteNum into h1
  put the locV of sprite spriteNum into v1
  put h1+(dx*75) into h2
  put v1+(dy*75) into v2
  repeat with i = 0 to step
    put float(i)/step into p
    set the locH of sprite spriteNum = (p*h2)+((1.0-p)*h1)
    set the locV of sprite spriteNum = (p*v2)+((1.0-p)*v1)
    updateStage
  end repeat
  put openSpotX-dx into openSpotX
  put openSpotY-dy into openSpotY
  if checkDone() then alert "You got it!"
end
```

The "checkDone" handler will look at each sprite and see if the current position matches the name of the cast member. It can do this because we used the final position of each piece as our cast member names.

```
on checkDone
  repeat with i = 3 to 17
    put the locH of sprite i into h
    put the locV of sprite i into v
    put (h-170)/75+1 into h
    put (v-90)/75+1 into v
    put the name of member the memberNum of sprite i into name
    if (value(word 1 of name) <> h) or→
(value(word 2 of name) <> v) then
      return FALSE
    end if
  end repeat
  return TRUE
end
```

There needs to be a *go to the frame* script, plus a score script assigned to each sprite that looks like this:

```
on mouseDown
  clickOnPiece(the clickOn)
end
```

This puzzle can be expanded to be a square of 6 by 6, a rectangle of 6 by 7, or several other rectangles that require less than 48 sprites. It can even be made into a 7 by 7 puzzle, if you are willing to sacrifice the border and any other extra graphics.

A game like this is just crying out for a timer, too. You could use the *startTimer* command and place the value of *the timer* divided by 60 to show how many seconds have gone by while the player tries to beat a certain time.

Meteor Shower Game

The last game type we will examine is an arcade-style game. Basically, in this game things fall out of the sky and you have to shoot them.

We'll start with a gun turret that slides along the bottom of the screen. We'll let the "j" and "l" keys control its movement. The spacebar will launch a missile or bullet.

Meanwhile, objects will randomly fall from the top of the screen. If you hit one with a bullet, it explodes. If an object hits the gun turret, you lose. We'll have the frequency of the falling objects increase slightly as you hit them.

You will need to create about five "meteors" and name them "object1" to "object5." Also, create a gun turret, stick it in sprite 5, and place it at the bottom of the screen. Last, you need to create a missile or bullet. Just a simple dot or short line will do. Name this "bullet." The objects and bullet need to be 1-bit graphics. Figure 25-9 shows what the game might look like.

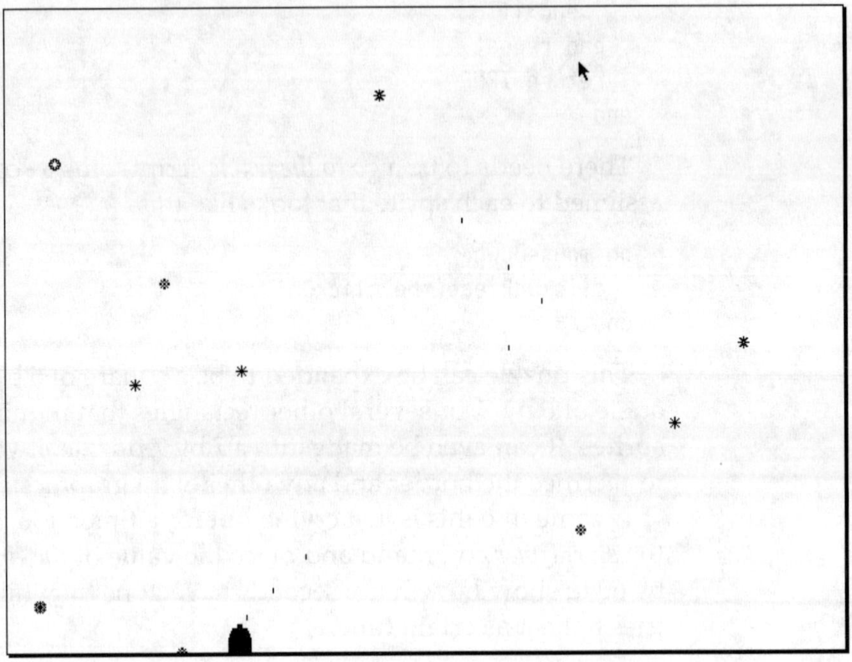

Figure 25-9: *The meteor shower game.*

One score script holds most of the handlers. It starts off by declaring some globals: "gunSprite" holds the sprite number of the turret; "speed" is the positive or negative movement of the turret along the bottom of the screen; "bulletSpriteList" and "objectSpriteList" hold the sprites being used as bullets traveling up and objects traveling down; and "objectDensity" handles how likely a new object is to appear at any moment.

```
global gunSprite, speed, bulletSpriteList, objectSpriteList,
objectDensity
```

The main routine is the *on exitFrame* handler. It uses the "speed" global to change the position of the turret. It makes sure the turret stops at the edges of the stage.

Then it decides whether a new object should be randomly dropped. It calls "newObject" to take care of this.

Last, the *on exitFrame* handler calls four handlers: one to move the bullets up, one to move the objects down, one to check for a bullet hitting an object, and one to check for an object hitting the turret.

```
on exitFrame

  put the locH of sprite gunSprite into h
  put speed+h into h -- move down
  if h < 10 then
    put 10 into h
    put 0 into speed
  else if h > 630 then
    put 630 into h
    put 0 into speed
  end if

  set the locH of sprite gunSprite = h

  if random(objectDensity) = 1 then newObject

  moveBullets
  moveObjects
  lookForCollision
  lookForDirectHit

  go to the frame
end
```

The *on keyDown* handler will take the "j" and "l" keys and reset the speed of the turret to correspond to the correct direction. We have the number 5 hard-coded here as the speed that the turret travels.

It also recognizes the spacebar as a signal to fire a new bullet. It calls the "fireBullet" handler in this case.

The "k" key is thrown in as a way to stop the turret from moving in either direction—a sort of "brakes" for the turret.

```
on keyDown
  if the key = "l" then
    put 5 into speed
  else if the key = "j" then
    put -5 into speed
  else if the key = " " then
    fireBullet
  else if the key = "k" then
    put 0 into speed
  end if
end
```

The "fireBullet" handler looks at all the sprites to find one that is empty. It then sets that sprite up to contain a "bullet" cast member, starting at the same location as the turret.

This sprite is also recorded in the "bulletSpriteList" so that another handler, "moveBullets," can remember to keep that sprite moving up.

```
on fireBullet
  repeat with i = 1 to 48
    if the memberNum of sprite i = 0 then
      puppetSprite i, TRUE
      set the memberNum of sprite i =→
the number of member "bullet"
      set the locH of sprite i = the locH→
of sprite gunSprite
      set the locV of sprite i = the locV→
of sprite gunSprite
      set the foreColor of sprite i = 255
      set the ink of sprite i = 36
      set the blend of sprite i = 100
      append(bulletSpriteList,i)
      exit
    end if
  end repeat
end
```

The "newObject" handler performs a task similar to that performed by the "fireBullet" handler. It looks at all the sprites for one that is empty. It then sets that sprite up to contain a randomly selected "object" cast member, starting at a random location at the top of the screen.

This sprite is also recorded in the "objectSpriteList" so that another handler can remember to keep that sprite moving down.

```
on newObject
  repeat with i = 1 to 48
    if the memberNum of sprite i = 0 then
      puppetSprite i, TRUE
      set the memberNum of sprite i = the number of member→
("object"&random(5))
      set the locH of sprite i = random(620)+10
      set the locV of sprite i = -5
      set the foreColor of sprite i = 255
      set the ink of sprite i = 36
      set the blend of sprite i = 100
      append(objectSpriteList,i)
      exit
    end if
  end repeat
end
```

The "moveBullets" and "moveObjects" handlers loop through all the sprites recorded in the "bulletSpriteList" and "objectSpriteList" and move them accordingly. When a bullet gets to the top of the stage, or an object gets to the bottom of the stage, the bullet or object is removed from its list and the sprite cleared.

```
on moveBullets
  repeat with i = count(bulletSpriteList) down to 1
    put getAt(bulletSpriteList,i) into spriteNum
    put the locV of sprite spriteNum into v
    if v < 0 then
      puppetSprite spriteNum, FALSE
      deleteAt(bulletSpriteList,i)
    else
      set the locV of sprite spriteNum = v-5
    end if
  end repeat
end
```

```
on moveObjects
  repeat with i = count(objectSpriteList) down to 1
    put getAt(objectSpriteList,i) into spriteNum
    put the locV of sprite spriteNum into v
    if v > 480 then
      puppetSprite spriteNum, FALSE
      deleteAt(objectSpriteList,i)
    else
      set the locV of sprite spriteNum = v+5
    end if
  end repeat
end
```

The "lookForCollision" handler loops through all of the bullet sprites and then loops through all of the object sprites to see if any of them intersect. If so, it quickly throws up another cast member, "explode," in its place and erases both the bullet and the object. It also decreases "objectDensity" so that objects appear more often.

```
on lookForCollision
  repeat with i = count(objectSpriteList) down to 1
    put getAt(objectSpriteList,i) into sprite1
    repeat with j = count(bulletSpriteList) down to 1
      if sprite sprite1 intersects→
getAt(bulletSpriteList,j) then
        set the memberNum of sprite sprite1 =→
the number of member "explode"
        updateStage
        puppetSprite sprite1, FALSE
        puppetSprite sprite→
getAt(bulletSpriteList,j), FALSE
        deleteAt(objectSpriteList,i)
        deleteAt(bulletSpriteList,j)
        put objectDensity-1 into objectDensity
      end if
    end repeat
  end repeat
end
```

The last handler in the score script checks all of the object sprites to see if any have collided with the turret. In this case, it just executes a *halt* to stop the game.

```
on lookForDirectHit
  repeat with j = count(objectSpriteList) down to 1
    if sprite gunSprite intersects→
getAt(objectSpriteList,j) then
      set the memberNum of sprite gunSprite→
= the number of member "explode"
      updateStage
      halt
    end if
  end repeat
end
```

In addition to the score script, the game uses an *on startMovie* handler in a movie script to set the global variables.

```
global gunSprite, speed, bulletSpriteList,→
objectSpriteList, objectDensity

on startMovie
  put [] into bulletSpriteList
  put [] into objectSpriteList
  put 0 into speed
  put 5 into gunSprite
  put 25 into objectDensity
  puppetSprite gunSprite, TRUE
end
```

This game is very far from finished. A field that shows your score could be the first improvement you would want to add. Also, something other than a *halt* should be done when the turret is hit. Perhaps the user should be given several lives. Also, different objects could be assigned different speeds—and maybe not even come straight down but at an angle. The objects themselves can be larger and more colorful. The turret can have a shield that appears when the user holds down the Shift key. Let your imagination run wild and remember those old arcade classics.

Moving On

Director is constantly being used to create games. The speed improvements in Director 5.0 mean that this will be truer than ever. A game can be the sole purpose of a Director movie, or it can be just one part of a larger product.

Next, let's return to the more serious side of Lingo and look at database processing techniques.

26 Sorting & Finding: Recursion

In Chapter 15, we talked about lists and how they can be used to store databases. There are some advanced database features, such as sorting and searching, that we can use to make Director databases even more powerful.

The *sort* command will automatically sort a linear or property list. However, there are limitations to this command. For one, it only sorts in ascending order. Also, it cannot sort anything but a simple linear list by value, or a simple property list by property. If you want to sort a list of lists by an element that is deep inside a sublist, for instance, you need to make your own sort routine.

The same is true of the list commands that deal with finding an item in a list. If the item is anything other than a basic element of a linear list, or a property in a simple property list, then you have to come up with your own way of finding the data.

Sorting Complex Lists

Suppose you have a list that is somewhat more complex than a basic linear list. Let's use some U.S. Census information available on the Internet for our example. Assume that we have already converted it into a Lingo list. The first few records in the list would look like this:

```
[[#name: "Alabama", #pop: [4048368, 4086715, 4130843,
4181248, 4220178, 4252982]], [#name: "Alaska", #pop: [553118,
569485, 587485, 598127, 602723, 603617]], [#name: "Arizona",
#pop: [3678757, 3746535, 3835366, 3944181, 4078567,
4217940]],
```

It is a list of lists. Each sublist contains two properties: the name of the state and a list of population numbers. The list of population numbers has six values that represent the population in the middle of the years 1990 to 1995.

The list is already sorted by state name. However, we want to re-sort the list by 1995 population. You can see how the *sort* command won't help us since we can specify which part of the sublist we want it to sort on. Furthermore, we could only use the *sort* command to put things in ascending order anyway. We want this sort to be in descending order, so that the most populated state is first in the list.

Basic Sort

So we need to turn to traditional computer science sorting algorithms. The basic sort routine is called *bubble sort* and works on a very simple principle.

Bubble sort loops through the entire list, comparing pairs of numbers. If the second number is greater than the first, it swaps them. It gets its name from the fact that the values seem to "bubble up" to the top of the list as they are sorted.

One pass through the list is not enough to ensure that all the items are sorted. There have to be as many loops as there are items, to make sure that the most misplaced item in the original list reaches its sorted destination.

Here is what our *bubble sort* handler looks like. The code is specific to the list of state populations shown above.

```
on bubbleSort year
  put year-89 into year
  repeat with i = 1 to count(list)
```

```
    repeat with j = 1 to count(list)-1
      if getAt(getProp(getAt(list,j),#pop), year)→
  < getAt(getProp(getAt(list,j+1),#pop), year) then
        put getAt(list,j) into v
        setAt(list,j,getAt(list,j+1))
        setAt(list,j+1,v)
      end if
    end repeat
  end repeat
end
```

The main action that goes on is the swapping at the heart of the handler. This handler takes a value like *95* and converts it to the corresponding position of that year's data in the population sublist (95 – 89 = 6). It then just compares pairs of values and swaps them if it doesn't like the order.

This type of processing will seem weird to those unfamiliar with it. Test it out, though, to see that it works. Try it on smaller lists and have the handler spit out the "list" variable as it goes along to see the gradual change.

A bubble sort works great, except that it takes a while to run. After all, if there are 50 records, and it has two nested loops, then it must perform 2,500 compares before finishing.

Divide & Conquer

A better way to sort is to use an algorithm called *Quick Sort*. This routine uses a technique called *recursion*.

Recursion means that a handler calls itself. What it does is divide a large task into two smaller tasks. Then it calls itself twice to handle these two smaller tasks individually. The routine will then divide these tasks further and call itself more times. Eventually, the tasks become so small that they are easy to handle. When the tasks cannot be divided anymore, the recursive routine has done its job and returns a value rather than calling itself again.

Many college computer science majors have met with their counselors and switched majors to business or the humanities after seeing this sort of thing. Recursion is actually the foundation of many programming techniques, but fortunately multimedia programming uses it only in rare cases.

Here is the recursive "quickSort" handler. It is a short handler that calls the "qSort" handler once. This "qSort" handler then divides the task over and over again.

```
-- Kicks off recursive sort routine
on quickSort year
  put year-89 into year
  qSort(year,1,count(list))
end

-- Recursive sort
on qSort year,first,last
  -- Use first value as the pivot
  put getAt(getProp(getAt(list,first),#pop), year) into pivot

  repeat while TRUE
    -- look for first low value
    repeat with i = 1 to last
      if getAt(getProp(getAt(list,i),#pop),year) <= pivot then
        put i into up
        exit repeat
      end if
    end repeat

    -- look for last high value
    repeat with i = last down to 1
      if getAt(getProp(getAt(list,i),#pop),year) >= pivot then
        put i into down
        exit repeat
      end if
    end repeat

    -- see if all swapping has been done for now
    if down <= up then
      exit repeat
```

```
      -- swap
    else
      put getAt(list,down) into v
      setAt(list,down,getAt(list,up))
      setAt(list,up,v)
    end if
  end repeat

  -- Call for two halves of list if necessary
  if up-1 > first then qsort(year,first,up-1)
  if up+1 < last then qsort(year,up+1,last)
end
```

The main gist of the "qSort" handler is that it picks a value in the list—the first value, in this case—as its *pivot value.* It then finds the earliest value in the list that is less than the pivot value and the latest value that is greater than the pivot value. It swaps these. Eventually, it gets to swapping the pivot value into the middle of the list. Then everything below this value is lower in the list than it is, and everything greater than this value is higher in the list than it is. However, these two halves of the list are not in any order. So it calls itself twice to better sort these two halves.

Eventually, the handler ends up sorting lists that only contain two or three elements. It doesn't need to call itself again at this point, because no more sorting needs to be done; you can assume that a list with one element is a sorted list.

Technically, this type of sort is much faster than a bubble sort. However, this is not the case with our example. With larger lists, say with 10,000 records, it will prove its speed.

Clever Sort

There is one final way to sort a list like this. It uses no established computer algorithm, yet it is much faster. It uses Lingo's *sort* command instead.

But wait a minute. Didn't we just talk about how you can't use *sort* to deal with complex lists like this one?

That's right, but we can change this list so that it is the type of list that *sort* works on. All we need to do is create a second list that uses the desired sort key as the property name of each entry. Then we sort the list with the *sort* command. Finally, we take this sorted list and repopulate the original list with the data—minus the property names.

```
on directorSort year
  put year-89 into year
  put [:] into sortedList

  -- create new list with properties
  repeat with i = 1 to count(list)
    put getAt(list,i) into state
    put getAt(getProp(state,#pop),year) into n
    addProp(sortedList,n,state)
  end repeat

  sort(sortedList)

  -- copy data back to original list
  put [] into list
  repeat with i = 1 to count(sortedList)
    append(list,getAt(sortedList,i))
  end repeat
end
```

By using Director's built-in *sort* command, we get results 10 times faster than our well-intentioned sort handlers. However, we don't get the list in descending order. Another simple handler can be written to reverse any list.

```
on reverseList
  put count(list) into last
  repeat with i = 1 to last/2+1
    put getAt(list,i) into v
    setAt(list,i,getAt(list,last-i+1))
    setAt(list,last-i+1,v)
  end repeat

end
```

The "reverseList" handler just moves through the first half of the list and swaps the items in the first half with items on the other side of the list.

Searching

Lingo lists have plenty of good seek-and-find functions like *getOne*, *findPos*, and *getProp* that can be used on basic linear or property lists. Complex lists, like our list of state populations, need custom handlers, however.

In this case we want to search our list of states for the one with a population closest to a certain number. This means we probably won't find a state that matches our number exactly, but we want to know which one is closest.

A basic requirement of a searchable list is that it be sorted. So we can use any one of our sort handlers above to sort the list by population. Now we can write a simple handler that looks for the first state in the list with a population less than our value. It then determines if that state, or the one just before it, is the closest.

```
on simpleFind year, pop
  put year-89 into year
  repeat with i = 2 to count(list)
    put getAt(getProp(getAt(list,i),#pop), year) into val2
    if val2 < pop then
      put getAt(getProp(getAt(list,i-1),#pop),→
year) into val1
      if abs(val1-pop) < abs(val2-pop) then→
return i-1
      else return i
    end if
  end repeat
end
```

The "simpleFind" handler loops through the list starting with the second state. It uses the *abs* function to determine which state has the closest population to our search value.

This isn't the fastest handler for this type of function. It needs to look down the list and check every item. If the list was thousands of records long, and the value it needed was at the bottom, it would have to look at nearly all the values.

A better way to do this would be to jump ahead to the middle of the list, if we know the value is at the end. If the search value is less than the population of a state in the middle of the list, then it knows it can find that value in the first half of the list. Otherwise, the value must be in the second half of the list.

You can see how much work has already been saved by dividing the list into two pieces. No reason to stop there. Might as well divide the remaining half into two pieces to save even more work. We should keep doing this until we find the value.

This is basically the same concept as our recursive sort routine. We are using a recursive seek handler to quickly home in on the desired value.

```
on recursiveFind year, pop
  put year-89 into year
  return rFind(year,pop,1,count(list))
end

on rFind year, pop, n1, n2
  -- See if we have narrowed it down to one
  if n1 = n2 then return n1
  put getAt(getProp(getAt(list,n1),#pop),year) into val1
  put getAt(getProp(getAt(list,n2),#pop),year) into val2

  -- See if we found exactly the value
  if val1 = pop then
    return n1
  else if val2 = pop then
    return n2

    -- See if we have narrowed to two
  else if n2 = n1+1 then
    -- Find closest value of the two
    if abs(val1-pop) < abs(val2-pop) then return n1
    else return n2
  end if
```

```
    -- Divide list in half and continue to look
    -- in the half that has our value
    put (n2-n1)/2+n1 into n
    put getAt(getProp(getAt(list,n),#pop),year) into val
    if val > pop then
      return rFind(year,pop,n,n2)
    else
      return rFind(year,pop,n1,n)
    end if
  end
```

Moving On

Director can be used to sort large, advanced databases of information. The list structure is a very robust part of Director and can be used for just about any type of data.

The programming concepts learned in this chapter, including bubble sort, recursion, and the seek method (which is sometimes called a "binary search"), are techniques that may be useful in a variety of different situations.

Now let's move back into the world of the user interface and look at how we can create windows outside of the stage.

27

Movies in a Window

One of the coolest features of Director and Lingo is the ability to create windows other than the stage. They are quick and easy to generate, and they work just like regular Director movies.

They work just like regular Director movies because that is exactly what they are. All you need to do to create a movie in a window (or *MIAW,* as they are nicknamed) is make a new movie. Set the movie to be small—say, 200 by 200 pixels. Then, save it as "win.dir" in your Director folder. Close that file and start a "new" movie. You may want to set the stage size back to 640 by 480.

Now type in the message window this simple command:

```
open window "win.dir"
```

A standard window will appear. On the Macintosh, it looks like Figure 27-1. On a Windows machine, it will look similar but more like a Windows-style window.

Figure 27-1: *A small empty window.*

You can get rid of this window by either clicking on the close box on the window or typing this in the message window:

```
close window "win.dir"
```

However, the window is not really gone. It has just been made invisible. The Lingo function *the windowList* will show us what windows are present. Even if we have "closed" this window, it still shows up in the list.

```
put the windowList

-- [(window "win.dir")]
```

We can make the window reappear by using the *open window* command again, or by making it visible.

```
set the visible of window "win.dir" = TRUE
```

We can get rid of the window once and for all by using the *forget window* command. This removes the window from memory entirely. It is important to do this, as leftover windows can take up enough memory to bring a movie to its knees.

```
forget window "win.dir"

put the windowList
-- []
```

We can also change many characteristics of the window. For instance, we can change the title of the window.

```
set the title of window "win.dir" = "My Window"
```

Of course it would be better to have the proper title of the window set to what we want before the window is visible. In this case, we don't want to use the *open window* command at all. We can use a combination of commands to create a new window, set it to run a movie file, change its title, and *then* make it visible.

```
on openWindow
   set myWin = window("MyWin")
   set the filename of myWin = "win.dir"
   set the title of myWin = "My Window"
   set the visible of myWin = TRUE
end
```

This simple handler creates a variable to hold the window definition. From that point on, we can refer to the window as just "myWin." It may be a good idea to make this variable a global if you plan on using it in other handlers—like one that closes the window, for instance.

TIP

Changing the title of a window does not change its name. *The window retains the original name set during its creation.*

The handler then assigns a movie file to the window. This is where it gets its size and content. Then the title is set to something other than the name of the window, and the window is made visible.

One other property of any window is its window type. You check it and set it with *the windowType of window* function. Exactly what these look like depend on whether you are on a Mac or Windows machine. Figures 27-2 to 27-15 show some samples.

Figure 27-2: *Window type -1, a movable standard window with a resize box but no zoom box.*

Figure 27-3: *Window type 1, a nonmovable thick-bordered box.*

Figure 27-4: *Window type 2, a nonmovable thin-bordered box.*

Figure 27-5: *Window type 3, a nonmovable box with a drop shadow.*

Figure 27-6: *Window type 4, a movable standard window without a resize or zoom box.*

Figure 27-7: *Window type 5, a movable box with a thick border.*

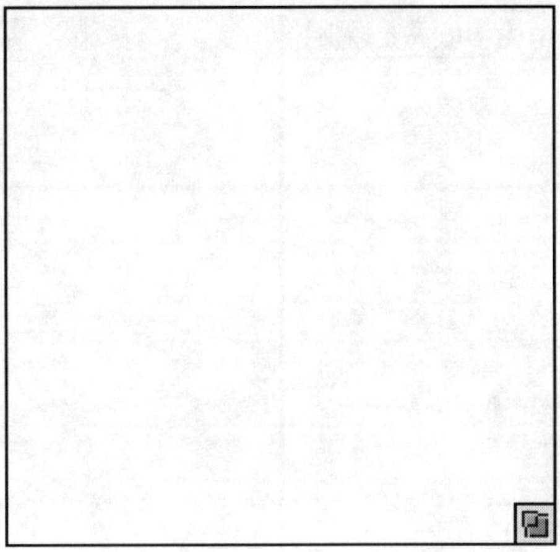

Figure 27-8: *Window type 6, a nonmovable thin-bordered box with a resize box.*

Figure 27-9: *Window type 7, a nonmovable box with a drop shadow and a resize box.*

Figure 27-10: *Window type 8, a movable standard window with a resize box and a zoom box.*

Figure 27-11: *Window type 12, a movable standard window with a zoom box but no resize box.*

Figure 27-12: *Window type 16, a round rect box.*

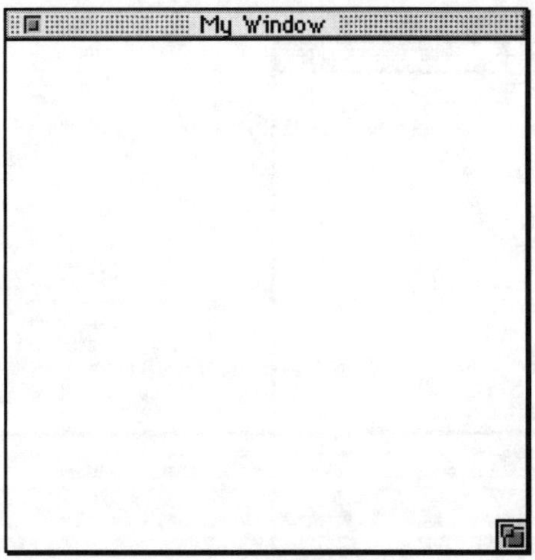

Figure 27-13: *Window type 48, a palette window with a resize box but no zoom box. Sometimes called a "windoid."*

Figure 27-14: *Window type 52, a palette window without a resize box or a zoom box.*

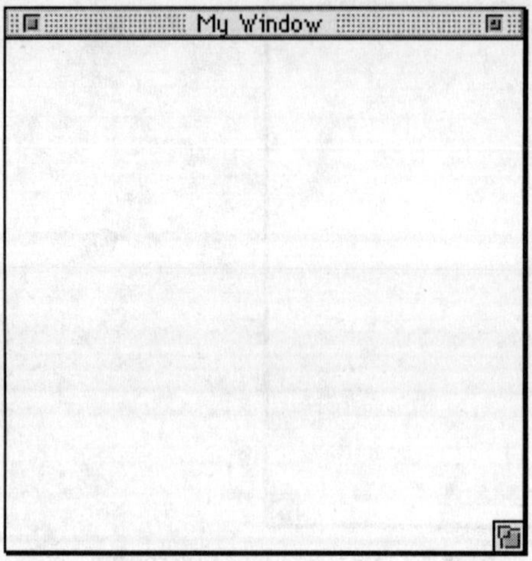

Figure 27-15: *Window type 56, a palette window with a resize box and a zoom box.*

There are other variations as well. However, not all of these windows work in both Director and projectors, and not all are available in Microsoft Windows. Just keep in mind that you need to check your windows when you're working in different environments and on different computers to make sure you get what you asked for.

In order to properly use things like the zoom box and resize box, there are some special handlers that respond to messages generated by these two functions: *on zoomWindow* and *on resizeWindow*.

When a user resizes or zooms, first the window is changed and then these handlers are called, if they exist in the movie that the window contains. You can use *the rect of window* to figure out what the new size of the window is and possibly change the contents of the window accordingly.

Let's look at an example. Create a movie that has a scrolling text field in its center. Make the movie about 200 by 200 pixels and make the text field about 5 pixels away from the top and sides and about 30 pixels away from the bottom. Figure 27-16 shows an example. The following movie script will resize the text field if the window size changes.

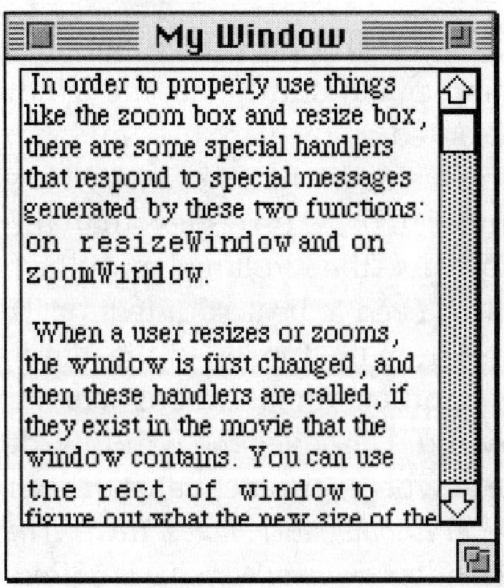

Figure 27-16: *A simple window with a text field.*

```
on zoomWindow
  resizeText
end

on resizeWindow
  resizeText
end

on resizeText
  global myWin
  put the rect of myWin into rec
  put the left of rec into l
  put the right of rec into r
  put the top of rec into t
  put the bottom of rec into b
  put rect(0,0,r-l-30,b-t-30) into castRect
  puppetSprite 1, TRUE
  set the rect of cast 1 = castRect
  set the locH of sprite 1 = 5
  set the locV of sprite 1 = 5
end
```

Our "resize" handler is called from either the *on resizeWindow* or the *on zoomWindow* handler. It assumes that the window it is dealing with is itself represented by the variable "myWin." It gets the rectangle of the window using *the rect of window*. Then it stretches the text field cast member to be 30 pixels less than the movie window. It has to be less because the scrolling bar of the field and the resize box of the window need to be accounted for. The sprite is then positioned 5 pixels from the top left of the window.

There are also new handlers for situations when the user clicks on the close box of a window, moves the window, deactivates the window by clicking elsewhere, or reactivates the window again: *on closeWindow*, *on moveWindow*, and *on deactivateWindow*, *on activateWindow*. The handler *on openWindow* is called when a movie is first opened in its window.

When you have more than one window present, you can change their order on the screen with the *moveToBack* and *moveToFront* commands. You can also check to see which window is active by checking the function *the activeWindow*.

The Lingo function *windowPresent(window)* is useful for avoiding errors generated by asking for a window that doesn't exist to do something. For instance, if you want to *forget* a window, you should check to make sure it exists.

```
if windowPresent(myWin) then forget(myWin)
```

Windows can communicate with the stage and each other with the *tell* command. You can send one or more Lingo commands this way. For instance, if you want a button in a window to call a handler called "myHandler" that is part of the stage's movie, use the *tell* command.

```
tell the stage to myHandler
```

You can also send any normal Lingo command rather than a call to a handler.

```
tell the stage to put "Hello" into field "test"
```

If you need more than one command to be sent, you can use the *tell* command in a slightly different way:

```
tell the stage
  put "Hello" into field "test"
  myHandler
end tell
```

Windows can also communicate with each other this way. You can *tell* another window to do something by using its window name or a global variable that represents the window.

```
tell window "myWin" to put "Hello" into field "test"
tell myWin to put "Hello" into field "test"
```

Windows can also be used to ask critical questions of users. You can set *the modal* of a window to *TRUE*, which will prevent any other interaction outside of the window from taking place. This means that the user is forced to interact only with the window.

For example, you can use a modal window to ask a question. Figure 25-17 shows an example.

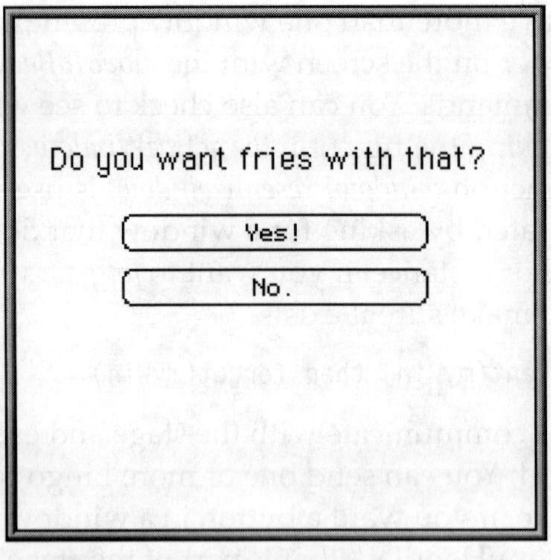

Figure 25-17: *A modal window.*

The code you need to create this window is the same as that of any other window handler. We just need to set *the modal* to *TRUE* in addition to the other things. We also select a *windowType* that is appropriate for this type of interface.

```
on openModalWindow
  global myWin5
  set myWin5 = window("ModalWin")
  set the filename of myWin5 = "ask.dir"
  set the windowType of myWin5 = 1
  set the modal of myWin5 = TRUE
  set the visible of myWin5 = TRUE
end
```

In turn, the answer buttons in the window need to *forget* the current window for us, since no stage interaction can happen until that is done. Here is the code for the "yes" button. It assumes that the window is represented by the global "myWin5."

```
on mouseUp
  global myWin5
  tell the stage to put "Yes" into field "test"
  forget myWin5
end
```

You can use windows for a variety of tasks. For instance, simple rectangle windows are a good way to overcome the 48-sprite limit in Director. You could have several windows adjacent to, or covering parts of, the stage.

Movies in a window have all the same capabilities as those with the stage. Director 4.0 had some limitations as far as transitions, but they work fine in Director 5.0.

Think about the possibilities of having multiple frames in one movie and using that movie as a library of dialog boxes. You can assign the same file to different windows if you wish, and then have the different windows showing different frames of that movie. For instance, frame one could be a yes/no dialog box, frame 2 could be an OK/Cancel dialog box, frame 3 could be a "please type your name" dialog box, etc. Then you could have the handler that opens this movie as a MIAW also have the MIAW jump to the frame of the dialog box you need.

Moving On

Movies in a window make our user-interface environment just about complete. We can now create dialog boxes, information windows, and tool palettes.

One last interface item we need to address is the pop-up menu. We'll take care of that next.

Moving On

28

Pop-Up Menus

Director allows us to make standard menus, but there is no pop-up menu function. Pop-up menus are interface objects that expand into single menus when clicked. Pop-up menus can appear anywhere on the stage.

However, we can use sprites and cast members to simulate this type of interface element. When the user clicks and holds on one of these cast members, the cast member expands to reveal a list of options. The user can then move the mouse down to select an item.

Text Pop-Up Menus

Figures 28-1 and 28-2 show a typical pop-up menu. The user clicks on the cast member and a list of options "pops up."

Figure 28-1: *The user is about to click on the pop-up menu.*

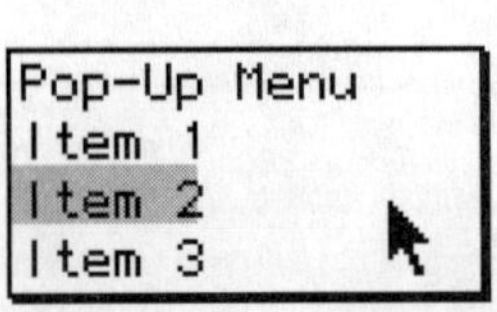

Figure 28-2: *The user has clicked on the pop-up menu and is holding down the mouse button while making a selection.*

This type of functionality can easily be accomplished with just a text field cast member. Make one that looks like Figure 28-2. You will need to set a 1-pixel border and a 1-pixel drop shadow. You will also need to set the field to "fixed" size. Then shrink the field on the stage so that only the first line of the field shows.

The field is now ready to be clicked. We need to place a script inside the text field cast member to handle the pop-up functionality.

```
on mouseDown

  put the clickOn into c
  put the memberNum of sprite c into m
  put (the lineHeight of member m)*→
(the lineCount of member m)+1 into h1
  put (the lineHeight of member m)+1 into h2
  put the rect of member m into r
  put rect(the left of r, the top of r,→
the right of r, the top of r + h1) into newRect
  put rect(the left of r, the top of r,→
the right of r, the top of r + h2) into originalRect
  set the rect of member m = newRect
  put 0 into lastHilite
  repeat while the mouseDown
    put the mouseLine into ml
    if the mouseCast <> m then
      exit repeat
    else if ml > 0 and ml <> lastHilite then
      hilite line ml of member m
      put ml into lastHilite
    else if ml <> lastHilite then
      exit repeat
```

```
    end if
  end repeat
  set the rect of member m = originalRect
  put ml
end
```

The first thing our handler does is get the sprite and cast member numbers and place them in the variables "c" and "m." Then it uses *the lineCount* and *the lineHeight* to figure out how high the text box really is. The height of the cast member when all the lines are showing is placed in "h1"; the height of the field when only the first item is showing is placed in "h2." These two variables are then used to calculate the "newRect" and "originalRect" variables, respectively.

The cast member is then set to the "newRect" rectangle to show all the menu items. It then loops while the user holds down the mouse. It changes the *hilite* to match the line the cursor is over, making sure not to use the *hilite* command more than once consecutively on a line. When you use the *hilite* command, it automatically removes the previous highlight.

If the user moves the mouse off of the field or releases the mouse button, the handler quits—but not before setting the rectangle of the field back to normal. The resulting menu item selected is placed in "ml."

A peculiar problem with this handler is that the *hilite* function doesn't produce a nice effect. It seems to highlight all but the last half of the last character on each line, as shown in Figure 28-2. We can fix this by using a more complex *hilite* statement.

```
on mouseDown
  put the clickOn into c
  put the memberNum of sprite c into m
  put (the lineHeight of member m)*→
(the lineCount of member m)+1 into h1
  put (the lineHeight of member m)+1 into h2
  put the rect of member m into r
  put rect(the left of r, the top of r,→
the right of r, the top of r + h1) into newRect
  put rect(the left of r, the top of r,→
```

```
the right of r, the top of r + h2) into originalRect
  set the rect of member m = newRect
  put 0 into lastHilite
  repeat while the mouseDown
    put the mouseLine into ml
    if the mouseCast <> m then
      exit repeat
    else if ml > 0 and ml <> lastHilite then
      if ml = 1 then put 1 into nl
      else put (the number of chars in line 1→
to ml-1 of field m)+2 into nl
      put (the number of chars in line 1 to ml→
of field m)+1 into n2
      hilite char nl to n2 of member m
      put ml into lastHilite
    else if ml <> lastHilite then
      exit repeat
    end if
  end repeat
  set the rect of member m = originalRect
  return ml
end
```

This handler figures out what the first character of the selected line is and what the last character of the selection line is. Then it uses these characters to *hilite* the area instead of the line. The difference is that we include the Return character at the end of each line. Figure 28-3 shows how much nicer this looks.

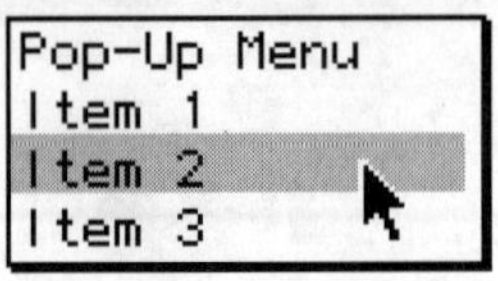

Figure 28-3: *The same pop-up menu with a better hilite command.*

Bitmap Pop-Up Menus

You can get away altogether from using text fields for pop-ups. Using bitmaps instead of text fields allows you to display more attractive text, and even graphic icons, in your pop-up menus.

Figure 28-4 shows the initial pop-up menu button on the stage. Figure 28-5 shows the bitmap that appears when the user clicks on the button. Figure 28-6 shows the first of a series of three bitmaps that represent the pop-up menu with different items selected. Two other cast members show each of the other two items selected.

Figure 28-4: *A pop-up menu button.*

Figure 28-5: *After the pop-up menu button has been pressed.*

Figure 28-6: *After the user selects the first item.*

The handler for this is actually simpler than the text field pop-ups. We just have to hard-code the height of each individual menu item, so that as the cursor moves we can follow it by changing the cast member of the sprite.

```
on mouseDown
  put the clickOn into c
  put the memberNum of sprite c into m
  repeat while the mouseDown
    put the mouseV into v
    put (v-the locV of sprite c)/16+1 into ml
    if not rollover(c) then
      exit repeat
    else
      set the memberNum of sprite c = the→
number of member ("popup3."&string(ml))
      updateStage
    end if
  end repeat
  put ml
end
```

The handler uses *16* as the height of each menu item. Next, it does some math to figure out which item is currently selected. It expects the names of the cast members to follow a pattern: "popup3.1," "popup3.2," etc. The item selected ends up in "ml," although invalid results can be stored there if the user has moved away from the sprite.

To prevent such invalid results we need to use *rollover* to see if the user is still over the sprite. If we used *the mouseCast*, it wouldn't work, since we are changing the member during the handler.

The advantages of a bitmap pop-up menu are many. For instance, you can choose any way you want to highlight the selected item: select a different shade, color, or font; or place a mark like a dot or a checkmark next to the selected item.

There are many other ways to do a pop-up menu with bitmaps. If you are concerned about file size, you may want to work out a way that uses more than one sprite and has individual bitmaps that represent only the highlighted items, as well as one larger "background" bitmap that shows all of the items in their grayed-out state. This way you have one grayed-out menu bitmap and several possible highlighted item bitmaps that appear on top of the pop-up menu bitmap as the user selects different items.

Option Pop-Up Menu

Another type of pop-up menu works by displaying one of the items in the menu initially then letting you click on it to choose another. Once you have chosen another item, that item is displayed when the pop-up menu returns to its condensed state. Figures 28-7, 28-8, and 28-9 show such a sequence of changes.

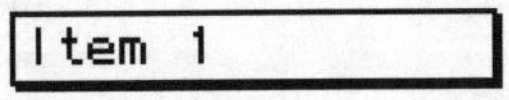

Figure 28-7: *An option pop-up that shows "Item 1" as the currently selected option.*

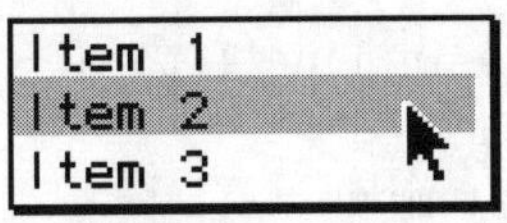

Figure 28-8: *While the user is selecting another option.*

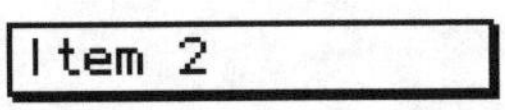

Figure 28-9: *After the user has selected "Item 2."*

We can pull this function off using the same text field from earlier in this chapter. However, the script is quite different. We actually embed the text of the field into the script and change it when the user clicks. Then, the text is changed to the selected option when the user releases.

```
on mouseDown
  put the clickOn into c
  put the memberNum of sprite c into m
  put "Item 1"&RETURN&"Item 2"&RETURN&"Item 3" into field m
  put (the lineHeight of member m)*(the→
lineCount of member m)+1 into h1
  put (the lineHeight of member m)+1 into h2
```

```
    put the rect of member m into r
    put rect(the left of r, the top of r, the→
right of r, the top of r + h1) into newRect
    put rect(the left of r, the top of r, the→
right of r, the top of r + h2) into originalRect
    set the rect of member m = newRect
    put 0 into lastHilite
    repeat while the mouseDown
      put the mouseLine into ml
      if the mouseCast <> m then
        exit repeat
      else if ml > 0 and ml <> lastHilite then
        if ml = 1 then put 1 into n1
        else put (the number of chars in line 1→
to ml-1 of field m)+2 into n1
        put (the number of chars in line 1 to ml→
of field m)+1 into n2
        hilite char n1 to n2 of member m
        put ml into lastHilite
      else if ml <> lastHilite then
        exit repeat
      end if
    end repeat
    set the rect of member m = originalRect
    put line ml of field m into field m
end
```

This type of pop-up menu can be used in all sorts of situations to answer questions, set user options, control movies, and swap sprites.

Moving On

Pop-up menus have been present for a long time in computer software. Now they are becoming common in multimedia products. They are particularly valuable because they allow a large number of options yet initially take up only a small amount of space on the stage.

Next, we will look at Lingo's most complex structure: the parent-child object.

29 Object-Oriented Programming (OOP)

Lingo programmers are divided into two groups when it comes to object-oriented programming: those who love it and use it as often as possible, and those who have no idea what it means and are scared to death of it. What that second group doesn't realize is that they have been doing object-oriented programming all along.

What Is Object-Oriented Programming?

Actually, just about all of Director is object-oriented. Even non-Lingo development is object-oriented. So, if you are one of the "scared to death" people, you are about to find out that there is nothing to be scared of.

When we think of simple programming, we usually divide everything into two pieces: the function and the data. For instance, a word processor is a functional piece of programming, without any data. The data is the document that you create.

With object-oriented programming we create *objects* instead of separate functions and data. Each object knows what it is and how to behave.

A good example is a bitmap cast member that has a script inside. The script knows how to react to the user clicking on the bitmap that contains it. The bitmap and the script inside it can be defined as an object.

Furthermore, objects can have properties. Our bitmap could have a name, a color depth setting, a width and height, and any number of other standard properties in Director.

Objects can then relate themselves to other objects. A sprite cell in the score, for instance, is an object. It combines a cast member, a script, an ink setting, a screen location, and other properties. Notice that the cast member that is part of this sprite cell object is also an object itself.

A scrolling text field is another good example of an object. It contains some text and has a scroll bar to the right. When the various elements of the scroll bar are clicked, the object knows how to behave by changing the text displayed in the field. Function and data are married into one object.

Parent-Child Scripts

The parent-child structure in Lingo is just an extension of the type of programming we have already been using. In previous chapters we put our global variable definitions at the top of the script cast member. This made them available for all of the handlers in the cast member. At their most basic, parent-child scripts do the same thing.

Let's take a look at a small parent script. Type it into a cast member and change the script type of the cast member to "parent."

```
property num

on new me, startNum
  put startNum into num
  return me
end

on beeper me
  repeat with i = 1 to num
    beep()
  end repeat
end
```

This is the parent script. It has one property, "num," and two handlers, "new" and "beeper." A parent script is like a template. We can create usable objects from this template. The objects we create are called *instances* or *children*. They share the handlers and properties of the parent, but properties may be set to different values in different children.

The *property* declaration for this script is just like the *global* declaration for normal script cast members. The exception is that these variables are only available to the children of this parent script and are individual, distinct variables in each child. In other words, setting "num" in one child will not change the value of "num" in another child.

The "new" handler is mandatory for the parent script and acts like a kind of *on startMovie* handler for it. When you want to create a child object, this handler runs to initialize any property variables you need. It also returns a variable that represents the new object. Inside the parent script, this variable is always represented as *me*. This *me* property should be included as the first parameter in every handler of the parent script.

TIP

The use of me *is by convention. You can actually use any variable name you want, but that is rarely done.*

To create a child object from a parent script, we will use the *new* command. In the message window, try the following:

```
set myObj1 = new(script "parent", 3)
```

This will create an instance of a child of that parent. The variable "myObj1" will represent, or *point to*, this child. We can create as many as we want, as long as we keep assigning them to different variables.

```
set myObj2 = new(script "parent", 7)
```

To access the handler inside a child, just include the variable that represents it in place of the *me* parameter. For instance, to execute the "beeper" handler in our current example, try this:

```
beeper(myObj1)
```

There should be three system beeps. This is because the "num" property in the child object represented by "myObj1" is set to 3. When the "beeper" handler is called, it uses this property to determine how many times to beep. If we called the "beeper" handler that is a part of the child "myObj2," we would get seven beeps, because the "num" property in that child was set to 7.

```
beeper(myObj2)
```

There is no magic to how the 3 and the 7 in the two children were set. We set them with a straightforward Lingo command in the *new* handler of the parent script when we created the children with the *new* command. Take a careful look at the parent script above to see how this was done.

Creating Objects

Let's use the parent-child structure to create something a little more graphical. We'll put circles on the stage and have them move around like bumblebees.

Each bee will be a child object created from a parent "bee" script. The only thing our bees will do is move around the stage in a bee-like fashion.

The parent script would look like this:

```
property spriteNum, moveLeft, moveRight, moveUp, moveDown
on new me, spriteNum0
  put spriteNum0 into spriteNum
  put random(7) into moveLeft
  put random(7) into moveRight
  put random(7) into moveUp
  put random(7) into moveDown
  puppetSprite spriteNum, TRUE
  set the locH of sprite spriteNum = random(640)
  set the locV of sprite spriteNum = random(480)
  return me
end
```

```
on buzz me
  put random(moveRight)-4 into x1
  put random(moveLeft)-4 into x2
  put random(moveDown)-4 into y1
  put random(moveUp)-4 into y2
  put the (locH of sprite spriteNum) +x1-x2 into x
  put the (locV of sprite spriteNum) +y1-y2 into y
  if x > 640 then put x-640 into x
  else if x < 0 then put x+640 into x
  if y > 480 then put y-480 into y
  else if y < 0 then put y+480 into y
  set the locH of sprite spriteNum = x
  set the locV of sprite spriteNum = y
end
```

This parent script contains five properties: one for the sprite number of the bee and four that represent how the bee will move. The "spriteNum" property is set immediately in the *new* handler to a sprite number that is passed as a parameter. We use the variable "spriteNum0" to pass the value into the *new* handler and then immediately pass that value along to the real property, "spriteNum."

The four "move…" variables are set to random numbers between 1 and 7. The sprite is puppeted and given a random position on the stage. We need to make sure that the bee cast members are already in the sprite channels before we call this "new" handler.

The only other handler in the script is the "buzz" handler. This handler, when called, uses the "move…" variables to tweak the position of the sprite. It also makes sure that if the sprite moves beyond the edge of the stage, it reappears on the other side.

The parent script should be named "bee," which is how we will identify it when we call the *new* handler. The script that creates the bees will be an *on startMovie* handler. This handler creates a global list called "beeList" and stores the pointers to each bee as elements in the list.

```
on startMovie
  global beeList
  put [] into beeList
  repeat with i = 1 to 5
    set temp = new(script "bee",i)
    append(beeList,temp)
  end repeat
end
```

There also needs to be an *on exitFrame* handler to go into the score frame script. This will just give each bee in the list a chance to "buzz" around.

```
on exitFrame
  global beeList
  repeat with i = 1 to count(beeList)
    buzz(getAt(beeList,i))
  end repeat
  go to the frame
end
```

Place bitmaps in the first five sprites—they could be drawings of bees, or just circles. The movie should now create five "bees," and they should start moving around the screen.

Take the time to observe each one. Notice how every bee has a slightly different behavior. One, for instance, may constantly be edging a little to the right. Another may be quickly moving downward.

Since we assign the "move..." properties of the bees during the *new* handler, each bee gets a set of characteristics that sticks with it throughout its life. If a bee gets a higher "moveRight" than a "moveLeft" number, it will have the characteristic of moving to the right over time.

Ancestor Scripts

When a child object is "born," it inherits all the handlers from its parent script. It also inherits the list of property variables from its parent, though it may have any value for each of these variables.

One special property that a parent-child object can have is *the ancestor* property. This variable can be set to another parent script. When that happens, the child inherits all of the handlers of that second parent, as well as those of the original parent.

The great thing about ancestors is that you can assign the same ancestor to several different children. You can even assign the same ancestor to children that have different parents. For instance, you could have two children with parent A and two children with parent B, and all of them could share ancestor C.

By assigning a parent script as the ancestor of an object, that object can use all of its handlers. The object would first check to see if the parent script contained the handler, then look to see if the ancestor script contained the handler.

Ancestor scripts can also have properties that can be set and used by the handlers inside the ancestor script. These properties aren't readily available to the child script, however, but they do modify the actions of the ancestor script's handlers.

Let's revisit the bumblebee program. What if there were two types of bee. One type runs away when you click on it; the other type stings you.

We'll create two parent scripts to act as ancestors for our bees. The first one will make a bee that runs away when you click it. We'll name this parent script cast member "bee type1."

```
property scamperCount, scamperDist

on new me
  put 0 into scamperCount
  return me
end

on click
  put 10 into scamperCount
  if random(2) = 1 then
    put 10 into scamperDist
  else
    put -10 into scamperDist
  end if
end
```

```
on action me, spriteNum
  if scamperCount < 1 then exit
  set the locH of sprite spriteNum =→
the locH of sprite spriteNum + scamperDist
  put scamperCount-1 into scamperCount
end
```

The *new* handler will initialize "scamperCount" to 0. When this property is set to 0, it means that the bee should behave normally.

The first handler, "click," will set "scamperCount" to 10 and assign either a 10 or –10 to "scamperDist." We will use this last property to determine how much of an extra horizontal offset we get when the bee is trying to get away from the cursor.

The "action" handler will be called from the "buzz" handler of our new bee objects. It checks to make sure that "scamperCount" is not 0. If it is greater than 0, it moves the bee 10 pixels to the right or left then decreases "scamperCount" by 1. This will mean that each time the user clicks on this type of bee, the bee will scamper away 100 pixels to the right or left.

Now let's create the second type of bee—one that stings when you click it. The parent script we will use as an ancestor in this case is similar to the last one. We'll call it "bee type2."

```
property stingCount

on new me
  put 0 into stingCount
  return me
end

on click
  put 10 into stingCount
end

on action me, spriteNum
  if stingCount < 1 then exit
  if stingCount = 1 then
    set the foreColor of sprite spriteNum = 255
  else
    set the foreColor of sprite spriteNum = random(255)
    put stingCount-1 into stingCount
  end if
end
```

This script is a little simpler in that it doesn't need to decide which direction it will take to scamper away. Instead, it sets the variable "stingCount" to 10 and then proceeds to repeatedly change the color of the bee while that counter decreases back to 0. The effect works best if the bee graphic is 1-bit or a simple circle.

The *on startMovie* handler and the *on exitFrame* hander stay the same for this improved bumblebee program. However, the "bee" parent script changes in two important places.

First, it randomly picks an ancestor script in the *new* handler. Second, it calls the "action" handler of that ancestor to check to see if the bee is in the process of a scamper-away or a sting.

```
property spriteNum, moveLeft, moveRight,→
moveUp, moveDown, ancestor

on new me, spriteNum0
  put spriteNum0 into spriteNum
  put random(6) into moveLeft
  put random(6) into moveRight
  put random(6) into moveUp
  put random(6) into moveDown
  puppetSprite spriteNum, TRUE
  set the locH of sprite spriteNum = random(640)
  set the locV of sprite spriteNum = random(480)
  if random(2) = 1 then set the ancestor of me→
= new(script "bee type1")
  else set the ancestor of me =→
new(script "bee type2")
  return me
end

on buzz me
  put random(moveRight+1)-1 into x1
  put random(moveLeft+1)-1 into x2
  put random(moveDown+1)-1 into y1
  put random(moveUp+1)-1 into y2
  put the locH of sprite spriteNum+x1-x2 into x
  put the locV of sprite spriteNum+y1-y2 into y
  if x > 640 then put x-640 into x
  else if x < 0 then put x+640 into x
```

```
    if y > 480 then put y-480 into y
    else if y < 0 then put y+480 into y
    set the locH of sprite spriteNum = x
    set the locV of sprite spriteNum = y
    action(me,spriteNum)
  end
```

There also needs to be an *on mouseDown* handler attached to each of the sprites. This will call the "action" handler through the child object to the ancestor script.

```
  on mouseDown
    global beeList
    click(getAt(beeList,the clickOn))
  end
```

Now, when you click on some of the bees, they will run away to the left or the right. Other bees will flash several colors very quickly when you click them. The bees are consistent in their behavior, since each bee has one or the other ancestor.

A similar-looking script can produce a different effect. We can change the *on startMovie* handler to create two child objects from the two ancestor scripts, then assign these children as the ancestors of the bees. This way, the bees share certain properties. All bees that run away will run away in unison when one is clicked. All the stinging bees will sting at the same time when one is clicked. The *on startMovie* handler looks like this:

```
  on startMovie
    global beeList
    put new(script "bee type1") into beeType1
    put new(script "bee type2") into beeType2
    put [] into beeList
    repeat with i = 1 to 5
      if random(2) = 1 then set temp =→
  new(script "bee",i,beeType1)
      else set temp = new(script "bee",i,beeType2)
      append(beeList,temp)
    end repeat
  end
```

The "bee" parent script just has to be changed to accept the "beeType…" variable as a third parameter, and use that parameter as an ancestor instead of choosing its own.

Linking Objects

Since references, or links, to objects are just variables, we can set properties of objects to link to other objects. For instance, a car insurance database may have objects for people and cars. Each person has a property called "car" that is a link to a car object. In turn, that car object may have a link back to the person with a property called "owner."

Let's revisit the *orbiting planets* script from Chapter 20. This time, let's make all the objects—the sun, planets, and moons—into objects. Each object will have a property that links it to the object it orbits.

```
property name, spriteDist, spriteNum,→
orbitBody, radius, period, pos, Xloc, Yloc, width

on new me, orbitBody0, color, width0,→
period0, radius0
  put radius0 into radius
  put period0 into period
  put width0/2 into width

  if objectP(orbitBody0) then set orbitBody =→
orbitBody0

  put 1 into pos

  -- Find a new sprite
  repeat with i = 1 to 48
    if the memberNum of sprite i = 0 then
      puppetSprite i, TRUE
      set the memberNum of sprite i = the→
number of member "Circle"
      set the foreColor of sprite i = color
      set the ink of sprite i = 8
      set the blend of sprite i = 100
```

```
        put i into spriteNum
        exit repeat
      end if
    end repeat

    return me
  end

  on orbit me
    put (the Xloc of the orbitBody of me) into ox
    put (the Yloc of the orbitBody of me) into oy

    put pos+1 into pos
    if pos > period then put 1 into pos

    put sin(2*pi()*float(pos)/period)*radius into y
    put -cos(2*pi()*float(pos)/period)*radius into x

    put (ox+x) into Xloc
    put (oy+y) into Yloc

    set the rect of sprite spriteNum =→
  rect(Xloc-width,Yloc-width,Xloc+width,Yloc+width)
  end
```

The *new* handler initializes a bunch of properties including the "radius" of the orbit, the "period" of the orbit, and the "width" of the object, in addition to setting the "pos" to 1. It also looks to see if we have passed it another object reference as the orbiting body. The "Sun" object is the only one for which we will not do this because it is stationary.

Next, the handler searches for the first empty sprite position and sets that sprite up to handle the object. It sets the color of the sprite to whatever the "color" parameter of the *new* handler specifies.

The "orbit" handler will position the object on the stage according to several variables. First, it gets the position of the orbiting body. Then it increases its own position along its orbit by 1. It uses trigonometry to convert "pos" and "radius" to an x and y coordinate. It needs to add the location of the body it orbits with its location around that object to get the real stage position. It then uses a *set the rect of sprite* function to position the sprite correctly.

The *on startMovie* handler will set up all of the objects. It stores the object references in individual variables, although we could have used a list in this situation similar to the one we used in the bumblebee scripts.

```
on startMovie
  global Sun, Mercury, Venus, Earth, Moon, Mars, Jupiter,→
Jupiter1,Mars, Jupiter, Jupiter2, Jupiter3, Jupiter4

  -- set up the sun
  put 320 into sunX
  put 240 into sunY
  set Sun = new(script "planetObj",5,18,0,0,0)
  set the Xloc of Sun = sunX
  set the Yloc of Sun = sunY
  set the rect of sprite the spriteNum of Sun =→
rect(310,230,330,250)

  -- set up the planets and moons
  set Mercury =→
new(script "planetObj",Sun,248,5,87.6,57.91/3)
  set Venus =→
new(script "planetObj",Sun,114,8,226.3,108.21/3)
  set Earth =→
new(script "planetObj",Sun,206,8,365.25,149.6/3)
  set Moon =→
new(script "planetObj",Earth,247,3,27.322,3.844*3)
  set Mars =→
new(script "planetObj",Sun,215,6,686.67,227.94/3)
  set Jupiter =→
new(script "planetObj",Sun,62,16,4263.2,778.34/3)
  set Jupiter1 =→
new(script "planetObj",Jupiter,9,3,1.769*4,4.213*3)
  set Jupiter2 =→
new(script "planetObj",Jupiter,89,3,3.551*4,6.705*3)
  set Jupiter3 =→
new(script "planetObj",Jupiter,13,3,7.155*4,10.693*3)
  set Jupiter4 =→
new(script "planetObj",Jupiter,35,3,16.689*4,18.81*3)
end
```

The first part of the *on startMovie* script will set up the sun as the initial object. It needs to specify the location of the object and draw it on the stage—because we will never call the "orbit" handler of this object, since it will remain stationary.

The rest of the handler creates all of the planets we will use, and their moons. The "period" numbers come from the actual number of days it takes each planet to orbit the sun. Notice the "365.25" for the Earth. For aesthetics, those numbers for the moon and the moons of Jupiter are increased beyond their actual values. Multiplying them by a factor of 4 makes things move faster. The same is true for the orbiting radius of the planets and moons, which are multiplied or divided by values to make the model—which is out of scale anyway—appear at a visually presentable scale.

The *on exitFrame* handler that appears in the frame score script just needs to call the "orbit" handler of each of the moving objects.

```
on exitFrame
  global Mercury, Venus, Earth, Moon, Mars, Jupiter,→
Jupiter1, Jupiter2, Jupiter3, Jupiter4

  orbit(Mercury)
  orbit(Venus)
  orbit(Earth)
  orbit(Mars)
  orbit(Moon)
  orbit(Jupiter)
  orbit(Jupiter1)
  orbit(Jupiter2)
  orbit(Jupiter3)
  orbit(Jupiter4)

  go to the frame
end
```

Business Uses for Objects

Now that we have used ancestor scripts and have linked objects to each other, let's briefly cover some less graphical applications of objects. You could use objects to create a linked, dynamic database.

Suppose you have a list of computer workstations and some information about them. Each workstation is an object. It has properties like "macOrPC," "processorSpeed," and "model."

In addition, it has other properties that link it to other objects: "CDdrive," "printer," and "scanner." Each of these objects has its own properties. For instance, a "CDdrive" would specify its "speed" and "manufacturer." A "printer" would have a property for "dotsPerInch."

Ancestors can be brought into this picture in several ways. One way is to have the ancestor of each object be the network that the computer is on. That way, each ancestor object could have a list of available network hard drives and printers as its properties. Those printers, in turn, could be linked to printer objects created from the same parent script as the printer objects attached to each individual computer.

Moving On

So what does object-oriented programming get you? The answer is *power*. These scripts are very powerful, considering that they are such small handlers. They are also far more adaptable to changing situations than scripts created by the standard approach to programming.

Don't feel the need to use parent-child scripts without a good reason, however. Very complex Lingo programs can be written without ever using this stuff. The best strategy is to work to understand its advantages and use object-oriented programming only when you feel it is the right way to do a job. A good rule of thumb is to identify when your program calls for "objects" that have "behaviors," like our bees or planets above, and go with object-oriented programming in those cases.

Next, let's look at the use of video and video-related media in Director; we'll discover how Lingo can help us to control them.

30 Media Control

Many multimedia projects use more than just text, sound, and graphics. Digital video and MIDI music are elements of Director movies that have their own special set of commands in Lingo.

Digital Video

Whether you are using QuickTime for Mac or Windows or Video for Windows files, the Lingo commands are the same. There is a whole suite of them, handling everything from the current position of the video, to the specifics of each track internal, to the video.

Standard Video Controls

The best way to explore these functions is to build our own video control movie. While you can use the standard video control bar provided by QuickTime, sometimes this may not fit your needs. The Lingo functions give you as much control over the video as this control bar—and more. Let's design a simple movie that will display a video and have a collection of our own buttons to control it. The result will look like Figure 30-1.

Figure 30-1: *Our video control station.*

To begin with, we will import a video clip into our movie. We'll make it a 160 by 120 QuickTime movie. Let's first go to the cast member's properties box and set it up so that the control bar is invisible, the mode is Paused, and it is set to Direct to Stage. That last option is your only choice on Windows machines. Figure 30-2 shows this properties dialog box set correctly for our requirements.

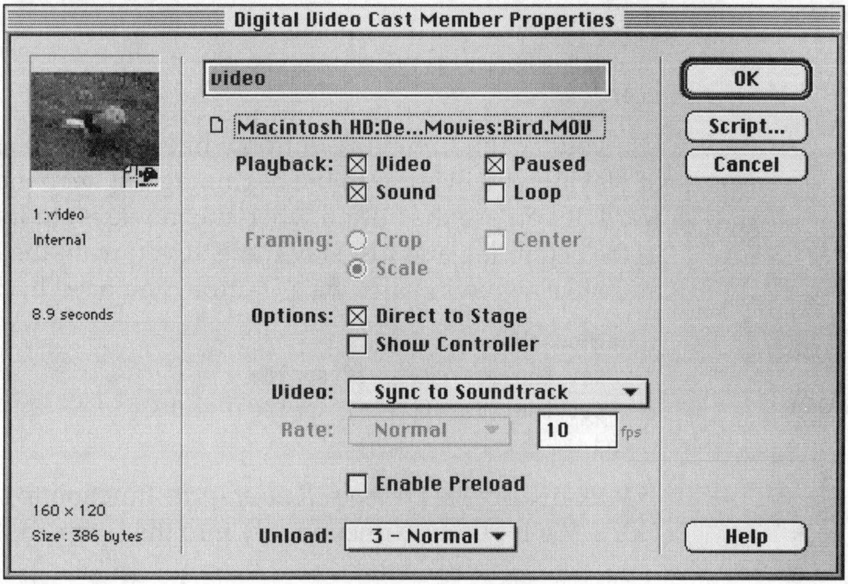

Figure 30-2: *Our video cast member's property box.*

Let's start by creating the "play" button. All this button needs to do is kick off the video and get it moving forward. The function that controls the speed of the video is *the movieRate of sprite*. This value is set to 0, initally, because of the "paused" property we set above. All we need to do is change it to *1* to have the video move forward at a normal pace.

```
on mouseUp
  set the movieRate of sprite 1 = 1
end
```

Using this button starts the video playing. It stops at the end. If you test *the movieRate of sprite* function when it has stopped, you will find that it returns to 0.

The next button we will script is the "rewind" button. This will just take the video back to the very first video frame. The function we need here is *the movieTime of sprite*. By setting it to 0, we take the video back to the beginning.

```
on mouseUp
  set the movieTime of sprite 1 = 0
end
```

If you try this "rewind" button while the video is in the middle of playing, it will jump to the beginning but keep moving forward. If you use the button when the movie is stopped, it will go to the beginning and just stay there. If you want the button to act more like a "rewind and wait" button, you need to change it thus:

```
on mouseUp
  set the movieRate of sprite 1 = 0
  set the movieTime of sprite 1 = 0
end
```

We can also use *the movieRate of sprite* function to pause the video. We'll put this functionality into the "stop" button.

```
on mouseUp
  set the movieRate of sprite 1 = 0
end
```

This "stop" button could also contain the same script as our "rewind and wait" button if you want the movie to return to the starting point when the user stops it.

The next two buttons show the versatility of *the movieRate of sprite* function. We have seen how setting this to 0 stops the video, and setting it to 1 moves the video forward at a normal rate. You can also set it to numbers greater than 1 to play the video faster, and numbers less than 0 to play the video backward. Here is the script for the "backward" button.

```
on mouseUp
  set the movieRate of sprite 1 = -1
end
```

Here is the script for the "fast play" button. The number can be changed to be greater than 2 for even faster play.

```
on mouseUp
  set the movieRate of sprite 1 = 2
end
```

Since neither of these scripts actually changes the current position of the video, their effects might not be noticeable if the video is at the very beginning or the very end. Therefore, use the "rewind" button before using the "fast play" button, and use the "backward" button only after the movie has been playing for a little while.

The "step" button further explores the video function: *the movieTime of sprite*. The function specifies where the video is currently positioned—in ticks. We can set this value and the video will update itself to that position. The "step" button will just add 30 ticks, or a half a second, to this value.

```
on mouseUp
  set the movieTime of sprite 1 = the movieTime→
of sprite 1 + 30
end
```

We could easily have used another number besides 30. We could even have used a negative number to step backward, or have the offset sent as a parameter.

The next two buttons are check boxes that control two properties of the video. The first one determines whether or not the video loops. Recall that earlier (in the properties box) we set the video not to loop. However, we can change this value in the script of the "loop" button by using *the loop of member*.

```
on mouseUp
  set the loop of member "video" = the hilite of member "loop"
end
```

Now, try some of the previous buttons once the *loop* property of the video has been set to TRUE. The "play," "backward," and "fast play" buttons will all obey the *loop* property.

The second *checkbox* button just sets the volume of the video to either 255, the maximum, or 0, which is off.

```
on mouseUp
  set the volume of sprite 1 =→
255*(the hilite of member "sound")
end
```

We could also set up a series of buttons, a pop-up menu, a text input box, or a slider to control the volume in smaller increments.

Let's also create an *on startMovie* handler that sets these two check boxes so that they are accurate even before the user touches them.

```
on startMovie
  set the hilite of member "Loop" = FALSE
  set the loop of member "video" = FALSE
  set the hilite of member "Sound" = TRUE
  set the volume of sprite 1 = 255
end
```

The next part of our video control station is a text display. This will let us observe three properties of the video as they change: *the movieRate, the movieTime* and *the volume.* We just use a simple *on exitFrame* script to constantly update this text.

```
on exitFrame
  put "Rate:"&&(the movieRate of sprite 1) into line 1 of text
  put "Time:"&&(the movieTime of sprite 1) into line 2 of text
  put "Volume:"&&(the volume of sprite 1) into line 3 of text
  put text into field "data"
  go to the frame
end
```

Now our control station lets us monitor the progress of the video as it changes.

To complete our control station movie, let's add some special effects buttons. The first one will enlarge the size of the video space. We can do this by setting *the rect of sprite* just like for any other Director element.

```
on mouseDown
  set the rect of sprite 1 = rect(140,0,460,240)
  repeat while the mouseDown
    updateStage
  end repeat
end
```

The script is an *on mouseDown* handler that changes the size of the sprite and waits for the user to release the mouse button. If you hold down this button, it will temporarily magnify the movie to the specified rectangle. You can also make the change permanent by using the *puppetSprite* command. This same script can also shrink or just reposition the video sprite.

The next button will take the location of the sprite and change it so that the video flies across the screen. We also include the commands needed to restart the video, so that you can see how the video is actually running while the sprite moves.

```
on mouseUp
  set the movieTime of sprite 1 = 0
  set the movieRate of sprite 1 = 1
  repeat with i = 1 to 600
    set the locH of sprite 1 = i
    set the locV of sprite 1 = I/3
    updateStage
  end repeat
end
```

The two "zoom" buttons let us have some more fun with the rectangle of the sprite. The first one will start the rectangle out small, and then expand it as the video runs.

```
on mouseUp
  set the movieTime of sprite 1 = 0
  set the movieRate of sprite 1 = 1
  repeat with i = 1 to 100
    put .01*i into p
    set the rect of sprite 1 =→
rect(314-p*80,181-p*60,314+p*80,181+p*60)
    updateStage
  end repeat
end
```

The second "zoom" button will expand the horizontal area of the video first, and then the vertical area. This will make the video look like an old television set that is warming up.

```
on mouseUp
  set the movieTime of sprite 1 = 0
  set the movieRate of sprite 1 = 1
  repeat with i = 1 to 100
    put .01*i into p
    set the rect of sprite 1 =→
rect(314-p*80,180,314+p*80,182)
    updateStage
  end repeat
  repeat with i = 1 to 100
    put .01*i into p
    set the rect of sprite 1 =→
rect(314-80,181-p*60,314+80,181+p*60)
    updateStage
  end repeat
end
```

We can also use *the blend of sprite* on video sprites. This allows us to fade a video in or out. The next two scripts perform a fade-in and a fade-out using *the blend*.

```
on mouseUp
  set the ink of sprite 1 = 32
  repeat with i = 0 to 100
    set the blend of sprite 1 = i
    updateStage
  end repeat
end

on mouseUp
  set the ink of sprite 1 = 32
  repeat with i = 100 down to 0
    set the blend of sprite 1 = i
    updateStage
  end repeat
end
```

Since you can play more than one video at a time, you can even use *the blend* to fade one video out while another fades in. This would make a nice transition between two videos.

Things like the fades and stretching will work properly only on Macintoshes. Windows machines require that video be played "direct to stage," which means they are basically laid on top of the Director movie and are not really an interactive part of it.

More Video-Related Lingo

There are a few more commands that might be useful when dealing with video.

The two functions *the quicktimePresent* and *the videoForWindowsPresent*, will allow you to check to see if users have either of these types of video support on their computers. You should check these if you are developing products that may be playing on machines where this is in question. You can then warn the user that video will not be available, or perhaps route the movie correctly to avoid the video segments.

The standard properties of a video cast member are also available for control by scripts: *the controller of member*, *the directToStage of member*, *the loop of member*, and *the pausedAtStart of member*.

Lingo also includes a whole set of commands that get or set track properties, including key frames, times, and types. Tracks are the elements of a video clip: video, sound channels, MIDI music, etc. They are each mentioned in the "Reference" section in the back of this book. A full discussion on digital video in Director, however, is a topic probably worthy of its own small book.

MIDI Music

Once you know how to handle QuickTime movies with Lingo, you should have no trouble bringing MIDI music into your projects. This is because QuickTime has the ability to handle MIDI "tracks." There are even a few shareware programs that allow you to convert standard MIDI files to small QuickTime movies. Some video editing programs will also allow you to add a MIDI track to a movie that already includes video and sound tracks.

The advantage of using MIDI music in Director movies is that you can include rich, lengthy soundtracks. These files are significantly smaller than a normal sound file and can sound fantastic if the computer it is playing on has a good sound card or MIDI device.

The need for the digital video sound commands in Lingo is even more critical when dealing with MIDI QuickTime movies. You will probably want to have the control bar hidden and yet use *the movieTime* and *the movieRate* to control it.

All you need to do to have a QuickTime MIDI piece play is to place the cast member that contains the link to the QuickTime file in a sprite on the stage. The cast member's properties of "paused" at start or "loop" will be obeyed, just as in a video QuickTime element.

Keep in mind that your user must have a MIDI-supporting version of QuickTime on their machine.

PC users have another option for using MIDI. Most PC sound cards support some sort of standard MIDI through the use of the media control interface, or *MCI*, communications protocols. On Windows machines, Lingo supports the *MCI* command, which will pass a message to the sound card. We can use this to play standard MIDI files.

Here is a set of simple handlers that play Windows MIDI files.

```
on playMIDI MIDIFile, waitTillDone
  global MIDIlength
  if the machinetype = 256 then
    stopMIDI
    mci "open"&&the pathname&MIDIFile&&→
"type sequencer alias song"
    mci "play song from 0"
    mci "status song length"
    put value(the result) into MIDIlength
    if waitTillDone then
      repeat while TRUE
        mci "status song position"
        if the result >= (MIDIlength) then exit repeat
      end repeat
```

```
      mci "close all"
    end if
  end if
end

on stopMIDI
  global MacMIDISpriteNum
  if the machinetype = 256 then
    mci "close all"
  end if
end
```

The "playMIDI" handler accepts the filename and a "waitTillDone" parameter. If you set the latter parameter to TRUE, the handler will wait until the file is done and close it for you. Otherwise, the movie will continue on while the sound is playing, and you need to be responsible for calling "stopMIDI" to close the file.

The MCI commands used simply open the file and assign the name "song" to it. They then ask that the sound card play that sound from the beginning. We use another MCI command to put the length of the sound file into *the result*.

In the "waitTillDone" loop, we check the status of the sound, to see if it has reached the end. If so, we close it. Here is another handler that does this same check for us.

```
on MIDIdone
  global MIDIlength
  mci "status song position"
  if the result < (MIDIlength) then return FALSE
  else return TRUE
end
```

We can also use Lingo to loop the MIDI file. The way we can do this is to constantly check to see if the file is done playing then start it again if it has. We can include this code in one handler that should be called from the *on exitFrame* handler in the score. This "loopMIDI" handler replaces the "openMIDI" handler.

```
on loopMIDI  MIDIFile
  global prepath, MIDIlength

  if the machinetype = 256 then
    mci "status song position"
    put value(the result) into r
    if not integerP(r) then
      mci "open"&&the pathname&MIDIFile&→
"type sequencer alias song"
      mci "play song from 0"
      mci "status song length"
      put value(the result) into MIDIlength
    else if (r >= MIDIlength) then
      mci "play song from 0"
    end if
  end if
end
```

Moving On

Both video and MIDI are good examples of external elements that can be used by Director with the help of Lingo. With Director 5.0's open architecture, it is probable that even more types of media may be added through third-party plug-ins.

Next, let's take a look at some ways to build tools with Director to automate some tasks for us. We can even use Lingo to permanently alter the score of a movie.

31

Building Tools

If you use Director on a regular basis to produce similar projects, you may have already seen the need for more specific tools to help you out. You can use Lingo to create tools that perform repetitive or difficult tasks on your movies.

Creating & Altering the Score

Before Director 5.0, Lingo did not have the power to make very many permanent changes to a movie. You could puppetSprite a sprite and change it temporarily, but you could not make a real change to the score; this could only be done manually, in the score window.

Now there is a whole set of new commands that let Lingo programs make real changes and save them as permanent parts of the movie. We can use this functionality to build custom tools to help us work in Director.

Score generation sessions allow us to use Lingo commands to make changes to the score just like we can do manually with the score window. The advantage of using Lingo to make these changes is that repetitive processes can be automated. In other words, tools can be built to add functionality to the Director authoring system.

Let's start by looking at these score-changing commands. The first one is a property called *the updateLock*. This is just a variable you need to set to FALSE before making changes.

To start making changes to the score, you need to execute the *beginRecording* command. Since events are recorded in the current frame, you may want to position Director's play head with a *go to frame* command first. A recording session ends with an *endRecording* command.

Once inside a recording session, you can use all sorts of familiar commands to change the score. For instance, you could use *the memberNum of sprite* to change cast members in a sprite channel. Unlike a puppetSprite-related command, this command will permanently change the score.

You could also add new cast members to the score by setting all of the sprite properties: *the memberNum, the locH, the locV, the ink, the foreColor, the backColor, the type,* and *the blend*. The cast member itself must exist in the score. To create a brand-new cast member, you can use a variation on the *new* command.

When you have finished making all the changes you want in a frame, you need to use one of several commands to make the changes "stick." The *updateFrame* command will do this then automatically move on to the next frame. The next changes you make will be to *that* frame. The *insertFrame* and the *duplicateFrame* commands will make the changes permanent then add a new frame after the current one. The next changes you make will be on that new frame.

Let's look at an example. Suppose we wanted a simple tool that would make a circle on the stage pulsate. This would mean that the first frame's circle would be a certain size, the second frame's would be a bit larger, and the next frame would return to the original size. This is something that cannot be done in Director without a lot of copying and pasting in the score window.

```
on pulsate
  put the rect of sprite 1 into r
  put r+rect(-5,-5,5,5) into r2
  set the updateLock = FALSE
  beginRecording
```

```
    repeat with i = 1 to 5
      set the rect of sprite 1 = r
      insertFrame
      set the rect of sprite 1 = r2
      insertFrame
    end repeat
  endRecording
end
```

This simple tool will take the rectangle of sprite 1 and use it to create a slightly bigger rectangle for variable "r2." It then loops five times, each time adding two new frames to the movie: one with the sprite the normal size, and one with the sprite a little bigger.

After running this script, you will see that it has generated 10 new frames. The element in sprite 1 of these frames alternates between the two sizes.

We can make this script a little more complex by trying to simulate a heartbeat instead of just a straight pulsating action.

```
on heartBeat
  put the rect of sprite 1 into r
  put r+rect(-5,-5,5,5) into r2
  set the updateLock = FALSE
  beginRecording
    repeat with i = 1 to 3
      set the rect of sprite 1 = r
      insertFrame
      set the rect of sprite 1 = r2
      insertFrame
      set the rect of sprite 1 = r
      insertFrame
      set the rect of sprite 1 = r2
      insertFrame
      set the rect of sprite 1 = r
      insertFrame
      set the rect of sprite 1 = r
      insertFrame
    end repeat
  endRecording
end
```

The "heartbeat" script is essentially the same as the "pulsate" script. We just insert a pattern of six frames that represent a heartbeat motion for sprite 1.

We can use *the locH* and *the locV* to move sprites around in the score. This example takes two sprites, calculates a midpoint for them, and causes them to converge over 25 new frames.

```
on convergeSprites
  -- get original locations
  put the locH of sprite 1 into h1
  put the locV of sprite 1 into v1
  put the locH of sprite 2 into h2
  put the locV of sprite 2 into v2

  -- find midpoint
  put (h1+h2)/2 into hm
  put (v1+v2)/2 into vm

  set the updateLock = FALSE
  beginRecording
    repeat with i = 0 to 25
      -- figure out the percent along the path
      put float(25-i)/25 into p1
      put float(i)/25 into p2

      -- set the first sprite
      put p1*h1+p2*hm into h
      put p1*v1+p2*vm into v
      set the locH of sprite 1 = h
      set the locV of sprite 1 = v

      -- set the second sprite
      put p1*h2+p2*hm into h
      put p1*v2+p2*vm into v
      set the locH of sprite 2 = h
      set the locV of sprite 2 = v

      insertFrame
    end repeat
  endRecording
end
```

We don't need to hard-code our sprite numbers for these types of tools. The Lingo function *the scoreSelection* will return a list that indicates which cells in the score have been selected. This way, we can have our tools work on those cells instead of just some predetermined sprite number(s).

The scoreSelection returns a list of lists. Each sublist represents a selected area of the score. These sublists contain four parameters: the first sprite, the last sprite, the first frame, and the last frame. For instance, [[3,6,1,5]] means that sprites 3 to 6 of frames 1 to 5 have been selected and [[3,6,1,5], [8,12,1,5]] means that sprites 3 to 6 and 8 to 12 of frames 1 to 5 have been selected. The numbers 0, –1, –2, –3, –4 , and –5 represent the script channel, sound channel 2, sound channel 1, the transition channel, the palette channel and the tempo channel, respectively.

The following script takes *the scoreSelection* and uses it to determine which sprites should be changed. It does this only for the first frame selected and ignores anything but the first selected group of cells.

What the tool does is something very useful: it properly spaces several sprites so that they are equally distant from each other. While Director 5.0's align tool lets you align items, it does not let you space them. This script uses the first and last selected sprites and spaces the rest evenly. It also lines up the vertical position of all of the sprites to an average position.

```
on alignAndSpace
  put the scoreSelection into ss
  put getAt(ss,1) into ss
  put getAt(ss,3) into frameNum
  put getAt(ss,1) into spriteNum1
  put getAt(ss,2) into spriteNum2
  put spriteNum2-spriteNum1+1 into numSprites
  if numSprites < 2 then exit
  go to frame frameNum
  put 0 into vVal
  repeat with i = spriteNum1 to spriteNum2
    put vVal+the locV of sprite i into vVal
  end repeat
  put vVal/numSprites into vVal
```

```
    put the locH of sprite (spriteNum1) into leftVal
    put the locH of sprite (spriteNum2) into rightVal
    put (rightVal-leftVal)/(numSprites-1) into hSpace
    set the updateLock = FALSE
    beginRecording
      repeat with i = spriteNum1 to spriteNum2
        set the locV of sprite i = vVal
        set the locH of sprite i =→
  leftVal+hSpace*(i-spriteNum1)
      end repeat
      updateFrame
    endRecording
    go to frame frameNum
  end
```

The "alignAndSpace" handler will calculate the left- and rightmost positions of the first and last sprites. It then figures out how far apart each one has to be from the previous one, in addition to calculating the average vertical position of the sprites. Then it starts a recording session, loops through the sprites to set them to their proper positions, and updates the frame. When it is done, it returns itself to the updated frame so you can see the change.

You can change more than just the sprite cells of a movie. Functions like *the frameScript*, *the frameSound1*, *the frameSound2*, *the frameTempo*, *the frameTransition*, and *the framePalette* can be used to assign new values to those elements. You can even use *the frameLabel* to change or create frame labels in the score during a recording session.

Other Useful Techniques

Lingo includes some other capabilities that may also be useful in creating tools. Some of these we have already dealt with in previous chapters.

Creating & Altering the Cast

You can also create new cast members on the fly. All you need to do is use the *new* command and pass as a parameter the type of cast member you want. Types include "#field," "#bitmap," "#sound," and "#button."

Once you have a new cast member, you can assign things to it. For instance, a new field can be given some text to hold. You can set the properties of the text, such as *the textFont* and *the lineHeight*, as well. You can do the same for existing text fields too.

Bitmap cast members can be populated using the file import techniques mentioned in Chapter 16. You could also use *the picture of member* to copy and paste bitmaps from member to member.

MIAWs

The best way to create tools is to make them "small movie in a window" (MIAW) files. MIAWs can use the *tell* command to communicate with the stage. This will allow you to put scripts, like the ones above, in MIAWs, and affect the score of the currently open movie.

You can have several of these tool windows open at a time, as long as you remember to set the "Pause when window inactive" property of those movies to FALSE. Otherwise, execution will halt in all windows if one goes inactive. This will allow you to have several of these tool windows open at the same time.

The best way to include a movie as a MIAW tool is to place it in the Xtras folder. Any movie placed there will become available as a tool under the Xtras menu. When you, or a user, selects the tool from the menu, the movie will appear in a window and will run in that window like a regular movie.

It is your responsibility to make sure this movie contains all the proper *tell* statements so that it can communicate what you want back to the stage.

A MIAW tool should also take care of handling the window-related messages mentioned in Chapter 27: "activateWindow," "closeWIndow," etc.

Text Functions

In addition to altering the score, don't forget that you have the power to alter text as well. You can use *the textStyle* and *the foreColor*, for instance, to change highlighted text. Use *the selection*, *the selStart*, and *the selEnd* to figure out what text has been selected.

One of the more powerful functions you may need is the ability to figure out which text field has been selected. You do this by taking *the selection* and comparing it to every *char selStart to selEnd of field* in the movie or in the current frame until you find a perfect match. This method is not perfect, however, as more than one field could possibly have exactly the same text in the same spot.

Moving On

Tool-building is one of the strengths of Director. Many other multimedia authoring systems make it impossible to add tools unless you can program extensions in languages like C.

Such extensions (Xtras, external Xobjects and XCMDs) still have their uses, however. In the next chapter, we will look at a few of these.

32

Beyond Lingo: Xtras & Xobjects

Even with all of the advances made in Director, from versions 3 through 5, there are still some basic things that Lingo cannot do without the use of the external code plug-ins called Xobjects. In Director 5, these are just referred to as *Xtras*.

You can make any Xobject or Xtra available to you by placing it in the Xtras folder of the Director folder on your hard drive. You can see what Xtras and Xobjects are available by typing **showXlib** in the message window.

```
showXlib
-- XLibraries:
--    Xtra: PrintOMatic_Lite
--    Xtra: OSUtil
-- "*Standard.xlib"
--    XObject: FileIO           Id:1020
--    XObject: SerialPort       Id:200
--    XObject: XCMDGlue         Id:2020
```

In Chapter 16 we introduced the idea of externals and learned how to use the basic FileIO Xobject. Now, let's take a look at some more of the most commonly used Xobjects.

You will find that most of these follow the same type of procedure for getting things done. Xobjects on the Macintosh could be files or resources attached to Director or a projector file. Xobjects in Windows are usually .DLL files. On the Macintosh, you can also use some XCMDs written for other programs like Hypercard.

You can find Xtras from several Internet sources. See the reference section at the back of this book for the Internet addresses.

Making Xtras available to your movies is as simple as placing them in the Xtras folder or using the *openXlib* command.

Printing

The PrintOMatic Lite Xtra greatly extends Director's printing capability. Without it, you only have the *printFrom* command, which is not a solution for most printing needs. The *printFrom* command prints only the stage. It is like getting a screen dump to the printer. However, it doesn't fare too well once puppetSprites are present. Sometimes it works, sometimes it doesn't.

The *printFrom* command is also of no use when the information you want printed isn't the information on the stage. For instance, a multimedia kiosk may need to print out text directions to a restaurant, or a game may need to spit out several pages of a small instruction booklet.

The PrintOMatic Lite Xtra gives us some basic printing capability that Director lacks. For one thing, it enables us to call up Print and Page Setup dialog boxes. It will also let us string together various elements—such as pictures and text cast members—into one document.

The simplest way to use this Xtra is just to use the *print* command. You can send a piece of text, a text cast member, or even a picture to the printer this way.

```
print "This is a test"
print field "printing test"
print member "bitmap"
```

This robust command also handles sprites, printing the cast member currently in that sprite, and it handles entire cast libraries as well.

```
print sprite 4
print castLib "cast7.cst"
```

The real power of the PrintOMatic Lite Xtra becomes apparent when you create document objects. You do this by using the *new* function, and using the name of the Xtra. If you are on a Windows machine, make sure you use the right name.

```
set printDoc = new(xtra "PrintoMatic_Lite")
```

Now that we have created a variable, "printDoc," that represents the document to be printed, we can build that document. We do this by using the *append* command. This next example will first place the word *Output:* in the document, and then the contents of a field.

```
append printDoc,"Output:"&RETURN
append printDoc, member "printing test"
```

If you want to call the Page Setup dialog, you must do so before using the *append* command. The syntax for this is *doPageSetup*. You can also use the *setDocumentName* command to change the official name of the document the user will see when the computer prints it.

```
doPageSetup printDoc
setDocumentName = "Output"
```

Once you are ready to print, just use *doJobSetup* to bring up the print dialog box. This function will return a TRUE if the user hits the Print button. You can then use the *print* command to send the document to the printer.

```
if doJobSetup(printDoc) then print printDoc
```

Rarely will you want to have such a sequence as described above. More typically, you will want to offer the user a Page Setup function and a Print function. The first function will set or reset the initial empty document, which will not really be created until the Print function is invoked. Here is a sample Page Setup function attached to a button.

```
on mouseUp
  global printDoc
  set printDoc = 0
  set printDoc = new(xtra "PrintOMatic_Lite")
  doPageSetup printDoc
end
```

This handler sets up a global "printDoc" variable to refer to the document. It clears any previously created document by setting the "printDoc" global to 0. Then it brings up the Page Setup dialog box.

Here is a handler for the print button.

```
on mouseUp
  global printDoc
  if not objectP(printDoc) then
    set printDoc = new(xtra "PrintOMatic_Lite")
  end if
  setDocumentName printDoc, "Test document"
  append printDoc, "Printing test"
  if doJobSetup(printDoc) then
    print printDoc
  end if
end
```

This handler first makes sure that a document has been created by the Page Setup button in the previous script. If not, it creates a new one. Then it sets the document name, populates it with some text, and brings up the Print dialog box. If the user hits Print, the document is printed.

The PrintOMatic Lite Xtra has all sorts of other commands to change the font, size, and style of text, and play with other printing settings as well. For more details, read over the short documentation booklet that comes in file format with the Xtra. PrintOMatic Lite is a cross-platform Xtra and should work basically the same on Macintosh and Windows machines.

OSUtil

A great utility Xtra for the Macintosh is OSUtil. This includes a whole suite of functions to return information about the user's computer and hard drive. Most important, it fills in some critical I/O functions that FileIO does not have, such as copying, moving, and renaming files.

Currently, OSUtil is only for the Macintosh. Keep checking online sources for a Windows version of either this utility Xtra or one that provides similar functions.

To use most of the functions in OSUtil, drop it into the Xtras folder before running Director. Then create a variable, "os," that will refer to the OSUtil's library of functions. We will use this variable almost every time we need to use an OSUtil command.

```
set os = new(xtra "OSutil")
put volumeFree(os,"Macintosh HD:")
-- 143818752
```

This first function returns the number of bytes available on the volume specified. We can also obtain other pieces of information about the volume, such as the number of files.

```
put volumeFiles(os,"Macintosh HD:")
-- 8932
```

We can get a list of volumes available as well.

```
put volumeList(os)
-- "Macintosh HD:Director 5:"
```

One command that does not need our "os" variable is the "getFileNamesInFolder" handler. This is not part of this Xobject but is a regular Lingo command. It just needs the full path of the folder and a 1 or 0, depending on whether you want invisible files to be included.

```
put getFileNamesInFolder("Macintosh HD:",0)
-- "Apple Extras:
Applications:
Astronomy Project:
```

```
Desktop Folder:
Director 4.0.4 folder:
Director 5:
Drawing Table:
Microsoft Word 6:
Netscape Navigator™ 2.0 Folder:
Power Mac 7500 & 8500 Read Me
SimpleText
System Folder:
Utilities:
Web:
What On Earth:
"
```

Notice that folders end with a : (colon), while files do not. You could use this function to get the names of the files in a folder full of pictures. Then you could list the files in a text field for the user to select one. The Lingo commands you learned in Chapter 16 to load a PICT file can then be used to display the picture. You can do similar things with text and sound files.

The real power of OSUtil is its ability to copy, rename, and move files. The commands for these are pretty straightforward.

```
fileCopy(os, "myFile1", "myFile2")
rename(os, "myFile2", "newFile")
move(os, "newFile", "Macintosh HD:new files:")
```

The *move* command accepts a filename as the source, then a path as the destination.

Another powerful command is the *createDir* function. This will create a new folder.

```
createDir(os, "Macintosh HD:", "new files")
```

The OSUtil is updated often by its author. Check the version you have for additional commands and documentation.

QuickTime VR

QuickTime VR is a very powerful cross-platform medium for displaying panoramic views and 3D objects. These types of files can be used inside of Director through the use of the QuickTime VR Xobject from Apple.

On the Macintosh side, you need the QuickTime VR XCMDs and the QuickTime VR Components files. On the PC, you need the QTVRW.QTC file. Unfortunately, the Lingo is different for each platform.

The details of using the QuickTime VR Xobject are explained in the documentation provided by Apple when you buy the authoring tools from them. They even have Mac and Windows "testbed" movies that include everything you need to try every function of QuickTime VR in Director.

Instead of repeating that explanation, let's take a look at a simpler set of handlers. Suppose you just want to display a panoramic QuickTime VR movie on the stage and are not really interested in advanced functionality. The following movie script will get the job done on the Macintosh.

```
global gPanoMovieID, gPanoSprite, gLastTimeRollover

on startMovie
  put 0 into gLastTimeRollover
  openxlib "QuickTime VR XCMDs"
end

on stopMovie
  closePanoMovie
  closexlib "QuickTime VR XCMDs"
end

on openPanoMovie fileName, spriteNum
  put spriteNum into gPanoSprite
  closePanoMovie

  put the rect of sprite gPanoSprite into r
  put the left of r &","& the top of r &","&
the right of r &","& the bottom of r into panoRect
```

```
    put PanoMovie("openMovie", "Direct", the→
  pathname&fileName, panoRect) into gPanoMovieID

    if gPanoMovieID contains "error" then
      alert gPanoMovieID
      put EMPTY into gPanoMovieID
      exit
    end if

    panoMovie "Direct", gPanoMovieID, "idle"
  end

  on closePanoMovie
    global gPanoMovieID
    if gPanoMovieID <> EMPTY then
      PanoMovie "Direct", gPanoMovieID, "dispose"
      put EMPTY into gPanoMovieID
    end if
  end

  on panoFrameScript
    global gLastTimeRollover, gPanoMovieID, gPanoSprite
    if rollover(gPanoSprite) then
      if gPanoMovieID <> EMPTY then
        PanoMovie "Direct", gPanoMovieID, "mouseOver"
        put the result into mouseOverResult

        if mouseOverResult <> 0 then
          if item 1 of mouseOverResult = "navg" then
            PanoMovie ("Direct", gPanoMovieID, "update")
          end if
          put TRUE into gLastTimeRollover
        else if rollover(gPanoSprite) then
          put TRUE into gLastTimeRollover
        else
          cursor 200
          cursor -1
          put FALSE into gLastTimeRollover
        end if
      end if
```

```
    else if gLastTimeRollover then
      cursor 200
      cursor -1
      put FALSE into gLastTimeRollover
      if gPanoMovieID <> EMPTY then PanoMovie→
  "Direct", gPanoMovieID, "idle"
    end if
  end
```

The three primary handlers here are "openPanoMovie," "closePanoMovie," and "panoFrameScript." This first one should be called to bring up the movie. It will position the movie to exactly cover the area marked by the object in its sprite channel.

```
openPanoMovie "DIA.mov", 1
```

In this case, there should be a simple rectangle in sprite channel 1 that is the proper dimensions for the QuickTime VR movie. While the movie is displayed, you should be calling "panoFrameScript" from within the *on exitFrame* handler of that frame. This will make sure the movie reacts and updates to mouse movement. It also resets the cursor when it leaves the QuickTime VR area.

When you want the QuickTime VR movie to go away, just use the "closePanoMovie" command.

Here are the same handlers, but with Windows-specific code.

```
global panoMovieObj, lastTimeRollover, panoSpriteNum

on StartMovie
  put FALSE into lastTimeRollover
  openxlib "QTVRW.QTC"
  openPanoMovie the pathname&"dia.mov", 1
end

on StopMovie
  closePanoMovie
  closeXlib "QTVRW.QTC"
end
```

```
on openPanoMovie fileName, spriteNum
  put spriteNum into panoSpriteNum
  closePanoMovie
  set panoMovieObj = QTVRW (mNew, "Pan")
  if not objectP(panoMovieObj) then
    alert "Can't open object"
    exit
  end if
  put panoMovieObj (mOpenMovie, fileName,→
the left of sprite spriteNum &","&→
the top of sprite spriteNum) into resultCode
  if resultCode = 0 then
    panoMovieObj (mDispose)
    alert "Unable to open panomovie"
    exit
  end if
  panoMovieObj (mUpdate)
end

on closePanoMovie
  if objectP (panoMovieObj) then
    panoMovieObj (mDispose)
  end if
end

on panoFrameScript
  if rollover(panoSpriteNum) then
    if objectP (panoMovieObj) then
      put panoMovieObj (mMouseOver) into mouseOverResult
      if mouseOverResult <> 0 then
        put item 1 of mouseOverResult into action
        if action = "navg" then
          put TRUE into lastTimeRollover
        else
          cursor 200
          cursor -1
          put FALSE into lastTimeRollover
        end if
      end if
    end if
```

```
    else if lastTimeRollover then
      cursor 200
      cursor -1
      put FALSE into lastTimeRollover
    end if
    if objectP(panoMovieObj) then panoMovieObj(mIdle)
  end
```

The QuickTime VR authoring kit goes into much more detail about other functions and the use of object movies. It is also quite likely that a new Xtra will eventually come out for Director 5 that will make QuickTime VR a normal cast member type and do away with the need for this Xobject.

stageToCast

A small Xobject that can prove to be useful is the stageToCast function. This Macintosh-only Xobject will grab the contents of a rectangle on the stage and place it in a new cast member.

It can be used to grab the result of drawing with trails, as you discovered in Chapter 18. You can have it capture what the user has drawn, or have it create multiple cast members by drawing something with trails and then capturing the result.

Here is a typical, short handler that captures the upper left portion of the stage. Note that you could set the coordinates differently to capture a different rectangular portion of the stage. The handler assumes that the Xobject is called "StageToCast.Xobj."

```
on getCastMember
  set stageToCast =  StageToCast.Xobj(mNew)
  put new(#bitmap) into newMemberNum
  set the picture of cast newMemberNum =→
stageToCast(mGetHandle, 0, 0, 300, 300)
  stageToCast(mDispose)
end
```

It also assumes that the Xobject has been loaded by being included in the Xtras folder or by an *openXlib* command in the *on startMovie* handler.

If you want to capture a series of cast members, you will probably want to use the *saveMovie* command every once in a while. This will help clear out memory buffers that get eaten by using the stageToCast Xobject.

The World of Xtras

There are dozens of useful Xobjects out there for Director 5.0 at the moment. Eventually, there may be hundreds. The best way to keep up with them is to look at Internet resources. The "Reference" section at the back of this book is a good place to start.

You can also access most XCMDs on the Macintosh in the same way you do with Hypercard, although now most Xobjects are being written specifically for Director as Xobjects.

Of course, you can create your own Xobjects too. You will need a good background in C or Pascal programming, and you'll need compilers for Macintosh, Windows, or both platforms. An understanding of the Macintosh and Windows toolbox subroutines is handy as well.

For those of you who are inclined to write your own Xobjects, you are strongly urged to consider the possibility that the functionality you want already exists in Lingo. The old Hypercard XCMD assumption that coding in C and Pascal will produce faster programs is not necessarily true with Director 5. Quite often you will find there is no performance increase at all over a simple Lingo handler.

The world of Xtras is changing rapidly now with the introduction of a new system of development for Director 5. You may have heard of MOA (Macromedia Open Architecture), which allows development companies to add everything from Lingo extensions to new transitions.

Moving On

Xtras pretty much complete the picture of what is possible in Lingo programming. With them, Lingo can be made even more powerful or can be fine-tuned to meet your specific needs.

Next, let's tie all of our knowledge together to see what is involved with finishing off a Director/Lingo-based multimedia product.

33 Tying It All Together

Once all of the content has been created, the design finalized, and the tricky Lingo handlers written, there are still a lot of details left before a project is done. Projectors need to be built, cast files and linked files need to be gathered, and cross-platform issues need to be addressed. The product may have to be mastered on CD-ROM or ported to a kiosk machine.

Let's take some time to review some of the common problems that occur in this final stage of development. In many cases, some simple Lingo scripts can help a great deal.

Reusable Projectors

If you are dealing with a single, small movie, you will probably just create a projector of it when you are done. This will keep your product down to one file, making it easy to transport and maintain.

However, larger projects require multiple movies, supporting files, and even several levels of folders. In these cases, as well as for single-file projects, it is often a good idea to create a stripped-down, simple projector for the project. This projector would do nothing more than play the first movie.

Such a projector would only have one script: a simple *on exitFrame* handler that would just use *play* or *go* to start the real movie. This script would be placed in the first frame.

```
on exitFrame
  play movie "main.dir"
end
```

This example would play a movie named "main.dir." You could create one projector for the Macintosh and one for Windows. Once you have created these two projectors, you should never have to make another set for the remainder of the project.

The movies you make, on the other hand, are cross-platform; so you will be able to play the same movie file with either projector. This can save a large amount of time during development, in addition to saving a lot of room on the final CD-ROM—especially during the last phase of the project when you could be building projectors, reviewing them, changing something small in the original movie, and building again.

The handler can be made a bit more robust. You could have it read its own name, for instance, and use that to figure out which movie file to play. This idea works well with Windows projectors.

```
on exitFrame
  put the movie into name
  put char 1 to offset(".",name) of name into name
  put name&"dir" into name
  play movie name
end
```

This handler will take the name of the Windows projector, cut off the ".exe" and replace it with a ".dir." You could do the same thing for projectors on the Macintosh, but the file naming would be strange. Instead, you may want to come up with another naming convention. For instance, the projector could be named "Project" and the movie could be named "Project file."

Running Your Movie in a Window on the Mac

The stage is an odd thing. It's this big block in the middle of the screen that doesn't move, and, worse, it takes up the entire screen.

When you build a Windows projector, you have the option of making the stage a window by itself. This gives the movie a nice application-like feel. It also looks much better on projectors that are less than 640 by 480.

On the Macintosh, the best you can do is use the Full Screen option when building a projector, to hide the rest of the Macintosh desktop. You cannot set the stage to appear inside a movable application-like window.

One trick you can use to get around this is to run your main presentation inside a movie in a window. To accommodate this, you can set your stage to be invisible. Here is an *on startMovie* handler that does this. It hides the stage and then opens a window and assigns the movie "main.dir" to that window.

```
on startMovie
  set the visible of the stage = FALSE
  set winObj = window("Presentation")
  set the fileName of window "Presentation" = "main.dir"
  set the visible of window "Presentation" = TRUE
end
```

You could also set the type, title, and position of the window before you make it visible.

Multiple Cast Files

A big advancement in Director 5 is the ability to have multiple casts. You can have several casts in one movie, plus many external casts. External casts are particularly useful, as they can be used by more than one movie.

There are a few Lingo commands to help you manage multiple casts. For instance, *the fileName of castLib* function will return the real file name of the cast. You can also use this property to *set* the filename to something else, so you can do some dynamic cast library swapping.

There are some simple cast library functions like *the number of castLibs*, *the name of castLib*, and *the number of members of castLib*. These do pretty much what you would expect. Here is a simple handler to show the names and number of members in all of the available cast libraries.

```
on showCastLibInfo
  repeat with i = 1 to the number of castLibs
    put the name of castLib i,→
the number of members of castLib i
  end repeat
end
```

The idea of multiple casts is so new to Director and Lingo that their aren't many "typical" uses for these Lingo commands yet. However, given that different cast libraries could have similar members with the same names, you could build some interesting programs around the technique of swapping out these libraries. One library, for instance, could have a deck of cards, as we used in Chapter 25. However, if the user selects another style of cards, then another cast library could be used.

Linked Cast Members

With cast members such as pictures and sounds, you have the option to have the actual cast member as a file with a link to it in the cast. This way, you can swap out files to change the cast member, instead of reimporting it every time. Digital video, on the other hand, is only allowed as a linked cast member.

There are a few Lingo commands that allow us to manipulate cast members. Just as with cast libraries, we can use *the filename* property to swap out files on the fly. Here is a script that assigns a new file to a digital video cast member.

```
on setVideo name
  set the filename of member "video" = name
end
```

The movie will use the new file the *next* time the cast member is used. This means that if the video is currently on the screen, it will not be swapped with the new one immediately.

Another important Lingo command is the *importFileInto* function. This allows you to import the actual bitmap or sound into a cast member.

It is often suggested that you use this function to bring media into casts when you are near the end of a project. That way, you can swap out pictures and sounds while constructing a movie, then bring them in when they are in a more finished state. Here is a typical example:

```
importFileInto member "picture", "picture.pct"
```

With the availability of multiple casts and an improved import function in Director 5, there are many options to make final production smoother.

Adding Resources to Mac Projectors

One of the advantages that Macintosh-only products have is the ability to add *resources* to a projector. These are like little files that are inside the projector file. You can see these resources with a program called ResEdit.

ResEdit comes bundled with many Macintosh development systems and other Apple programs. When you use it to open a Director projector, you get a window that looks like Figure 33-1.

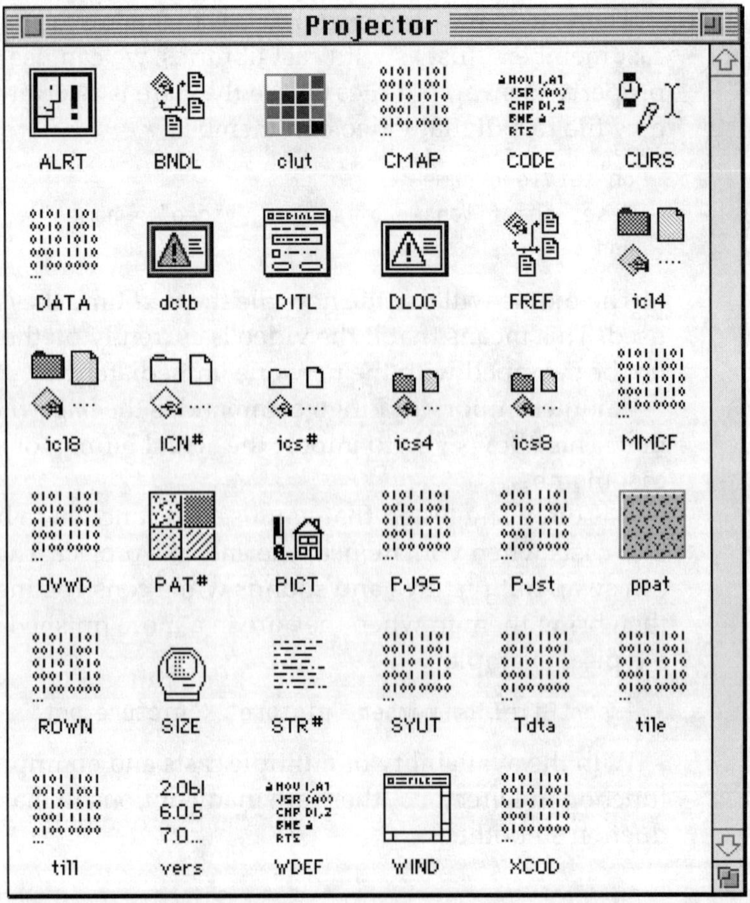

Figure 33-1: *A ResEdit window showing the resources in a Director projector.*

Double-clicking on any of the icons will bring up a window that shows all of that specific type of resource in the file. For instance, if you double-click on CURS, you will see a window that looks like Figure 33-2.

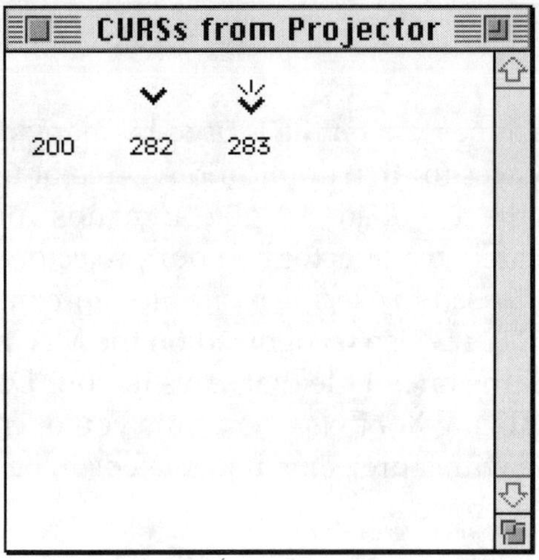

Figure 33-2: *The cursor resources of a Director Projector.*

You can double-click on one of the cursors to edit it, or even create a new one. The number underneath each cursor icon in Figure 33-2 represents the number you can use with the *cursor* Lingo command. You can also cut and paste cursors from one projector or another application to your projector.

The other types of resources that are handy are font resources and Xobject resources. You can get either one of these from a font or Xobject file then use ResEdit to copy and paste into the Director projector. Any fonts or Xobjects that are included in the projector are automatically available to it when it runs.

You can also use ResEdit to edit the resources of the Director 5.0 Resources file. This file is used to build all projectors. So, placing cursors or other things inside it will ensure that they will be included in any projectors you make.

Lingo.ini

On Windows machines, an *.ini* file is used by many programs to store user preferences for that application. Director uses a *lingo.ini* file that contains the text of any Lingo commands you want executed immediately by Director by your projectors.

Typically, this is used to execute *openXlib* commands. In Director 5, the lingo.ini file is also recognized on the Macintosh.

Creating or editing an .ini file that stays in your Director folder is handy for initializing Xobjects every time you open Director. To use a lingo.ini file with a projector, it just needs to be placed in the same folder as the projector.

Cross-Platform Issues

One of the biggest headaches for developers is getting their finished products to look the same on both Mac and Windows platforms. While Director is a cross-platform development tool, issues like fonts, color palettes, and video and sound formats tend to foul up the product when played on a system it was not developed on.

Fonts

When computers first started to use font technology to display text, the most important part of the font was the screen bitmap image. These fonts were created specifically for onscreen display, because that's where they were used.

As computers were used more and more for word processing and desktop publishing, the font industry focused on laserwriter output rather than screen display. As a result, most fonts are created for printing.

Now that the world of multimedia and the Internet increases the importance of onscreen font presentation, these fonts are falling short. Still, there are quite a few, like the Mac fonts Geneva, New York, Monaco, and Courier, that are well-suited for screen display.

Unfortunately, these are not always the fonts you want to use. Even worse, the same fonts don't exist on the Windows platform. Therefore, we need to specify how the fonts map from system to system.

The way Director does this is with a font map file. You can get this file by using the Save Font Map function in the Movie Properties dialog box of any movie. You can make changes to it and re-import it with the accompanying Load Font Map function.

The font map file is a basic text file and is pretty self-explanatory. Most of the lines show which font maps to which font when the movie is moved to another system. That part of the file looks like this:

```
Mac:Chicago       => Win:System
Mac:Courier       => Win:"Courier New"
Mac:Geneva        => Win:"MS Sans Serif"
Mac:Helvetica     => Win:Arial
Mac:Monaco        => Win:Terminal
Mac:"New York"    => Win:"MS Serif"
Mac:Symbol        => Win:Symbol  Map None
Mac:Times         => Win:"Times New Roman" 14=>12 18=>14
                     24=>18 30=>24

Win:Arial             => Mac:Helvetica
Win:"Courier"         => Mac:Courier
Win:"Courier New"     => Mac:Courier
Win:"MS Serif"        => Mac:"New York"
Win:"MS Sans Serif"   => Mac:Geneva
Win:Symbol            => Mac:Symbol  Map None
Win:System            => Mac:Chicago
Win:Terminal          => Mac:Monaco
Win:"Times New Roman" => Mac:"Times" 12=>14 14=>18 18=>24
                         24=>30
```

You can change or add to these lists. The only reason for the quotes around some of the font names is so that font names with multiple word descriptions are handled correctly.

One of the odd things about the default font map is that the Times to Times New Roman map has a size translation part. You can see on the preceding page how 14 point is translated to 12 point when going from Mac to Windows. While it is nice to see an example of this, it is annoying because this mapping makes no sense. At most sizes, the two fonts actually translate back and forth to each other quite nicely. The first thing you should do when creating your own font map is to delete this size translation.

Also, note that the translation is not very accurate. Times and Times New Roman look very much the same, but they are different fonts. So words will wrap differently because character widths are slightly different. The only way to avoid this is to use the Rich Text cast members in Director, which translates the text to a bitmap for screen display.

Also, remember that just because a font is on your machine doesn't mean it is on everyone else's. The only fonts you can rely on are Courier, Times, New York, Helvetica, Chicago, and Monaco on the Mac, and Times New Roman, Arial, and Courier New on Windows.

Courier and Courier New are particularly useful, as they are monospaced fonts. This means that you can create tables that will line up in text fields across platforms. These two fonts match up in character widths identically on both platforms at normal sizes.

Color Palettes

The standard consumer computer has a 640 by 480 screen and 8-bit color. This means it can display only 256 different colors at one time.

A set of 256 colors is called a palette. You can switch palettes, so that the monitor is showing a custom set of 256, but you can never show more than 256 colors on these basic machines.

The trouble comes when you need to show two screen elements that use different palettes. These can be two pictures in your Director movie. In this case, one of the two pictures will be forced into the other's palette and look very bad. You need to avoid this in situations where you expect users with 8-bit color computers to be using your product.

You can also have your Director movie and another program conflict with each other: for instance, a Director movie that doesn't use the whole screen and lets some of the Mac or Windows desktop show through.

The desktop, and the objects on it, are probably displayed with the system palette. This is a special palette used by most programs. The Mac system palette and the Windows system palette are different.

When your movie uses a different palette than that of the other screen elements, those other elements will be color-distorted. You can solve this problem by either taking over the whole screen, or by using only the system palette in your movie.

The problem with that last solution is that, as mentioned previously, the Mac and Windows system palettes are different. What works great on one machine will mess up the color on another.

There is no great solution for this. Many products are built using only the Macintosh system palette, making sure to take over the whole screen on the Windows side so that the color shift is not apparent. The same would hold true if you used your own custom palette and took over the whole screen on both platforms.

Video

Using QuickTime video is the best cross-platform solution. Windows .AVI files are nice on the Windows side, but they can't be seen on the Mac, whereas QuickTime can be seen on both platforms.

The only thing you need to do is remember to flatten any cross-platform QuickTime movies. This means that the Macintosh resources are incorporated into the main part of the video file, which will ensure that they translate to Windows.

There are several great utilities out there to flatten your video files. The QuickTime movie player on the Mac also lets you save movies as cross-platform. Popular video editing programs give you this option as well.

Sound

Most of the sound capabilities in Director translate nicely between platforms. However, you need to be aware that some of the compression types do not work on Windows. Stick to the standard types of Mac AIFF sounds or Window WAVE sounds and you should be okay.

Also, the capabilities of Windows to play multiple sounds at once is very limited. Director does as good a job as it can to mix sounds, but sound cards in PC machines can only really handle one device at a time. So, playing video with sound and then trying to play sound from Director's audio track at the same time doesn't work on Windows computers.

Keep your end user's machine in mind when putting the sound together for your project. The only way to ensure proper playback is to test your product on as many machines as possible. Remember that Windows computers can use a variety of different sound cards that claim to be compatible with one another but often aren't when you push them to the limits.

File Paths

An obvious difference between platforms is the way folders and files are separated in path names. This is called the path delimiter. On Windows machines, the backslash ("\") is the path delimiter; on the Macintosh, it is a colon (:).

The cross-platform problem with this comes when you build path names in Lingo handlers. You can't just assume that the path delimiter will be a backslash or a colon; you need code that will cover both.

The following handler sets a global called "pathDel" to the proper path delimiter. You can use this global in your scripts when you need to create path names.

```
on getPathDel
  global pathDel
  if the machineType = 256 then
```

```
put "\" into pathDel
  else put ":" into pathDel
end
```

Another useful handler is one that converts a pathname to fit the current operating system.

```
on convertPath name
  if the machineType = 256 then
    put "\" into pathDel
    put ":" into wrongPathDel
  else
    put ":" into pathDel
    put "\" into wrongPathDel
  end if

  set the itemDelimiter = wrongPathDel
  put "" into newname
  repeat with i = 1 to the number of items in name
    if i > 1 then put pathDel after newname
    put (item i of name) after newname
  end repeat
  return newname
end
```

Moving On

Finishing a multimedia project is quite a task. Many producers say that you should budget at least a third of your time for the problems that come up at the last minute. Many of these problems will only be apparent after testing.

This "Expert Lingo" section covered a lot of different topics. Hopefully, what you've learned here will help you through some of the most difficult development tasks.

Coming up, Section IV takes an in-depth look at Shockwave and your ability to use Director and Lingo to make rich multimedia for the Internet.

SECTION IV

Shockwave

34

Introduction to Shockwave

With the introduction of Shockwave for Director in October of 1995, the usefulness of Lingo greatly increased. Now Director movies can be viewed inside Internet browsers as a part of World Wide Web pages. Thousands of developers jumped at the chance to create rich multimedia on the Internet for the first time. Let's look at how to use Lingo to make the best Shockwave movies.

First of all, what is Shockwave? It is a method of playing Director movies as part of Internet World Wide Web pages. The World Wide Web is the part of the Internet, along with e-mail and other functions, that allows users to search for and display information from all over the world in a mixed-media format currently dominated by text and graphics.

The World Wide Web displays information created with a simple language called hypertext markup language, or HTML. Pages of HTML are usually little more than simple text documents with some added control features that style the text or perform more advanced functions like presenting text in table format. See the resources section at the end of this book for a list of places on the Internet where you can go for more information about HTML.

Web pages can also contain bits of media. Until recently, the only types of media you could include were pictures and text. Now, thanks to the plug-in architecture of browsers, you can place a variety of things inside Web pages, provided the end user also has that plug-in installed in their browser's folder.

A Director movie is one of the things you can place on a Web page, thanks to the Shockwave plug-in. The plug-in, along with its technical documentation, is located at

http://www.macromedia.com/director.html.

Shockwave technology is in a state of flux at the moment. Improvements are being made by Macromedia on a monthly basis, and better tools and plug-ins will probably be available by the time this book reaches your hands. If you are serious about Shockwave development, keep checking the Macromedia site for up-to-date information.

Getting Shockwave to Work

Contrary to what many developers believe, you don't have to do anything to a Director movie to convert it to a Shockwave movie. Most normal movies will work just fine with no special considerations.

What you *can* do, however, is to use the Afterburner program to compress the movie. This simple program, provided at the aforementioned Macromedia Internet site, will compress your movie file to make it as small as possible, for Internet transfer. This is important, since you want to minimize file transfer times for your end users to give them a better experience.

Using Afterburner is simple. It is just an Xtra that appears in the Xtras menu. Just select it and it will prompt you for a file to "burn." Then assign a new name, preferably the same name but with a *.dcr* filename extension at the end.

A .dcr file is compressed and cannot be opened by Director again. The Shockwave plug-in can use either the original Director movie or the compressed .dcr.

The next step is to embed your movie into an HTML page. To do this, we use an HTML command inside the Web page. Here is an example:

```
<EMBED SRC="mymovie.dcr" WIDTH=480 HEIGHT=240>
```

This command will embed the movie "mymovie," which is in the same directory as the Web page, and give it a 480 by 240 box. You could also include the full pathname of the movie.

```
<EMBED SRC="http://www2.csn.net/~rosenz/mymovie.dcr"
WIDTH=480 HEIGHT=240>
```

Two other parameters of this HTML command are "palette" and "textfocus." The "palette" parameter can be either "background" or "foreground," depending on whether you want the movie to impose its palette on the page or vice-versa. The "textfocus" parameter can either be "onstart," to have the movie immediately recognize keyboard input; "onmouse," to have the movie accept keyboard input only after the user has clicked within the rect of the movie; or "never," to have the shockwave movie never accept keyboard input. Here is an example:

```
<EMBED SRC=" mymovie.dcr" WIDTH=480 HEIGHT=240
PALETTE=background TEXTFOCUS=never>
```

A problem you might have to deal with is setting up your Internet server to handle Shockwave movies. You do this by properly setting MIME (Multipurpose Internet Mail Extension) types for Shockwave.

If you have your own server, then you need to add the MIME type *application/x-director* to apply to files with .dcr, .dir, and .dxr extensions. Otherwise, you have two options. You can ask your server administrator to add this MIME type to the server, or you can ask the administrator to tell you how to set up custom MIME types for your part of the server only.

Making Good Shockwave Movies

There is one factor in making Director movies for the Internet that is far more important than all others: file size.

Shockwave movies need to be totally downloaded to the user's machine before they begin to play. The fastest standard modem loads less than 3K per second. This means that a 100K Director movie takes longer than half a minute to start playing for the typical Web surfer at optimum conditions.

The best way to go about creating Shockwave movies is to make every byte count. This means that Shockwave development needs to be very different than CD-ROM development. In the latter case you have over 600 megabytes of space available.

But just because you need to worry about every byte of data in your movies doesn't mean you can't be creative. Here is a list of ideas that allow you to make great movies while keeping the file size down.

- Use 1-bit bitmap graphics when you can. They are small and their color can be set by the foreground property of the sprite.
- Limit sounds as much as possible. They are the biggest file-size hogs. Use only 8-bit mono sounds. Try using short sound loops rather than long compositions.
- Find parts of your graphics that are identical, and substitute a single graphic for the identical portions by placing the graphic in multiple sprites.
- Use the tiling option to create custom tiles to apply to Director rectangles or circles. This method can be used to make small but interesting backgrounds.
- Use ink effects to present altered views of graphics. For instance, use another ink for the down state of a button, rather than a totally different cast member.

- Try using graphics that are 2-bit or 4-bit. The 2-bit graphics, in particular, are handy because they can include black, white, and two shades of gray.
- Use the Trails setting for sprites to get them to draw things on the stage.
- If an image has a large area that is one color, make sure it is really only one color and not a dithered pattern. One-color areas will compress much better.
- Always compress your files with the Afterburner. Do not use raw Director movies.

What Shockwave Movies Can't Do

There are plenty of Director functions that are not available to Shockwave productions. All are functions directly related to the fact that the movies are being played in a browser and accessed over the Internet.

For one, you cannot have linked media across the Internet. This means no digital video. QuickTime and AVI video can be played separately with other plug-ins or viewers. However, you can have the user load files like these, as well as cast member libraries and Xtras, as long as the user has them in a special support file on their hard drive.

Other file-access types of Lingo commands do not work: *importFileInto*, *saveMovie*, *open*, and *mci*. Movies in a window are also not operable with Shockwave. Neither is *printFrom*.

Also, the tempo channel in the score is severely crippled. None of the "wait for" options work. This can be corrected by using some simple Lingo handlers, however. For instance, here is an *on exitFrame* handler that waits until the sound in channel 2 is finished playing.

```
on exitFrame
  is soundBusy(2) then go to the frame
end
```

Troubleshooting

Remember that Shockwave is a very new technology. There are lots of bugs. Some of them are in the Shockwave plug-in, while others are in the Internet browsers. Engineers are working hard on both sides to make the entire experience more stable. Until they have solved all the problems, here are some troubleshooting tips:

- Make sure your browser uses the plug-in architecture. Presently, only Netscape 2.0 and the Microsoft Internet Explorer for Macintosh can handle Shockwave. More may be added by the time you read this.
- Set your browser's disk cache to at least 10MB of space—more if possible.
- Set the memory size of the browser on the Mac, and the memory cache of the browser on Windows, to at least 8MB.
- There are problems with placing Shockwave movies inside HTML tables, so don't attempt to do so.
- If you have problems accessing every Shockwave site you try, there is probably something wrong with your browser setup. If you have trouble with one Shockwave site but can successfully access others, then the problem is likely to be with that one bad site.

Moving On

The best way to get acquainted with what you can and can't do in Shockwave is to look at other Internet sites that use it. Appendix H in the back of this book has a list of the best examples of Shockwave sites on the Web.

Next, let's take a look at some new Lingo commands that Shockwave movies can utilize.

35

Shockwave Lingo

There is a new set of Lingo commands that work specifically with Shockwave movies. These all have to do with various aspects of network communications. By using them, you can have functions that go to other pages or functions that load other movies or text files over the Internet. Note, however, that these new Lingo commands are not understood by Director itself, so they will cause error messages while you are developing your movies in the Director application, and they will only work when the movie is loaded into your Internet browser.

Links

You can make your Shockwave movies act like sophisticated image maps that link to other Web pages. The *gotoNetPage* command can be placed in any Lingo handler and will signal the browser to load another page.

The only parameter for this command is the URL (Uniform Resource Locator), or Internet address, of this new page. A button that uses this command may look like this:

```
on mouseUp
  gotoNetPage("http://clevermedia.com")
end
```

The new page will begin to load immediately, but while the transfer takes place the Shockwave movie will continue to run. You can have the full path of the new page, as above; or you can have a relative path if the page is located in the same directory as the current page or one below it in the file system directory.

You can also use the command to send instructions back to the server. A *gotoNetPage* that calls a server-side script or application would be recognized just as any other call from the HTML page. That way, if you do CGI or Java scripting, you can use this command in much the same way you use some HTML forms to submit data.

The *gotoNetPage* command can take a second parameter as well. This parameter lets you target a Netscape frame or new browser window. It works the same way as a TARGET attribute in an HTML link tag.To use it, you should first be familar with Netscape windows and frames. This second parameter will specify the name of an existing frame or window target, or use "_blank" to specify that you want to open a new window. Here is an example:

```
on mouseUp
  gotoNetPage("http://clevermedia.com", "_blank")
end

on mouseUp
  gotoNetPage("http://clevermedia.com", "sideframe")
end
```

Another type of link involves swapping Shockwave movies. The *gotoNetMovie* command will load another movie into the same embedded spot as the current one. It is very much like the standard Lingo *play* command.

```
on mouseUp
  gotoNetMovie("movie2.dcr")
end
```

You can use a relative path or full path for this command as well. Make sure that the new movie is the same size as the old one, because it will have to exist in the embedded space already created by the first movie.

You can use this command to separate your Shockwave presentation into smaller parts, so that the first one can play quickly and the loading times for the rest of the parts are spread out between movies. It is interesting to note that with the *gotoNetMovie* command, global variables will retain their values between the movies.

You can also use this command to allow simple program branching. For instance, if the user has three options that go to three screens, you may not want to load all three screens at once—which will take a while—but rather load the initial screen first as its own movie and allow the user to choose which of the three options they want to go to. Then, the movie will use *gotoNetMovie* to get just that one screen, which would be another movie.

Reading Text

Shockwave movies have the ability to load a text file over the Internet. This means you could have lists of data on your server space that the movie can access through Lingo commands.

The *getNetText* command will request a text file. It accepts the Internet address of that text file as its only parameter. The file request is executed immediately, but nothing is immediately returned by the *getNetText* function.

```
getNetText("http://www2.csn.net/~rosenz/PGG/courses.txt")
```

In order to find out when the text file transfer is done, you need to use the *netDone()* function. This will return True when the file has been completely transferred.

Furthermore, you need to make sure the browser is given time to perform the file transfer. If you just use a *repeat* loop until *netDone()* is true, then the Netscape browser for the Macintosh will never get the time to do the transfer, since the Shockwave move is caught in a loop. Also, the repeat loop locks the browser from getting any mouse-click messages that occur even outside the Shockwave movie area of the screen. Instead, you need to allow your movie to play on, looping through a frame if necessary, until the transfer is done. Here is a frame script that does this.

```
on exitFrame
  if not netDone() then
    go to the frame
  else
    put netTextResult() into text
  end if
end
```

The previous handler also introduces the *netTextResult()* function. This just returns the text that the *getNetText()* function asked for.

Another useful command that can be used in conjunction with the *getNetText* command is the *netError()* function. When a transfer is completed, this function returns *OK* if everything is fine, and an error message otherwise.

TIP

Remember that when you use repeat *loops in Shockwave, it not only stops the Director movie from doing anything else but also freezes the browser.*

Other Functions

Two other functions are also available. One is *preLoadNetThing*, which loads an Internet file, whether it is an HTML Web page or another Shockwave movie, into the user's disk cache.

This means that it will just transfer it from the Internet Web site to the user's machine so that when that element is needed, it can be quickly loaded from the disk drive rather than slowly transferred over the Internet.

Remember that the browser has ultimate control over the cache. It can quickly throw away the file you intentionally preloaded. Use *preLoadNetThing* with this in mind.

Xobjects & External Files

You can also access Xobjects, cast libraries, and linked media, like digital video, from Shockwave, provided that the file is present in the user's plug-in folder with the Shockwave plug-in. On Windows machines, the Xobjects need to be buried one folder deeper than the plug-in in a directory called either "NP16DSW" or "NP32DSW," respectively, depending on whether a Windows 3.1 or Windows 95 machine is being used. On Macintosh computers, this folder is named "NP-Mac68K-Dir-Shockwave" or "NP-PPC-Dir-Shockwave."

There are many advantages in placing cast libraries in this support folder. You can get these files to a user by supplying the files on your Web site and allowing the user to download them prior to viewing the Shockwave movie that uses them.

Improvements are made monthly, so be sure to check the Shockwave section of the Macromedia Web site as well as independent sources listed in Appendix H of this book for updated information on how to use linked media.

You need to use the *openXlib* command in your Shockwave movie before you have access to an Xobject. If the user does not have the Xobject in the proper place, they will get an error message. So this type of functionality is probably something you only want to use for intranets or special sites.

Note that the use of Xobjects violates some of the security ideas that govern other server-client communication. For instance, by using the FileIO Xobject, you can read, write, and delete files from the user's hard drive.

Of course, the solution to this problem is just to be very careful. A good use of the FileIO function is to write out a user preferences file that can be read by that movie or another Shockwave movie, so that each individual user can customize the site for their own needs.

Moving On

If you find yourself using these special Shockwave commands, you are probably the type of developer that needs to keep tabs on the latest developments. Make sure you keep checking Macromedia's Web site for new features. Also, check out the Shockwave resources listed in Appendix H at the back of this book.

Next, in our final chapter, let's look at techniques to make better Shockwave movies.

36 Shockwave Techniques

To create a Shockwave movie, you need to do little more than make a regular Director movie and stick it up on the Internet. However, this is quite a different environment than playing a movie from a CD-ROM or the hard disk.

A good Shockwave movie should not annoy your users by taking too long to download. You should always consider whether the user is getting an experience that matches expectations after waiting for the movie to load.

Splash Screen Movies

A great technique to adopt if you are developing large Shockwave movies is to embed a Shockwave movie that is a picture relating to the original Shockwave movie into the HTML page as a small placeholder—say, under 10K. This movie will load quickly then immediately use *gotoNetMovie* to start loading the real movie.

These splash screen movies can consist of very simple graphics or text. They can also have small, short animations. The idea is to give the user something to look at while the real movie is being downloaded.

Make the splash screen movie useful if you can. For instance, if your Shockwave product is a game, you might want to have instructions, or possibly credits.

Splash screen movies are also useful if you are not comfortable with the idea of the Macromedia logo appearing as your movie loads. By having a splash screen movie that is as small as possible, this logo will not appear for long, and may never even get the chance to show itself.

Users Without Shockwave

If you need to make sure your pages are viewable using any browser, then you'll want to cover yourself in case the Web surfer who comes to your page doesn't have Shockwave.

There are several ways to do this. The simplest is to use the <NOEMBED> tag in your HTML page. This works with the <EMBED> tag to propose an option to some browsers to display something else in place of the Shockwave movie.

```
<EMBED SRC="myShock.dcr" WIDTH=300 HEIGHT=200>
<NOEMBED><IMAGE SRC="shockSub.gif"></NOEMBED>
```

The idea here is that browsers that understand the <EMBED> tag will also understand that they must ignore anything between <NOEMBED> and </NOEMBED>.

Another way to do this is to use some light *Javascript* programming. Javascript is a scripting language understood by the Netscape 2.0 family of browsers, and possibly others in the future. But since the only browser that uses Javascript also uses Shockwave, we can include the following code in the HTML page:

```
<SCRIPT LANGUAGE="JavaScript">
document.write( '<EMBED SRC="myShock.dcr WIDTH=300
HEIGHT=200">' );
</SCRIPT>
```

The *document.write* command in Javascript will just pass along the text string as part of the HTML page.

However, this still doesn't solve the problem of what happens when a surfer comes along who has a browser that understands <EMBED> and Javascript but who hasn't downloaded the Shockwave plug-in yet. Right now, the Netscape 2.0 browser will automatically prompt the user to go and get the plug-in, but the user can still refuse.

The best way to handle all situations is to have a set of HTML pages for your site that runs with Shockwave and also have one that uses standard HTML. When the user comes to the first page of your site, have a small Shockwave movie embedded there that uses *gotoNetPage* to jump to the Shockwave version of that page and the entire site. If the user does not have Shockwave, the movie will never run and the page will remain as is.

Of course, you can always just ask the user directly: "Do you have Shockwave?" and allow them to go to one version of your site or the other. This will also be a desirable option for someone who needs fast access to your site and doesn't want to be bothered with the longer download times.

Shockwave Footprint

Another factor you need to keep in mind is the footprint, or stage size, of your movie. If you plan to make a movie that takes over the entire screen, remember that the browser will take a few pixels to the left and the right of the screen. It is best to limit your movie's width to no more than 592 pixels. Remember that your development machine might be set to handle monitors that are 800 or more pixels wide, but most users are still using 640 by 480 screens.

The height of a movie is also a concern. Netscape's browser, for instance, usually takes up a large part of the top of the screen with buttons and tools. While these areas can be hidden by the user, many users don't know how or don't want to do this. Your best bet is to assume that you only have about 300 pixels to play with vertically. Otherwise, you risk the chance that users will not be able to see your entire movie on the screen at one time.

TIP

Director movies can only have widths that are multiples of 16. Heights can be any number.

Moving On

Shockwave movies have another difference from other types of Director movies: you can see most of the Shockwave movies in existence just by surfing the Web. To do the same with the rest of the Director movies in existence, you would have to buy a lot of CD-ROMs, visit thousands of kiosks, and sneak into a lot of board room meetings.

This means that you can keep tabs on what others are developing pretty easily. It will quickly become obvious which developers are ahead of the pack. Keep watching their sites.

This overview of Shockwave completes our look at Lingo. While all major topics have been covered comprehensively, the reference section to come will go into more detail about some individual commands. The problem-solving guide in Appendix G will help you find resources inside this book, while Appendix H, "A List of Director Resources on the World Wide Web," will help you find up-to-date information on the Internet.

SECTION

V

Lingo Reference A–Z

Lingo Reference

What follows is a complete reference listing of Lingo commands and some syntax. Macromedia already provides Director owners with a complete "Lingo Dictionary." This reference guide can be used alone or in conjunction with that book.

In many cases, the "Lingo Dictionary" is excessively wordy. For instance, it constantly restates that setting a property to 1 will enable that property, and that setting it to 0 will disable that property. In this reference section I attempt to be more concise. We present only the information you need, in a compact format, so that you can identify and use the syntax you want.

In cases where detailed information is needed about a command, you can refer to both this guide and the "Lingo Dictionary," as well as the earlier chapters in this book.

Lingo has so many elements, however, that you sometimes may have to resort to testing a command yourself to see exactly how it works in different situations. You are encouraged to do this.

This section starts with symbols and then continues with entries in alphabetical order. The most useful part of this guide may be the "Also" listing under each command. This is a good way to explore the depth of Lingo and quickly identify and find related commands.

Items labeled as functions or properties return values. Most, but not all, properties can be set as well as tested. When you see the brackets, [], in the description of a command, it means that part of the parameter list is optional.

#

SYMBOL DECLARATION

What it looks like (in the message window)

```
put #thing
-- thing
put [#this: 5, #that: 7] into list
put getProp(list,#this)
-- 5
```

What it is

When you use # before a group of alphanumerics, the whole string is called a symbol. In the above example, *#thing* is a symbol. These are variables like numbers and strings, but they don't represent anything other than simple labels that you create and use as you wish.

Often, symbols are used as the properties of a list, as we do above. They operate faster than strings (i.e. ["this": 5, "that":7]) and are much more descriptive than numbers. You can also pass them into your handlers as parameters or have them returned as handler results.

Another use is as descriptive variable contents. For instance, a "size" variable could have values like #small, #medium, or #large.

You can test and compare variables that contain symbols with each other just as you would compare other variables. You can convert symbols to strings with the *string* function.

Also

symbolP(), string

+, –, *, /

MATH OPERATORS

What they look like (in the message window)

```
put 8+4
-- 12
put 8-4
-- 4
put 8*4
-- 32
put 8/4
-- 2
```

What they are

These are mathematical operators that can be used in a variety of situations in Lingo. Generally, any place you can use a number or variable that represents a number, you can instead put two or more numbers or variables there and use them as operators.

--

COMMENT SYNTAX

What it looks like (in a handler)

```
-- This handler does absolutely nothing
on doNothing
  nothing
end
```

What it is

Any text placed on the same line after this double-dash mark will not be interpreted at all by Director. Use it as often as possible to clarify the meaning of your code.

&, &&

CONCATENATION OPERATORS

What they look like (in the message window)

```
put "A"&"B"
-- "AB"
put "A"&&"B"
-- "A B"
put "A"&"B"&&"C"&"D"
-- "AB CD"
```

What they are

These two operators will merge any two strings. The && will add a space between them.

( )

MATH OPERATORS

What they look like (in the message window)

```
put 8+4*3
-- 20
put (8+4)*3
-- 36
```

What they are

Parentheses in Lingo work the same way they do in written math equations. They change the order in which operations are done, to reflect what you really mean. In the example above, we use parentheses to make sure that the addition is done before the multiplication.

<, <=, =, >=, >, <>

COMPARISON OPERATORS

What they look like (in the message window)

```
put 4 < 5
-- 1
put 4 <= 5
```

```
-- 1
put 4 = 4
-- 1
put 5 >= 4
-- 1
put 5 > 4
-- 1
put 5 <> 4
-- 1
```

What they are

These are the basic comparison operators. In order, they are as follows: less than, less than or equal to, equal to, greater than or equal to, greater than, not equal to. Use them to compare two number or variables. You can also use the = and <> to compare strings. If you use the others to compare strings, you will get results that reflect their alphabetical order.

[ ]

LIST SYNTAX

What they look like (in the message window)

```
put [1,2,3]
-- [1, 2, 3]
```

What they are

Brackets tell Director that you are defining a list. Use [] to represent a blank linear list and [:] to represent a blank property list.

"

STRING SYNTAX

What they look like (in the message window)

```
put "Lingo"
-- "Lingo"
```

What they are

Quotes tell Director that you are defining a string.

¬

CONTINUATION SYMBOL

What it looks like (in a handler)

```
on doThis
  put the long date && the long time¬
into field "whatever"
end
```

What it is

This symbol tells Director that you wish to continue the same line of Lingo on the next line. You can use this to make your code easier to read instead of letting Director wrap the text for you.

abort

COMMAND

What it looks like (in a handler)

```
on myHandler x
  if the shiftDown then abort
  return x*2
end
```

What it is

The *abort* command will exit a handler and also stop the handler that called it, the handler that called that one, and so on. It will not, however, exit Director or the projector.

The difference between the *abort* command and the *exit* command is that *exit* will only stop that one handler, while the handler that called it will continue on.

In the above example, a handler is called with one parameter. If the user is holding down the Shift key, the *abort* command causes that handler and the ones that lead up to it to stop. Otherwise, the handler returns twice the value of the parameter.

Also

exit, halt

abs(*number*)

MATH FUNCTION

What it looks like (in the message window)

```
put abs(-7)
-- 7
put abs(7)
-- 7
```

What it is

This function returns the absolute value of an integer or a floating-point number. The absolute value of a number is simply the number without a positive or negative component—in other words, it is always positive.

activeWindow

MIAW FUNCTION

What it looks like (in a button script)

```
on mouseUp
  if the activeWindow = the stage then alert "I am the stage"
  else alert "I am a window"
end
```

What it is

This function returns the name of the window that is executing that Lingo line. If the above script is run by a MIAW, then the result of *the activeWindow* will be the name of the window, for instance *(window "myWin")*. Otherwise, the result will be *(the stage)*.

This is useful when you have a piece of code that is sometimes run as part of a MIAW and sometimes run by the stage, and it is important for the code to know the difference.

actorList

OBJECT-ORIENTED PROGRAMMING PROPERTY

What it looks like (in the message window)

```
add the actorList, new(script "parentScript")
set the actorList = []
```

What it is

This is a special list that you can populate with child objects, as we do in the first line of the example above. When you do this, Director will know to send "enterFrame" messages to each child object in the *the actorList*. That message will trigger any *on enterFrame* handlers inside those child objects.

To clear *the actorList,* just use the second line in our example.

Also

new

add *list, element*

LIST COMMAND

What it looks like (in the message window)

```
put [1,2,3,4] into list
add list, 5
put list
-- [1,2,3,4,5]
```

What it is

For an unsorted linear list, the *add* command will append the new element to the end of a list. For a sorted linear list (see *sort*), the new element will be added in its proper place.

Also

addAt, addProp, append, setAt, sort

addAt *list, position, element*

LIST COMMAND

What it looks like (in the message window)

```
put [1,2,3,4] into list
addAt list, 3, 5
put list
-- [1,2,5,3,4]
```

What it is

This list command will insert a new element into a linear list in the position that you specify. In the above example, we insert the number 5 at the third position in the list.

Also

add, addProp, append, sort

addProp *list, property, value*

LIST COMMAND

What it looks like (in the message window)

```
put [#name: "Alice", #age: 26] into list
addProp list, #number, 3834
put list
-- [#name: "Alice", #age: 26, #number: 3834]
```

What it is

This command will add a new property and its value to a property list. If the list is unsorted, it appends the property; if sorted, it inserts the property in its proper place.

If *AddProp* is used and the property already exists, it will be added a second time. However, using *setAProp* will add a new property to a list only if the property doesn't already exist, and replace the value of the property if it already does exist.

Also

add, setAProp, sort

alert *string*

COMMAND

What it looks like (in a button script)

```
on mouseUp
  alert "You pushed me!"
end
```

What it is

This command brings up a simple dialog box displaying the string, and generates a system beep. The parameter must be a string. You can use the *string* function to create a string from a number or list for use in this command.

The *alert* command is very useful for displaying simple messages, like errors and "about" boxes. You can also use this to send debugging messages at times when the debugger may not be available—such as with projectors and shockwave applications.

Note that there is a limit on the number of characters you can fit into this window. It depends on system font settings. Try to keep it under 150 characters, and test out the alert box in the cases of long strings to make sure.

Also

string

align of member *member*

FIELD MEMBER PROPERTY

What it looks like (in the message window)

```
put the align of member "text"
-- "left"
set the align of member "text" to "center"
```

What it is

This is a property of a text field that can be tested and set. Acceptable values are: "left," "right," and "center." Make sure that at least one character is in the text field.

ancestor

OBJECT-ORIENTED PROGRAMMING PROPERTY

What it is

This property of an object can be set to point to another parent script. When that happens, the child inherits all of the handlers of that second parent, as well as those of the original parent. This means that all of the handlers of the ancestor are available for the child script to use.

Also

new, property

and

LOGICAL OPERATOR

What it looks like (in the message window)

```
put TRUE and FALSE
-- FALSE
put TRUE and TRUE
-- TRUE
```

What it is

You can use *and* inside any Lingo syntax that requires a logical expression—like *if...then* or *repeat* statements. It will perform a logical "and" on two expressions. This means that the result will only be true if both expressions are true, and false if either or both are false.

Also

or, not

A

append *list, value*

LIST COMMAND

What it looks like (in the message window)

```
put [1,2,3] into list
append list, 5
put list
-- [1, 2, 3, 5]
```

What it is

This will place a new value at the end of a linear list.

Also

add, addAt, addProp

atan *number*

MATH FUNCTION

What it looks like (in the message window)

```
put atan(1.0)
-- .7854
```

What it is

This function returns the arctangent of a number. In the above example, for instance, we get the arctangent of 1, which is equivalent to pi divided by four.

The "1" would represent the slope of a line, which would be a diagonal line going up and to the right. The result, one-fourth pi, would represent the number of radians in a 45 degree angle, which is the angle the line is at. Thus, you can use *atan* to translate line slopes to angles. Refer to a basic trigonometry book for more information on arctangents.

Also

sin, cos, tan, pi

autoTab of member *member*

FIELD MEMBER PROPERTY

What it looks like (in a handler)

```
on makeAutoTab
  set the autoTab of member "text" = TRUE
end
```

What it is

This property determines, when the Tab key is hit, whether the text field could possibly be selected as the next field to be edited by the user. Usually, you would have several editable text fields set with this property turned on. Then the user could use the Tab key to move between fields. You can test and set this property with Lingo or manually in the member information box.

Also

editable of member

backColor of member *member*

FIELD MEMBER PROPERTY

What it looks like (in the message window)

```
set the backColor of member "text" = 215
```

What it is

This property corresponds to the background color of a text field. You can test and set its value. Remember that if you are using an 8-bit palette, the numbers correspond to the colors in the palette, while 16- and 32-bit movies mean that the number corresponds to the color value.

Also

the backColor of sprite, the foreColor of member

B

backColor of sprite *spriteNumber*

SPRITE PROPERTY

What it looks like (in a button handler)

```
on mouseDown
  set the backColor of sprite (the clickOn) = 215
  updateStage
  repeat while the mouseDown
  end repeat
end
```

What it is

Director boxes and ovals have both a foreground color and a background color. So do 1-bit graphics. This Lingo command allows you to temporarily change the background color or just get its value.

In the above example, we change the background color of a sprite to red when the user clicks down, and then we wait until the mouse is lifted. After the frame is finished playing, the color will return to its original value. We can make the change stick with a *puppetSprite* command.

This command is also useful for 8-bit graphics, as it determines which color will be transparent when using the "background transparent" ink setting.

Also

the foreColor of sprite, the backColor of member

BACKSPACE

CONSTANT

What it looks like (in a handler)

```
on keyDown
  if the key = BACKSPACE then
    put EMPTY into field "text"
  end if
end
```

What it is
This constant refers to the character equivalent of the Delete key on the Mac and the backspace key on a Windows machine. In the above example, we intercept the backspace character and clear a text field when the user hits it.

Also
keyDown, keyUp, numToChar, charToNum

beep *number*

COMMAND

What it looks like (in a handler)

```
on checkValue n
  if n = 42 then beep(2)
end
```

What it is
This command just sounds the system beep the number of times specified as the parameter. The system beep is set in the control panels of the operating system.

Be careful when using this in a product. Your system beep might be a nice "ding" and "quack," but one of your customers may set their system beep to something more disgusting.

Also
alert, soundLevel

beepOn

SYSTEM PROPERTY

What it looks like (in a handler)

```
on startMovie
  set the beepOn = TRUE
end
```

B

What it is
When you set this system property to true, the computer will beep any time the user tries to click on a part of the Director stage where there is no active sprite. An active sprite is one that has a script assigned to it.

The default for this property is false. The example above will activate this functionality. Use it in cases where you want to signal the user that areas of the stage are either active or inactive.

Also
exitLock

beginRecording

SCORE COMMAND

What it looks like (in a handler)

```
on resetColors
  beginRecording
    repeat with i = 1 to 48
      set the foreColor of sprite i = 255
    end repeat
    updateFrame
  endRecording
end
```

What it is
This signifies the start of a recording session. The beginRecording and endRecording commands surround a set of Lingo lines that would be used to permanently change the score. In the above example, we simply set all the foreground colors of all the sprites in the current frame to black.

Also
endRecording, updateFrame, Chapter 31

blend of sprite *spriteNumber*

SPRITE PROPERTY

What it looks like (in a handler)

```
on fadeOut spriteNum
  repeat with i = 100 down to 0
    set the blend of sprite spriteNum to i
    updateStage
  end repeat
end
```

What it is

This property lets you blend a sprite with whatever is behind it. A value of 100 will make the sprite opaque, while a value of 0 will make the sprite invisible. Anything in between will attempt to blend the sprite with graphics underneath. This all depends on the ink setting of the sprite as well.

This Lingo command can be used in handlers like the one above, or in conjunction with puppetSprites. You can also set the blend of a sprite manually in the sprite information box.

You are supposed to only use blend values on sprites that are set to “matte,” “blend,” “background transparent,” or “mask” ink in the score.

Also

ink of sprite, Chapter 7

border of member *member*

FIELD MEMBER PROPERTY

What it looks like (in the message window)

```
put the border of member "text"
-- 0
set the border of member "text" = 5
```

What it is

This property represents the border around a text cast member. You can test it and set it to a new value with Lingo by using this property.

bottom of sprite *spriteNumber*

SPRITE PROPERTY

What it looks like (in the message window)

```
put the bottom of sprite 6
-- 356
```

What it is

This property returns the position, in pixels, of the bottom of the sprite on the stage. You cannot set this property directly, but you can adjust it using the *rect of sprite.*

Also

top of sprite, left of sprite, right of sprite, width of sprite, height of sprite, rect of sprite

boxDropShadow of member *member*

FIELD MEMBER PROPERTY

What it looks like (in the message window)

```
put the boxDropShadow of member "text"
-- 0
set the boxDropShadow of member "text" = 5
```

What it is

This property represents the drop shadow around a text cast member. It is in pixels. You can test it and set it to a new value with Lingo by using this property.

boxType of member *member*

FIELD MEMBER PROPERTY

What it looks like (in the message window)

```
put the boxType of member "text"
-- #adjust
set the boxDropShadow of member "text" = #scroll
```

B

What it is

This property lets you test or set the type of a text cast member. Possible values are #adjust, #scroll, #fixed, and #limit. These correspond to the types that you can set manually in the text member property box.

buttonStyle

SYSTEM PROPERTY

What it looks like (in a handler)

```
on startMovie
  set the buttonStyle = 1
end
```

What it is

This is a simple system property that can be set to 0 or 1. When set to 0, the user can click on a button, hold down the mouse, roll the cursor away from that button and over another button, and that second button will become active. If set to 1, the user has to lift up the mouse and click on the second button separately to activate it.

This only works on prefab Director buttons, not any bitmap buttons you might create—although of course the functionality can be simulated with Lingo.

buttonType of member *member*

BUTTON MEMBER PROPERTY

What it looks like (in the message window)

```
put the buttonType of member "button"
-- #pushButton
set the buttonType of member "button" = #checkBox
```

What it is

This property lets you test or set the type of a button cast member. Possible values are #pushButton, #checkBox, and #radioButton. These correspond to the types you can set manually in the button member property box.

C

cancelIdleLoad *number*

COMMAND

What it looks like (in a button handler)

```
on mouseDown
  cancelIdleLoad 42
  go to frame "next"
end
```

What it is

First, you need to use the *idleLoadTag* command to tag all of the cast members that have been queued for loading. Then, you use that same tag number with the *cancelIdleLoad* command to cancel this loading if you need to.

Also

idleLoadTag, idleLoadDone, idleLoadMode, idleLoadPeriod, finishIdleLoad

case

SYNTAX

What it looks like (in a handler)

```
on decide n
  case n of
    1 : go to frame "a"
    2 : go to frame "b"
    3 :
      set myGlobal = 0
      go to frame "c"
    otherwise
      go to frame "d"
  end case
end
```

What it is

This is a multibranch condition statement. You use a single variable or expression, in this case "n," and then list its possible values and what to do in each event. At the end, you can use the *otherwise* syntax to take care of values you do not list.

The actual variable or expression can be a number, string, or any Lingo element with a value. Each branch in the *case* statement can have one or more lines of code.

Also
if...then

C

castLibNum of sprite *spriteNumber*

SPRITE PROPERTY

What it looks like (in a handler)

```
on switchLib libNum
  set the castLibNum of sprite 5 = libNum
end
```

What it is
This property allows you to test and set the cast library of a cast member in a sprite. This could be useful if you have two or more cast libraries, in or linked to one movie, that have similar members. You could have a sprite switch between the *same* cast member (by number) in different casts.

center of member *memberNumber*

DIGITAL VIDEO PEOPERTY

What it looks like (in the message window)

```
set the center of member "video" to TRUE
```

What it is
This property corresponds to the "center" property of a digital video sprite. You can use it to set the property via Lingo. It determines if cropping of the video is from the center or the upper left corner of the video. It only has an effect if the *crop of member* is set to true.

Also
crop of member

centerStage

SYSTEM PROPERTY

What it looks like (in a handler)

```
on nextMovie
  set the centerStage = TRUE
  go to movie "next.dir"
end
```

What it is

This property determines whether the next movie to be played is centered or not. You must use it before jumping to another movie in order for it to work.

changeArea of member *member*

TRANSITION MEMBER PROPERTY

What it looks like (in the message window)

```
set the changeArea of member "specialWipe" = TRUE
```

What it is

This lets you test and set a property of a transition cast member. The property is the same as the changing area property found in the cast members information box.

When set to true, the transition only applies to the changing area. When set to false, the transition applies to the whole stage.

channelCount of member *member*

SOUND MEMBER PROPERTY

What it looks like (in the message window)

```
put the channelCount of member "sound"
-- 2
```

What it is

This returns the number of channels that a sound has. In the above example, the sound has two channels, which means that it is in stereo.

char *whichChar* [to *otherChar*] of *string*

STRING FUNCTION

What it looks like (in the message window)

```
put "abcdefg" into s
put char 3 of s
-- "c"
put char 3 to 5 of s
-- "cde"
```

What it is

This function allows you to extract one or more characters from a string. Using the *to* part of the expression is optional if you only need one character.

Also

word, line, item, offset, length, Chapter 9

charPosToLoc (member *member*, *number*)

FIELD MEMBER FUNCTION

What it looks like (in the message window)

```
put charPosToLoc(member "text", 42)
-- point(132,31)
```

What it is

This handy little function will return the distance, in pixels, from the upper left corner of a text field to the position of a character in the text field. It has nothing to do with screen position.

This function can be used cleverly in tools. It actually returns the position of the bottom left corner of the character you ask for. The first parameter specifies the text field, and the second specifies the character in that field.

By using the coordinates returned, you can examine where the word wraps are in a field, what the actual widths of characters, words, and phrases are, and even check to make sure that text isn't wrapping beyond the size of the stage.

Also

locToCharPos

chars(*string, firstChar, lastChar*)

STRING FUNCTION

What it looks like (in the message window)

```
put chars("abcdefg",3,5)
-- "cde"
put chars("abcdefg",2,2)
-- "b"
```

What it is

This function just lets you extract characters from inside another string. You can get the same result by using "char a to b of string."

Also

char, offset

charToNum *character*

STRING FUNCTION

What it looks like (in the message window)

```
put charToNum("A")
-- 65
```

What it looks like (in a handler)

```
on keyDown
  if charToNum(the key) = 27 then
    alert "Escape key hit"
  end if
end
```

What it is

This function converts a character to its number equivalent. The number corresponds to the ASCII (American Standard Code for Information Interchange) code.

This is useful for figuring out what key the user presses, when the key is not a simple letter or number. You can also convert any lowercase letter (numbers 97 to 122) to uppercase by subtracting 32 and using *numToChar* to convert back to a character.

Also
numToChar

checkBoxAccess

SYSTEM PROPERTY

What it looks like (in a handler)

```
on startMovie
  set the checkBoxAccess to 2
```

What it is
This setting changes how the Director standard check boxes and radio buttons behave. When set to 0, the default value, they behave normally, allowing the user to turn them on and off. When set to 1, the user can only turn them on but not back off again. When set to 2, the user cannot turn them either on or off. In this last case, you would use scripts to change the state of the buttons.

Also
hilite of member, checkBoxType

checkBoxType

SYSTEM PROPERTY

What it looks like (in a handler)

```
on startMovie
  set the checkBoxType = 2
end
```

What it is
This system property allows you to specify how you want Director standard check box buttons to look. When set to 0, the default, they fill with an "X." When set to 1, they have a black box when selected. When set to 2, they will fill with black when selected.

Also
checkBoxAccess, hilite of member

checkMark of menuItem *whichItem* of *whichMenu*

MENU BAR PROPERTY

What it looks like (in a handler)

```
on checkMyItem
  set the checkMark of menuItem "My Item" of menu "My Menu"→
= TRUE
end
```

What it is

This property represents the checkmark in front of a menu item on a custom menu bar. Set it to true or false to place or remove a checkmark.

Also

installMenu, enabled of menuItem

chunkSize of member *member*

TRANSITION PROPERTY

What it looks like (in the message window)

```
set the chunkSize of member "myTrans" = 8
```

What it is

This allows you to set the smoothness value of a custom transition. The number can range from 1 to 128. It basically corresponds to the number of pixels changed with each screen refresh. A higher number will allow for a faster transition, while a lower number will appear smoother.

clearFrame

SCORE COMMAND

What it looks like (in a handler)

```
on clearItOut frameNum
  go to frame frameNum
  beginRecording
    clearFrame
    updateFrame
  endRecording
end
```

What it is

When you are using the score generation commands, *clearFrame* will clean out all of the sprites and other channels. The above handler will go to a frame and then clean out everything in that frame.

Also

beginRecording, updateFrame

clearGlobals

COMMAND

What it looks like (in a handler)

```
on startOver
  clearGlobals
  go to frame 1
end
```

What it is

This command simply sets the value of all global variables used to 0. It is useful for resetting a movie or project completely, as the above example does. For instance, you may have a game that uses all sorts of globals to keep score and such. Instead of re-initializing all these globals to 0 with separate Lingo lines, you can just use *clearGlobals*.

Note that this will not affect local variables. So if you wanted to clear all globals except for one, you could do something like this to save the global "myGlobal."

```
on startOver
  global myGlobal
  put myGlobal into temp
  clearGlobals
  put temp into myGlobal
  go to frame 1
end
```

Also
global

clickLoc

FUNCTION

What it looks like (in a handler)

```
on mouseDown
  put the clickLoc into cLoc
end
```

What it is
This returns the point where the user last clicked. The value is a point on the stage.

Also
point, locToCharPos, mouseH, mouseV, clickOn

clickOn

FUNCTION

What it looks like (in a handler)

```
on mouseDown
  put the clickOn into spriteNum
end
```

What it is

Returns the number of the sprite that the user just clicked. The sprite must be "active" by having at least a dummy script assigned to it.

You would only use this function at the beginning of an *on mouseDown* or *on mouseUp* handler as shown above. It is useful in button handlers.

You can use *the clickOn* in a movie or frame score script. Just be sure to handle the case where the user clicks outside of any sprite. In these instances, the value returned will be 0.

Also

rollover, mouseCast

C

close window *window*

MIAW COMMAND

What it looks like (in the message window)

```
on closeMIAW
  close window "myWindow"
end
```

What it is

This will not actually dispose of a movie in a window but will instead hide it. You can then use *the visible of window* property to show the window again. Use the *forget window* command to completely get rid of a window.

You can pass either a window name or its number in *the windowList* to this command.

Also

forget window, open window, windowList, visible of window

C

closeResFile *filename*

COMMAND

What it looks like (in a handler)

```
on stopMovie
  closeResFile
end
```

What it is

This will close any resource files you have used. It is a Macintosh-only command. You can use the command by itself, as above, to close all resource files. Or you can use it with a specific file or path name.

Also

openResFile, showResFile

closeXlib *filename*

COMMAND

What it looks like (in a handler)

```
on stopMovie
  closeXlib
end
```

What it is

This closes any Xobjects, XCMDs, XFCNs or DLLs that you have opened with *openXlib*. You don't need to use the .DLL extension. If you leave out the file name, it will close all of the Xobjects.

Also

openXlib, showXlib

C

colorDepth

SYSTEM PROPERTY

What it looks like (in a handler)

```
on startMovie
  set the colorDepth to 8
end
```

What it is

This property allows you to get or set the color depth of the monitor. This corresponds to how many colors the monitor can show at one time. An 8 means that the computer can show 256 colors; a 1 means that the computer can show only black and white; a 16 means thousands of colors; and a 32 means millions.

Most PCs and all Macs will let you set the color depth manually in the control panels of a video control application.

You cannot use this command to set the depth on a Windows machine, though—only on Macs. This is a good way on Macs to make sure that the user is in 8-bit mode if that is what you want. The handler above does this.

Acceptable values are 1, 2, 4, 8, 16, and 32. If a Macintosh has more than one monitor, then the value is the greatest color depth of a monitor that has a piece of the stage there. Setting the value in this case will set the color depth of all monitors.

Also

colorQD, switchColorDepth

C

colorQD

SYSTEM PROPERTY

What it looks like (in the message window)

```
put the colorQD
-- 1
```

What it is

For Macs only. This tells you, with a true or false value, whether color QuickDraw is available. You can use this to identify Macs that cannot display color, such as some early Powerbooks.

Also

colorDepth

commandDown

SYSTEM PROPERTY

What it looks like (in a handler)

```
on keyDown
  if the key = "g" and the commandDown then
    alert "Command-G!"
  end if
end
```

What it is

This simply returns true if the command key is held down, and false otherwise. On a Windows machine, it refers to the Control key.

Also

controlDown, optionDown, shiftDown, key, keyDown

constrainH(*sprite, number*), constrainV(*sprite, number*)

SPRITE FUNCTIONS

C

What it looks like (in the message window)

```
put the left of sprite 1
-- 50
put the right of sprite 1
-- 150
put constrainH(1,40)
-- 50
put constrainH(1,100)
-- 100
put contstrainH(1,160)
-- 150
```

What it is

These functions take a sprite number and an integer as parameters. It will then check to make sure that the integer is within the bounds of the horizontal or vertical location of the sprite, and return a value that is within those bounds otherwise.

For example, the sprite referred to in the example above stretches from 50 to 150 pixels horizontally on the screen. Since 40 is too far to the left, it returns 50 instead. The number 160 is too far to the right, so it returns 150 instead. The number 100 is between 50 and 150, so 100 is returned, as numbers like 95, 137, etc. would be.

Yes, that's right—you can do this same thing using *if...then* statements, *min max* functions, and a variety of other techniques.

Also

constraint of sprite, left of sprite, right of sprite

constraint of sprite *sprite*

SPRITE PROPERTY

What it looks like (in the message window)

```
set the constraint of sprite 6 to 9
```

What it is

The above example takes the bounding rectangle of sprite 9 and makes sure that sprite 6 never leaves it. You would use this sort of command in conjunction with making a sprite "movable" in the score or using the Lingo *locH* and *locV* functions. It uses the registration point of the sprite to determine if the user or script is trying to make it leave the area.

This is useful when you want to enable the user to move a sprite around on the stage by dragging it with the mouse but want to make sure the user stays within a certain area.

Also

rect, regPoint, locH, locV, constrainH, constrainV

contains

STRING FUNCTION

What it looks like (in the message window)

```
put "abcdefg" contains "bcd"
-- 1
```

What it is

This function compares two strings to see if the second string is contained in the first string. It returns true or false.

Also

=, offset

C

continue

COMMAND

What it looks like (in a handler)

```
on mouseDown
  continue
end
```

What it is

Use this command to resume the playing of a movie after you use the *pause* command.

Also

pause, delay, pauseState

controlDown

SYSTEM PROPERTY

What it looks like (in a handler)

```
on keyDown
  if the key = "g" and the controlDown then
    alert "Control-G!"
  end if
end
```

What it is

This simply returns true if the Control key is held down, and false otherwise.

Also

commandDown, optionDown, shiftDown, key, keyDown

controller of member *member*

DIGITAL VIDEO MEMBER PROPERTY

What it looks like (in the message window)

```
set the controller of member "video" to FALSE
```

What it is

You can use this property to show or hide the video controller of a video cast member. The *directToStage* property of a digital video cast member must be set to true to show the controller.

Also

directToStage

copyToClipBoard member *member*

COMMAND

What it looks like (in the message window)

```
copyToClipBoard member "text"
```

What it is

This places a cast member into the system clipboard. You can use this in custom tools to copy members from one cast to another. You can also copy things like text cast members to the clipboard for users to paste into other applications.

Also

pasteClipBoardInto

cos(*number*)

MATH FUNCTION

What it looks like (in the message window)

```
put cos(pi())
-- -1.0
```

C

What it is
This function returns the cosine of a number. Use radians, not degrees, for the parameter.

Also
sin, tan, atan, pi

count *list*

LIST FUNCTION

What it looks like (in the message window)

```
put ["a","b","c"] into myList
put count(myList)
-- 3
```

What it is
This function returns the number of items in either a linear list or a property list.

Also
Chapter 15

cpuHogTicks

SYSTEM PROPERTY

What it looks like (in the message window)

```
set the cpuHogTicks = 10
```

What it is
This undocumented property determines how much the movie tries to use processor time. The default is 20. Set it to a lower number to let the system and other programs have more processor time; set it higher for Director to "hog" processor time. Effect varies—experiment in your free time.

C

crop of member *member*

DIGITAL VIDEO MEMBER PROPERTY

What it looks like (in the message window)

```
set the crop of member "video" = TRUE
```

What it is

This comes into play when the video member and the sprite are different sizes on the screen. When set to true, it means that the video appears in its standard size, and edges are cut off if the sprite is smaller than the video. If it is set to false, then the video is scaled to fit exactly inside the sprite.

Also

center of member

cursor *number*, cursor [*member*, *member*]

COMMAND

What it looks like (in a handler)

```
on exitFrame
  if rollover(3) then cursor(2)
  else cursor(0)
end
```

What it is

This command allows you to change the cursor. You can use it two ways. The first is to pass it a number that corresponds to a standard cursor or a Macintosh cursor resource number. The second way to use it is to pass the names of two cast members that correspond to a custom cursor and a cursor mask.

The example above will change the cursor to a crosshair when the user rolls over sprite 3. See Chapter 17 for details.

Note that Director does not have complete control over the cursor. If the user moves the cursor outside of the stage, for instance, the cursor command will not work. Also, if another element, like a QuickTime VR movie or a system extension, takes control of the cursor, Director has no way of knowing there was a change. In these cases, you need to execute a *cursor(-1)* followed by a *cursor(x)*, where x is your cursor, in order to force the cursor to change.

Also

cursor of sprite, Chapter 17

C

cursor of sprite *sprite*

SPRITE PROPERTY

What it looks like (in a handler)

```
on mouseDown
  go to frame "a"
  set the cursor of sprite 6 to 3
end
```

What it is

This property allows you to set the movie so that the cursor will change when it passes over a particular sprite. See Chapter 17 for complete details.

This property has several flaws, such as not responding correctly to puppets, and sticking around when the movie goes to another frame. Better functionality can be gotten from using *the mouseCast*, *rollover,* and *cursor* commands in an *on exitFrame* handler.

Also

cursor, Chapter 17

date

SYSTEM PROPERTY

What it looks like (in the message window)

```
put the date
-- "5/18/96"
put the abbr date
-- "Sat, May 18, 1996"
put the short date
-- "5/18/96"
put the long date
-- "Saturday, May 18, 1996"
```

What it is

This function returns a string with the date in various formats. It gets the actual date and the formats from the operating system. Therefore, if your program is run on a European computer, it is likely that the above date would read "18/5/96."

Also

time

delay *ticks*

COMMAND

What it looks like (in a handler)

```
on exitFrame
  if the shiftDown then delay(600)
end
```

What it is

This command adds a certain number of ticks to the current frame. It doesn't actually pause the Lingo code at that place—it just makes the frame last longer. You cannot use this inside a repeat loop to create a pause.

delete *stringExpression*

STRING COMMAND

What it looks like (in the message window)

```
put "abcdefg" into s
delete char 3 of s
put s
-- "abdefg"
```


What it is

This command allows you to delete a part of a string. The string can be a variable or a text cast member. You can use *char*, as above, or similar modifiers such as *word*, *line*, or *item* to define what is to be deleted.

Also

char, word, line, item

deleteAt(*list,number*)

LIST COMMAND

What it looks like (in the message window)

```
put [1,2,3,4,5] into list
deleteAt(list,2)
put list
-- [1,3,4,5]
```

What it is

This list command allows you to remove one item from either a linear or property list. Make sure that there are at least that many items in a list before trying to delete an item that isn't there.

Also

deleteProp

D

deleteFrame

SCORE COMMAND

What it looks like (in a handler)

```
on killFrame
  beginRecording
    deleteFrame
  endRecording
end
```

What it is

During a score generation session, you can use this command to completely remove the current frame from the score. In the above example, we start a simple score generation sequence and just delete the current frame.

Also

beginRecording, endRecording, updateFrame

deleteOne *list, value*

LIST COMMAND

What it looks like (in the message window)

```
put [1,2,3,2,1] into list
deleteOne list, 2
put list
-- [1,3,2,1]
```

What it is

This list command deletes an element from a linear list. It will find and delete the first element that matches the second parameter of the command, and leave any others untouched.

Also

deleteAt, deleteProp

deleteProp *list, property*

LIST COMMAND

What it looks like (in the message window)

```
put [#name: "Gary", #acct: 14, #misc: 3] into list
deleteProp(list,#misc)
put list
-- [#name: "Gary", #acct: 14]
```

What it is

This command will delete a property and its value from a property list.

Also

deleteAt

depth of member

BITMAP MEMBER PROPERTY

What it looks like (in the message window)

```
put the depth of member "picture"
-- 8
```

What it is

This property can tell you the color depth of a bitmap cast member. An 8, for instance, means that it is 8-bit or 256 colors. You cannot change this value with Lingo.

deskTopRectList

SYSTEM PROPERTY

What it looks like (in the message window)

```
put the deskTopRectList
-- [rect(0,0,640,480)]
```

What it is
This property returns a list of rects that represent the positions of all of the monitors. The example above shows a typical one-monitor setup. If there were a second monitor, a second rect would be in the list.

Also
rect

digitalVideoTimeScale

SYSTEM PROPERTY

What it looks like (in the message window)

```
put the digitalVideoTimeScale
-- 600
```

What it is
With this system property you can test and set the fractions of a second the system uses to display digital video. If set to 0, it will default to the value set in the video currently playing.

This is a setting most people will not need to bother with unless they're trying fancy tricks with Lingo and digital video.

digitalVideoType of member

DIGITAL VIDEO MEMBER PROPERTY

What it looks like (in the message window)

```
put the digitalVideoType of member "video"
-- #quickTime
```

What it is
This member property allows you to check to see if the member is a QuickTime movie (#quickTime) or Video For Windows (#videoForWindows) movie.

Also
type of member

directToStage of member

DIGITAL VIDEO MEMBER PROPERTY

What it looks like (in the message window)

```
set the directToStage of member "video" = TRUE
```

What it is

This property determines if the video member is shown directly on the screen, ignoring sprites that should be in front of it and ink settings. In Windows, this is your only option. On the Mac you can set this property to false and distort the video in a number of ways with sprite properties.

do *string*

COMMAND

What it looks like (in the message window)

```
do "put 2*3"
-- 6
put "alert"&&QUOTE&"Hello world."&QUOTE into a
do a
```

What it is

This command executes any Lingo syntax contained in the string. One way to use it is to construct string variables based on user input or program status and then use *do* to execute that string.

Note that you must initalize any local variables before using them in a *do* command.

dontPassEvent

COMMAND

What it looks like (in a handler)

```
on mouseDown
  beep(1)
  dontPassEvent
end
```

D

What it is
This command prevents the message that a handler answered from being passed to the next level in the message hierarchy. For instance, if the above handler were in a script assigned to a sprite, it would prevent the "mouseDown" message from going to the frame score script.

Also
pass

doubleClick

SYSTEM PROPERTY

What it looks like (in a handler)

```
on mouseUp
  if the doubleClick then beep(1)
end
```

What it is
This function is supposed to tell you when the user has double-clicked. However, it is not a very smart function, as it simply returns true if the user has clicked the mouse button two times quickly. This means that the user can click two times, on two different parts of the stage, and it will return true.

Another way that this function can perform incorrectly could go this way: The user double-clicks on a button. That button actually only takes the first click and jumps to another frame. On that other frame is a different button that appears in the same spot as the first. That second button thinks that it just got a double click because it gets the "mouseDown" from the second click and *the doubleClick* is true because the two clicks occurred one right after the other.

A safer way to handle double clicks is to use a global variable to record the first time that the user clicked on that object, and then check that time when the user makes the second click to see if they are close enough to make a double click.

Also
mouseDown, mouseUp

D

drawRect of window *windowName*

MIAW PROPERTY

What it looks like (in the message window)

```
put the drawRect of window "myMovie"
-- rect(0,0,256,100)
set the drawRect of window "myMovie" to rect (0,0,128,50)
```

What it is

This property represents the physical rectangle of the movie playing in a movie in a window. You can do really funky things by setting this rectangle to another value. In the the above example, we scale the movie by 50 percent. The window stays the same size, but the movie inside it shrinks. You can also create panning effects.

Note that in the above example the bitmaps and shapes are scaled; however, the text and odd objects like the check boxes only change position to fit into the scaled movie but remain the same size.

Also

rect

dropShadow of member *member*

FIELD MEMBER PROPERTY

What it looks like (in the message window)

```
set the dropShadow of member "text" = 2
```

What it is

This property corresponds to the drop shadow property of a text field that you can also set manually. With Lingo, you can change this shadow on the fly to create some pretty nifty effects.

D

duplicate *list*

LIST COMMAND

What it looks like (in the message window)

```
put [1,2,3,4,5] into list1
put list1 into list2
setAt(list2,3,9)
put list2
-- [1,2,9,4,5]
put list1
-- [1,2,9,4,5]

put [1,2,3,4,5] into list1
put duplicate(list1) into list2
setAt(list2,3,9)
put list2
-- [1,2,9,4,5]
put list1
-- [1,2,3,4,5]
```

What it is

This command creates a separate copy of a list. The need for this is demonstrated by the above example. The first part shows the variable "list2" set to represent the same list as "list1." Thus, when a change is made to "list2," the change also seems to occur in "list1." This is because both variables represent the same list.

With the duplicate command, you actually create a new list for the second variable. From that point on, the two lists are unrelated.

duplicate member *member [, member]*

CAST COMMAND

What it looks like (in the message window)

```
duplicate member "text"
duplicate member "text", member 42
```

What it is

This command just creates a copy of the cast member. You can leave the second parameter blank to allow the copy to be placed in the next available spot, or specify a number.

D

duplicateFrame

SCORE COMMAND

What it looks like (in a handler)

```
on dupFrame x
  beginRecording
    repeat with I = 1 to x
      duplicateFrame
    end repeat
  endRecording
end
```

What it is

You can use this command to create copies of the current frame during a score generation session.

Also

beginRecording

duration of member *member*

DIGITAL VIDEO MEMBER PROPERTY, TRANSITION MEMBER PROPERTY

What it looks like (in the message window)

```
put the duration of member "video"
```

What it is

This corresponds to the duration property of either a digital video member or a transition member. In the case of the transition member, you can use this to change the transition duration. The value is in ticks.

editable of member *member*

FIELD MEMBER PROPERTY

What it looks like (in the message window)

```
set the editable of member "text" = TRUE
```

What it is

This property determines whether the user can click and type in a text field on the stage when the movie is playing. You can set it manually in the field information box.

There are two ways to make a text field editable with Lingo. The first is to use this property; the second is to use *the editable of sprite* property.

Also

editable of sprite, autoTab of member

editable of sprite *spriteNumber*

SPRITE PROPERTY

What it looks like (in the message window)

```
set the editable of sprite 6 = TRUE
```

What it is

When this property is set to true, the user can click and type in the field member that is in that sprite channel. You can accomplish the same thing by setting *the editable of member* property of the member. By using this property, however, you can have the same member editable on one frame and noneditable on another. This property can be set manually in the score.

Also

editable of member

EMPTY

CONSTANT

What it looks like (in the message window)

```
put EMPTY
-- ""
```

What it is

This is a string constant that represents a text string with no characters. It is the equivalent of "".

emulateMultiButtonMouse

SYSTEM PROPERTY

What it looks like (in the message window)

```
set the emulateMultiButtonMouse = TRUE
```

What it is

This property allows you to equate pressing the right mouse button on a Windows machine with pressing the mouse button and holding down the Control key on a Mac.

Also

the rightMouseDown, the rightMouseUp

enabled of menuItem *whichMenuItem* of menu *whichMenu*

MENU PROPERTY

What it looks like (in the message window)

```
set the enabled of menuItem "overview" of menu "help" = TRUE
```

What it is

This property determines if a menu item in the menu bar is active and selectable or inactive and grayed-out. You can use names or numbers for the parameters here. Just make sure that the menu and menu item actually exist before trying to test or set them.

E

Also
installMenu, checkMark of menuItem

end, end case, end if, end repeat

SYNTAX

What they are
The word "end" is used at the end of handlers, *case* statements, *if* statements and *repeat* statements.

Also
on, case…of, if…then, repeat…while

endRecording

SCORE COMMAND

What it is
Used at the end of a score recording session, in conjunction with a *beginRecording* command.

Also
beginRecording

ENTER

CONSTANT

What it looks like (in the message window)

```
on keyDown
  if the key = ENTER then beep()
end
```

What it is
This constant represents the Enter key on the Macintosh and the number pad Enter key on PCs.

Also
RETURN

erase member *member*

CAST COMMAND

What it looks like (in the message window)

```
erase member "text"
```

What it is

This removes a cast member from a cast. You can use a name or a number as the parameter, and even specify the library with an "of castLib" extension.

exit

COMMAND

What it looks like (in a handler)

```
on doSomething
  global a, b
  put 3 into a
  if the shiftDown then exit
  put 5 into b
end
```

What it is

This command will quit a handler immediately. The handler that called it will continue running. This is a good way to jump out of a handler mid-way and prevent the rest of the code from executing. In the example above, if the Shift key is down, only the variable "a" is changed, because the handler terminates before it gets to the last line.

Also

abort, halt, quit

exit repeat

COMMAND

What it looks like (in a handler)

```
on mouseDown
  repeat while rollover(1)
    if not the mouseDown then exit repeat
  end repeat
end
```

What it is

This command simply jumps out of a *repeat* loop. The handler continues with the next line after the *end repeat*. You can use it when a loop needs to have more than one reason to stop, as in the example above. You can also use it to make very complex loops.

Also

repeat…while, next repeat

exitLock

SYSTEM PROPERTY

What it looks like (in a handler)

```
on startMovie
  set the exitLock = TRUE
end
```

What it is

According to the official documentation, setting this property to true will disable the Command+period and Command+W from quitting projectors in Macs, and Control+period and Control+-W from quitting projectors in Windows. However, when tested this command only affected the Command+Q key combination. You can set it to true to prevent the user from quitting your projectors that way.

Use this command with caution. It has been known to cause side effects with sounds.

exp *number*

MATH FUNCTION

What it looks like (in the message window)

```
put exp(2)
-- 7.3891
```

What it is

This function returns the natural logarithm base, or "e," to a power.

Also

power, log

FALSE

CONSTANT

What it looks like (in the message window)

```
put FALSE
-- 0
```

What it is

This constant is the same as 0. You should use this constant in situations where you want to set properties to true or false so that it is easier to read your code.

Also

TRUE

field *member*

SYNTAX

What it looks like (in the message window)

```
put "this" into member "text"
put "this" into field "text"
```

E

What it is
This is just another way to refer to cast members that are text fields. You can supply either a name or a number. The two lines in the example above do the same thing.

fileName of castLib *cast*

CAST PROPERTY

What it looks like (in the message window)

```
put the fileName of castLib "icons"
-- "c:\project\icons.cst"
```

What it is
This property of a cast can be tested and set. If the movie is internal, it just returns the same path name as the movie. Otherwise, it returns the path name of the cast library.

You can use this property to swap out cast libraries. This way, you can have similar libraries with similar cast members at the same locations. Then you can swap the files to change the appearance of the movie.

fileName of member *member*

MEMBER PROPERTY

What it looks like (in a handler)

```
on swapMember
  set the fileName of member "video" = "video1.mov"
  end
```

What it is
This property allows you to test and set the file that is linked to a cast member. A good use for this property is to switch the video file a digital video cast member is linked to. You could use it for other linked cast members as well, such as sounds and pictures but not text.

fileName of window *window*

MIAW PROPERTY

What it looks like (in a handler)

```
on openWin
  set newWin = window("my window")
  set the fileName of newWin = "miaw.dir"
  set the visible of window newWin = TRUE
end
```

What it is

This property allows you to test and set the file that is associated with a movie in a window. A handler like the one above can be used in place of an *open window* command.

Also

open window

filled of member *member*

SHAPE MEMBER PROPERTY

What it looks like (in the message window)

```
set the filled of member "square" = TRUE
```

What it is

You can use this property to change the appearance of rectangle and oval-shape cast members.

Also

foreColor of member, pattern of member

findEmpty *member*

CAST FUNCTION

What it looks like (in the message window)

```
put findEmpty(member "text")
-- 34
```

What it is

This function will return the number of the next empty cast member after the one you give as a parameter.

Also

new

findPos *list, property*

LIST FUNCTION

What it looks like (in the message window)

```
put [#a: 1, #b: 2, #c: 3] into list
put findPos(list,#b)
-- 2
```

What it is

This function will return the position of a property in a property list.

Also

findPosNear, getOne

findPosNear *list, property*

LIST FUNCTION

What it looks like (in the message window)

```
put [#a: 1, #f: 2, #z: 3] into list
sort(list)
put findPosNear(list,#g)
-- 2
```

What it is

This list function will return the position of the property in the list, or the position with a property that is closest in value to what you want. It only works with sorted lists.

Also

findPos

finishIdleLoad *loadTag*

COMMAND

What it looks like (in a button handler)

```
on mouseDown
  finishIdleLoad 42
  go to frame "next"
end
```

What it is

First, you need to use the *idleLoadTag* command to tag all of the cast members that have been queued for loading. Then use that same tag number with the *finishIdleLoad* command to complete this loading.

Also

cancelIdleTag, idleLoadTag, idleLoadDone, idleLoadMode, idleLoadPeriod

fixStageSize

SYSTEM PROPERTY

What it looks like (in the message window)

```
set the fixStageSize = TRUE
```

What it is

This property allows you to specify whether or not the stage resizes itself when the next movie is played. This is the same as the option in the movie properties dialog box.

Also

centerStage

float *number*

MATH FUNCTION

What it looks like (in the message window)

```
put float(1)
-- 1.0
```

What it is

This converts an integer to a floating-point number. It has no effect on, but does no damage to, a number that is already a floating-point number. It is a good idea to convert integers to floating-point numbers inside calculations if you expect them to interact accurately with floating-point numbers.

Also

integer, floatPrecision, floatP

floatP *number*

FUNCTION

What it looks like (in the message window)

```
put floatP(1)
-- 0
put floatP(1.0)
-- 1
```

What it is

Returns true if the number is a floating-point number, and false otherwise.

Also

integerP, voidP

floatPrecision

SYSTEM PROPERTY

What it looks like (in the message window)

```
put the floatprecision
-- 4
set val = 3.4
put val / pi()
-- 1.0823
set the floatprecision = 8
put val / pi()
-- 1.08225361
set the floatprecision = 1
put val / pi()
-- 1.1
```

What it is

This property determines how many decimal places are possible in floating-point numbers. The maximum is 19 and the default is 4.

font of member *member*

FIELD MEMBER PROPERTY

What it looks like (in the message window)

```
set the font of member "text" = "Courier"
set the font of char 3 of word 4 of line 2 of field "text" =→
"Courier"
```

What it is

This property allows you to set the font of an entire field. You can set the font of a specific piece of a field by using modifiers like those in the second line of the example above. When tested, this property returns the font of the first character in the field unless you specify another character.

Setting this property will have no effect if there are no characters in the field.

Also

fontSize of member, fontStyle of member, foreColor of member, lineHeight of member

F

fontSize of member *member*

FIELD MEMBER PROPERTY

What it looks like (in the message window)

```
set the fontSize of member "text" = 12"
set the fontSize of char 3 of word 4 of line 2 of field→
"text" = 12
```

What it is

This property allows you to set the font size of an entire field. You can set the size of a specific piece of a field by using modifiers like those in the second line of the example above. When tested, this property returns the size of the first character in the field unless you specify another character.

Setting this property will have no effect if there are no characters in the field.

Also

font of member, fontStyle of member, foreColor of member, lineHeight of member

fontStyle of member *member*

FIELD MEMBER PROPERTY

What it looks like (in the message window)

```
set the fontStyle of member "text" = "Bold"
set the fontStyle of char 3 of word 4 of line 2 of field→
"italic, underline"
```

What it is

This property allows you to set the font style of an entire field. You can set the style of a specific piece of a field by using modifiers like those in the second line of the example above. When tested, this property returns the style of the first character in the field unless you specify another character.

Setting this property will have no effect if there are no characters in the field.

Also
font of member, fontSize of member, foreColor of member, lineHeight of member

foreColor of member *member*

FIELD MEMBER PROPERTY

What it looks like (in the message window)

```
set the foreColor of member "text" = 35
set the fontStyle of char 3 of word 4 of line 2 of field 17
```

What it is
This property allows you to set the color of the text of an entire field. You can set the color of a specific piece of a field by using modifiers like those in the second line of the example above. When tested, this property returns the color of the first character in the field unless you specify another character.

Setting this property will have no effect if there are no characters in the field.

Also
font of member, fontStyle of member, lineHeight of member

foreColor of sprite

SPRITE PROPERTY

What it looks like (in a button handler)

```
on mouseDown
  set the foreColor of sprite (the clickOn) = 215
  updateStage
  repeat while the mouseDown
  end repeat
end
```

What it is
Director boxes and ovals have both a foreground color and a background color. So do 1-bit graphics. This Lingo command allows you to temporarily change the foreground color, or just get its value.

In the above example, we change the foreground color of a sprite to red when the user clicks down, and then we wait until the mouse is lifted. After the frame is finished playing, the color will return to its orginal value. We can make the change stick with a *puppetSprite* command.

Also
the backColor of sprite, the foreColor of member

F

forget window *window*

MIAW COMMAND

What it looks like (in a handler)

```
on closeWin
  forget window "myWin"
end
```

What it is
This command will close and delete a movie in a window from memory.

Also
close window

frame

SCORE FUNCTION

What it looks like (in the message window)

```
put the frame
-- 12
```

What it is
This function returns the number of the current frame.

Also
frameLabel, label, marker

frameLabel

SCORE PROPERTY

What it looks like (in the message window)

```
put the frameLabel
-- "page 1"
```

What it is

This property lets you find out the frame label of the current frame. During a score generation session, you can also change it.

This property will return a 0 if there is no frame label in the score. This could spell trouble if you have code that expects a string.

Also

marker, label, frame

framePalette

SCORE PROPERTY

What it looks like (in the message window)

```
put the framePalette
-- 2
```

What it is

This property represents the cast member number of the palette assigned to that frame in the score. It returns a value of –1 if there is no special palette assigned to the frame in the score. You can also set this property during a score generation session.

Also

beginRecording, frameLabel, frameScript, frameSound1, frameSound2, frameTempo, frameTransition

F

frameRate of member *member*

DIGITAL VIDEO MEMBER PROPERTY

What it looks like (in the message window)

```
set the frameRate of member "video" = 12
```

What it is

This property can be set to alter the frame rate, in frames per second, of a QuickTime digital video cast member. The highest value is 255 frames per second. If you set this value to –1, the video plays at its normal rate. If you set this value to –2 the video plays as fast as possible.

Also

movieRate of sprite, movieTime of sprite

frameScript

SCORE PROPERTY

What it looks like (in the message window)

```
put the frameScript
-- 5
```

What it is

This property represents the cast member number of the script assigned to that frame in the score. It returns a 0 if there is no script assigned to the frame in the score. You can also set this property during a score generation session.

Also

beginRecording, frameLabel, framePalette, frameSound1, frameSound2, frameTempo, frameTransition

frameSound1, frameSound2

SCORE PROPERTIES

What it looks like (in the message window)

```
put the frameSound1
-- 3
```

What it is

These properties represent the cast member number of the sounds assigned to that frame in the score. The first property is for sound channel 1, and the second is for sound channel 2. It returns a 0 if there is no sound assigned to the channel of that frame in the score. You can also set this property during a score generation session.

Also

beginRecording, frameLabel, framePalette, frameScript, frameTempo, frameTransition

framesToHMS *frames, tempo, dropFrame, showFractional*

FUNCTION

What it looks like (in the message window)

```
put framesToHMS(600,12,FALSE,TRUE)
-- " 00:00:50.00 "
```

What it is

This function just does a little bit of math for you. It takes the number of frames and the tempo and returns a string with a length of time. The format is hours, minutes, seconds, and fractions of a second, as in the example above. The preceding space may be filled with a "–" if the value is negative, and the last space may be filled with a "d" if the third parameter is true. If the fourth parameter is true, you get a real decimal value for the leftover seconds. If the fourth parameter is false, you get the number of frames left over, placed after the seconds.

You guessed right if you thought that this entire function can be replaced with your own Lingo custom handler.

Also
HMStoFrames

frameTempo

SCORE PROPERTY

What it looks like (in the message window)

```
put the frameTempo
-- 15
```

What it is
This property represents the tempo of the current frame in the score. It returns the movie's tempo if there is no special tempo assigned to the frame in the score. You can also set this property during a score generation session.

Also
beginRecording, frameLabel, framePalette, frameScript, frameSound1, frameSound2, frameTransition

frameTransition

SCORE PROPERTY

What it looks like (in the message window)

```
put the frameTransition
-- 8
```

What it is
This property represents the cast member number of the transition assigned to that frame in the score. It returns a 0 if there is no special transition assigned to the frame in the score. You can also set this property during a score generation session.

Also
beginRecording, frameLabel, framePalette, frameScript, frameSound1, frameSound2, frameTempo

freeBlock

SYSTEM PROPERTY

What it looks like (in the message window)

```
put the freeBlock
-- 384725
```

What it is
This property tells you the size of the largest block of free memory in bytes. Each new cast member needs to be loaded into a single block of memory. Thus, if the value of this property is smaller than the size of a cast member, Director will not be able to load it.

Also
freeBytes, memorySize, ramNeeded

freeBytes

SYSTEM PROPERTY

What it looks like (in the message window)

```
put the freeBytes
-- 573924
```

What it is
This property tells you how many bytes of memory are free for Director to use.

Also
freeBlock, memorySize, ramNeeded

frontWindow

MIAW FUNCTION

What it looks like (in the message window)

```
put the frontWindow
-- 0
```

What it is

This function returns the number of the window that is at the front. If the value is 0, then the stage is at the front. If the value is <void> then a Director palette or editing window is at the front. The number corresponds to a window's position in *the windowList*.

Also

the windowList, moveToFront

getaProp *list, property*

LIST FUNCTION

What it looks like (in the message window)

```
put [#a: 11, #b: 22, #c: 33] into list
put getaProp(list,#b)
-- 22
```

What it is

This function returns the value that matches the property specified in a property list. Unlike the *getProp* function, *getaProp* only returns a <void> if the property is not there, rather than an error message.

You can also use this function with linear lists, in which case it operates the same as *getAt*.

Also

getProp, getAt, getOne, findPos

getAt *list, position*

LIST FUNCTION

What it looks like (in the message window)

```
put [11,22,33,44] into list
put getAt(list,3)
-- 33
```

What it is

This function returns the value at the position specified of either a linear or property list. Make sure that there are at least that many items in the list, or else an error message will pop up.

Also

getProp, getaProp, getOne, findPos

getLast *list*

LIST FUNCTION

What it looks like (in the message window)

```
put [1,2,3,4] into list
put getLast(list)
-- 4
```

What it is

This function returns the last value of a linear or property list. It is the same as "getAt(list,count(list))."

Also

count

G

G

getLatestNetID

SHOCKWAVE FUNCTION

What it looks like (in a handler)

```
on exitFrame
  global textID
  getNetText("mytext.txt")
  getLatestNetID() into textID
end
```

What it is

This function returns the ID number of a command like *getNetText*, *gotoNetMovie*, *gotoNetPage*, or *preLoadNetThing*. You can then use it with functions like *NetDone*, *netError*, *nettLastModDate*, and *netTextResult*.

Also

getNetText, *gotoNetMovie*, *gotoNetPage*, or *preLoadNetThing*, *NetDone*, *netError*, *nettLastModDate*, and *netTextResult*.

getNetText *url*

SHOCKWAVE COMMAND

What it looks like (in a handler)

```
on exitFrame
  getNetText("mytext.txt")
end
```

What it is

This command starts loading a text file from across the Internet. You know when it is done by checking the *netDone* function. Then, you can get the text by using the *netTextResult* function.

Also

netDone, *netError*, *netTextResult*, *getLatestNetID*

getNthFileNameInFolder *path, number*

FUNCTION

What it looks like (in a handler)

```
on listFiles
  put 1 into i
  repeat while TRUE
    put getNthFileNameInFolder(the pathname, i) into t
    if t = EMPTY then exit repeat
    put t
  end repeat
end
```

What it is

This function returns the name of a file in a folder. If there are not that many files in a folder, or the path does not exist, it returns an empty string.

You can use this function to see what is inside a folder. Folders are listed as well as files.

You are right in thinking that this is an unusual function. After all, most of the file functions are part of the FileIO Xobject, but this one is a standard Director command.

getOne *list, value*

LIST FUNCTION

What it looks like (in the message window)

```
put [11,22,33,44] into list
put getOne(list,33)
-- 3
```

What it is

This function returns the position or property in a list that contains the value. It works with both property and linear lists. If there is more than one instance of that value in the list, it returns the first.

Also

getPos, findPos

getPos *list, value*

LIST FUNCTION

What it looks like (in the message window)

```
put [11,22,33,44] into list
put getOne(list,33)
-- 3
```

What it is

This function returns the position in a list that contains the value. It works with both property and linear lists. If there is more than one instance of that value in the list, it returns the first.

The difference between this command and *getOne* is that this will return the position, not the property, when a property list is concerned.

Also

getOne, findPos

getProp *list, property*

LIST FUNCTION

What it looks like (in the message window)

```
put [#a: 11, #b: 22, #c: 33] into list
put getaProp(list,#b)
-- 22
```

What it is

This function returns the value that matches the property specified in a property list. Unlike the *getaProp* function, *getProp* generates an error message if the property is not there or if you try to use it on a linear list.

Also

getaProp, getAt, getOne, findPos

getPropAt *list, position*

LIST FUNCTION

What it looks like (in the message window)

```
put [#a: 11, #b: 22, #c: 33] into list
put getPropAt(list,2)
-- #b
```

What it is

This function returns the property, not the value, at a location in a property list.

Also

getaProp, getProp, getAt, getOne

global *variable, variable, variable...*

SYNTAX

What it looks like (in the message window)

```
global a, b, c
```

What it is

This word precedes all global variable declarations. You can make a variable a global by either using this syntax in every handler that uses it or by placing a *global* command at the top of a script cast member. In the latter case, the variable is made a global in all of the handlers in the script member.

Also

property, showGlobals, clearGlobals

go

COMMAND

What it looks like

```
go 2 -- jump to frame 2
go to 2 -- jump to frame 2
go to frame 2 -- jump to frame 2
go "contents" -- jump to frame "contents"
go to "contents" -- jump to frame "contents"
go to frame "contents" -- jump to frame "contents"

go to movie "newmovie.dir" -- jump to frame 1 of
"newmovie.dir"
go to frame 2 of movie "newmovie.dir" -- jump to frame 2 of
"newmovie.dir"
go to frame "contents" of movie "newmovie.dir" -- jump to
frame "contents" of "newmovie.dir"

go loop -- go to the marker to the left in the score
go next -- go to the marker to the right in the score
go previous -- go to the two markers to the left in the score
```

What it looks like (jn a handler)

```
-- The following button handler will jump
-- to a random frame from a list
on mouseUp
  put ["frameA","frameB","frameC"] into frameList
  put random(count(frameList)) into r
  go to frame getAt(frameList,r)
end
```

What it is

This command has many appearances, as you can tell from the examples above. It basically moves the play head in the score to a specific spot in the movie or to another movie.

Also

play, label, marker

gotoNetMovie *url*

SHOCKWAVE COMMAND

What it looks like (in a handler)

```
on exitFrame
  gotoNetMovie("next.html")
end
```

What it is

This command tells the Internet browser to replace the current Shockwave movie with another one. This new movie should be the same screen size as the one asking for it. The load will begin immediately, while the current movie keeps playing. When the load is done, the new movie will replace the old one.

Also

getLatestNetID

gotoNetPage *url, target*

SHOCKWAVE COMMAND

What it looks like (in a handler)

```
on exitFrame
  gotoNetPage("next.html")
end
```

What it is

This command tells the Internet browser to jump to another html page. You can use the target parameter to send this command to another frame or window by placing its name there. To create a new window, use "_blank" as the second parameter.

Also

getLatestNetID

halt

COMMAND

What it looks like (in a handler)

```
on checkInput input
  if input < 1 then halt
end
```

What it is

This simply stops a movie. It is useful because it will only stop the movie while you are authoring in Director, but it will quit a projector. Use it instead of *quit* for this reason.

Also

quit, abort, exit

height of member *member*

BITMAP MEMBER PROPERTY

What it looks like (in the message window)

```
put the height of member "graphic"
-- 232
```

What it is

This property represents the height, in pixels, of a bitmap cast member. It does not take into account any stretching that is done on the sprite level. For this reason, it is not a good idea to use this property for shape members, since they are often stretched to a different size on the stage than the original cast member.

Also

width of member, height of sprite, rect

height of sprite *spriteNum*

SPRITE PROPERTY

What it looks like (in the message window)

```
put the height of sprite 4
-- 43
```

What it is

This property represents the height, in pixels, of bitmap and shape cast members in the score. Since these can be stretched on the stage, this number may not correspond to the *height of member* property.

Also

width of sprite, height of member, rect

hilite *fieldExpression*

COMMAND

What it looks like (in the message window)

```
hilite line 2 of field "text"
```

What it is

This command will allow you to select a piece of text on the screen. The highlight will appear as if the user selected the text. You can use any string modifier, like *char, word, item,* or *line*. You need to refer to a field. This will not work with rich text cast members and string variables.

Also

field, selStart, selEnd

hilite of member *member*

BUTTON MEMBER PROPERTY

What it looks like (in the message window)

```
set the hilite of member "button" = TRUE
```

What it is

This property corresponds to the check in the check box and the button in the radio button. You can, and should, use Lingo to set these when needed.

hMStoFrames *hms, tempo, dropFrame, fractional*

FUNCTION

What it looks like (in the message window)

```
put HMStoFrames(" 00:00:50.00 ", 30, FALSE, TRUE)
-- 600
```

What it is

This command is the opposite of *framesToHMS*. It essentially converts a string that represents time, plus a few other variables, to the total number of frames.

Also

framesToHMS

idleHandlerPeriod

SYSTEM PROPERTY

What it looks like (in the message window)

```
set the idleHandlerPeriod = 15
```

What it is

This is the number of ticks between "idle" messages. Director sends an "enterFrame" message after it draws the screen on a new frame. Then it generates "idle" messages until it is time to move on to the next frame, at which time it generates an "exitFrame" message. By decreasing this number, you can fit more "idle" messages between the "enterFrame" and "exitFrame" messages. Setting its value to 0, its default value, will make it send "idle" messages as frequently as it can.

idleLoadDone(*loadTag*)

SYSTEM FUNCTION

What it looks like (in a handler)

```
on exitFrame
  if idleLoadDone(tag) then go next
  else go to the frame
end
```

What it is

This function returns a true if all the members that share that tag are done loading.

Also

idleLoadTag

idleLoadMode

SYSTEM PROPERTY

What it looks like (in the message window)

```
set the idleLoadMode = 3
```

What it is

This property determines how vigorously Director tries to load members with the *preLoad* and *preLoadMember* commands. 0 means that no loading is done, 1 means that loading is done between frames, 2 means that loading is done during "idle" time, and 3 means that loading is done as often as possible.

Also

preLoad, preLoadMember

I

idleLoadPeriod

SYSTEM PROPERTY

What it looks like (in the message window)

```
set the idleLoadPeriod = 30
```

What it is

The default number for this property is 0, which means that there is no hesitation when Director decides to load a cast member. However, setting this property will make it wait a certain number of ticks first.

idleLoadTag *number*

COMMAND

What it looks like (in the message window)

```
set the idleLoadTag = 2
```

What it is

This attaches a number, or tag, to all of the cast members that are waiting to be loaded. You can then use this tag in commands and functions like *cancelIdleLoad* and *idleLoadDone*.

Also

cancelIdleLoad, idleLoadDone

idleReadChunkSize

SYSTEM PROPERTY

What it looks like (in the message window)

```
set the idleReadChunkSize = 200000
```

What it is

You can use this property to limit the number of bytes that Director loads at one time.

if...then

SYNTAX

What it looks like

```
if a = 1 then go to frame "a"
if a = 1 then
  go to frame "a"
end if

if a = 1 then go to frame "a"
else go to frame "b"

if a = 1 then
  go to frame "a"
else
  go to frame "b"
end if

if a = 1 then
  go to frame "a"
else if a = 2 then
  go to frame "b"
else
  go to frame "c"
end if

if a > 0 then
  if a = 1 then
    go to "a"
  else
    go to "b"
  end if
end if
```

What it is

This is a key piece of syntax for any programming language. The examples above illustrate the many ways in which it can be used. Remember that you can also nest these statements, as in the last example.

Also

case

ilk *list*, ilk(*item, type*)

FUNCTION

What it looks like (in the message window)

```
put [1,2,3] into list
put ilk(list)
-- #linearlist
put ilk(list,#linearlist)
```

What it is

You can use this command to test the type of a list variable in two ways. By using the function with only one parameter, it will return a value that signifies what type of list you are dealing with: #linearlist, #proplist, #rect, or #point. By using it with two parameters, you can compare the variable to a type and it will return a true or false. In this case, you can also use the type #list, which will return a true if the variable is any type of list at all.

importFileInto member *member, fileName*

CAST COMMAND

What it looks like (in the message window)

```
importFileInto "graphic", "graphic.bmp"
```

What it is

Although this command may seem useful for accessing external files, it is actually meant for importing media into a cast when you are done with a project. You can also use the "castLib" modifier to specify which cast library to load the file into.

For accessing external pictures and sounds, see the FileIO(mReadPICT) command in Chapter 16, and the *sound playFile* command.

inflate *rectangle, widthChange, heightChange*

FUNCTION

What it looks like (in the message window)

```
put rect(50,50,100,100) into r
put inflate(r,10,20) into r
put r
-- rect(45,40,105,110)
```

What it is

This function just takes care of a tricky piece of math for you. It will expand, or shrink if you use negative numbers, a rectangle.

Also

rect

ink of sprite *spriteNumber*

SPRITE PROPERTY

What it looks like (in a handler)

```
on mouseDown
  set the ink of sprite (the clickOn) = 2
  updateStage
end
```

What it is

This property allows you to set the ink of a sprite with Lingo. For a list of inks and their numbers, see "Tables & Charts" in the reference section of this book. The above example turns a sprite to "reverse" for a moment when it is clicked.

Also

backColor of sprite, blend of sprite, foreColor of sprite

insertFrame

SCORE COMMAND

Same as *DuplicateFrame*

inside (*point, rectangle*)

FUNCTION

What it looks like (in the message window)

```
put point(50,50) into p
put rect(40,40,60,60) into r
put inside(p,r)
-- 1
```


What it is

This function returns a true if the point is located inside the rectangle.

Also

intersect, point, rect

installMenu *member*

MENU COMMAND

What it looks like (in a handler)

```
on startMovie
  installMenu
end
```

What it is

This makes that cast member the current menu. See Chapter 17 for more details on how to set up your own custom menu. Using a 0 in place of a member will turn the custom menu off.

integer *number*

MATH FUNCTION

What it looks like (in the message window)

```
put integer(3.14)
-- 3
```

What it is

This function will round a floating-point number to the nearest integer. It will have no effect on, but do no harm to, a number that is already an integer.

Also

float, string

integerP *number*

FUNCTION

What it looks like (in the message window)

```
put integerP(5)
-- 1
put integerP(5.5)
-- 0
```

What it is

This function will tell you whether or not a number is an integer.

Also

floatP, voidP

intersect *rectangle, rectangle*

FUNCTION

What it looks like (in the message window)

```
put intersect(rect(40,40,60,60),rect(50,50,70,70))
-- 1
```

What it is

This function will return true if the two rectangles overlap.

Also

inside, map, rect

itemDelimiter

SYSTEM PROPERTY

What it looks like (in the message window)

```
set the itemDelimiter = ","
put item 2 of "4,5,6,7,8"
-- "5"
```

What it is

This property allows you to determine what separates items in string lists. For instance, a string like "5/6/7/8/9" might need a "/" as the *itemDelimiter*, while a string like "5,6,7,8,9" would use a comma. The default value is a comma, but once you change it, it remains that new value through the life of your session.

Here's a trick: you can set this property to a "\" or a ":" to separate folders in path names on the PC and Mac. With the string "c:\director\project\myfile.dir" you could get each folder using the *item* modifier to deconstruct that string.

key

SYSTEM FUNCTION

What it looks like (in a handler)

```
on keyDown
  put the key into field "text"
end
```

What it is

This property returns the character of the last key pressed.

Also

keyCode, keyDown, keyUp, keyDownScript, keyUpScript

keyCode

SYSTEM FUNCTION

What it looks like (in a handler)

```
on keyDown
  put the keyCode into field "text"
end
```

What it is

This property returns the character number of the last key pressed, rather than a one-character string.

Also

key, keyDown, keyUp, keyDownScript, keyUpScript

keyDownScript, keyUpScript

SYSTEM PROPERTIES

What they look like (in a handler)

```
-- This script will intercept the "q" key
-- and make sure a Cmd-Q is routed to a
-- special "quit" handler.
on startMovie
  set the keyDownScript = "handleKeys"
end
on handleKeys
  if the key = "q" and the commandDown then
    quitHandler
  else
    pass
  end if
end
```


What they are

These properties allow you to set up a Lingo command or handler to intercept all key presses. The messages "keyUp" and "keyDown" get sent to these handlers first. If you wish them to continue up the message hierarchy, make sure you include a *pass* command in the handler.

Also

on keyDown, on keyUp, pass

keyPressed

SYSTEM PROPERTY

What it looks like (in a handler)

```
on wait
  repeat while the keyPressed <> RETURN
  end repeat
end
```

What it is
This is essentially the same as the *key* property, except that it is updated within repeat loops.

Also
key, keyCode

label *string*

FUNCTION

What it looks like (in the message window)

```
put label("contents")
-- 7
```

What it is
This function returns the number of the frame with the string as its marker. If the marker does not exist, it returns a 0.

Also
labelList, marker

labelList

MOVIE PROPERTY

What it looks like (in the message window)

```
put the labelList
-- "contents
chapter1
chapter2"
```

What it is
This property returns a list of all of the markers in the score, in order, one per line.

Also
label, marker

last *chunkExpression*

STRING FUNCTION

What it looks like (in the message window)

```
put the last char of "abcdef"
-- "f"
```

What it is

This function allows you to get the last character, word, item, or line of a string.

Also

char, word, item, line

lastClick

SYSTEM PROPERTY

What it looks like (in a handler)

```
on exitFrame
  if the lastClick > 3000 then
    go to frame "restart"
  end if
end
```

What it is

This property represents the time, in ticks, since the user last pressed the mouse button.

Also

lastEvent, lastKey, lastRoll

lastEvent

SYSTEM PROPERTY

What it looks like (in a handler)

```
on exitFrame
  if the lastEvent > 3000 then
    go to frame "restart"
```

```
    end if
  end
```

What it is
This property represents the time, in ticks, since the user last pressed the mouse button, moved the mouse, or pressed a key.

Also
lastClick, lastKey, lastRoll

lastFrame

SYSTEM PROPERTY

What it looks like (in the message window)

```
put the lastFrame
-- 72
```

What it is
This property returns the number of the last, final, rightmost, highest-numbered frame in the movie.

lastKey

SYSTEM PROPERTY

What it looks like (in a handler)

```
on exitFrame
  if the lastKey > 3000 then
    go to frame "restart"
  end if
end
```

What it is
This property represents the time, in ticks, since the user last pressed a key.

Also
lastClick, lastEvent, lastRoll

lastRoll

SYSTEM PROPERTY

What it looks like (in a handler)

```
on exitFrame
  if the lastRoll > 3000 then
    go to frame "restart"
  end if
end
```

What it is

This property represents the time, in ticks, since the user last moved the mouse.

Also

lastClick, lastEvent, lastKey

left of sprite *spriteNumber*

SPRITE PROPERTY

What it looks like (in the message window)

```
put the left of sprite 5
-- 450
```

What it is

This property returns the position, in pixels, of the left side of the sprite on the stage. You cannot set this property directly; instead, use the *rect of sprite* property.

Also

right of sprite, bottom of sprite, top of sprite, width of sprite, height of sprite, rect of sprite

length *string*

STRING FUNCTION

What it looks like (in the message window)

```
put "abcde" into s
put length(s)
-- 5
```

What it is

This function returns the number of characters in a string. It is the same as saying "the number of chars in."

Also

chars, offset

line *whichLine* [to *otherLine*] of *string*

STRING FUNCTION

What it looks like (in the message window)

```
put "abcdefg"&RETURN&"hijk"&RETURN&"lmn" into s
put line 2 of s
-- "hijk"
put line 2 to 3 of s
-- "hijk
lmn"
```

What it is

This function allows you to extract one or more lines from a string. Using the *to* part of the expression is optional if you only need one line.

Also

char, word, item, offset, length

lineCount of member *member*

FIELD MEMBER FUNCTION

What it looks like (in the message window)

```
put the lineCount of member "text"
```

What it is

This function looks at how the words in a text field wrap, and figures out the total number of lines that the user sees on the screen. You can use this routine to make sure that text in automatically filled fields does not grow off the screen. Very useful for tool-building.

Also

linePosToLocV, locVToLinePos, locToCharPos, charPostoLoc

L

lineHeight(member *member*, *lineNumber*), lineHeight of member *member*

FIELD MEMBER PROPERTIES

What they look like (in the message window)

```
put lineHeight(member "text",1)
-- 16
put the lineHeight of member "text"
-- 16
put the lineHeight of line 1 of member "text"
-- 16
set the lineheight of line 1 of member "text" = 18
```

What they are

These field properties tells you how many pixels high each line in a field is. You can use the first syntax structure above to get this value, or the second syntax structure to get and set this value.

Since fields revert to standard line spacing after they quit and restart a movie, you may end up having several statements like the last example above in your *on startMovie* handler.

Also

align of member, font of member, fontSize of member, fontStyle of member

linePosToLocV(*member*, *lineNumber*)

FIELD MEMBER FUNCTION

What it looks like (in the message window)

```
put linePosToLocV(member "text", 5)
-- 80
```

What it is

This function returns the position of the line of a text field, in pixels, from the top of the field. This is relative to the top of the field, which is always position 0, and independent of its stage position.

Also

lineCount, locVToLinePos, charToPosLoc, posLocToChar

L

lineSize of member *member*

SHAPE MEMBER PROPERTY

What it looks like (in the message window)

```
set the lineSize of member "line" = 7
```

What it is

This property allows you to determine the border width of boxes and ovals, and the thickness of lines.

Also

lineSize of sprite

lineSize of sprite *spriteNumber*

SPRITE PROPERTY

What it looks like (in the message window)

```
set the lineSize of sprite 6 = 7
```

What it is

This property allows you to determine the border width of boxes and ovals, and the thickness of lines.

Also
lineSize of member

list(*item1, item2, item3...*)

LIST FUNCTION

What it looks like (in the message window)

```
put list(1,2,3,4) into list
put list
-- [1,2,3,4]
```

What it is
This is just an odd way to create a linear list, instead of using brackets right off the bat.

listP *list*

FUNCTION

What it looks like (in the message window)

```
put [1,2,3,4] into list
put listP(list)
-- 1
```

What it is
This function will tell you whether or not the parameter is a list.

Also
ilk

loaded of member *member*

MEMBER PROPERTY

What it looks like (in a handler)

```
on exitFrame
  if the loaded of member "picture" = FALSE then
    go to frame "alternative"
  end if
end
```

What it is

This property will tell you if a cast member has already been loaded into memory.

Also

preLoad, unload

loc of sprite *spriteNumber*

SPRITE PROPERTY

What it looks like (in the message window)

```
put the loc of sprite 5
-- point(50,60)
```

What it is

This property tells you the position of a sprite on the stage. It returns this value as a point. For bitmaps, it corresponds to the registration point. For fields and shapes, it corresponds to the upper left corner of the sprite.

You use this, as well as the *locH* and *locV*, to test and set the position of a sprite.

Also

point, locH of sprite, locV of sprite, rect of sprite, left of sprite, right of sprite, bottom of sprite, top of sprite, regPoint of member

locH of sprite *spriteNumber*, locV of sprite *spriteNumber*

SPRITE PROPERTIES

What they look like (in the message window)

```
put the locH of sprite 5
-- 50
set the locV of sprite 5 = 80
```

What they are

These two properties represent the location of a sprite on the stage. For bitmaps, they correspond to the registration point. For fields and shapes, they correspond to the upper left corner of the sprite.

You can set these properties, in conjunction with the *updateStage* and/or *puppetSprite* commands, to move sprites around the stage using Lingo.

Also

loc of sprite, rect of sprite, updateStage, puppetSprite

locToCharPos(member *member, point*)

FIELD MEMBER FUNCTION

What it looks like (in the message window)

```
put locToCharPos(member "text", point(50,50))
-- 67
```

What it is

This function looks at the field member on the stage and figures out which character is closest to the point you specify.

Also

charPosToLoc, linePosToLocV, locVtoLinePos, lineCount of member

locVToLinePos(member *member*, *locV*)

FIELD MEMBER FUNCTION

What it looks like (in the message window)

```
put locVToLinePos(member "text", 150)
-- 5
```

What it is

This function looks at the field member on the stage and figures out which line is closest to the vertical position you specify.

Also

charPosToLoc, locToCharPos, linePosTolocV, lineCount of member

log *number*

MATH FUNCTION

What it looks like (in the message window)

```
put log(4)
-- 1.3863
```

What it is

Returns the natural logarithm of the parameter.

Also

exp

loop of member *member*

DIGITAL VIDEO MEMBER PROPERTY

What it looks like (in the message window)

```
set the loop of member "video" = TRUE
```

What it is

This property corresponds to the “loop” setting of a digital video cast member.

machineType

SYSTEM PROPERTY

What it looks like (in the message window)

```
put the machineType
-- 256
```

What it is

This property tells you what type of operating system the movie is playing on. The value of 256 means it is playing on a Windows machine. Any other value means it is playing on a Macintosh. This property has been effectively replaced by *the platform* property.

Also

platform, colorDepth, colorQD

map(*targetRectOrPoint*, *sourceRect*, *destinationRect*)

FUNCTION

What it looks like (in the message window)

```
set the rect of sprite 1 = map(the rect of sprite 1, the→
rect of sprite 2, the rect of sprite 3)
```

What it is

This function performs some math for you by taking the relationship between the second and third parameters and applying it to the first. For example, if the "sourceRect" is half the size of the "destinationRect" and is on the opposite side of the stage, then the value returned will be half the size of the "targetRect" on the opposite side of the stage (more or less). This function also works with a point as the first parameter.

Also

rect, point

margin of member *member*

FIELD MEMBER PROPERTY

What it looks like (in the message window)

```
set the margin of member "text" = 2
```

What it is

This property corresponds to the inner margin of a text field.

Also

border of member, boxType of member, boxDropShadow of member

marker *number*

SCORE FUNCTION

What it looks like (in the message window)

```
put marker(-1)
-- "a"
```

What it is

This function allows you to look forward or backward in the score and figure out what frames have labels. A parameter of 0 will look at the current frame, and frames before the current frame, until it finds one with a label. A parameter of –1 will not look at the current frame but look backward through the score for the next frame with a label. A parameter of 1 will look for the next frame forward in the score with a label. A parameter of 2 will look for the second frame forward with a label. You can use any positive or negative number to look further forward or backward.

Also

label, labelList

max(*number1, number2, number3, etc*)

MATH FUNCTION

What it looks like (in the message window)

```
put max(3,4)
-- 4
```

What it is

This simple function just returns the highest number in the parameter list.

Also

min

maxInteger

SYSTEM PROPERTY

What it looks like (in the message window)

```
put the maxInteger
-- 2147483647
```

What it is

For reference, this property gives you the largest integer supported by the computer.

mci *string*

COMMAND

What it looks like (in the message window)

```
mci "play song1"
```

What it is

This command sends a string directly to a PC sound card. It only works on Windows machines.

media of member *member*

MEMBER PROPERTY

What it looks like (in the message window)

```
set the media of member "picture2" = the media of member→
"picture1"
```

What it is

This property represents the actual contents of a cast member. The above example copies the contents of one cast member into another cast member.

Also

type of member

memberNum of sprite *spriteNumber*

SPRITE PROPERTY

What it looks like (in the message window)

```
put the memberNum of sprite 4
-- 65
set the memberNum of sprite 4 = the number of member→
"picture"
```

What it is

This property tells you which cast member is assigned to a sprite channel in the current frame. You can set this value temporarily in conjunction with an *updateStage* and/or *puppetSprite* command, or you can set it permanently inside a score generation session.

This property was called "castNum" before Director 5.

Also

number of member

M

memorySize

SYSTEM PROPERTY

What it looks like (in the message window)

```
put the memorySize
-- 102400
```

What it is

Tells you the total amount of memory, in bytes, allocated to Director or your projector.

Also

freeBlock, freeBytes

mod

MATH FUNCTION

What it looks like (in the message window)

```
put 7 mod 3
-- 1
put 8 mod 3
-- 2
put 9 mod 3
-- 0
```

What it is

There are two ways to look at this function. Mathematically, it takes the first number, divides by the second number, and gives you the remainder. A more useful way to look at it is that it restricts the number to a range. In the above example, the range is 0 to 2.

modal of window *window*

MIAW PROPERTY

What it looks like (in the message window)

```
set the modal of window "mywin" = TRUE
```

What it is

This property determines whether a movie in a window is considered "modal." This simply means that no other window can become active while this window is active. If the user attempts to click elsewhere, it has no effect.

modified of member *member*

MEMBER PROPERTY

What it looks like (in the message window)

```
put the modified of member "text"
-- 0
```

What it is

This property tells you whether a cast member has changed since the movie file was opened.

mouseCast

FUNCTION

What it looks like (in a handler)

```
on exitFrame
  put the mouseCast into a
  if a > 0 then put a
end
```

What it is

This function returns the number of the cast member that the cursor is currently over. If the cursor is not over a member, then it returns a –1.

This is similar to the *rollover* function, except that the *rollover* function tests a single sprite, while the *mouseCast* function returns the number of a cast member.

If you need to find out which cast member the user clicked on in a *mouseDown* or *mouseUp* script, use "the memberNum of sprite the clickOn" instead, as the user can move the mouse quickly and change the value of *mouseCast* inadvertently before your code gets to execute.

Also
rollover, clickOn, memberNum

mouseChar, mouseWord, mouseItem, mouseLine

FUNCTIONS

What they look like (in the message window)

```
on exitFrame
  put the mouseCast into mcast
  put the mouseChar into mchar
  if mcast > 0 then
    if char mchar of field mcast = " " then
      cursor(2)
    else
      cursor(0)
    end if
  else
    cursor(0)
  end if
end
```


What they are
These functions will tell you which character, item, line, and word the cursor is currently positioned over. If the cursor is not over a field, then all of these functions return a –1.

In the simple example above, the scipt changes the cursor whenever the user moves it over a space in the text.

Also
itemDelimiter

mouseDown, mouseUp

SYSTEM FUNCTIONS

What they look like (in the message window)

```
put the mouseDown
-- 0
put the mouseUp
-- 1
```

What they are

These functions simply return a true only if the mouse button is currently down in the case of the first function and up in the case of the second. Don't confuse them with the *on mouseDown* or *on mouseUp* event handlers. These are functions that return a true or false, while the handlers interact with messages.

Also

mouseUp, on mouseDown, on mouseUp, rightMouseDown, rightMouseUp

mouseDownScript, mouseUpScript

SYSTEM PROPERTIES

What they look like (in a handler)

```
on startMovie
  set the mouseDownScript = "handleClick"
  set the mouseUpScript = "beep()"
end
on handleClick
  put "click!"
  pass
end
```

What they are

These properties can be set so that the movie sends all "mouseDown" and/or "mouseUp" messages to a certain handler, or executes a certain Lingo script. Make sure you include a *pass* command if you wish the message to continue down the message hierarchy.

Also
kepDownScript, keyUpScript

mouseH, mouseV

SYSTEM PROPERTIES

What they look like (in a handler)

```
on exitFrame
  put the mouseH into field "h"
  put the mouseV into field "v"
  go to the frame
end
```

What they are
These two properties represent the horizontal and vertical positions of the cursor on the stage.

move member *member* [to member *member*]

CAST COMMAND

What it looks like (in the message window)

```
move member "text1"
move member "text2" to member 35
move member "text2" to member 30 of castLib "myLib"
```

What it is
This command will let you move cast members around the cast library. The first example above will place it in the next available space.

Also
new

moveableSprite of sprite *spriteNumber*

SPRITE PROPERTY

What it looks like (in the message window)

```
set the moveableSprite of sprite 5 = TRUE
```

What it is

When you set this property to true, it allows the user to click and drag the sprite around the stage. You can set this property manually in the score window as well.

moveToBack window *window*, moveToFront window *window*

MIAW COMMANDS

What they look like (in the message window)

```
moveToFront window "myWindow"
```

What they are

These two commands let you move any windows you have created to the back or the front of the interface.

Also

windowList

movie, movieName

SYSTEM PROPERTY

What it looks like (in the message window)

```
put the movie
-- "mymovie.dir"
```

What it is

This property returns the name of the current movie file. These two properties are identical.

Also

moviePath

movieFileFreeSize

MOVIE PROPERTY

What it looks like (in the message window)

```
put the movieFileFreeSize
-- 4729
```

What it is

This property tells you how much wasted space there is in a movie file. You can use the "Save and Compact" menu function to reduce the wasted space in a movie file.

movieFileSize

MOVIE PROPERTY

What it looks like (in the message window)

```
put the movieFileSize
-- 498464
```


What it is

This returns the file size, in bytes, of the current movie.

moviePath, pathName

MOVIE PROPERTY

What it looks like (in the message window)

```
put the moviePath
-- "c:\director\movie.dir"
```

What it is

These equivalent functions return the full path name of the current movie.

Also

movie

movieRate of sprite *spriteNumber*

DIGITAL VIDEO PROPERTY

What it looks like (in the message window)

```
set the movieRate of sprite 5 = 1
```

What it is

This poorly named property is for digital video cast members. When set to 1, the video plays at normal rate. Set to 0, the video stops. Set to –1, the video plays backward. You can also use other integer values—the movie can play faster in forward or reverse.

Also

movieTime of sprite, frameRate

movieTime of sprite *spriteNumber*

DIGITAL VIDEO PROPERTY

What it looks like (in the message window)

```
set the movieTime of sprite 6 = 0
```

What it is

This property represents the time, in ticks, of the current frame of the video. You can set this property to different values to control the video.

Also

movieRate of sprite

multiSound

SYSTEM PROPERTY

What it looks like (in the message window)

```
put the multiSound
-- 1
```

What it is

This property will tell you whether the current computer has more than one sound channel.

name of castLib *number*

CAST PROPERTY

What it looks like (in the message window)

```
put the name of castLib 2
-- "icons.cst"
```

What it is
This property tells you the name of a library. You can set this property as well as test it.

name of member *member*

MEMBER PROPERTY

What it looks like (in the message window)

```
put the name of member 4
-- "text"
```

What it is
This gives you the name of a cast member, if you supply the number. You can also set this property to change the names of cast members.

Also
number of member

name of menu *number*

MENU PROPERTY

What it looks like (in the message window)

```
put the name of menu 2 into menuName
```

What it is
This function will tell you what the name of a menu is, from the number that you supply. To change this name, you need to use the *installMenu* command.

Also

installMenu, name of menuItem

name of menuItem *number* of menu *nameOrNumber*

MENU PROPERTY

What it looks like (in the message window)

```
put the name of menuItem 3 of menu "File"
-- "Quit"
```

What it is

This function will tell you what the name of a menuItem in a menu is, from the number that you supply. You can change this property as well.

Also

name of menu, installMenu

name of window *window*

MIAW PROPERTY

What it looks like (in the message window)

```
set the name of window "myWindow" to "yourWindow"
```

What it is

You can supply a number or a MIAW variable to get this property value. Or you could change this property from one value to another as in the example above.

Also

windowList, title of window

name of Xtra *nameOrNumber*

XTRA PROPERTY

What it looks like (in the message window)

```
set the name of xtra "cool" to "funky"
```

What it is

This property corresponds to the name of an Xtra. You can change the name, as in the example above.

netAbort *number*

SHOCKWAVE COMMAND

What it looks like (in a handler)

```
on exitFrame
  if not netDone(1) then netAbort(1)
end
```

What it is

This command lets you cancel an operation like *getNetText*, *gotoNetMovie*, *gotoNetPage* or *preLoadNetThing*. The parameter refers to the ID number of the operation, which can be obtained by a *getLatestNetID* function.

Also

getNetText, gotoNetMovie, gotoNetPage, preLoadNetThing, getLatestNetID

netDone *number*

SHOCKWAVE FUNCTION

What it looks like (in a handler)

```
on exitFrame
  if not netDone(1) then go to the frame
end
```

What it is
This function becomes true once an operation like *getNetText, gotoNetMovie, gotoNetPage* or *preLoadNetThing* is done. The parameter refers to the ID number of the operation, which can be obtained by a *getLatestNetID* function.

Also
getNetText, gotoNetMovie, gotoNetPage, preLoadNetThing, getLatestNetID

netError *number*

SHOCKWAVE FUNCTION

What it looks like (in a handler)

```
on exitFrame
  if not netDone() then go to the frame
  else if netError() <> "OK" then
    alert "There was a problem."
  end if
end
```

What it is
This function returns an "OK" once an operation like *getNetText, gotoNetMovie, gotoNetPage* or *preLoadNetThing* is done. If there is a problem, it will return a message that describes the error. The parameter refers to the ID number of the operation, which can be obtained by a *getLatestNetID* function.

Also
getNetText, gotoNetMovie, gotoNetPage, preLoadNetThing, getLatestNetID

netLastModDate *number*

SHOCKWAVE FUNCTION

What it looks like (in a handler)

```
on exitFrame
  global urlDate
  if not netDone() then go to the frame
  else put netLastModDate() into urlDate
end
```

What it is

This function returns the last modified date of an item on the Internet that was obtained with a *preLoadNetThing* command. The parameter refers to the ID number of the operation, which can be obtained by a *getLatestNetID* function.

Also

preLoadNetThing, getLatestNetID

netMIME *number*

SHOCKWAVE FUNCTION

What it looks like (in a handler)

```
on exitFrame
  global mimeType
  if not netDone() then go to the frame
  else put netMIME() into mimeType
end
```

What it is

This function returns the MIME type of an item on the Internet that was obtained with a *preLoadNetThing* command. The parameter refers to the ID number of the operation, which can be obtained by a *getLatestNetID* function.

Also

preLoadNetThing, getLatestNetID

netTextResult *number*

SHOCKWAVE FUNCTION

What it looks like (in a handler)

```
on exitFrame
  if not netDone() then go to the frame
  else put netTextResult() into field "text"
end
```

What it is

This function allows you to retrieve the text obtained from the *getNetText* command. It only works after the *netDone* returns a true, indicating that the text retrieval is complete. The parameter refers to the ID number of the operation, which can be obtained by a *getLatestNetID* function.

Also

getNetText, getLatestNetID

new(type), new(type, castLib *castLib*), new(type, member *member* [of castLib *castLib*])

CAST COMMAND

What it looks like (in the message window)

```
put new(#field) into a
put a
-- 45
```

What it is

This command creates a new cast member. The type can be any one of the following: #bitmap, #button, #digitalVideo, #field, #fileLoop, #movie, #picture, #richText, #script, #shape, #sound, #palette, #transition.

This command returns a value, as a function, that is the number of the new cast member.

Also
type of member

new (script *script, parameter1, parameter2, etc...*)

OBJECT-ORIENTED PROGRAMMING COMMAND

What it looks like (in the message window)

```
set myObj = new(script "parent", 3, "this", "that")
```

What it is
This function creates a new instance of a parent script and returns a pointer to that instance (child). It replaces the "birth" command used in previous versions of Director.

next repeat

COMMAND

What it looks like (in a handler)

```
on myHandler
  repeat while TRUE
    if the shiftDown then next repeat
    if the mouseDown then exit repeat
  end repeat
end
```

What it is
This is a command that can be used inside a repeat loop to tell the movie to skip the rest of the Lingo in the loop and start it all over again.

Also
repeat, exit repeat

not

LOGICAL OPERATOR

What it looks like (in the message window)

```
put not TRUE
-- 0
put not FALSE
 -- 1
```

What it is

This function returns the opposite true/false value of the parameter.

Also

and, or

nothing

COMMAND

What it looks like (in the message window)

```
on doSomething what
  if what = 1 then
    nothing
  else
    beep()
  end if
end
```

What it is

This command does exactly what it says: nothing. It is simply a placeholder to make your code more readable.

number of *what*, number of *whats*

FUNCTION

What it looks like

```
put the number of members
put the number of castLib "castLib"
put the number of castLibs
put the number of members of castLib "castLib"

put the number of member "name"

put the number of menus
put the number of menuItems

put the number of chars in myString
put the number of words in myString
put the number of items in myString
put the number of lines in myString

put the number of Xtras
```

What it is

This function counts the number of different types of items in a variable or of a system element. The examples above show how diverse this function is. However, in all cases it is pretty obvious what it does.

numToChar(*number*)

FUNCTION

What it looks like (in the message window)

```
put numToChar(65)
-- "A"
```

What it is

This function takes a character number and converts it to the actual character.

Also

charToNum

objectP *variable*

FUNCTION

What it looks like (in the message window)

```
put objectP(myObj)
-- 1
```

What it is

This function will tell you if a variable is an object created as an instance of a parent script or as an instance of an Xobject or Xtra.

Also

new, voidP

offset *searchString, string*

STRING FUNCTION

What it looks like (in the message window)

```
put offset("d", "abcdef")
-- 4
put offset("$", "The amount I want to spend is $40")
-- 31
```

What it is

This function will return the position where the searchString is first found in the string. If the character is not found, it returns a 0. Remember that Lingo considers lowercase and uppercase the same in situations like this.

Also

contains, starts

offset(*rectangle*, *horizontalDifference*, *verticalDifference*)

FUNCTION

What it looks like (in the message window)

```
put offset(rect(10,20,10,20),1,2)
-- rect(11,22,11,22)
```

What it is

This function returns a rectangle that is the same as the first parameter except that the position has changed according to the other two parameters. Positive numbers will move it to the lower right, negative numbers to the upper left. You can also accomplish this by adding two rectangles.

Also

inflate, rect

on

HANDLER PREFIX

What it looks like

```
on startMovie
on stopMovie
on stepMovie

on mouseDown
on mouseUp

on rightMouseDown
on rightMouseUp

on keyDown
on keyUp

on enterFrame
on exitFrame
on idle

on timeOut

on activateWindow
on closeWindow
```

```
on deactivateWindow
on moveWindow
on openWindow
on resizeWindow
on zoomWindow
```

What it is

The word *on* is used as a prefix before a handler name. The handler can be one of the predefined ones above or your own custom handler. All of the above handler names respond to their corresponding messages. Your own handlers need to be explicitly called as commands or functions.

open *documentName* with *application*, open *application*

COMMAND

What it looks like (in the message window)

```
open "text.txt" with "write.exe"
```

What it is

This command allows you to start another application. The movie or projector will continue to play in the background. If the file or application is not in the same folder, you must specify the full path name.

open window *fileOrWindow*

MIAW COMMAND

What it looks like (in the message window)

```
open window "miaw.dir"
```

What it is

This command creates a new movie in a window. If you use a filename, it will look for and open that file as the MIAW. Otherwise, you must use the *fileName of window* property to set the file first.

Also

fileName of window, close window, title of window, visible of window

openResFile *filename*

COMMAND

What it looks like (in the message window)

```
openResFile "xcmds"
```

What it is

On the Macintosh, this command will open and access a file that has additional resources, such as Xobjects, cursors, or fonts.

Also

closeResFile, showResFile

openXlib *filename*

COMMAND

What it looks like (in the message window)

```
openXlib "fileio.dll"
```

What it is

This command opens an Xobject file. On Windows, these usually end with .dll, but you can leave that extension of the command if you wish.

Also

closeXlib

optionDown

SYSTEM PROPERTY

What it looks like (in the message window)

```
put the optionDown
-- 0
```

What it is

This property is true if the Option key is held down on the Macintosh or the Alt key is held down on the PC.

Also
commandDown, controlDown, shiftDown

or

LOGICAL OPERATOR

What it looks like (in the message window)

```
put TRUE or FALSE
-- TRUE
put TRUE or TRUE
-- TRUE
put FALSE or FALSE
-- FALSE
```

What it is
You can use *or* inside any Lingo syntax that requires a logical expression—like *if...then* or *repeat* statements. It will perform a logical "or" on two expressions. This means that the result will be true if either of the expressions are true, and false only if both are false.

Also
and, not

pageHeight of member *member*

FIELD MEMBER PROPERTY

What it looks like (in the message window)

```
put the pageHeight of member "text"
-- 200
```

What it is
This property tells you how high, in pixels, the visible part of the text field is. For "fixed" fields, this is the same as its actual height, but for "scrolling" fields it is the size of the scrolling box window on the stage.

Also
height of member, lineCount of member

palette of member *member*

BITMAP MEMBER PROPERTY

What it looks like (in the message window)

```
put the palette of member "picture"
-- 43
```

What it is

This property represents the number of the cast member that contains the special palette needed by a bitmap cast member. If the palette assigned to the bitmap is not a cast member but rather a system palette or other built-in palette, it returns a negative number. See *paletteRef* for more information about built-in palettes.

You can set this property, thus changing which palette a cast member uses on the fly.

Also

paletteRef

paletteMapping

SYSTEM PROPERTY

What it looks like (in the message window)

```
set the paletteMapping = TRUE
```

What it is

This property determines whether Director will attempt to remap the palettes of bitmaps as it imports them.

paletteRef

BITMAP MEMBER PROPERTY

What it looks like (in the message window)

```
set the paletteRef of member "picture" = #systemMac
```

What it is

This is similar to *palette of member*, except that it uses symbols to represent built-in palettes. Possible values are #systemMac, #systemWin, #rainbow, #grayscale, #pastels, #vivid, #NTSC, #metallic, #systemWinDir4.

Also

palette of member

param *number*

FUNCTION

What it looks like (in a handler)

```
on myHandler
  repeat with i = 1 to the paramCount
    put param(i)
  end repeat
end
```

What it is

This function allows you to access a variable number of parameters for a custom handler. In the example above, for instance, the handler expects no parameters, but if you suppy them the loop will send their values to the message window.

Also

paramCount

paramCount

FUNCTION

What it looks like (in a handler)

```
on myHandler
  repeat with i = 1 to the paramCount
    put param(i)
  end repeat
end
```

What it is

This will return the number of paramaters fed to a handler. In the above example, no paramters are expected, but the *paramCount* will accurately return the number of parameters passed to it, whether it is 0 or 100.

Also

param

pass

COMMAND

What it looks like (in a handler)


```
on mouseUp
  beep()
  pass
end
```

What it is

This command will signal Director to pass the message that triggered a handler on to another event handler. For instance, the handler above could be a score script that would cause a beep when the user clicked on the sprite. Since the handler includes a *pass* command, the message would go on to trigger another *on mouseUp* handler that could be in the cast script.

Also

dontPassEvent

pasteClipBoardInto member *member*

COMMAND

What it looks like (in the message window)

```
pasteClipBoardInto member "text"
```

What it is

This places the contents of the system clipboard into a cast member. You can use this in custom tools to copy members from one cast to another. Any cast member type can be copied and pasted. You can also copy things from other applications into cast members this way. You can do this for pictures, sounds or text.

Also

copyToClipBoard

pathName, moviePath

MOVIE PROPERTY

What it looks like (in the message window)

```
put the pathName
-- "c:\director\movie.dir"
```

What it is

These equivalent functions return the full pathname of the current movie.

Also

movie

pattern of member *member*

SHAPE MEMBER PROPERTY

What it looks like (in the message window)

```
set the pattern of member "circle"
```

What it is

This property corresponds to the pattern that is assigned to a shape cast member. The cast member must have the filled property turned on to have a pattern. The value of this property corresponds to the order of the patterns in the Director pattern palette.

Also

filled of member, foreColor of member, backColor of member

pause

COMMAND

What it looks like (in a handler)

```
on exitFrame
  pause
end
```

What it is

This command will stop the play head from moving forward. The movie will then stay on the current frame until a *continue* or *go* command is executed, say by a button on that frame.

However, this command will foul up any puppets or rollover scripts. It is much better to use a "go to the frame" in the *on exitFrame* handler.

Also

continue, go, pauseState, delay

pausedAtStart of member *member*

DIGITAL VIDEO MEMBER PROPERTY

What it looks like (in the message window)

```
set the pausedAtStart of member "video" = TRUE
```

What it is

This property corresponds to the same option in the digital video member's information box. It determines if a video starts playing as soon as it is shown on the stage or waits for a user action or Lingo command to start.

Also

movieRate

pauseState

MOVIE PROPERTY

What it looks like (in the message window)

```
put the pauseState
```

What it is

This property tells you whether the movie is currently paused. Use the *pause* command to pause a movie; use the *continue* command to resume.

Also

pause, continue

perFrameHook

MOVIE PROPERTY

What it is

This old Lingo command is outdated. It will still work, however, if you wish to assign an Xobject, Xtra, or method to execute with every frame. Use the *on enterFrame* handler to accomplish this now.

Also

enterFrame, exitFrame

pi

MATH FUNCTION

What it looks like (in the message window)

```
put pi()
-- 3.1416
```

What it is

This function will return pi to as many digits as *the floatPrecision* allows—usually four. Use this function in conjunction with *sin, cos, tan* and *atan* functions to make your code easier to read and debug.

Also

floatPrecision, sin, cos, tan, atan

picture of member *member*

BITMAP MEMBER PROPERTY

What it looks like (in the message window)

```
set the picture of member "picture" = the picture of member→
"pic1"
```


What it is

This property represents the image in the cast member. You can use it to swap pictures, as we are doing in the example above. It also works with Macintosh PICT file format cast members.

Also

media of member

pictureP *variable*

FUNCTION

What it looks like (in the message window)

```
put pictureP(myPic)
-- 1
```

What it is

This function will test a variable and tell you whether or not it is a picture.

Also

picture of member, type of member

platform

SYSTEM PROPERTY

What it looks like (in the message window)

```
put the platform
-- "Macintosh, PowerPC"
```

What it is

This property returns a string that corresponds to the type of machine the movie is running on. Possible values are "Macintosh, 68K," "Macintosh, PowerPC," "Windows, 16," and "Windows, 32." The last two correspond to Windows 3.1 and Windows 95/NT, respectively.

Also

the machineType, colorQD, colorDepth

play [frame] *frame,* play [frame *frame* of] movie *movieName*

COMMAND

What it looks like

```
play frame "chapter1"
play frame "chapter12" of movie "section2.dir"
```

What it is

This command is similar to the go command, but with two important differences. First, the *play* command will remember what frame of what movie Director is playing when it jumps to the new position or movie. Then, when a *play done* is executed, or the movie jumps to the end, it will know to go back to the frame and movie it came from. The second difference is that it will suspend a handler that uses the play command and wait for that movie or sequence to end before the original handler resumes.

Also

go, play done

play done

COMMAND

What it looks like

```
play done
```

What it is

This command should be used in conjunction with a *play* command. It signals that the sequence to be played is done.

Also

play

point(*horizontalPosition, verticalPosition*)

FUNCTION

What it looks like (in the message window)

```
put  point(100,100) into myPoint
put myPoint * 2
-- point(200, 200)
put myPoint / 5
-- point(20, 20)
put myPoint + 2
-- point(102, 102)
put myPoint + point(2,2)
-- point(102, 102)
put myPoint + point(2,20)
-- point(102, 120)
```

What it is

This function will create a Director point variable. These variables are used to represent position on the stage or any location expression. A point is often returned by graphics-related functions. The examples above demonstrate using the point function with arithmetic operators.

Also

rect

P

power(*number, exponent*)

MATH FUNCTION

What it looks like (in the message window)

```
put power(4,3)
-- 64
```

What it is

This function returns the result of the first paramater raised to the power of the second parameter. You can also use decimal or negative numbers for either parameter.

Also

sqrt

preLoad [[*frameNum*,] *frameNum*]

COMMAND

What it looks like:

```
preLoad
preLoad 20
preLoad 15,20
```

What it is

This command tells Director to start loading cast members. The first example above will start loading all cast members in the current frame to the last frame. The second example will start loading all cast members in the current frame to frame 20. The last example will load in cast members in frames 15 though 20.

Also

preLoadMember, preLoadEventAbort

preLoad of member *member*

DIGITAL VIDEO MEMBER PROPERTY

What it looks like (in the message window)

```
set the preLoad of member "video" = TRUE
```

P

What it is

This corresponds to the "enable preload" option in the digital video cast member information box. When set to false, it will exclude the member from being loaded into memory before it is needed.

Also

preLoadRAM

preLoadEventAbort

SYSTEM PROPERTY

What it looks like

```
set the preLoadEventAbort = TRUE
```

What it is

When set to true, this property will allow a preload command to be aborted when the user clicks the mouse or presses a key. The idea is to allow users to get a faster reaction from the program.

Also

preLoadMember, preLoadFrame

preLoadMember [[*member*,] *member*]

COMMAND

What it looks like (in the message window)

```
preLoadMember
preLoadMember "picture1"
preLoadMember "picture1", "picture13"
put preLoadMember("picture1", "picture13") into lastLoaded
```

What it is

This command allows you to load members into memory. The first example above will try and load all cast members. The second example will load only that one cast member. The third example loads a range of members. The loading will stop if Director has no more memory to load in members. If used as a function, this command will return the number of the last member loaded, so you know how many members were loaded and which ones couldn't fit into memory.

Also

preLoadFrame, preLoadEventAbort

preLoadMode of castLib *castLib*

MOVIE PROPERTY

What it looks like (in a handler)

```
on startMovie
  set the preLoadMode of castLib "icons" = 2
end
```

What it is

You can choose three ways that you want cast libraries to be loaded. Setting the value to 0 will mean that the library is loaded when needed. Setting it to 1 or 2 means that the library will be loaded either before frame 1 or after frame 1, respectively. This corresponds to the "load cast" setting in the movie information dialog box.

Also

preLoadMovie

preLoadNetThing *uri*

SHOCKWAVE COMMAND

What it looks like (in a handler)

```
on startMovie
  preLoadNetThing "next.dcr"
end
```

What it is

This command allows you to tell the browser to get a file from across the Internet and store it in the disk cache. You can use this to predict what Shockwave movie or other element the user will need next and get it to them before they know they want it.

Also

gotoNetPage, gotoNetMovie

preLoadRAM

FUNCTION

What it looks like (in a handler)

```
on startMovie
  set the preLoadRAM = 1000000
end
```

What it is

This property lets Director know how much memory to set aside for loading digital video. This is useful for limiting the memory your video uses so that there is room for other cast members.

printFrom *fromFrame* [,*toFrame*] [,*percent*]

COMMAND

What it looks like (in a handler)

```
on mouseDown
  printFrom the frame, the frame, 100
end
```

What it is

This command sends a series of frames to the printer. You can specify a range of frames and a percentage reduction (100, 75, 50, or 25). Unfortunately, there is no way to bring up a "page setup" dialog or even specify that you want to print in landscape mode or anything like that. You can do these things with Xobjects, however. When you try to print at 100 percent, it attempts to print text as styled text, while at other sizes it prints them as bitmaps. This command does not handle puppeted or movable sprites very well.

property *property1, property2, property3, ...*

SYNTAX

What it looks like (in the message window)

```
property var1, gamescore, positionXY
```

What it is

This piece of syntax is used at the top of parent scripts to declare all of the object's properties. All of the variables declared are shared by each of the handlers in the parent script.

Also

new, global

puppet of sprite *spriteNumber*

SPRITE PROPERTY

What it looks like (in a handler)

```
on mouseDown
  if the puppet of sprite 5 = TRUE then
    set the locH of sprite 5 = 200
  end if
end
```

What it is

This property tells you whether the sprite has been puppeted. You can also set this value, as a substitute for the *puppetSprite* command.

Also

puppetSprite

puppetPalette *palette, speed, numberOfFrames*

COMMAND

What it looks like (in the message window)

```
puppetPalette "Gray", 20
```

What it is

The *puppetPalette* command takes control of the frame palettes in the movie. You can import a new palette as a cast member. Use that cast member's name as the parameter for the *puppetPalette* command.

The second parameter is the speed of the transition: 1 is the slowest and 60 is the fastest. Assuming that our palette named "Gray" is a palette with 256 levels of gray, this command would gradually shift the colors on the stage to shades of gray. A very nice effect.

You can also have a third parameter: the number of frames over which you want the change to take place. This means that you can combine the palette change with other changes on your stage as well.

With the *puppetPalette* command control of the palettes will not return to Director until you issue a *puppetPalette 0* command.

Also

puppetSprite, puppetSound, puppetTempo, puppetTransition

P

puppetSound *member,* puppetSound *channel, member*

COMMAND

What it looks like (in a handler)

```
on mouseDown
  puppetSound "hello"
  updateStage
end
```

```
-- The following handler will play a
-- random sound from a list
on exitFrame
  put ["sound1","sound2","sound3"] into soundList
  put random(count(soundList)) into r
  puppetSound getAt(soundList,r)
  updateStage
end
```

What it is

This command takes control of one of the sound channels and lets us play sounds at any time we want. Just as with puppetSprites, we need to use the *updateStage* command to trigger the sound, or the sound will not start until the next frame.

To return control of sound to the score, issue a *puppetSound 0* command.

Also

puppetPalette, puppetSprite, puppetTempo, puppetTransition

puppetSprite *spriteNumber, trueOrFalse*

COMMAND

P

What it looks like (in the message window)

```
on mouseDown
  puppetSprite 5, TRUE
  set the locH of sprite 5 = 200
end

-- The following handler will put a
-- random member in a sprite channel
on randomPicture spriteNum
  put ["pic1","pic2"," pic3"] into picList
  put random(count(picList)) into r
  puppetSprite spriteNum, TRUE
  set the memberNum of sprite spriteNum = the number of→
member getAt(picList,r)
  updateStage
end
```

What it is

This command allows you to take and keep control of a sprite. Once you use the command, the behavior of the sprite depends on Lingo commands, not on the score. You can then change the position and appearance of a sprite. Updates occur every frame and every time you use the updateStage command.

To return control of the sprite to the score, use FALSE as the second parameter.

Also

puppetPalette, puppetSound, puppetTempo, puppetTransition

puppetTempo *number*

COMMAND

What it looks like (in a handler)

```
on exitFrame
  puppetTempo 20
end
```

What it is

This command lets you override the score's tempo channel. The parameter represents the number of frames per second of the new tempo. The frame rate will remain the same until you issue another puppetTempo command or until the tempo changes in the score.

Also

puppetPalette, puppetSound, puppetSprite, puppetTransition

puppetTransition *transition, time, chunkSize, onlyChangedArea*

COMMAND

What it looks like (in a handler)

```
on mouseDown
  puppetTransition 20
  go to frame "q"
end
```

What it is

The *puppetTransition* command allows you to control the next transition, which occurs either when the movie enters a frame or when you issue the *updateStage* command. All you need to do is place your *puppetTransition* command just before any command that will create a change—for example, a *go to the frame*, or *go to frame "a."*

The *puppetTransition* takes up to four parameters, but only the first one is required. This first parameter is the transition number. There are 52 transitions built into Director. A complete list of all 52 transitions can be found in the "Tables & Charts" appendix of this book.

P

The second parameter is the time it takes, in 1/4-second increments, for the transition to complete. In the above example, the 8 means that we want the transition to last for 2 seconds. This number should be taken with a grain of salt, however, because some effects don't use it and others may take too long on slow computers to make your deadline. It is best to experiment with the transitions you would like to use.

The third parameter is the chunk size of the transition. With each step the transition takes, a certain number of pixels are changed. This value helps determine how many. By setting this value higher, you will loose the smoothness of the transition. However, you will also gain some speed. This can help if you absolutely need a transition to finish on time.

The last parameter is a true or false value that determines if the transition will occur in only the portion of the stage that changed. This will create a very different effect for some transitions. A "push right" transition—number 12—will seem to push the entire stage to the right, replacing it with the new stage, if the value is false. However, if only a small portion of the stage has changed, and the value is set to true, then the push will only happen in a small area of the stage.

The most common problem with *puppetTransition*, and also with normal transitions placed in the score, is that you may wish to place one on a looping frame. If a frame is looping and a transition is also present, that transition will continue to happen over and over again. You may not see it because after the first transition the stage hasn't changed, so the transition is happening from B to B instead of from A to B. But you will see the effects of this continuous transitioning: response times will be slowed, and cursors on the Macintosh will appear to blink on and off.

You can easily fix this problem by not having score and puppet transitions inside loops. For the score, create another, identical frame just before the looping one, and place the transition in there. Then the second frame has the loop. That way, the movie enters the first frame, does its transition, and then loops on the second frame.

Also

puppetPalette, puppetSound, puppetSprite, puppetTempo

purgePriority of member *member*

MEMBER PROPERTY

What it looks like (in the message window)

```
set the purgePriority of member "picture" = 1
```

What it is

This allows you to set the purge priority of a cast member. This is the same property as the "purge priority" in the cast member information box. Possible values are 0 = Never purge, 1 = Purge Last, 2 = Purge Next, 3 = Purge Normal. The setting determines a cast member's chance of being purged from memory when not in use.

put

COMMAND

What it looks like

```
put myVariable
put a+b
put 3 into myVariable
put a into b
put "and" into t
put "this " before t
put "that" after t
```

What it is

This command is one of the basic foundations of Lingo. It is very similar to the *set* command, which has some additional powers.

Using the *put* command without an *into* extension will place whatever it is into the message window. Otherwise, the results of the expression will go into the variable specified.

You can use all of the standard modifiers, such as *char*, *item*, *word*, or *line*, on either side of the *into*. You can also use *before* and *after* modifiers with strings.

Also

set

quickTimePresent

SYSTEM PROPERTY

What it looks like (in a handler)

```
on startMovie
  if the quickTimePresent then
    alert "You need QuickTime to play this movie."
    halt
  end if
end
```

What it is

This property tells you whether QuickTime is present on the computer that the movie is playing on.

quit

COMMAND

What it looks like (in a handler)

```
on mouseDown
  quit
end
```

What it is

This command will cause a projector to quit. It will also attempt to quit Director. A better command to use would be the *halt* command, since that command will stop the movie from playing only when you are authoring in Director, but it will not try to quit.

Also

halt, restart, shutDown

QUOTE

CONSTANT

What it looks like

```
put QUOTE&"Hi"&QUOTE into t
```

What it is

This constant represents the quote character. It comes in handy when you need to place quotes inside a string with Lingo.

ramNeeded *firstFrame, lastFrame*

FUNCTION

What it looks like

```
on mouseUp
  if ramNeeded(5,7) > the freeBytes then
    go to frame 8
  else
    go to frame 5
  end if
end
```

What it is
This function calculates the amount of memory needed to display a series of frames.

Also
freeBytes, freeBlock, size of member

random *number*

FUNCTION

What it looks like (in the message window)

```
put random(3)
-- 2
put random(3)
-- 3
```

What it is
This function returns a random number from 1 to the number supplied.

Also
randomSeed

randomSeed

SYSTEM PROPERTY

What it looks like (in the message window)

```
set the randomSeed = the ticks
```

What it is
Computers use a complex algorithm to generate random numbers. This algorithm starts with a single number. That number corresponds to this property. You can ensure a random-looking sequence generated by the *random* function by setting it to something semi-random like *the ticks* above. Or you can set it to a specific number and have the *random* function return the same seqence of numbers.

Also
random

rect(*left*, *top*, *right*, *bottom*), **rect**(*topLeftPoint*, *bottomRightPoint*)

FUNCTION

What it looks like (in the message window)

```
put rect(50,60,100,200) into myRect
put rect(point(50,60),point(100,200) into myRect
put rect(100,100,100,100) into myRect
put myRect+rect(10,10,10,10)
-- rect(110,110,110,110)
put myRect*2
-- rect(200,200,200,200)
```

What it is

This function will create a Director rectangle variable. These variables are used to represent position and size on the stage or any position and size expression. A rect is often returned by graphics-related functions. You can also use arithmetic with rectangles.

Also

point

rect of member *member*

MEMBER PROPERTY

What it looks like (in the message window)

```
put the rect of member "picture"
-- rect (0,0,270,345)
```

What it is

With this property you can get the size of a bitmap, shape, or digital video member.

Also

rect of sprite, rect, height, width

R

rect of sprite *spriteNumber*

SPRITE PROPERTY

What it looks like (in the message window)

```
set the rect of sprite 5 = rect(100,100,200,200)
```

What it is

This property allows you to test and set the position and size of a sprite on the stage. Used in conjunction with *puppetSprite* and *updateStage*, you can reposition and scale any visible sprite.

Also

rect, rect of member, inflate, map, locH of sprite, locV of sprite

rect of window *window*

MIAW PROPERTY

What it looks like (in the message window)

```
set the rect of window "myWin" = rect(100,100,300,200)
```

What it is

This property allows you to test and set the coordinates of a movie in a window relative to the position of the stage.

Also

drawRect of window

regPoint of member *member*

BITMAP MEMBER PROPERTY

What it looks like (in the message window)

```
set the regPoint of member "picture" = point(0,0)
```

What it is

This property allows you to set the registration point of a bitmap cast member. Director automatically sets this point to the center of a bitmap but allows you to change it in the paint window as well as with this Lingo property.

The registration point is the point in the bitmap that will line up with the exact horizontal and vertical location of the member on the stage.

repeat

SYNTAX

What it looks like

```
repeat while the shiftDown
  put "This shift key is down"
end repeat

repeat while TRUE
  put "I will write this forever"
end repeat

repeat with i = 1 to 100
  put i
end repeat

repeat with i = 100 down to 1
  put i
end repeat

repeat with x in [1,5,3,7]
  put x
end repeat
```

What it is

The repeat loop syntax takes several forms, all illustrated above. The *repeat...while* loop will continue to execute the internal code until the *while* condition is true. If you supply a true or a 1 as the *while* condition, the loop will go on forever. In this case an *exit* or an *exit repeat* command would be used to stop the loop. The third example shows a *repeat...with* loop that will loop 100 times, and the variable "i" will be set to the number of each loop. The fourth example shows a *repeat...with* loop that uses the *down to* modifier to count backward. The last example shows a *repeat...with...in list* loop that will set "x" to one of the values in the list each time through the loop until all values have been used.

Also

exit repeat, next repeat

restart

COMMAND

What it looks like (in a handler)

```
on mouseDown
  restart
end
```

What it is

This Macintosh-only command will restart the computer.

Also

shutDown, halt, quit

result

FUNCTION

What it looks like (in the message window)

```
put square(3)
-- 9
square(3)
put the result
-- 9
```

What it is

This function will recall the returned value from the last function called. In the above example, the custom handler "square" will return the square or a number. First, we grab the value of this the regular way. Then, we simply call the function first, and then use *the result* to get the returned value. Both of these techniques give the same result.

Also

return

RETURN

CONSTANT

What it looks like (in a handler)

```
on keyDown
  if the key = RETURN then
    alert "Don't hit the Return key!"
  end if
end
```

What it is

This constant represents the character generated by a Return key. You can also use it to build strings with multiple lines. For instance, "this line"&RETURN&"that line."

Also

numToChar

return *value*

COMMAND

What it looks like (in a hander)

```
on square n
  put n*n into n2
  return n2
end
```

What it is

This command will cause a custom handler to exit, and return the value supplied to whatever called it. You can return a number, string, list, or any other type of data.

Also

result

right of sprite *spriteNumber*

SPRITE PROPERTY

What it looks like (in the message window)

```
put the left of sprite 5
-- 450
```

What it is

This property returns the position, in pixels, of the right side of the sprite on the stage. You cannot set this property directly.

Also

left of sprite, bottom of sprite, top of sprite, width of sprite, height of sprite, rect of sprite

rightMouseDown, rightMouseUp

SYSTEM FUNCTIONS

What they look like (in the message window)

```
put the mouseDown
-- 0
put the mouseUp
-- 1
```

What they are

R

These functions simply return a true only if the right mouse button is currently down in the case of the first function and up in the case of the second. Don't confuse them with the *on rightMouseDown* or *on rightMouseUp* event handlers. These are functions that return a true or false, while the handlers interact with messages.

On the Macintosh, which has no right mouse button, setting the *emulateRightMouseButton* property to true will make the mouse button act as the right mouse button if the user holds down the Control key.

Also

emulateRightMouseButton, mouseDown, mouseUp, on mouseDown, on mouseUp

rollover *spriteNumber*

FUNCTION

What it looks like (in a handler)

```
on exitFrame
  if rollover(5) then beep()
end
```

What it is

This function will tell you if the cursor is over a sprite. The cursor can be over more than one sprite at a time if the sprites overlap. This function only detects if the cursor is over the rectangle of that sprite, not over a specific shape. To detect if the cursor is over a nonrectangular bitmap, you have to set the ink of the bitmap to "matte" and use the *mouseCast* function.

Also

mouseCast

rollover

SYSTEM PROPERTY

What it looks like (in the message window)

```
put the rollover
-- 26
```

What it is

This undocumented property will tell you which sprite the cursor is currently over. If it is over more than one sprite because they overlap, then it returns the highest sprite number.

Also

mouseCast

romanLingo

SYSTEM PROPERTY

What it looks like (in the message window)

```
set the romanLingo = TRUE
```

What it is
Some charcter sets, like those in the Japanese alphabet, use more than 256 characters. If your system is set to use character sets like these, the *romanLingo* will be set to false. When this happens, Lingo may be slower. You may wish to override this setting by changing the *romanLingo* to true. Most users will never need to worry about this property.

runMode

SYSTEM PROPERTY

What it looks like (in a handler)

```
on startMovie
  put the runMode into field "display"
end
```

What it is
This undocumented property will return an "Author" if you are in Director and a "Projector" if the movie is running as or from a projector. This property currently returns "Projector" if running in Shockwave.

Also
machineType

R

sampleRate of member *member*

SOUND MEMBER PROPERTY

What it looks like (in the message window)

```
put the sampleRate of member "audio"
-- 11
```

What it is

This property tells you the sample rate of a sound, in kiloHertz.

Also

sampleSize of member

sampleSize of member *member*

SOUND MEMBER PROPERTY

What it looks like (in the message window)

```
put the sampleSize of member "audio"
-- 8
```

What it is

This property tells you whether a sound is 8-bit or 16-bit.

Also

sampleRate of member

save castLib *castLib, [pathname]*

COMMAND

What it looks like (in the message window)

```
save castLib "icons.cst"
```

What it is

This command saves a cast library. If you include the path name parameter, it will make a new copy of the library.

Also

saveMovie

saveMovie [*pathname*]

COMMAND

What it looks like (in the message window)

```
saveMovie
```

What it is

This command saves the current movie. This will allow you to keep any changes you have made, either manually or through cast member or score generation changes. And because it cleans up memory, it is also handy when you're having memory problems with Xtras that are tools.

Also

save castLib

score

MOVIE PROPERTY

What it looks like (in the message window)

```
set the score = media of member "film loop"
```

What it is

This strange property allows you to replace the score of a movie with the score embedded into a film loop cast member.

scoreColor of sprite *spriteNumber*

SCORE PROPERTY

What it looks like (in the message window)

```
set the scoreColor of sprite 8 = 3
```

What it is

This property allows you to test and set the color of a cell in the score. The number, which can go from 0 to 5, corresponds to the colors shown on the left side of the score. You can set this color manually in the score window. You must have the colored score option turned on in the perferences to see this change.

scoreSelection

SCORE FUNCTION

What it looks like (in the message window)

```
put the scoreSelection
-- [[3,6,1,5]]
```

What it is

the scoreSelection returns a list of lists. Each sublist represents a selected area of the score. These sublists have four numbers: the first sprite, the last sprite, the first frame, and the last frame. For instance, [[3,6,1,5]] means that sprites 3 to 6 of frames 1 to 5 have been selected; [[3,6,1,5], [8,12,1,5]] means that sprites 3 to 6 and 8 to 12 of frames 1 to 5 have been selected. The numbers 0, –1, –2, –3, –4 , and –5 represent the script channel, sound channel 2, sound channel 1, the transition channel, the palette channel, and the tempo channel.

This command is useful for building tools with the score generation commands.

Also

beginRecording

script of menuItem *menuItem* of menu *menu*

MENU PROPERTY

What it looks like (in the message window)

```
set the script of menuItem "chapter 1" of menu "Jump to" =→
"go to frame 65"
```

What it is

This property represents the script that a menu item in a custom menu will execute when selected. This property is initially set in the *installMenu* command by the menu field member. You can change this property on the fly from that point on.

Also

installMenu, checkMark of menuItem, enabled of menuItem

S

scriptNum of sprite *spriteNumber*

SPRITE PROPERTY

What it looks like (in the message window)

```
put the scriptNum of sprite 4
-- 34
```

What it is

This property corresponds to the script member that is assigned to the sprite in the current frame of the score. You can also set this property during a score generation session. Make sure you only assign score scripts to sprite channels and not movie scripts.

Also

beginRecording

scriptsEnabled of member *member*

MOVIE MEMBER PROPERTY

What it looks like (in the message window)

```
set the scriptsEnabled of member "littleMovie" = FALSE
```

What it is

This property allows you to turn off the scripts embedded in a linked movie cast member. You cannot use this property for any other cast member type.

scriptText of member *member*

SCRIPT MEMBER PROPERTY

What it looks like (in the message window)

```
put the scriptText of member "myScript" into t
```

What it is

This property will allow you to get and set the script of a script cast member or another type of cast member that has a script embedded in it. The above example put this text into the variable "t." You cannot use this property in projectors or protected movies, since the text of each script has been stripped out.

scriptType of member *member*

SCRIPT MEMBER PROPERTY

What it looks like (in the message window)

```
put the scriptType of member "myScript"
-- #MOVIE
```

What it is

This property will tell you what type of script a member is: #MOVIE, #SPRITE, #FRAME, or #PARENT.

Also

scriptText of member

scrollByLine member *member, amount*

FIELD MEMBER COMMAND

What it looks like (in the message window)

```
scrollByLine member "text", -1
```

What it is

This command will cause a "scrolling" or "fixed size" field to scroll up or down by one line. You can use positive or negative numbers, depending on which direction you want to scroll. A "line" in this case is a visual line on the screen, and it has nothing to do with the placement of Returns in the field.

Also

scrollByPage, scrollTop

scrollByPage member *member, amount*

FIELD MEMBER COMMAND

What it looks like (in the message window)

```
scrollByPage member "text", -1
```

What it is

This command will cause a "scrolling" or "fixed size" field to scroll up or down by one page. You can use positive or negative numbers, depending on which direction you want to scroll in. A "page" in this case is about equal to the amount of text that can be seen in the field area at one time.

Also

scrollByLine, scrollTop

scrollTop of member *member*

FIELD AND TEXT MEMBER PROPERTY

What it looks like (in the message window)

```
set the scrollTop of member "text" = 100
```

What it looks like (in a handler)

```
-- This handler resets a few scrolling
-- fields when a movie starts
on startMovie
  set the scrollTop of member "text1" = 0
  set the scrollTop of member "text2" = 0
  set the scrollTop of member "text3" = 0
end
```

What it is

This lets you set what portion of a field or rich text member is shown. It works in cases where these members only show a portion of the entire member on the stage because they are set to "scrolling" or "fixed size." You set this property by pixels, allowing you to determine exactly which part is displayed.

Also

scrollByLine, scrollByPage

searchCurrentFolder

SYSTEM PROPERTY

What it looks like (in the message window)

```
set the searchCurrentFolder = TRUE
```

What it is

This property determines whether the current folder is searched when Director is looking for movies or linked media.

Also

searchPath

searchPath, searchPaths

SYSTEM PROPERTY

What it looks like (in the message window)

```
set the searchPath = ["f:\pictues\"]
addAt(the searchPath, "g:\images\")
```

What it is

This system property is a list that can contain several paths for Director to search for movies or linked files. You can use the standard list functions to alter this property.

The *searchPath* and the *searchPaths* properties are one and the same.

Also

searchCurrentFolder

selection

SYSTEM PROPERTY

What it looks like (in a handler)

```
on keyDown
  if the key = "c" and the commandDown then
    put the selection into text
  end if
end
```

What it is

This property holds the text that the user has selected in an editable text field. It is useful for getting just the text that is selected, but it will not tell you which field the user is selecting it in.

Also

selStart, selEnd

selection of castLib *castLib*

CAST LIBRARY PROPERTY

What it looks like (in the message window)

```
set the selection of castLib "icons" = [[3,5],[8,12]]
```

What it is

This property corresponds to the items selected in the cast library window. The list that it returns, or can be set to, can contain several ranges of cast members. The above example, for instance, will select members 3 to 5 and 8 to 12.

Also

scoreSelection

selEnd, selStart

SYSTEM PROPERTIES

What it looks like (in the message window)

```
set the selStart = 24
set the selEnd = 145
```

What it is

These two properties represent the starting and ending points of the selection in the currently editable text field. You can test and set them.

Also

selection

set

COMMAND

What it looks like (in the message window)

```
set a = 3
set b = 3+4
set c = "text"
set the ink of sprite 5 = 8
set the name of member "this" = "that"
```

What it is

This basic command can put values into variables and set properties. It is similar to the *put* command and can be interchanged with it in many circumstances. It has the extra ability, though, of working with Lingo properties, as in the last two examples above.

Also

put

setAProp *list, property, value*

LIST COMMAND

What it looks like (in the message window)

```
put [#a: 1,#b: 2,#c: 3] into list
setAProp(list,#b,7)
put list
-- [#a: 1, #b: 7, #c: 3]
setAProp(list,#d,9)
put list
-- [#a: 1, #b: 7, #c: 3, #d: 9]
```

What it is

This list command will set the value of a property in a property list to a new value. It differs from *setProp* because if the property is not already in the list, it will just add it.

Also

setProp, setAt

setAt *list, number, value*

LIST COMMAND

What it looks like (in the message window)

```
put [1,2,3,4] into list
setAt(list,3,8)
put list
-- [1,2,8,4]
```


What it is

This list function will change the value of an item in a linear or property list. If the item does not exist, you will get an error message.

Also

getAt, setProp, setAProp

setCallBack

SYSTEM PROPERTY

What it looks like (in the message window)

```
setCallBack myXCMD, TRUE
```

What it is

This Macintosh-only property deals with what happens when unsupported callbacks are made to an XCMD or XFCN. When it is set to true, unsupported callbacks cause an error message.

setProp *list, property, value*

LIST COMMAND

What it looks like (in the message window)

```
put [#a: 1,#b: 2,#c: 3] into list
setProp(list,#b,7)
put list
-- [#a: 1, #b: 7, #c: 3]
```

What it is

This list command will set the value of a property in a property list to a new value. If the property is not already in the list, it generates an error message.

Also

setAProp, setAt

S

setTrackEnabled(sprite *sprite*, *track*, *enabled*)

DIGITAL VIDEO COMMAND

What it looks like (in the message window)

```
setTrackEnabled(sprite 3, 2, TRUE)
```

What it is

This command allows you to enable or disable tracks in a digital video sprite. You can use this to create some interesting effects if your video editing program gives you control over the tracks you produce. For instance, you could have a sound track that is in English and another sound track in Japanese, then enable and disable the ones you want for different settings in your movie.

Also

trackCount, trackEnabled, trackStartTime, trackStopTime, trackType

shapeType of member *member*

SHAPE MEMBER PROPERTY

What it looks like (in the message window)

```
set the shapeType of member "oval" = #roundRect
```

What it is

This property allows you to control the type of shape a shape member is. The possible values are: #rect, #roundRect, #oval, and #line.

shiftDown

SYSTEM PROPERTY

What it looks like (in a handler)

```
on keyDown
  if the key = "g" and the shiftDown then
    alert "Shift-G!"
  end if
end
```

What it is

This simply returns true if the Shift key is held down and false otherwise.

Also

commandDown, controlDown, optionDown, key, keyDown

showGlobals

COMMAND

What it looks like (in the message window)

```
showGlobals
-- Global Variables
-- version = "5.0"
x1 = 446
y1 = 91
x2 = 451
y2 = 433
mode = #wait
```

What it is

This makes Director list all of the global variables and their values in the message window.

Also

clearGlobals, showLocals

showLocals

COMMAND

What it looks like (in a handler)

```
on thisHandler
  put 5 into s
  put 6 into t
  showLocals
end
```

What it is

Use this command in a handler to make Director list all of the local variables and their values in the Message window.

Also

showGlobals

showResFile *whichFile*

COMMAND

What it looks like (in the message window)

```
openResFile "myRes"
showResFile "myRes"
-- **
closeResFile
```

What it is

This command will list all of the resources in an open resource file. It is a Macintosh-only command.

Also

openResFile, closeResFile

showXlib [*filename*]

COMMAND

What it looks like (in the message window)

```
showXlib
-- XLibraries:
--    Xtra: PrintOMatic_Lite
--    Xtra: OSUtil
-- "*Standard.xlib"
--    XObject: FileIO          Id:1020
--    XObject: SerialPort      Id:200
--    XObject: XCMDGlue        Id:2020
```

What it is

This command will display all of the available Xtras and Xobjects. If you supply a filename, it will display only those inside that file.

Also

openXlib, closeXib

shutDown

COMMAND

What it looks like (in a handler)

```
on mouseUp
  shutDown
end
```

What it is

On a Macintosh, this command will shut down the computer. On a Windows machine, this command will exit Windows.

Also

restart, quit, halt

sin(*number*)

MATH FUNCTION

What it looks like (in the message window)

```
put sin(pi())
-- -0.0000
```

What it is

This function returns the sine of a number. Use radians, not degrees, for the parameter.

Also

cos, tan, atan, pi

size of member *member*

MEMBER PROPERTY

What it looks like (in the message window)

```
put the size of member "picture"
-- 38743
```

What it is

This property tells you the size of any cast member, in bytes.

sort *list*

LIST COMMAND

What it looks like (in the message window)

```
put [4,2,7,3] into list
sort(list)
put list
-- [2,3,4,7]
```

What it is

This command quickly sorts a list. For linear lists, the sort is by value. For property lists, the sort is by property. The sort is always in ascending order. Once a list is sorted, the *add* and *addProp* commands will place items in their proper sorted position in that list and findPosNear will work.

Also

add, addProp, findPosNear

sound close *channel*

COMMAND

What it looks like (in the message window)

```
sound close 1
```

What it is

This stops and closes a sound that was opened with the *sound playFile* command.

Also

sound playFile

sound fadeIn *channel,* [*ticks*], sound fadeOut *channel,* [*ticks*]

COMMANDS

What it looks like (in the message window)

```
sound fadeIn 1, 120
```

What it is
This command tells Director to fade in or out the sound in a sound channel. You specify the ticks, or let Director determine it based on the tempo (over about 15 frames).

sound of member *member*

DIGITAL VIDEO MEMBER PROPERTY

What it looks like (in the message window)

```
set the sound of member "video" = FALSE
```

What it is
This property lets you turn the sound of a digital video member on or off.

Also
volume of sprite

sound playFile *channel, fileName*

COMMAND

What it looks like (in the message window)

```
sound playFile 1, "scream.aif"
```

What it is
This command will let you stream sounds from sound files on the disk. You can play files formatted in either wave or AIFF. On Windows machines, these are files with extensions .WAV or .AIF. On Macintosh computers, the type of file will depend on the sound editing program you are using.

Also
sound close, sound stop

sound stop *channel*

COMMAND

What it looks like (in the message window)

```
sound stop 1
```

What it is

This command will stop a sound that is playing in a sound channel.

Also

puppetSound, soundBusy, play sound

soundEnabled

SYSTEM PROPERTY

What it looks like (in the message window)

```
set the soundEnabled = FALSE
```

What it is

This property lets you turn the sound on or off.

Also

soundLevel, volume of sound, sound of member

soundLevel

SYSTEM PROPERTY

What it looks like (in the message window)

```
set the soundLevel = 7
```

What it is

This property lets you change the overall system volume. A value of 0 is silence, while a value of 7 is the loudest.

Also

soundEnabled, volume of sprite

sourceRect of window *window*

MIAW PROPERTY

What it looks like (in the message window)

```
put  the sourceRect of window "myWin"
-- rect(100,100,540,380)
```

What it is

Every movie has its default screen position as part of its properties. When you open a movie as a movie in a window, the position of this window may differ from this original setting as you move it around. This property will allow you to examine what the original value was.

Also

rect of window

sprite *spriteNumber* intersects *spriteNumber*

SPRITE FUNCTION

What it looks like (in the message window)

```
if sprite 1 intersects sprite 2 then alert "touching!"
```

What it is

This function will tell you if the bounding rectangles of two sprites overlap.

Also

sprite...within

sprite *spriteNumber* within *spriteNumber*

SPRITE FUNCTION

What it looks like (in the message window)

```
if sprite 2 within sprite 1 then alert "inside"
```

What it is

This function will tell you whether the bounding rectangle of the first sprite is within the bounding rectangle of the second sprite.

Also

sprite...intersects

spriteBox *sprite, left, top, right, bottom*

COMMAND

What it looks like (in the message window)

```
spriteBox 5,50,60,150,160
```

What it is

This command lets you change the rectangle of a sprite on the stage. This command is rarely used, as you can just set the *rect* of a sprite.

Also

rect of sprite

sqrt *number*

MATH FUNCTION

What it looks like (in the message window)

```
put sqrt(4)
-- 2.0
```

What it is

This function returns the square root of a number.

Also

power, floatPrecision

stage

EXPRESSION

What it looks like (in the message window)

```
put the rect of the stage
-- rect(0,0,640,480)
set the visible of the stage = FALSE
```

What it is

This expression lets you refer to the stage, rather than a window, when using properties like *rect*, *visible*, or other MIAW properties. You can also use it with the *tell* command to refer to the main movie rather than a MIAW.

stageBottom, stageLeft, stageRight, stageTop

MOVIE PROPERTIES

What it looks like (in the message window)

```
put the stageBottom
-- 480
```

What it is

These four properties indicate the position on the screen of the sides of the stage. You cannot set these properties. You can also get these values with *the rect of stage.*

Also

the stage

S

stageColor

MOVIE PROPERTY

What it looks like (in the message window)

```
set the stageColor = 255
```

What it is
This property allows you to test and set the background color of the stage. The number corresponds to the color palette that the movie is using.

starts

FUNCTION

What it looks like (in the message window)

```
if "abcdef" starts "abc" then beep()
```

What it is
This function is a quick way to tell if a string starts with another string.

Also
contains

startTimer

COMMAND

What it looks like (in the message window)

```
put the timer
-- 33924
startTimer
put the timer
-- 342
```

What it is
In addition to the system clock, which will tell you the time, and *the ticks*, which starts when the computer is turned on, there is a third time counter: the timer. You can reset this counter to 0 with the *startTimer* command.

Also
timer

stillDown

FUNCTION

What it looks like (in a handler)

```
on mouseDown
  myHandlerToDoALotOfStuff
  if the stillDown then beep()
end
```

What it is

This function will tell you if the mouse button is still being held down after an *on mouseDown* handler begins. It differs from *mouseDown* in that it will know if the user has lifted up the button and pressed again between the start of the handler and the *stillDown*.

Also

mouseDown

stretch of sprite *spriteNumber*

SPRITE PROPERTY

What it looks like (in the message window)

```
put the stretch of sprite 5
-- 1
set the stretch of sprite 5 = FALSE
```

What it is

This property tells you if the sprite is displaying the cast member at its actual size or if it has been stretched. It will change automatically when you adjust the size by setting the sprite's rectangle or by using the *spriteBox* command. You can use a command like the last line of the example above to reset the sprite to its original size.

Also

rect of sprite

string *value*

FUNCTION

What it looks like (in the message window)

```
put string(7)
- "7"
put string([1,2,3])
-- "[1, 2, 3]"
```

What it is

This function converts any value to a string. If you pass it a string as a value, it will just return that same value.

Also

integer, value

stringP *value*

FUNCTION

What it looks like (in the message window)

```
put stringP(4)
-- 0
put stringP("text")
-- 1
```

What it is

This function tells you whether the value is a string.

Also

integerP, voidP, listP

switchColorDepth

SYSTEM PROPERTY

What it looks like (in the message window)

```
set the switchColorDepth = TRUE
```

What it is

This property determines if, when a new movie is loaded, the monitor switches color depth to match the new movie—same as a movie properties dialog box's check box. This only works on the Macintosh.

Also

colorDepth

symbolP *value*

FUNCTION

What it looks like (in the message window)

```
put symbolP(4)
-- 0
put symbolP(#a)
-- 1
```

What it is

This function will tell you whether a value is a symbol.

Also

#, *integerP, stringP, voidP*

TAB

CONSTANT

What it looks like (in a handler)

```
on keyDown
  if the key = TAB then
    alert "TAB key hit"
  end if
end
```

What it is

This constant corresponds to the Tab key on the keyboard and the tab character in strings.

Also

RETURN, BACKSPACE, EMPTY

tan(*number*)

MATH FUNCTION

What it looks like (in the message window)

```
put tan(pi())
-- 0.0000
put tan(pi()/2)
-- INF
put tan(pi()/4)
-- 1.0000
```

What it is

This function returns the tangent of a number. Use radians, not degrees, for the parameter.

Also

cos, *sin, atan, pi*

tell *MIAW* to *command*

COMMAND

What it looks like

```
tell window "myWin" to myHandler

tell myWin
  myHandler
  myOtherHandler
end
```

What it is

This command allows you to pass commands to other windows. You can pass either a single line or command, as in the first example, or a whole series of commands. You can also have a window tell *the stage* to do something.

Also

the stage

text of member *member*

FIELD MEMBER PROPERTY

What it looks like (in the message window)

```
set the text of member "myText" = "Hello world"
```

What it is

This property refers to the text in a field cast member. It is the same as just referring directly to the cast member as *field*.

Also

field

ticks

SYSTEM PROPERTY

What it looks like (in the message window)

```
put the ticks
-- 87203
```

What it is

This property counts time in 1/60 of a second. The counting starts when the computer is switched on.

Also

timer, time

time

SYSTEM PROPERTY

What it looks like (in the message window)

```
put the time
-- "12:15 AM"
put the abbr time
-- "12:15 AM"
put the short time
-- "12:15 AM"
put the long time
-- "12:15:55 AM"
```

What it is

This function returns a string with the time in various formats. It gets the actual time and the formats from the operating system.

Also

date

timeoutKeyDown, timeOutMouse, timeoutPlay

SYSTEM PROPERTIES

What they look like (in a handler)

```
on startUp
  set the timeoutKeyDown = TRUE
  set the timeoutMouse = TRUE
  set the timeoutPlay = TRUE
end
```

What they are

These three properties determine if the *timeoutLapsed* is reset when a user presses a key or clicks the mouse button, or a new movie plays.

Also

timeoutLapsed

timeoutLapsed, timeoutlength

SYSTEM PROPERTY

What it looks like (in a handler)

```
on exitFrame
  if timeoutLapsed = (the timeoutLength / 2) then
    put "Hello. Are you there?" into field "remark"
  end if
end
```

What it is

The time counter *timeoutLapsed* will increase until an event occurs that resets it. When the *timeoutLapsed* equals the *timeoutLength*, a "timeout" message is generated and the *timeoutScript* is executed. You can set the *timeoutLength* to any number of ticks.

Also

timeoutKeyDown, timeoutMouse, timeoutPlay, timeoutScript

timeoutScript

SYSTEM PROPERTY

What it looks like (in the message window)

```
on startMovie
  set the timeoutScript = "go to frame 1"
end
```

What it is

This line of Lingo is executed whenever a "timeout" event occurs. A "timeout" message is also generated that could trigger an *on timeout* handler if it exists.

Also

timeoutLapsed, timeoutLength, timeoutKeyDown, timeoutMouse, timeoutPlay

timer

SYSTEM PROPERTY

What it looks like (in the message window)

```
put the timer
-- 33924
startTimer
put the timer
-- 342
```

What it is

In addition to the system clock, which will tell you the time, and *the ticks*, which starts when the computer is turned on, there is a third time counter: the timer. You can reset this counter to 0 with the *startTimer* command.

Also

startTimer

timeScale of member *member*

DIGITAL VIDEO MEMBER PROPERTY

What it looks like (in the message window)

```
put the timeScale of member "video"
-- 600
```

What it is

Returns the time unit that the video member is based on. For instance, the above example shows a time scale that is based on 1/600 of a second.

Also

digitalVideoTimeScale

title of window *window*

MIAW PROPERTY

What it looks like (in the message window)

```
set the title of window "myWin" = "Please select"
```

What it is

This property allows you to specify what appears in the title bar of a movie in a window. Do not confuse it with the name of the window. This is just the text that appears in the MIAW's title bar.

Also

name of window, titleVisible of window, windowType of window

titleVisible of window *window*

MIAW PROPERTY

What it looks like (in the message window)

```
set the titleVisible of window "myWin" = FALSE
```

What it is
This property lets you control whether the movie in a window's title is displayed in the title bar. Note that the title is a different property than the name of the window. Also note that some window types do not have title bars at all.

Also
title of window, windowType of window

top of sprite

SPRITE PROPERTY

What it looks like (in the message window)

```
put the top of sprite 6
-- 156
```

What it is
This property returns the position, in pixels, of the top of the sprite on the stage. You cannot set this property directly.

Also
bottom of sprite, left of sprite, right of sprite, width of sprite, height of sprite, rect of sprite

trace

SYSTEM PROPERTY

What it looks like (in the message window)

```
set the trace = TRUE
```

What it is
When this property is turned on, Director throws debugging statements to the message window when the movie is running. You can use this to debug, as an alternative to using the debugger.

Also
traceLoad, traceLogFile

traceLoad

SYSTEM PROPERTY

What it looks like (in the message window)

```
set the traceLoad = 2
```

What it is

This property allows you to see information about memory and cast members as Director loads and unloads them from memory. This information gets written to the message window.

When set to 1, only the cast member names are displayed. When set to 2, you get the cast member name, frame number, movie name, and file seek offset. This last item refers to how far Director had to go to find the cast member in the file. When this number is huge, say over 50,000, you may want to rearrange your cast order or use a preload command for this cast member if timing is important.

Also

trace, traceLogFile

traceLogFile

SYSTEM PROPERTY

What it looks like (in the message window)

```
set the traceLogFile = "trace.txt"
```

What it is

Setting this property to a filename will cause all trace and traceLoad information to be written to a file as well as the message window. It will also write out any *put* statements that you target to the message window in your program. It is a useful debugging tool when running in Director, although it does not work in projectors. Make sure to set this property to *EMPTY* to close the file. Remember not to use this property in finished products, or any message window *put* statements for that matter, to avoid slowing down a projector. However, you may wish to use this function as an easy way to write out user behavior data from a projector.

Also
trace, traceLoad, put

trackCount(member *member*), trackCount(sprite *spriteNumber*)

DIGITAL VIDEO FUNCTION

What it looks like (in the message window)

```
put trackCount(member "video")
-- 3
```

What it is
This function will tell you how many tracks are in a digital video member. You can specify the member or the sprite.

trackEnabled(sprite *sprite*, *track*)

DIGITAL VIDEO FUNCTION

What it looks like (in the message window)

```
put trackEnabled(sprite 3, 2)
-- 1
```

What it is
This function tells you if a track in a digital video sprite is enabled or disabled. You can set this with the *setTrackEnabled* command.

Also
setTrackEnabled, trackCount, trackStartTime, trackStopTime, trackType

trackNextKeyTime(sprite *spriteNumber*, *track*), trackPreviousKeyTime(sprite *spriteNumber*, *track*)

DIGITAL VIDEO FUNCTIONS

What it looks like (in the message window)

```
put trackNextKeyTime(sprite 3,1)
-- 429496729
```

What they are:

These two functions will tell you when is the next or previous key frame of a digital video sprite.

Also

movieTime, trackType

trackNextSampleTime(sprite *spriteNumber*, *track*), trackPreviousSampleTime(sprite *spriteNumber*, *track*)

DIGITAL VIDEO FUNCTIONS

What it looks like (in the message window)

```
put the trackNextSampleTime(sprite 3, 1)
-- 2
```

What they are:

These two commands will locate the surrounding samples in a track of a digital video sprite.

Also

movieTime, trackType

trackStartTime(member *member*, *track*), **trackStartTime(sprite** *spriteNumber*, *track*), **trackStopTime(member** *member*, *track*), **trackStopTime(sprite** *spriteNumber*, *track*)

DIGITAL VIDEO FUNCTIONS

What it looks like (in the message window)

```
put the trackStartTime(member "video", 1)
-- 300
```

What they are

These commands will tell you when tracks start and stop in a digital video member or sprite.

Also

trackCount, trackType

trackText(sprite *spriteNumber*, *track*)

DIGITAL VIDEO FUNCTION

What it looks like (in the message window)

```
put trackText(sprite 1, 5)
-- "Music begins"
```

What it is

This function can read the text embedded in text tracks of digital video sprites.

Also

trackType

trackType(member *member*, *track*), trackType(sprite *spriteNumber*, *track*)

DIGITAL VIDEO FUNCTIONS

What it looks like (in the message window)

```
put trackType(member "video", 1)
-- #video
```

What it is

This function will get the track type of digital video member or sprite. Possible values are: #video, #sound, #text, and #music.

Also

trackCount

trails of sprite *spriteNumber*

SPRITE PROPERTY

What it looks like (in a hander)

```
on mouseDown
  put the clickOn into s
  set the trails of sprite s = TRUE
  repeat while the stillDown
    set the locH of sprite s = the mouseH
    set the locV of sprite s = the mouseV
    updateStage
  end repeat
end
```

What it is

This property corresponds to the "trails" property of a sprite in the score window. When set to true, the sprite leaves an image of itself anywhere it is positioned on the stage. This image is temporary and can be erased when another object is moved over it or there is a transition. Use this command in conjunction with the *updateStage* and/or the *puppetSprite* commands.

transitionType of member *member*

TRANSITION MEMBER PROPERTY

What it looks like (in the message window)

```
put the transitionType of member 1
-- 23
```

What it is

This property lets you get the transition number from a transition cast member. These numbers are the same as the ones used with the *puppetTransition* command and can be found in the "Tables & Charts" appendix of this book.

TRUE

CONSTANT

What it looks like (in the message window)

```
put TRUE
-- 1
```

What it is

This constant is the same as 1. You should use this constant in situations where you want to set properties to true or false so that it is easier to read your code.

Also

FALSE

type of member *member* [of castLib *castLib*]

MEMBER PROPERTY

What it looks like (in the message window)

```
put the type of member "thing"
-- #bitmap
```

What it is
This property tells you the type of a cast member. It used to be called *castType* in earlier versions of Director. Possible values are: #bitmap, #button, #digitalVideo, #field, #filmLoop, #movie, #picture, #richText, #script, #shape, #sound, #palette, and #transition.

Also
type of sprite

type of sprite *spriteNumber*

SPRITE PROPERTY

What it looks like (in the message window)

```
put the type of sprite 3
-- 16
```

What it is
This odd property will return a 0 if there is nothing in a sprite, and 16, for some reason, if there is. You can use this property to clear a sprite by setting it to 0. To get a better idea of what type of object is in a sprite, use this: "put the type of member (the memberNum of sprite 3)."

Also
type of member

union rect *rectangle, rectangle*

FUNCTION

What it looks like (in the message window)

```
put union rect(100,100,200,200), rect(150,150,250,250)
-- rect(100,100,250,250)
```

What it is
This functon will return a rectangle that completely contains both rectangle parameters.

Also
rect, map

unLoad [[from *frameNumber*, to] *frameNumber*]

COMMAND

What it looks like (in a handler)

```
on exitFrame
  unLoad 3, 6
end
```

What it is

This command will remove cast members from memory. They are still present in the file, of course, but are just no longer available for the quickest access by the movie, which will reload them automatically if needed. This allows you to keep your memory clean and ready to quickly load other cast members.

You can use this command either by itself, which means that all the unused members are cleared, or with a single frame or range of frames.

Also

unLoadMember, preLoad, preLoadMember, purgePriority of member

unloadMember [[from *member* to] *member*]

COMMAND

What it looks like (in a handler)

```
on exitFrame
  unLoadMember "picture"
end
```


What it is

This command will remove cast members from memory. They are still present in the file, of course, but are just no longer available for the quickest access by the movie, which will reload them automatically if needed. This allows you to keep your memory clean and ready to quickly load other cast members.

You can use this command either by itself, which means that all the unused members are cleared, or with a single member or range of members. You can also specify the cast library.

Also
unLoad, preLoad, preLoadMember, purgePriority of member

unLoadMovie *movieName*

COMMAND

What it looks like (in a handler)

```
on startMovie
  unLoadMovie "other.mov"
end
```

What it is
This command allows you to unload an entire movie that is no longer in use, to clear up memory. The same basic rules apply from the *unLoad* command.

Also
preLoadMovie, unLoad, unLoadMember

updateFrame

SCORE COMMAND

What it looks like (in a handler)

```
on resetColors
  beginRecording
    repeat with i = 1 to 48
      set the foreColor of sprite i = 255
    end repeat
    updateFrame
  endRecording
end
```

What it is
This command causes changes to the score to be permanently applied during a recording session. The *beginRecording* and *endRecording* commands surround a set of Lingo lines that would be used to permanently change the score. In the above example, we simply set all the foreground colors of all the sprites in the current frame to black.

Also
beginRecording, endRecording

updateLock

SCORE PROPERTY

What it is
You can set this to true to prevent changes to the stage being made during a score generation session. Suppose you wanted to change one frame relative to another. You can set this property to true when you jump to the frame you don't want to change, and then false again when you are ready to make a change. This command is really just for your peace of mind when making score generation handlers; it adds no real functionality.

Also
beginRecording, udpateFrame

updateMovieEnabled

MOVIE PROPERTY

What it looks like (in a handler)

```
on startMovie
  set the updateMovieEnabled = TRUE
end
```

What it is
If you set this property to true, then the movie will be saved, including any changes to cast member or the score, when Director or a projector jumps to another movie.

updateStage

COMMAND

What it looks like (in a handler)

```
on moveIt
  repeat with i = 1 to 639
    set the locH of sprite 1 = i
    set the locH of sprite 2 = (640-i)
    updateStage
  end repeat
end
```

What it is

This command tells Director to take into account any changes you have made to sprites through Lingo, and update the stage to reflect those changes. In the above example, two sprites are changed and those changes visually happen at the same time because there is only one *updateStage*. In order to make the changes last between frames, you need to use the *puppetSprite* command. Note that changes to cast members—fields, for instance—happen immediately and do not wait for the *updateStage* command.

Also

puppetSprite

value(*string*)

FUNCTION

What it looks like (in the message window)

```
put value("3")
-- 3
put value("3+4")
-- 7
put value("[1,2,3]")
-- [1,2,3]
```

U

What it is
This function interprets a string and returns a numerical value. It is useful for converting strings to numbers, or building and solving mathematical equations like the second example. You can also use this function to convert strings to lists as in the third example.

Also
integer, string

version

GLOBAL VARIABLE

What it looks like (in the message window)

```
put version
-- "5.0"
```

What it is
This global variable will tell you what version of Director you are running under, or what version of Director the projector was created with. It is unusual in that it is the only global variable pre-initalized by Director. Note that it doesn't need a *the* in front of it.

video of member *member*

DIGITAL VIDEO MEMBER PROPERTY

What it looks like (in the message window)

```
set the video of member "video" = FALSE
```

What it is
This property allows you to disable or enable the showing of a video member entirely.

videoForWindowsPresent

SYSTEM PROPERTY

What it looks like (in the message window)

```
put the videoForWindowsPresent
-- 0
```

What it is

This property tells you whether the video for Windows system software is present on the computer. You need this to play .AVI files on Windows. .AVI files cannot be played on a Macintosh.

Also

quickTimePresent

visible of sprite *spriteNumber*

SPRITE PROPERTY

What it looks like (in the message window)

```
set the visible of sprite 1 = FALSE
```

What it is

This property allows you to show and hide sprite channels. The effect happens immediately and needs no *updateStage* command. It also persists over frame changes. You can set this property manually in the score window, but all sprites revert to visible once the movie is reloaded.

visible of window *window*

MIAW PROPERTY

What it looks like (in the message window)

```
set the visible of window "myWin" = FALSE
```

What it is
This property allows you to show and hide movies in a window. Remember that just because you hide a window doesn't mean you don't have to *close window* to really make it go away.

Also
close window

voidP *variable*

FUNCTION

What it looks like (in the message window)

```
put voidP(someVariableIHaventUsedYet)
-- 1
```

What it is
This function will tell you whether a variable is set to <void>. It will return a false if the variable is anything else: a number, string, list, pointer, etc.

Also
integerP, stringP, listP

volume of sound *channel*

SCORE PROPERTY

What it looks like (in the message window)

```
set the volume of sound 1 = 128
```

What it is
This property allows you to set the volume of a sound channel individually. Values range from 0 to 255.

Also
soundLevel, volume of sprite

volume of sprite *spriteNumber*

DIGITAL VIDEO MEMBER PROPERTY

What it looks like (in the message window)

```
set the volume of sprite 3 = 128
```

What it is

This property allows you to set the volume of a digital video sprite. Values range from 0 to 255.

Also

volume of sound, soundLevel

width of member *member*

BITMAP MEMBER PROPERTY

What it looks like (in the message window)

```
put the width of member "graphic"
-- 323
```

What it is

This property represents the width, in pixels, of a bitmap cast member. It does not take into account any stretching that is done on the sprite level. For this reason, it is not a good idea to use this property for shape members, even though you can.

Also

height of member, width of sprite, rect

width of sprite *spriteNum*

SPRITE PROPERTY

What it looks like (in the message window)

```
put the width of sprite 4
-- 43
```

What it is

This property represents the width, in pixels, of bitmap and shape cast members in the score. Since these can be stretched on the stage, this number may not correspond to the *width of member* property.

Also

height of sprite, width of member, rect

windowList

MIAW FUNCTION

What it looks like (in the message window)

```
put the windowList
-- [window ("miaw"), window ("myWin")]
```

What it is

This property shows a list of all of the movies present in a window. When referring to a window by number, the number corresponds to the order in this list.

Also

open window, name of window

windowPresent("*windowName*")

MIAW FUNCTION

What it looks like (in the message window)

```
put windowPresent("myWin")
-- TRUE
```

What it is
This function allows you to test to see if a movie in a window is currently open.

Also
windowList

windowType of window *window*

MIAW PROPERTY

What it looks like (in the message window)

```
set the windowType of window ("myWin") = 49
```

What it is
This property determines what type of window appearance a movie in a window has. See Appendix C, "Tables & Charts," for a complete list.

Also
titleVisible of window

wordWrap of member *member*

FIELD MEMBER PROPERTY

What it looks like (in the message window)

```
set the wordWrap of member "text" = TRUE
```

What it is
This property, which corresponds to one you can set manually in the text field information box, determines whether text in the field wraps around to fit or the ends of lines are just cut off.

xFactoryList(*fileName*)

FUNCTION

What it looks like:

```
put xFactoryList("myX") into xlist
```

What it is

This function is similar to *showXlib*, except that you can place its value in a variable. If you pass it an *EMPTY* as a parameter, it will give you a list of all Xobjects.

Also

showXlib

zoomBox *spriteNumber*, *spriteNumber* [, *ticks*]

COMMAND

What it looks like (in the message window)

```
zoomBox 2,3,120
```

What it is

This command creates the neat visual effect of a zooming box that quickly moves from the rectangle of the first sprite to the rectangle of the second sprite. The second sprite can be in the next frame if there is no sprite in the current frame. This will happen as fast as possible unless you supply a third parameter of the number of ticks for this to happen over.

SECTION

VI

Appendices

appendix A

About the Online Companion

To find out more about Lingo go to Ventana's *Macromedia Director 5 Online Companion*. It's your one-stop location for Macromedia Director resources on the Internet. The Companion was created to provide up-to-date information for readers of Ventana's books about Macromedia Director products.

Among the resources at the *Macromedia Director 5 Online Companion* are the update pages. The update pages have been created to keep you aware of developments since the book's release. If information changes, or if errors are discovered in Ventana's Macromedia Director 5 books, you will find correct, timely information on the update pages.

Are you interested in other books about Macromedia Director? The *Macromedia Director 5 Online Companion* links to Ventana's online bookshop. In the bookshop, you can find out about all of Ventana's books, and order them online at a discounted price.

The *Macromedia Director 5 Online Companion* also features resources that don't directly relate to the book, such as reviews of software that you can use with Macromedia Director, complete with downloadable demos! You will also find articles written by Macromedia Director users from across the Internet.

Still need more? The *Macromedia Director 5 Online Companion* is not a dead-end page. The Internet Resources page features links and information on Web pages, newsgroups, and e-mail discussion groups that contain useful information about Macromedia Director that you won't find anywhere else.

To access the *Macromedia Director 5 Online Companion*, connect to Ventana's site via the World Wide Web at: **http://www.vmedia.com/director.html**

appendix **B**

About the Companion CD-ROM

The CD-ROM included with your copy of *A Comprehensive Guide to Lingo* contains valuable software programs and example files from the appropriate chapters.

To view the CD-ROM using:

- Windows 3.1/Windows 95/Windows NT: Double-click on the LAUNCHME.EXE file from your Windows Explorer or File Manager.
- 68K Mac: Double-click on the 68K Mac LAUNCHME icon after opening the CD on your desktop.
- PowerPC Mac: Double-click on the PowerPC LAUNCHME icon after opening the CD on your desktop.

You'll see a menu screen offering several choices. See "Navigating the CD-ROM" below for your option choices.

Navigating the CD-ROM

Your choices for navigating the CD-ROM appear on the opening screen. You can view Software, browse the Hot Picks, learn more about Ventana, or quit the CD.

The Resources section allows you to open an HTML file in your Web browser with links to Macromedia Director 5 resources on the Internet.

If the Ventana Viewer does not run properly on your machine, you can also access the material on the CD-ROM manually. You can find the various files in their respective directories in the same location as the LAUNCHME file.

Technical Support

Technical support is available for installation-related problems only. The technical support office is open from 8:00 A.M. to 6:00 P.M., Monday through Friday and can be reached as follows:

Phone: (919) 544-9404 extension 81
Faxback Answer System: (919) 544-9404 extension 85
E-mail: help@vmedia.com
FAX: (919) 544-9472
World Wide Web: http://www.vmedia.com/support
America Online: keyword Ventana

Limits of Liability & Disclaimer of Warranty

The author and publisher of this book have used their best efforts in preparing the CD-ROM and the programs contained in it. These efforts include the development, research, and testing of the theories and programs to determine their effectiveness. The author and publisher make no warranty of any kind expressed or implied, with regard to these programs or the documentation contained in this book.

The author and publisher shall not be liable in the event of incidental or consequential damages in connection with, or arising out of, the furnishing, performance, or use of the programs, associated instructions, and/or claims of productivity gains.

Some of the software on this CD-ROM is shareware; there may be additional charges (owed to the software authors/makers) incurred for their registration and continued use. See individual program's README or VREADME.TXT files for more information.

appendix C

Tables & Charts

Machine Types

These values are returned by *the machineType* property.

Number	Machine
1	Macintosh 512Ke
2	Macintosh Plus
3	Macintosh SE
4	Macintosh II
5	Macintosh IIx
6	Macintosh IIcx
7	Macintosh SE/30
8	Macintosh Portable
9	Macintosh IIci
11	Macintosh IIfx
15	Macintosh Classic
16	Macintosh IIsi
17	Macintosh LC
18	Macintosh Quadra 900
19	PowerBook 170
20	Macintosh Quadra 700
21	Classic II
22	PowerBook 100
23	PowerBook 140
24	Macintosh Quadra 950

Number	Machine
25	Macintosh LCIII
27	PowerBook Duo 210
28	Macintosh Centris 650
30	PowerBook Duo 230
31	PowerBook 180
32	PowerBook 160
33	Macintosh Quadra 800
35	Macintosh LC II
42	Macintosh IIvi
45	PowerMac 7100/70
46	Macintosh IIvx
47	Macintosh Color Classic
48	PowerBook 165c
50	Macintosh Centris 610
52	PowerBook 145
53	PowerComputing 8100/100
73	PowerMac 6100/60
76	Macintosh Quadra 840av
256	IBM PC-type machine

ASCII Character Chart

These character numbers are used by the *numToChar* and *charToNum* functions. Some characters, especially those from 127 and higher, vary from font to font. The characters shown are common ones, in this case from the "Times" font.

Key/character	Number
Enter key	3
Delete key	8
Tab key	9
Line feed	10
Return key	13
Clear key	27
Left arrow	28
Right arrow	29
Up arrow	30
Down arrow	31
Space	32
!	33
“	34
#	35
$	36
%	37
&	38
‘	39
(	40
)	41
*	42
+	43
,	44
-	45
.	46
/	47
0	48
1	49
2	50
3	51
4	52
5	53
6	54
7	55
8	56
9	57

Key/character	Number
:	58
;	59
<	60
=	61
>	62
?	63
@	64
A	65
B	66
C	67
D	68
E	69
F	70
G	71
H	72
I	73
J	74
K	75
L	76
M	77
N	78
O	79
P	80
Q	81
R	82
S	83
T	84
U	85
V	86
W	87
X	88
Y	89
Z	90
[	91
\	92
]	93

Key/character	Number
^	94
_	95
‘	96
a	97
b	98
c	99
d	100
e	101
f	102
g	103
h	104
i	105
j	106
k	107
l	108
m	109
n	110
o	111
p	112
q	113
r	114
s	115
t	116
u	117
v	118
w	119
x	120
y	121
z	122
{	123
|	124
}	125
~	126
	127
Ä	128
Å	129

Key/character	Number
Ç	130
É	131
Ñ	132
Ö	133
Ü	134
á	135
à	136
â	137
ä	138
ã	139
å	140
ç	141
é	142
è	143
ê	144
ë	145
í	146
ì	147
î	148
ï	149
ñ	150
ó	151
ò	152
ô	153
ö	154
õ	155
ú	156
ù	157
û	158
ü	159
†	160
°	161
¢	162
£	163
§	164
•	165
¶	166
ß	167
®	168
©	169
™	170
´	171

Key/character	Number
¨	172
≠	173
Æ	174
Ø	175
∞	176
±	177
≤	178
≥	179
¥	180
µ	181
∂	182
∑	183
∏	184
π	185
∫	186
ª	187
º	188
Ω	189
æ	190
ø	191
¿	192
¡	193
¬	194
√	195
ƒ	196
≈	197
∆	198
«	199
»	200
…	201
	202
À	203
Ã	204
Õ	205
Œ	206
œ	207
–	208
—	209
“	210
”	211
‘	212
’	213

Key/character	Number
÷	214
◊	215
ÿ	216
Ÿ	217
⁄	218
¤	219
‹	220
›	221
ﬁ	222
ﬂ	223
‡	224
·	225
‚	226
„	227
‰	228
Â	229
Ê	230
Á	231
Ë	232
È	233
Í	234
Î	235
Ï	236
Ì	237
Ó	238
Ô	239
	240
Ò	241
Ú	242
Û	243
Ù	244
ı	245
ˆ	246
˜	247
¯	248
˘	249
˙	250
˚	251
¸	252
˝	253
˛	254
ˇ	255

Ink Numbers

These numbers correspond to the ink settings for *the ink of sprite* property.

Number	Ink	Description
0	Copy	Takes the entire object as a rectangle and places it on the stage, overlapping anything under the rectangle completely. This ink animates the fastest.
1	Transparent	All colors are transparent, causing the object to "mix" with the background.
2	Reverse	Takes the color of the background or object behind the sprite and makes it the opposite color in the palette.
3	Ghost	Makes white pixels transparent and black pixels turn white. Colors will disappear on a white background and reverse on a black background.
4	Not Copy	Reverses the object.
5	Not transparent	Reverses the object and then makes it transparent. Useful for making pictures look like photo negatives.
6	Not reverse	Reverses the object and then takes the color of the background or object behind the sprite and makes it the opposite color in the palette.
7	Not ghost	Makes white pixels transparent and black pixels turn white. Colors will disappear on a white background and look normal on a black background.
8	Matte	Takes the image, traces around its actual shape using the background color as a guide, and then displays the image as opaque.
9	Mask	Takes a 1-bit cast member that you placed in the next cast member slot, and uses it to define the area of the sprite that is opaque.
32	Blend	Uses the blend property of the sprite to mix the object and the background's colors.
33	Add pin	Adds the value of the object and the background's colors, but makes sure that it does not exceed the maximum value.
34	Add	Adds the value of the object and the background's colors, but makes sure that it does not exceed the minimum value.
35	Subtract Pin	Subtracts the value of the object from the background's colors. If the value is less than the minimum, the colors wrap around the spectrum.
36	Background transparent	Makes the background color of the object completely transparent.
37	Lightest	Shows the lightest pixels between the object and the background.
38	Subtract	Subtracts the value of the object from the background's colors. If the value is less than the minimum, the colors wrap around the spectrum.
39	Darkest	Shows the darkest pixels between the object and the background.

Transition Numbers

Use these numbers to select transitions with the *puppetTransition* command.

Number	Definition
01	Wipe right
02	Wipe left
03	Wipe down
04	Wipe up
05	Center out, horizontal
06	Edges in, horizontal
07	Center out, vertical
08	Edges in, vertical
09	Center out, square
10	Edges in, square
11	Push left
12	Push right
13	Push down
14	Push up
15	Reveal up
16	Reveal up, right
17	Reveal right
18	Reveal down, right
19	Reveal down
20	Reveal down, left
21	Reveal left
22	Reveal up, left
23	Dissolve, pixels fast *
24	Dissolve, boxy rectangles
25	Dissolve, boxy squares
26	Dissolve, patterns

Number	Definition
27	Random rows
28	Random columns
29	Cover down
30	Cover down, left
31	Cover down, right
32	Cover left
33	Cover right
34	Cover up
35	Cover up, left
36	Cover up, right
37	Venetian blinds
38	Checkerboard
39	Strips on bottom, build left
40	Strips on bottom, build right
41	Strips on left, build down
42	Strips on left, build up
43	Strips on right, build down
44	Strips on right, build up
45	Strips on top, build left
46	Strips on top, build right
47	Zoom open
48	Zoom close
49	Vertical blinds
50	Dissolve, bits fast *
51	Dissolve, pixels *
52	Dissolve, bits *

* These transitions will not work on monitors that are set to 32 bits.

Cast Member Types

These types are used by the *type of member* property.

#bitmap	#picture
#button	#richText
#digitalVideo	#script
#field	#shape
#filmLoop	#sound
#movie	#transition
#palette	

appendix D

New Lingo in Director 5

Here is a list of new and changed elements in Director 5. The table also shows if the new element has a Director 4 equivalent.

New Element	Director 4 Equivalent
activeWindow	
alignment of member	textAlign of field
autoTab of member	
backColor of member	backColor of cast
beginRecording	
border of member	
boxDropShadow	
boxType of member	
buttonType	
cancelIdleLoad	
case	
castLibNum of sprite	
center of member	
center of member	center of cast

New Element	Director 4 Equivalent
changeArea of member	
channelCount of member	
charPosToLoc	
chunkSize of member	
clearFrame	
controller of member	controller of cast
crop of member	
crop of member	crop of cast
deleteFrame	
depth of member	depth of cast
desktopRectList	
digitalVideoTimeScale	
digitalVideoType of member	
dropShadow of member	
duplicate member	duplicate cast
duplicate(list)	
duplicateFrame	
duration of member	
duration of member	duration of cast
editable of member	
emulateMultiButtonMouse	
end case	
endRecording	
erase member	erase cast
fileName of castLib	
fileName of member	fileName of cast
filled of member	
finishIdleLoad	
font of member	textFont of field
fontSize of member	textSize of field

New Element	Director 4 Equivalent
fontStyle of member	textStyle of field
foreColor of member	foreColor of cast
frameLabel	
framePalette	
frameRate of member	frameRate of cast
frameScript	
frameSound1	
frameSound2	
frameTempo	
frameTransition	
frontWindow	
height of member	
height of member	height of cast
hilite of member	hilite of cast
idleHandlerPeriod	
idleLoadDone	
idleLoadMode	
idleLoadPeriod	
idleLoadTag	
idleReadChunkSize	
insertFrame	
keyPressed	
lineCount of member	
lineHeight of member	textHeight of field
linePosToLocV	
lineSize of member	
loaded of member	loaded of cast
loc of sprite	
locToCharPos	
locVToLinePos	

New Element	Director 4 Equivalent
loop of member	
loop of member	loop of cast
margin of member	
media of member	
member	
member	cast
memberNum of sprite	
memberNum of sprite	castNum of sprite
modified of member	modified of cast
move member	move cast
name of castLib	
name of member	name of cast
new	
number of castLib	
number of castLibs	
number of member	number of cast
number of members	castmembers
number of members	number of castmembers
number of members of castLib	
on activateWindow	
on closeWindow	
on moveWindow	
on resizeWindow	
on rightMouseDown	
on rightMouseUp	
on zoomWindow	
openWindow	
otherwise	
pageHeight of member	
palette of member	palette of cast
paletteMapping	

New Element	Director 4 Equivalent
paletteRef	
pattern	
picture of member	picture of cast
platform	
preLoad of member	preLoad of cast
preLoadMember	preLoadCast
preLoadMode of castLib	
preLoadMovie	
purgePriority of member	purgePriority of cast
rect of member	
rightMouseDown, the	
rightMouseUp, the	
sampleRate	
sampleSize	
save castLib	
score	
scoreSelection	
scriptsEnabled	
scriptText of member	scriptText of cast
scriptType	
scrollByLine	
scrollByPage	
scrollTop of member	
selection of castLib	
setCallBack	
shapeType	
size of member	size of cast
sound of member	
sound of member	sound of cast
text of member	text of cast
timeScale of member	

New Element	Director 4 Equivalent
trackCount(member)	
trackCount(sprite)	
trackEnabled	
trackNextKeyTime	
trackNextSampleTime	
trackPreviousKeyTime	
trackPreviousSampleTime	
trackStartTime	
trackStopTime	
trackText	
trackType	
transitionType of member	
type of member	
type of member	castType of cast
unloadMovie	
updateFrame	
updateLock	
video of member	video of cast
width of member	width of cast
windowPresent	
wordWrap of member	

Here is a list of Lingo elements that are obsolete in Director 5.

birth
instance
factory
closeDA
openDA
when...then constructs

appendix E

Keyboard & Mouse Shortcuts

File Menu	Shortcut
New Movie	Cmd-N
New Cast	Cmd-Option-N
Open	Cmd-O
Close	Cmd-W
Save	Cmd-S
Import	Cmd-R
Export	Cmd-Shift-R
Page Setup	Cmd-Shift-P
Print	Cmd-P
General Preferences	Cmd-U
Quit	Cmd-Q

Edit Menu	Shortcut
Undo	Cmd-Z
Repeat	Cmd-Y
Cut	Cmd-X
Copy	Cmd-C
Paste	Cmd-V
Clear	Delete
Duplicate	Cmd-D
Select All	Cmd-A
Find Text	Cmd-F
Find Handler	Cmd-Shift-;
Find Cast Member	Cmd-;
Find Selection	Cmd-H
Find Again	Cmd-Option-F
Replace Again	Cmd-Option-E
Exchange Cast Members	Cmd-E
Launch External Editor	Cmd-,

View Menu	Shortcut
Next Marker	Cmd-Right arrow
Previous Marker	Cmd-Left arrow
Zoom In	Cmd- +
Zoom Out	Cmd- –
Show Grid	Cmd-Shift-Option-G
Snap to Grid	Cmd-Option-G

Insert Menu	Shortcut
Insert Frame	Cmd-]
Remove Frame	Cmd-[

Modify Menu	Shortcut
Cast Member Properties	Cmd-I
Cast Member Script	Cmd-'
Sprite Properties	Cmd-Shift-I
Sprite Script	Cmd-Shift-'
Movie Properties	Cmd-Shift-D
Movie Casts	Cmd-Shift-C
Font	Cmd-Shift-T
Paragraph	Cmd-Shift-Option-T
In-Between	Cmd-B
In-Between Special	Cmd-Shift-B
Bring to Front	Cmd-Shift-Up arrow
Move Forward	Cmd-Up arrow
Move Backward	Cmd-Down arrow
Send to Back	Cmd-Shift-Down arrow
Align	Cmd-K
Tweak	Cmd-Shift-K

Control Menu	Shortcut
Play	Cmd-Option-P
Stop	Cmd-.
Rewind	Cmd-Option-R
Step Backward	Cmd–Option-Left arrow
Step Forward	Cmd–Option-Right arrow
Loop Playback	Cmd-Option-L
Volume: Mute	Cmd-Option-M
Toggle Breakpoint	Cmd-Shift-Option-K
Watch Expression	Cmd-Shift-Option-W
Ignore Breakpoints	Cmd-Shift-Option-I
Step Script	Cmd-Shift-Option-Down arrow

Control Menu	Shortcut
Step Into Script	Cmd-Shift-Option-Right arrow
Run Script	Cmd-Shift-Option-Up arrow
Recompile All Scripts	Cmd-Shift-Option-C

Window Menu	Shortcut
Toolbar	Cmd-Shift-Option-B
Tool Palette	Cmd-7
Text Inspector	Cmd-T
Stage	Cmd-1
Control Panel	Cmd-2
Markers	Cmd-Shift-M
Score	Cmd-4
Cast	Cmd-3
Paint	Cmd-5
Text	Cmd-6
Field	Cmd-8
Color Palettes	Cmd-Option-7
Video	Cmd-9
Script	Cmd-0
Message	Cmd-M
Debugger	Cmd-'(back quote)
Watcher	Cmd-Shift-'(back quote)

Stage	Shortcut
Open cast member editor	Double-click sprite
Open paint window	Cmd-5
Inks pop-up	Cmd-click
Toggle record light on and off	Option-click
Real-time record	Control-Spacebar-drag sprite on the stage
Display shortcut menu for selection	Control-click

Cast Window & Cast Editor Window	Shortcut
Open cast member editor	Double-click a paint, text, palette, or script cast member or select the cast member and press Return
Cast member script	Cmd-' (apostrophe)
Switch selected cast member selection	Option-double-click thumbnail with score
Display cast member info	Control-click cast thumbnail
Open script in new window	Option-Script button
Center of stage	Cmd-Shift-
Cast to Time	Cmd-Shift-Option-L
New cast member	Cmd-Shift-A
Previous cast member	Cmd-Left arrow
Next cast member	Cmd-Right arrow
Previous cast member in new window	Cmd- Option-Left arrow
Next cast member in new window	Cmd- Option-Right arrow
Scroll up on window	Page up
Scroll down one window	Page down
Scroll to top left of cast window	Home
Scroll to show last occupied	End
Type-select by cast member	Type number

appendix F

Lingo by Subject

The following is a list of Lingo commands, functions and properties arranged by subject. The purpose is to make it easier to locate a command quickly, and allow you to see what other commands are in the same category.

Buttons
buttonStyle
buttonType of member
hilite of member

Cast Libraries
castLibNum
fileName of castLib
name of castLib
save castLib

Cast Member Loading
cancelIdleLoad
finishIdleLoad
idleHandlerPeriod
idleLoadDone
idleLoadMode
idleLoadPeriod
idleLoadTag
idleReadChunkSize
preLoad
preLoad of member
preLoadEvenAbort
preLoadMember
preLoadMode of castLib
preLoadRam
purgePriority of member
ramNeeded
unLoad
unLoadMember
unLoadMovie
updateStage

Constants
BACKSPACE
EMPTY
ENTER
FALSE
QUOTE
RETURN
TAB
TRUE

Conversion
integer
string
value

Cursors
cursor
cursor of sprite

Digital Video
center of member
controller of member
crop of member
digitalVideoTimeScale

digitalVideoType of member
directToStage of member
duration of member
frameRate of member
loop of member
movieRate of sprite
movieTime of sprite
pausedAtStart of member
preLoad of member
quickTimePresent
setTrackEnabled
sound of member
timeScale of member
trackCount
trackCount of member
trackEnabled
trackNextKeyTime
trackNextSampleTime
trackPreviousKeyTime
trackPreviousSampleTime
trackStartTime
trackStopTime
trackText
trackType
video of member
videoForWindowsPresent
volume of sprite

Fields

autoTab of member
backColor of member
border of member
boxDropShadow of member
boxType of member
charPosToLoc
dropShadow of member
editable of member
editable of sprite
field
font of member
fontSize of member
fontStyle of member
foreColor of member
hilite
hilite of member
lineCount of member
lineHeight
lineHeight of member
linePosToLocV
lineSize of member
locToCharPos
locVToLinePos
margin of member
pageHeight of member
scrollByLine
scrollByPage
scrollTop
text of member
wordWrap of member

File & Path Names

movie
movieName
moviePath
path
pathName
searchCurrentFolder

Handler Commands & Functions

dontPassEvent
param
paramCount
pass
result

Handlers

on activateWindow
on closeWindow
on deactivateWindow
on enterFrame
on exitFrame
on idle
on keyDown
on keyUp
on mouseDown
on mouseUp
on moveWindow
on openWindow
on resizeWindow
on rightMouseDown
on rightMouseUp
on startMovie
on stepMovie
on stopMovie
on timeOut
on zoomWindow

Keyboard

commandDown
controlDown
key
keyCode
keyDownScript
keyPressed
keyUpScript
optionDown
shiftDown
stillDown

Lists

[ ]
add
addAt
addProp
append
count
deleteAt
deleteOne
deleteProp
duplicate
findPos
findPosNear
getAProp
getAt
getLast
getOne
getPos
getPropAt

ilk
list
listP
setAProp
setAt
setProp
sort

Logic
<
<=
=
>=
>
<>
and
not
or

Math
+
-
*
/
abs
atan
cos
exp
float
floatPrecision
integer
log
max
maxInteger
mod
pi
power
random
randomSeed
sin
sqrt
tan

Members
align of member
channelCount of member
duplicate member
erase member
fileName of member
findEmpty
height of member
importFileInto
loaded of member
media of member
modified of member
move member
name of member
new
palette of member
paletteRef of member
picture of member
rect of member
regPoint of member
sampleRate of member
sampleSize of member
scriptsEnabled of member
scriptText of member
scriptType of member
size of member
type of member
width of member

Memory & File Size
freeBlock
freeBytes
memorySize
movieFileFreeSize
movieFileSize

Menu Bar
checkMark of menuItem
enabled of menuItem
installMenu
name of menu
name of menuItem
script of menuItem

Miscellaneous Commands
abort
alert
beep
case
clearGlobals
copyToClipBoard member
do
exit
exit repeat
getNthFileNameInFolder
global
if...then
mci
next repeat
nothing
open
pasteClipBoardInto
member
printFrom
put
quit
repeat
restart
saveMovie
set
showGlobals
showLocals
shutDown
startTime
zoomBox

Miscellaneous System Properties & Functions
beepOn
buttonStyle
centerStage
checkBoxAccess
checkBoxType
colorDepth
colorQD
cpuHogTicks
deskTopRectList

emulateMultiButtonMouse
exitLock
fixStageSize
itemDelimiter
machineType
maxInteger
multiSound
paletteMapping
perFrameHook
platform
quickTimePresent
romanLingo
runMode
searchPath
searchPaths
setCallBack
stage
stageBottom
stageColor
stageLeft
stageRight
stageTop
switchColorDepth
trace
traceLoad
traceLogFile
updateMovieEnabled
version
videoForWindowsPresent

Mouse
clickLoc
clickOn
doubleClick
emulateMultiButtonMouse
mouseCast
mouseChar
mouseDown
mouseDownScript
mouseH
mouseItem
mouseLine
mouseUp
mouseUpScript
mouseV
mouseWord
rightMouseDown
rightMouseUp
rollover

Movie Flow
continue
delay
framesToHMS
go
halt
HMStoFrames
pause
pauseState
play
play done
play movie

Movie in a Window
activeWindow
close window
drawRect of window
fileName of window
frontWindow
forget window
modal of window
moveToBack window
moveToFront window
name of window
open window
rect of window
sourceRect of window
tell
title of window
titleVisible of window
visible of window
windowList
windowPresent
windowType of window

Object-Oriented Programming
actorList
ancestor
new
objectP
property

Points & Rectangles
inflate
inside
intersect
map
offset
point
rect
union rect

Predicates
floatP
integerP
listP
objectP
pictureP
stringP
symbolP
voidP

Puppets
puppetPalette
puppetSound
puppetSprite
puppetTempo
puppetTransition

Score
frame
frameLabel
framePalette
frameScript
frameSound1
frameSound2
frameTempo

frameTransition
label
labelList
marker
score
scriptNum of sprite
volume of sound

Score Generation
beginRecording
deleteFrame
duplicateFrame
endRecording
insertFrame
scoreColor of sprite
scoreSelection
updateFrame
updateLock

Selection
selection
selection of castLib
selEnd
selStart

Shapes
filled of member
pattern of member
shapeType of member

Sounds
sound close
sound fadeIn
sound fadeOut
sound playFile
sound stop
soundEnabled
soundLevel

Sprites
backColor of sprite
blend of sprite
bottom of sprite
constrainH
constraint of sprite
constrainV
foreColor of sprite
height of sprite
ink of sprite
left of sprite
lineSize of sprite
loc of sprite
locH of sprite
locV of sprite
memberNum of sprite
moveableSprite of sprite
puppet of sprite
puppetSprite
rect of sprite
right of sprite
scriptNumof sprite
sprite...intersects
sprite...within
spriteBox
stretch of sprite
top of sprite
trails of sprite
type of sprite
visible of sprite
width of sprite

Strings
char
chars
charToNum
contains
delete
last
length
line
numToChar
offset
starts
string
stringP
value

Time
date
startTimer
ticks
time
timer

Transitions
changeArea of member
chunkSize of member
transitionType of member

User Inaction
lastClick
lastEvent
lastFrame
lastKey
lastRoll
timeOut
timeOutKeyDown
timeOutLapsed
timeOutlength
timeOutMouse
timeOutScript
timer

Xtras
closeResFile
closeXlib
name of Xtra
openResFile
openXlib
showXlib
xFactoryList

appendix G

Problem-Solving Guide

This is an alternative index of subjects covered in this book. It is arranged by category, from basic to more complex needs, to make it easy for you to find what you want quickly.

Task	Solution
Buttons	
How to give a button proper behavior	Chapter 4, Lesson 10; Chapter 11
How to make quick and simple buttons	Chapter 4, Lesson 7
How to make a list of buttons that are related to each other	Chapter 13
How to program a group of check boxes	Chapter 13
How to program a group of radio buttons	Chapter 13
How to make sliders	Chapter 13

Task	Solution
Animation	
How to make an object blink on and off	Chapter 5, Lesson 11
How to alternate between two objects in the same space	Chapter 5, Lesson 12, Lesson 13
How to move sprites around on the stage	Chapter 5, Lesson 14, Lesson 15
How to make simple 3-D animation	Chapter 7, Lesson 19
How to sync sound and animation	Chapter 5, Lesson 13
How to tell if two sprites are touching	Chapter 6, Lesson 17
How to make text move across the stage	Chapter 20
User Control of Sprites	
How to let the user move a sprite with the mouse	Chapter 6, Lesson 16
How to let the user click and drag a sprite	Chapter 6, Lesson 16
How to let the user draw with the mouse	Chapter 18
Sound	
How to play a sound that is not in the score	Chapter 8, Lesson 21
How to play a sound file	Chapter 8, Lesson 21
How to fade sounds	Chapter 8, Lesson 21
How to incorporate MIDI into movies	Chapter 29
How to play a random sound	*puppetSound*
Text	
How to import text files	Chapter 16
How to make hypertext links in a text field	Chapter 9, Lesson 24; Chapter 12
How to let the user select from a list of options	Chapter 14
How to let the user enter some new text	Chapter 14
How to reset scrolling fields so they are at the top every time	*scrollTop*

Task	Solution
Movie Flow	
How to make the movie pause for a few seconds	Chapter 3, Lesson 6
How to make the movie wait for a user action	Chapter 3, Lesson 4, Lesson 5
How to make a movie return to an "attact loop"	Chapter 17
How to jump to a random frame	*go*
User Interface	
How to make your own menu bar	Chapter 17
How to change the cursor	Chapter 17, *cursor, cursor of sprite*
How to create a window separate from the stage	Chapter 27
How to make pop-up menus	Chapter 28
How to prevent the user from quitting with a Cmd-Q	*exitLock*
How to ensure that the user sees a "credits" page on a Cmd-Q	*exitLock, keyDownScript*
Images	
How to display a random picture	*puppetSprite*
How to import a picture from a file	Chapter 16
How to stretch and shrink sprites	Chapter 7, Lesson 19
How to make an object change color	Chapter 7, Lesson 20
How to make an object blend in with the background	Chapter 7, Lesson 20
How to invert or otherwise color distort an image	Chapter 7, Lesson 20
How to display a bitmap with scroll bars	Chapter 24

Task	Solution
Miscellaneous	
How to tell the date and time	Chapter 21; *date, time*
How to initalize global variables at the start of a movie	Chapter 11
How to let the user copy and paste	Chapter 21; *copyToClipBoard, pasteClipBoardInto*
How to tell what type of computer the user has	Chapter 21; *machineType, platform*
How to sort a list of items	Chapter 26
How to control digital video	Chapter 29
How to print out frames and members	Chapter 32
How to tell if the user's computer has video capability	*quickTimePresent, videoForWindows-Present*
How to execute a Lingo command that the user has typed in	*do*

appendix **H**

A List of Director Resources on the World Wide Web

Key Resources

Ventana's Director 5 Online Companion:
http://www.vmedia.com/director.html
A list of resources, tools and information about Ventana's Director books.

CleverMedia (Gary Rosenzweig's Director Page):
http://clevermedia.com
Resources, tips, shockwave games, and tools.

Maricopa Community College "Director Web":
http://hakatai.mcli.dist.maricopa.edu/director/index.html
The most comprehensive Director/Lingo site on the Internet. Contains many sections, links to other resources, and companies. Also the best list of Shockwave movies available.

Yahoo's Director listing:
http://www.yahoo.com/Business_and_Economy/Companies/Computers/Software/Macromedia/Products/Director/
Check here for new resources.

Director & Lingo information

Direct-L Daily Digest:
http://hakatai.mcli.dist.maricopa.edu/director/digest/today.txt
A dump of this very overcrowded but very useful listserve about Director and Lingo.

Direct-L Index:
http://hakatai.mcli.dist.maricopa.edu/director/digest/index.html
Use this page to search Direct-L.

Macromedia's Tech Notes:
http://www.macromedia.com/AYS/Tech.support/Technotes/Director/index.html
A list of official technical notes and suggestions. Often Lingo subjects.

UpdateStage:
http://www.xensei.com/users/gcm/
An excellent page, updated weekly, with all sorts of tips and information.

List of Undocumented Lingo:
http://hakatai.mcli.dist.maricopa.edu/director/tips/unlingo/index.html
A list of some of the commands and uses of Lingo that are not in the official documentation.

Director Click Zone:
http://www.ddce.cqu.edu.au/IMU/tools/director/
A site with Xtras, tools, and Director and Lingo information.

Dan Pilkenton's Director Tips & Tricks:
http://www.best.com/~danp/tips.html
A page of hints.

Kurt Cagle's Lingo and Code Page:
http://www.blarg.net/~cagles/lingo/
Text of some papers on Lingo.

Mark Castle's Lingo Examples:
http://www.best.com/~mcastle/examples.html
Tools and scripting examples.

New York University Center for Advanced Technology:
http://found.cs.nyu.edu/
General information.

Raul Silva's Digital Wonderland:
http://www.tezcat.com/~raul/
Tools and resources.

Daniele Russo's Library of XObjects:
http://c4dm.nyu.edu/russo/xobject.html

Macromedia's List of Xobjects and Xtras:
http://www.macromedia.com/Toys/Resources/Director/Resources/index.html
A collection of Xobjects and Xtras.

Shockwave

Maricopa Community College "Director Web":
http://hakatai.mcli.dist.maricopa.edu/director/shockwavelist.html
The most comprehensive list of Shockwave movies available.

ShockeR:
http://www.shocker.com/shocker/cool.html
A list of Shockwave sites, including the cool site of the week.

Macromedia's Shocked Site of the Day:
http://www.macromedia.com/Tools/Shockwave/Gallery/Epicenter/index.html
Plus a complete archive and the Shockwave "Epicenter."

Shockwave FAQ:
http://hakatai.mcli.dist.maricopa.edu/director/shocklist/faq.html
A great independent resource of information about Shockwave.

Shock-Baubles:
http://www.pcslink.com/~sbullock/abtboble.htm
A collection of small Shockwave movies that you can use on your own Web pages. You can also contribute your own.

Gary Masson's Shockwave Links:
http://silver.nbnet.nb.ca:8080/
A good list of links.

Turntable Media:
http://www.turntable.com:80/shockwave/
A short list of sites.

Music Related Shockwave Sites:
http://www.teleport.com/~arcana/shockwave/
A collection of music-related sites, plus lots more.

The Tape Gallery Shockwave List:
http://www.adweb.co.uk/dp/voicegal/shockwav/sitewrap.htm

University of Missouri - Columbia:
http://shenzi.cc.missouri.edu/shockwave/index.html

Online Magazines

c|net:
http://www.itp.tsoa.nyu.edu/~review/
Online magazine of the TV show. Excellent source of news.

NewMedia:
http://www.hyperstand.com/
NewMedia magazine's online companion.

HotWired:
http://www.hotwired.com/frontdoor/index.html
Wired magazine's online counterpart.

Fusion:
http://shell.conknet.com/~d_abad/fusion/FUSION.HTMLX
A magazine about Director and multimedia in general.

Review|ITP:
http://www.itp.tsoa.nyu.edu/~review/
Published by students at New York University's Interactive Telecommunications Program.

Key Third-Party Companies

CyberActive:
http://www.pwr.com/cyberactive/
Xtras, resources, and tools.

Electronic Ink:
http://www.rahul.net/peterv/
Some Xtras.

FileFlex HQ:
http://www.component-net.com/fileflex/fileflex-hq.html
The home page of the FileFlex Xtra.

g/matter:
http://www.gmatter.com
Produces Xobjects, information guides, and other materials for Director.

Media Lab:
http://www.medialab.com/
Demos of some Xtras.

MediaSpark:
http://mfusion.com/mspark/
Some tools.

Nine Trees Design:
http://www.pacific.net/~david/ntd/ntd_director.html
Script examples and resources.

Xtra Media:
http://www.xtramedia.com/
Xtras and Lingo tips.

Visionary Designs:
http://www.visdesigns.com/
A "Developers Consortium."

Index

A

D

G

H

I

K

L

Q

R

S

T

U

V

W

X

Z

Power Publishing on the Web!

Walking the World Wide Web, Second Edition

$39.95, 800 pages, illustrated, part #: 298-4

More than 30% new, this book now features 500 listings and an extensive index of servers, expanded and arranged by subject. This groundbreaking bestseller includes a CD-ROM enhanced with Ventana's exclusive PerpetuWAVE technology; updated online components that make it the richest resource available for Web travelers; Netscape Navigator; and a hypertext version of the book.

Internet Power Toolkit

$49.95, 1200 pages, illustrated, part #: 329-8

Plunge deeper into cyberspace with this advanced guide to Internet tools, techniques and possibilities. Channel the array of Internet utilities and advice into increased productivity and profitability on the Internet. The CD-ROM features a wide variety of tools and utilities including Netscape plug-ins, e-mail, file management, multimedia, online monitoring, searching and more.

The Windows NT Web Server Book

$49.95, 680 pages, illustrated, part #: 342-5

A complete toolkit for providing services on the Internet using the Windows NT operating system. This how-to guide includes adding the necessary World Wide Web server software, comparison of the major Windows NT server packages for the Web, becoming a global product provider and more! The CD-ROM features Alibaba™ Lite (a fully licensed Web server), support programs, scripts, forms, utilities and demos.

Java Programming for the Internet

$49.95, 800 pages, illustrated, part #: 355-7

Create dynamic, interactive Internet applications with Java Programming for the Internet. Expand the scope of your online development with this comprehensive, step-by-step guide to creating Java applets. Includes four real-world, start-to-finish tutorials. The CD-ROM has all the programs, samples and applets from the book, plus shareware. Continual updates on Ventana's *Online Companion* will keep this information on the cutting edge.

Official Netscape JavaScript Book

$29.99, 400 pages, illustrated, part #: 465-0

Add life to Web pages—animated logos, text-in-motion sequences, live updating and calculations—quickly and easily. Sample code and step-by-step instructions show how to put JavaScript to real-world, practical use.

The Comprehensive Guide to VBScript

$34.99, 408 pages, illustrated, part #: 470-7

The only encyclopedic reference to VBScript and HTML commands and features. Complete with practical examples for plugging directly into programs. The companion CD-ROM features a hypertext version of the book, along with shareware, templates, utilities and more.

Books marked with this logo include a free Internet *Online Companion*™, featuring archives of free utilities plus a software archive and links to other Internet resources.

ORDER [illegible] VENTURE [illegible] THIS ORDER FORM AND
MAIL OR FAX IT TO [illegible] WITH PAYMENT FOR QUICK SHIPMENT.

Payment enclosed

Signature

MACROMEDIA

End-User License Agreement

PLEASE READ THIS DOCUMENT CAREFULLY BEFORE BREAKING THE SEAL ON THE MEDIA PACKAGE. THIS AGREEMENT LICENSES THE ENCLOSED SOFTWARE TO YOU AND CONTAINS WARRANTY AND LIABILITY DISCLAIMERS. BY BREAKING THE SEAL ON THE MEDIA ENVELOPE, YOU ARE CONFIRMING YOUR ACCEPTANCE OF THE SOFTWARE AND AGREEING TO BECOME BOUND BY THE TERMS OF THIS AGREEMENT. IF YOU DO NOT WISH TO DO SO, DO NOT BREAK THE SEAL. INSTEAD, PROMPTLY RETURN THE ENTIRE PACKAGE, INCLUDING THE UNOPENED MEDIA PACKAGE, TO THE PLACE WHERE YOU OBTAINED IT, FOR A FULL REFUND.

1. Definitions

(a) "Macromedia« Software" means the software program included in the enclosed package, and all related updates supplied by Macromedia.

(b) "Macromedia Product" means the Macromedia Software and the related documentation and models and multimedia content (such as animation, sound, and graphics), and all related updates supplied by Macromedia.

2. License. This Agreement allows you to:
(a) Use the Macromedia Software on a single computer.

(b) Make one copy of the Macromedia Software in machine-readable form solely for backup purposes. You must reproduce on any such copy all copyright notices and any other proprietary legends on the original copy of the Macromedia Software.

(c) Certain Macromedia Software is licensed with additional rights as set forth in the Supplementary Rights Addendum that may be included in the package for this Macromedia Product.

3. Supplementary Licenses
Certain rights are not granted under this Agreement, but may be available under a separate agreement. If you would like to enter into a Site or Network License, please contact Macromedia.

4. Restrictions

You may not make or distribute copies of the Macromedia Product, or electronically transfer the Macromedia Software from one computer to another or over a network. You may not decompile, reverse engineer, disassemble, or otherwise reduce the Macromedia Software to a human-perceivable form. Youmay not modify, rent, resell for profit, distribute, or create derivativeworks based upon the Macromedia Software or any part thereof. You will notexport or reexport, directly or indirectly, the Macromedia Product into any country prohibited by the United States Export Administration Act and the regulations thereunder.

5. Ownership

The foregoing license gives you limited rights to use the Macromedia Software. Although you own the disk on which the Macromedia Software is recorded, you do not become the owner of, and Macromedia retains title to, the Macromedia Product, and all copies thereof. All rights not specifically granted in this Agreement, includin Federal and International Copyrights, are reserved by Macromedia.

6. Limited Warranties

(a) Macromedia warrants that, for a period of ninety (90) days from the date of delivery (as evidenced by a copy of your receipt): (i) when used with a recommended hardware configuration, the Macromedia Software will perform in substantial conformance with the documentation supplied as part of the Macromedia Product; and (ii) that the media on which the Macromedia Software is furnished will be free from defects in materials and workmanship under normal use. EXCEPT AS SET FORTH IN THE FOREGOING LIMITED WARRANTY, MACROMEDIA DISCLAIMS ALL OTHER WARRANTIES, EITHER EXPRESS OR IMPLIED, INCLUDING THE WARRANTIES OF MERCHANTABILITY, FITNESS FOR A PARTICULAR PURPOSE, AND NON-INFRINGEMENT. IF APPLICABLE LAW IMPLIES ANY WARRANTIES WITH RESPECT TO THE MACROMEDIA PRODUCT, ALL SUCH WARRANTIES ARE LIMITED IN DURATION TO NINETY (90)

DAYS FROM THE DATE OF DELIVERY. No oral or written information or advice given by Macromedia, its dealers, distributors, agents, or employees shall create a warranty or in any way increase the scope of this warranty.

(b) SOME STATES DO NOT ALLOW THE EXCLUSION OF IMPLIED WARRANTIES, SO THE ABOVE EXCLUSION MAY NOT APPLY TO YOU. THIS WARRANTY GIVES YOU SPECIFIC LEGAL RIGHTS AND YOU MAY ALSO HAVE OTHER LEGAL RIGHTS WHICH VARY FROM STATE TO STATE.

7. Exclusive Remedy Your exclusive remedy under Section 6 is to return the Macromedia Software to the place you acquired it, with a copy of your receipt and a description of the problem. Macromedia will use reasonable commercial efforts to supply you with a replacement copy of the Macromedia Software that substantially conforms to the documentation, provide a replacement for the defective media, or refund to you your purchase price for the Macromedia Software, at its option. Macromedia shall have no responsibility with respect to Macromedia Software that has been altered in any way, if the media has been damaged by accident, abuse, or misapplication, or if the non conformance arises out of use of the Macromedia Software in conjunction with software not supplied by Macromedia.

8. Limitations of Damages

(a) MACROMEDIA SHALL NOT BE LIABLE FOR ANY INDIRECT, SPECIAL, INCIDENTAL OR CONSEQUENTIAL DAMAGES (INCLUDING DAMAGES FOR LOSS OF BUSINESS, LOSS OF PROFITS, OR THE LIKE), WHETHER BASED ON BREACH OF CONTRACT, TORT (INCLUDING NEGLIGENCE), PRODUCT LIABILITY, OR OTHERWISE, EVEN IF MACROMEDIA OR ITS REPRESENTATIVES HAVE BEEN ADVISED OF THE POSSIBILITY OF SUCH DAMAGES AND EVEN IF A REMEDY SET FORTH HEREIN IS FOUND TO HAVE FAILED OF ITS ESSENTIAL PURPOSE.

(b) Macromedia's total liability to you for actual damages for any cause whatsoever will be limited to the greater of $500 or the amount paid by you for the Macromedia Software that caused such damages.

(c) SOME STATES DO NOT ALLOW THE LIMITATION OR EXCLUSION OF LIABILITY FOR INCIDENTAL OR CONSEQUENTIAL DAMAGES, SO THE ABOVE LIMITATION OR EXCLUSION MAY NOT APPLY TO YOU.

9. Basis of Bargain

The limited warranty, exclusive remedies, and limited liability set forth above are fundamental elements of the basis of the bargain between Macromedia and you. Macromedia would not be able to provide the MacromediaSoftware on an economic basis without such limitations.

10. Government End Users

The Macromedia Product is "Restricted Computer Software." RESTRICTED RIGHTS LEGEND Use, duplication, or disclosure by the Government is subject to restrictions as set forth in subparagraph (c)(1)(ii) of the Rights in Technical Data and Computer Software clause at DFARS 252.227-7013. Manufacturer: Macromedia, Inc., 600 Townsend, San Francisco, CA 94103

11. General

This Agreement shall be governed by the internal laws of the State of California. This Agreement contains the complete agreement between the parties with respect to the subject matter hereof, and supersedes all prior or contemporaneous agreements or understandings, whether oral or written. All questions concerning this Agreement shall be directed to: Macromedia, Inc., 600 Townsend, San Francisco, CA 94103, Attention: Chief Financial Officer.

Suzanne Porta
Publisher Programs Associate
Macromedia, Inc.
600 Townsend Street, Suite 310
San Francisco, CA, 94103 USA
e-mail: sporta@macromedia.com